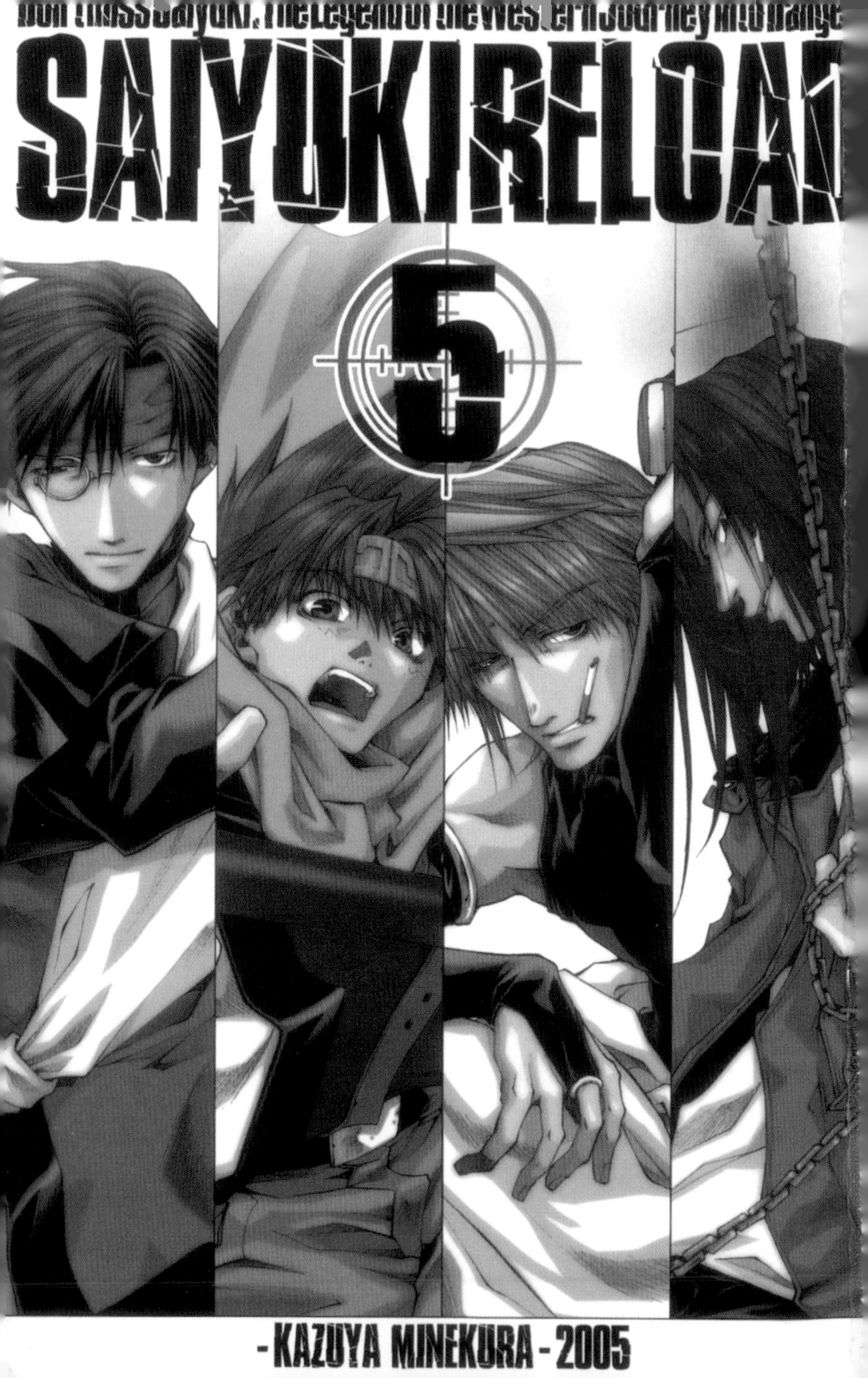
SAIYUKI RELOAD
5
- KAZUYA MINEKURA - 2005

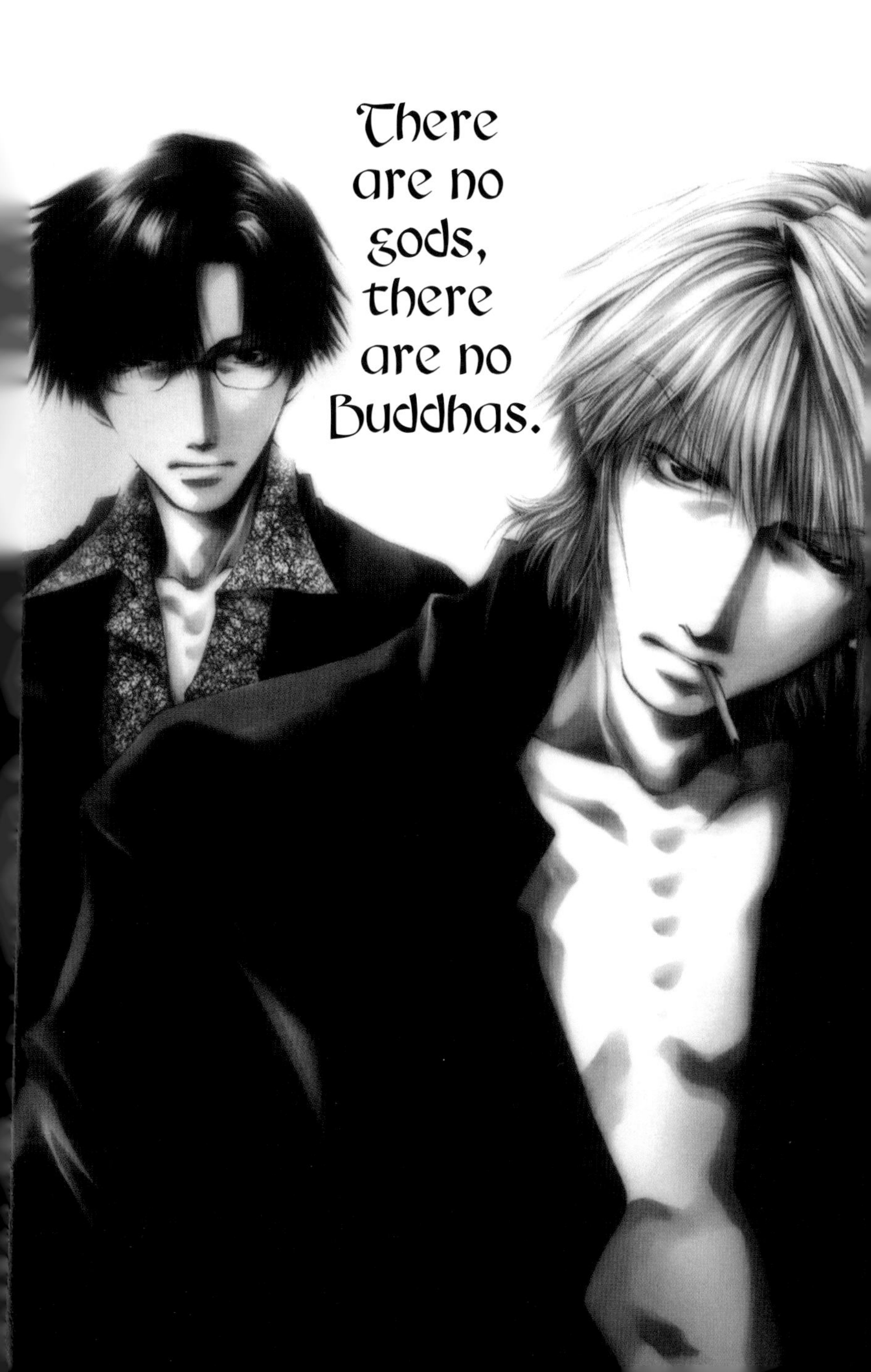
There are no gods, there are no Buddhas.

SAIYUKI RELOAD

The world begins to go crazy. You can't take your eyes off them.

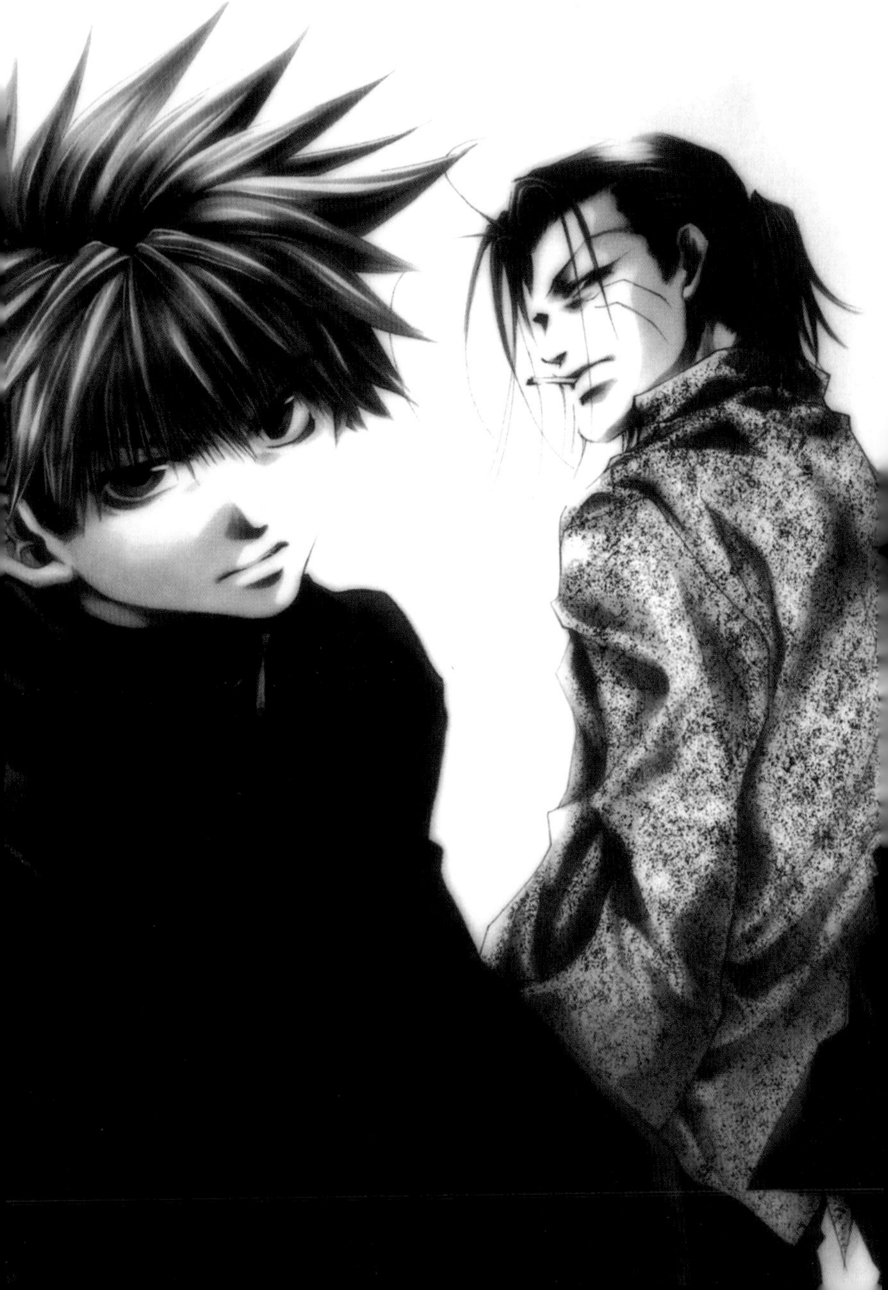

CONTENTS

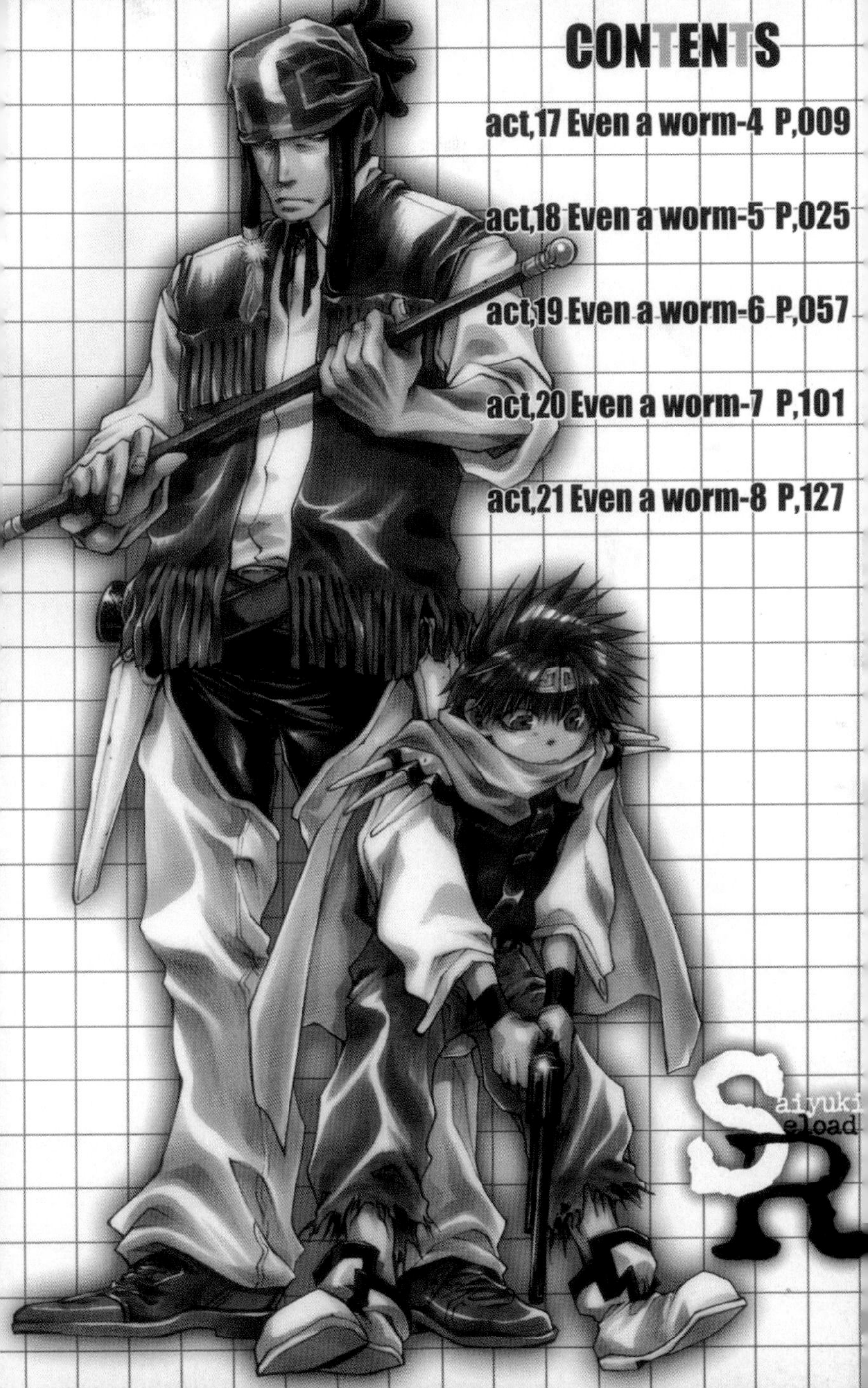

Saiyuki Reload

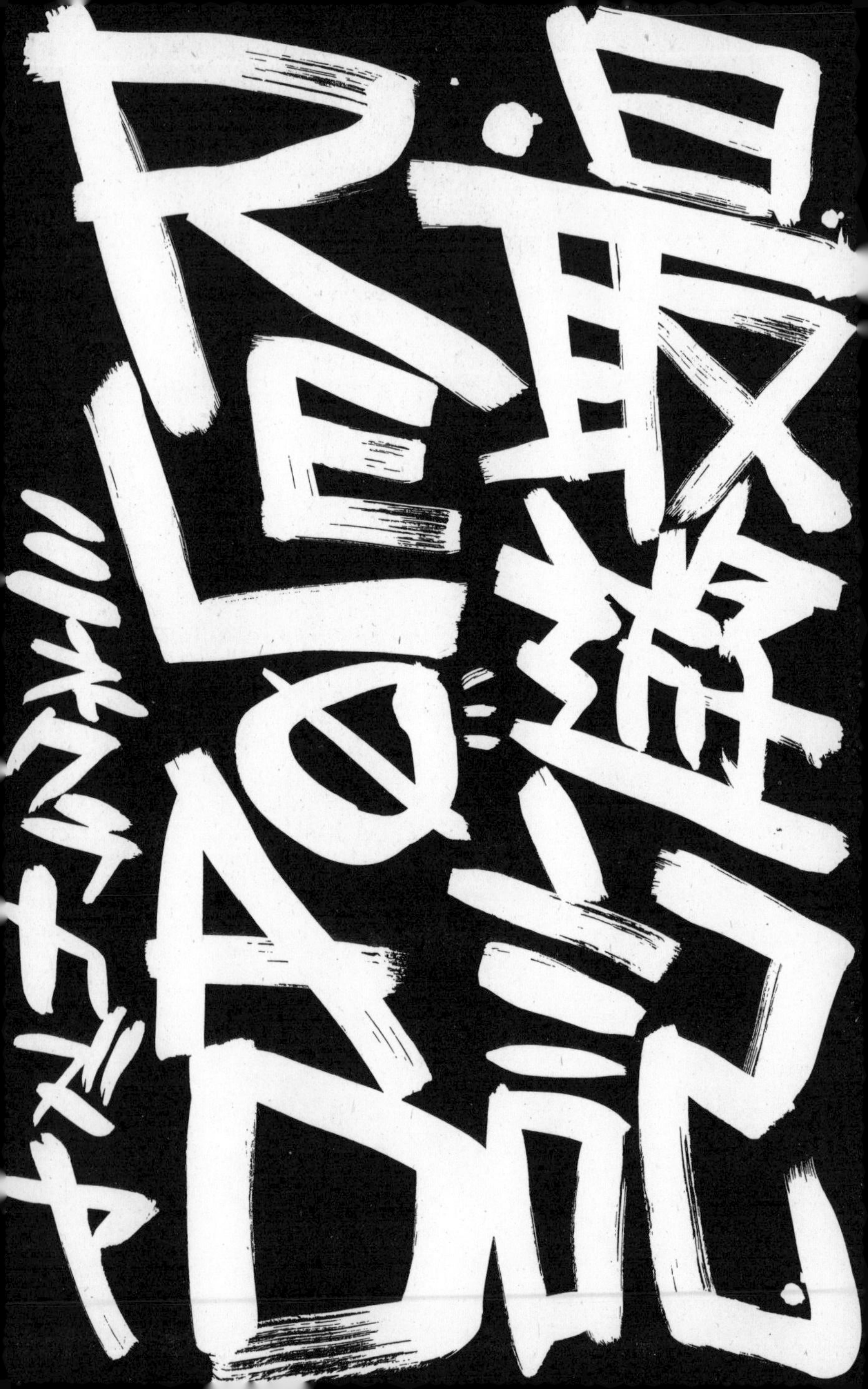
最遊記
RELOAD
ミネクラカズヤ

Saiyuki Reload Vol. 5
Created by Kazuya Minekura

Translation - Athena Nibley and Alethea Nibley
English Adaptation - Lianne Sentar
Associate Editor - Peter Ahlstrom
Retouch and Lettering - Bowen Park
Production Artist - Jihye "Sophia" Hong
Cover Artist - Kyle Plummer

Editor - Lillian Diaz-Przybyl
Digital Imaging Manager - Chris Buford
Production Manager - Elisabeth Brizzi
VP of Production - Ron Klamert
Publisher - Mike Kiley
Editor in Chief - Rob Tokar
President and C.O.O. - John Parker
C.E.O. and Chief Creative Officer - Stuart Levy

A **TOKYOPOP**® Manga

TOKYOPOP Inc.
5900 Wilshire Blvd. Suite 2000
Los Angeles, CA 90036

E-mail: info@TOKYOPOP.com
Come visit us online at www.TOKYOPOP.com

ISBN: 1-59816-180-6

First TOKYOPOP printing: September 2006
10 9 8 7 6 5 4 3 2 1
Printed in the USA

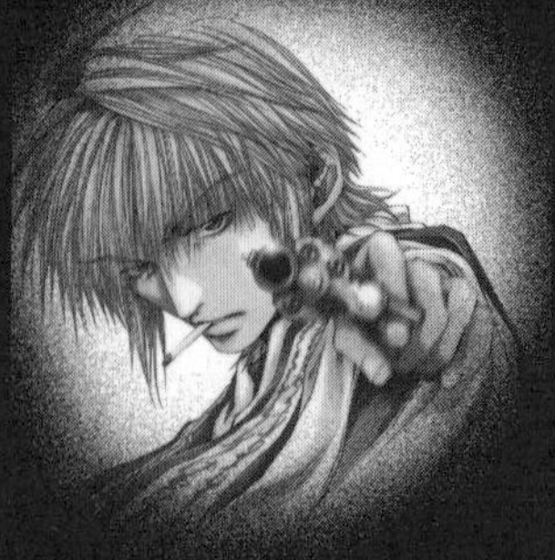

Genjyo Sanzo –

A very brutal, worldly priest. He drinks, smokes, gambles and even carries a gun. He's looking for the sacred scripture of his late master, Koumyou Sanzo. He's egotistical, haughty and has zero sense of humor, but this handsome 23-year-old hero also has calm judgment and charisma. His favorite phrases are "Die" and "I'll kill you." His main weapons are the Maten Sutra, a handgun, and a paper fan for idiots. He's 177cm tall (approx. 5'10"), and is often noted for his drooping purple eyes.

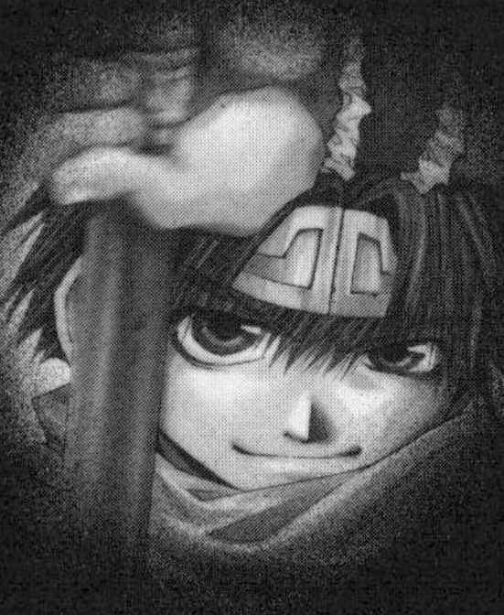

Son Goku –

The brave, cheerful Monkey King of legend; an unholy child born from the rocks where the aura of the Earth was gathered. His brain is full of thoughts of food and games. To pay for crimes he committed when he was young, he was imprisoned in the rocks for five hundred years without aging. Because of his optimistic personality, he's become the mascot character of the group; this 18-year-old of superior health is made fun of by Gojyo, yelled at by Sanzo and watched over by Hakkai. He's 162cm tall (approx. 5'4"). His main weapon is the Nyoi-Bo, a magical cudgel that can extend into a sansekkon staff.

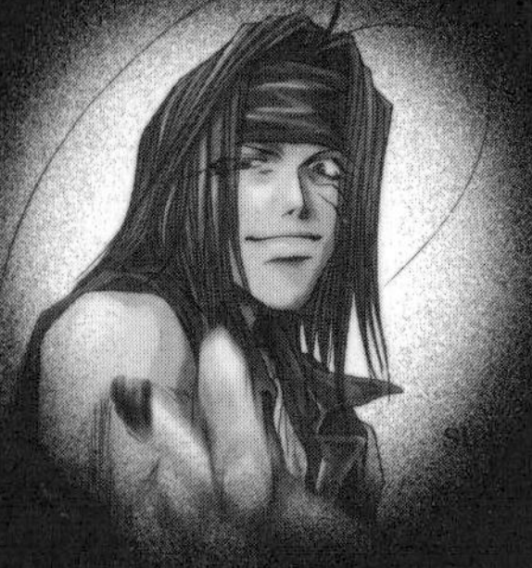

Sha Gojyo –

Gojyo is a lecherous kappa (water youkai). His behavior might seem vulgar and rough at first glance (and it is), but to his friends, he's like a dependable older brother. He and Goku are sparring partners, he and Hakkai are best friends and he and Sanzo are bad friends (ha ha!). Sometimes his love for the ladies gets him into trouble. Because of his unusual heritage, he doesn't need a limiter to blend in with the humans. His favorite way of fighting is to use a shakujou, a staff with a crescent-shaped blade connected by a chain; it's quite messy. He's 184cm tall (approx. 6'), has scarlet hair and eyes and is a 22-year-old chain smoker.

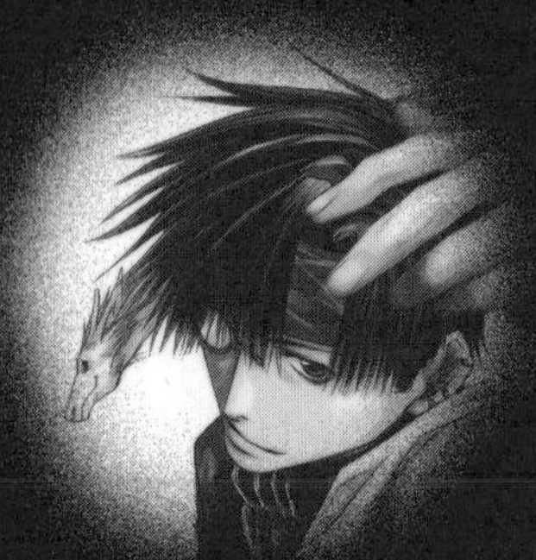

Cho Hakkai –

A pleasant, rather absent-minded young man with a kind smile that suits him nicely. It's sometimes hard to tell whether he's serious or laughing to himself at his friends' expense. His darker side comes through from time to time in the form of a sharp, penetrating gaze, a symbol of a dark past. As he's Hakuryu's (the white dragon) owner, he gets to drive the Jeep. Because he uses kikou jutsu (Chi manipulation) in battle, his "weapon" is his smile (ha ha!). He's 22 years old, 181cm tall (approx. 5'11") and his eyes are deep green (his right eye is nearly blind). The cuffs he wears on his left ear are Youkai power limiters.

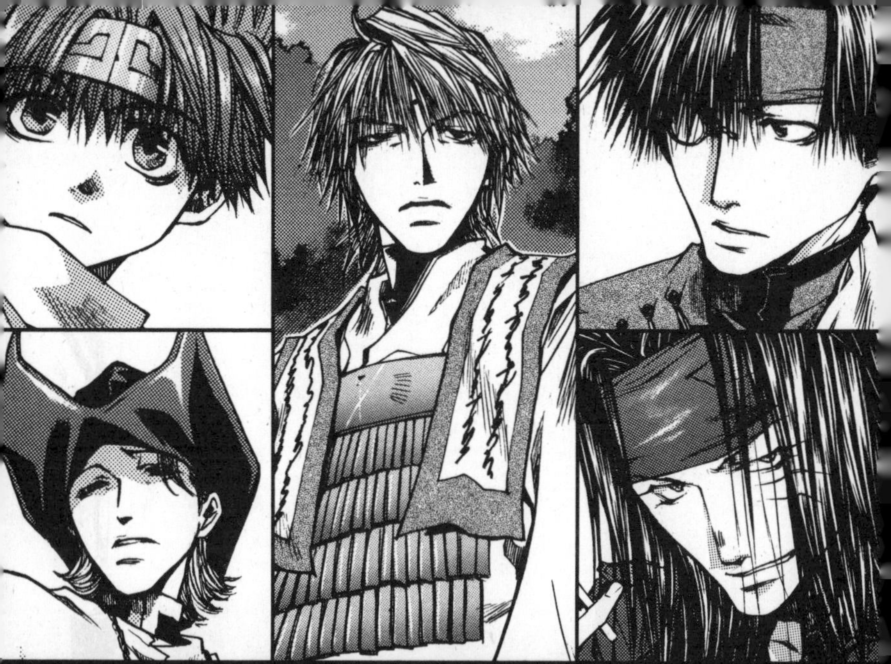

The Story So Far

Chaos has ravaged Shangri-La. During an attempt by dark forces to revive the Ox King Gyumaoh, the combination of science and youkai magic sent a Minus Wave surging through the land that drove all youkai berserk, thus causing mass violence and upsetting the peaceful balance between the races. Now it's up to four companions--the youkai Son Goku, Sha Gojyo, and Cho Hakkai, and the human Priest Genjyo Sanzo--to travel West and stop the experiment that plagues the world. It's an excellent plan...save for the fact that the four companions suffer from "teamwork issues."

In buried tales, Sanzo discovered just how powerful--and vulnerable--the small monster he claimed from the mountains really is. He took responsibility for the child, despite his distaste for the task. And two men thrown together by fate discovered how intertwined purity and sin can be...not to mention love and violence.

But in our reluctant heroes' current travels, Hakkai, Gojyo, and Goku were randomly attacked by a number of youkai-hating humans--potentially undead humans with eerie yellow eyes. The foreign "Bishop" Hazel and his servant Gat appeared a short time later, claiming to control the power to revive dead humans with youkai souls. But those Hazel revives also have yellow eyes, and our heroes suffer yet another surprise attack at the hands of these "saved" humans. Although Hazel and Gat say they're fighting the berserk youkai, do they consider the youkai in Sanzo's party just as worthy of defeat?

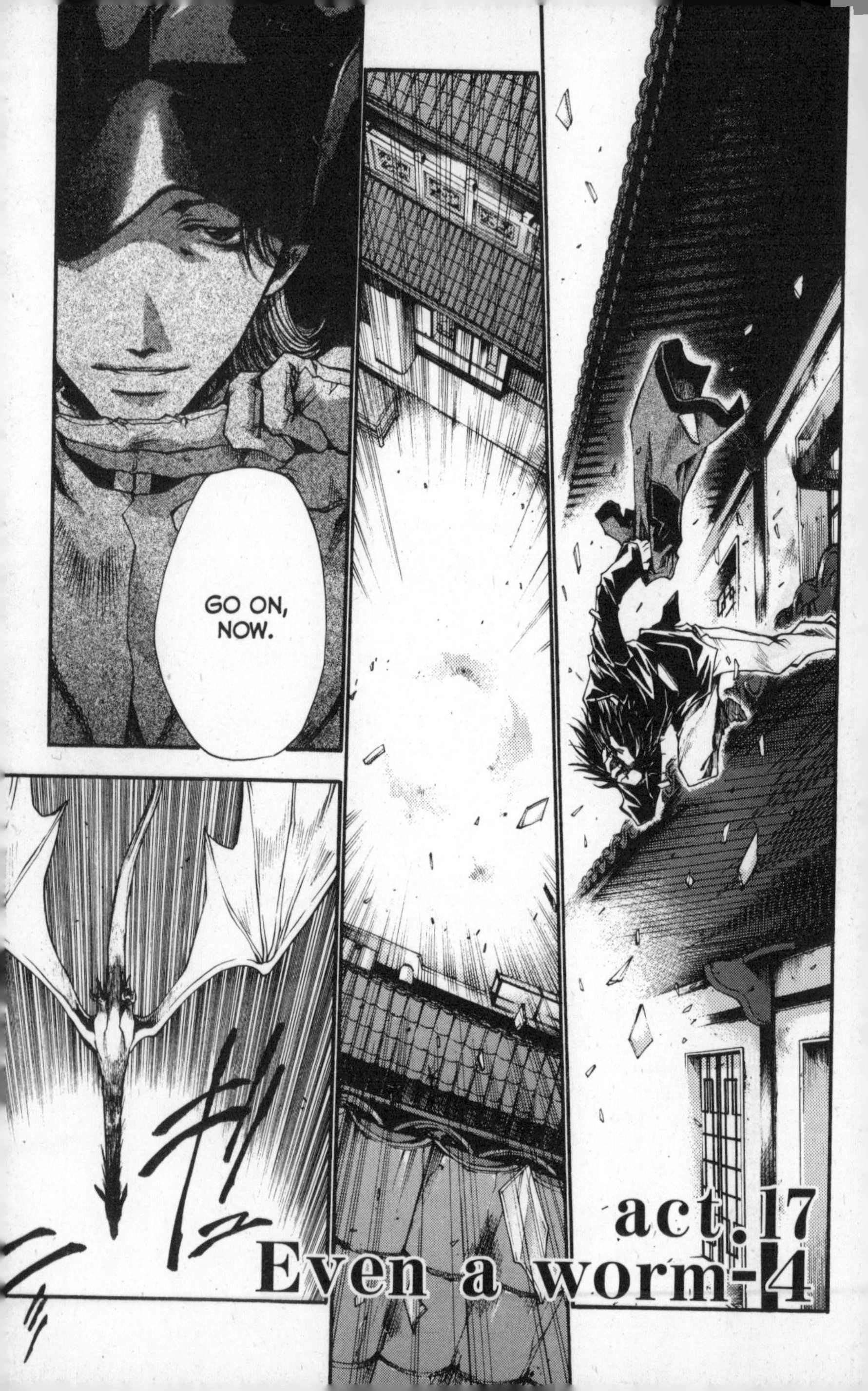
GO ON, NOW.
act. 17
Even a worm-4

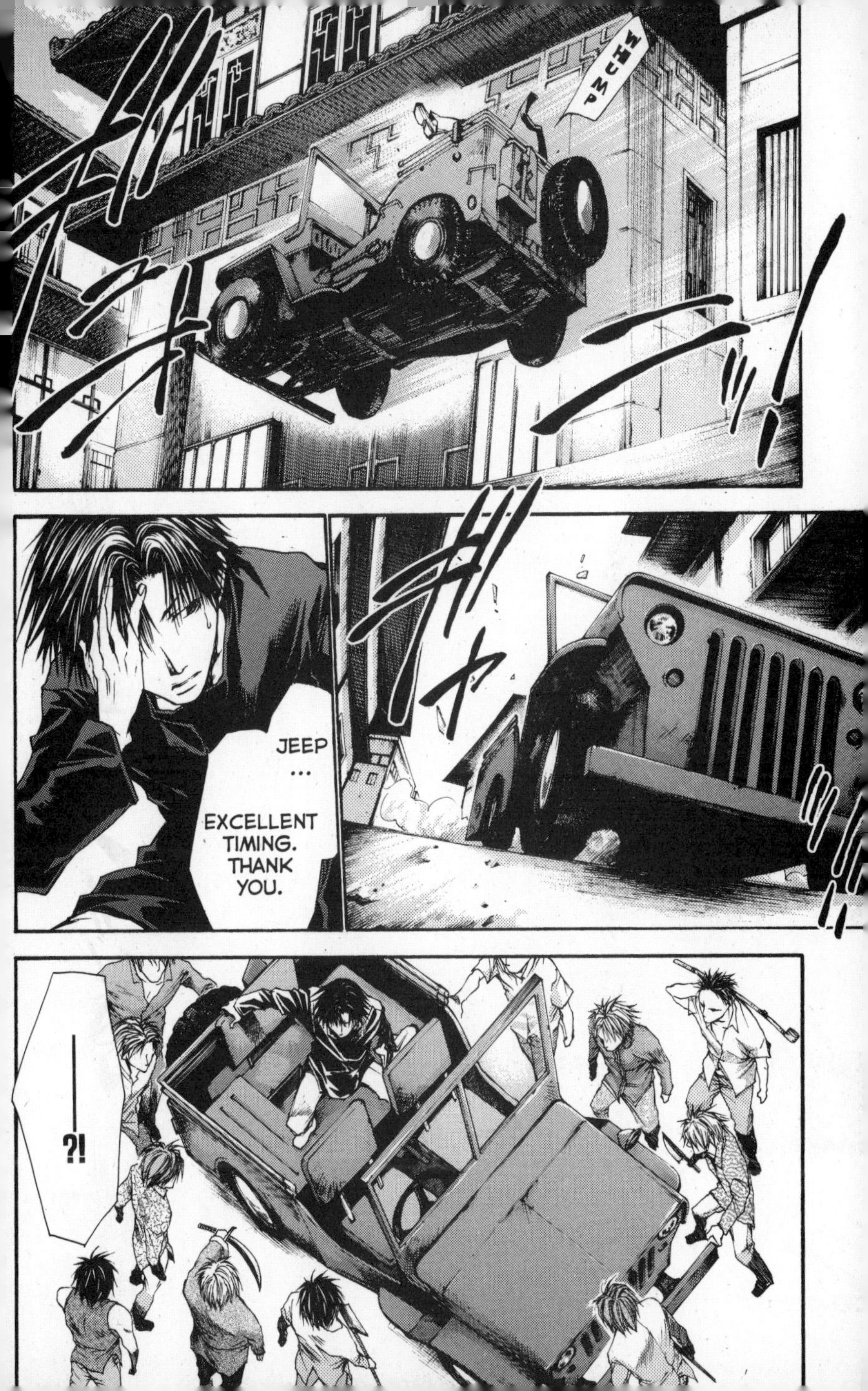
WHUMP
JEEP
...
EXCELLENT TIMING. THANK YOU.
——?!

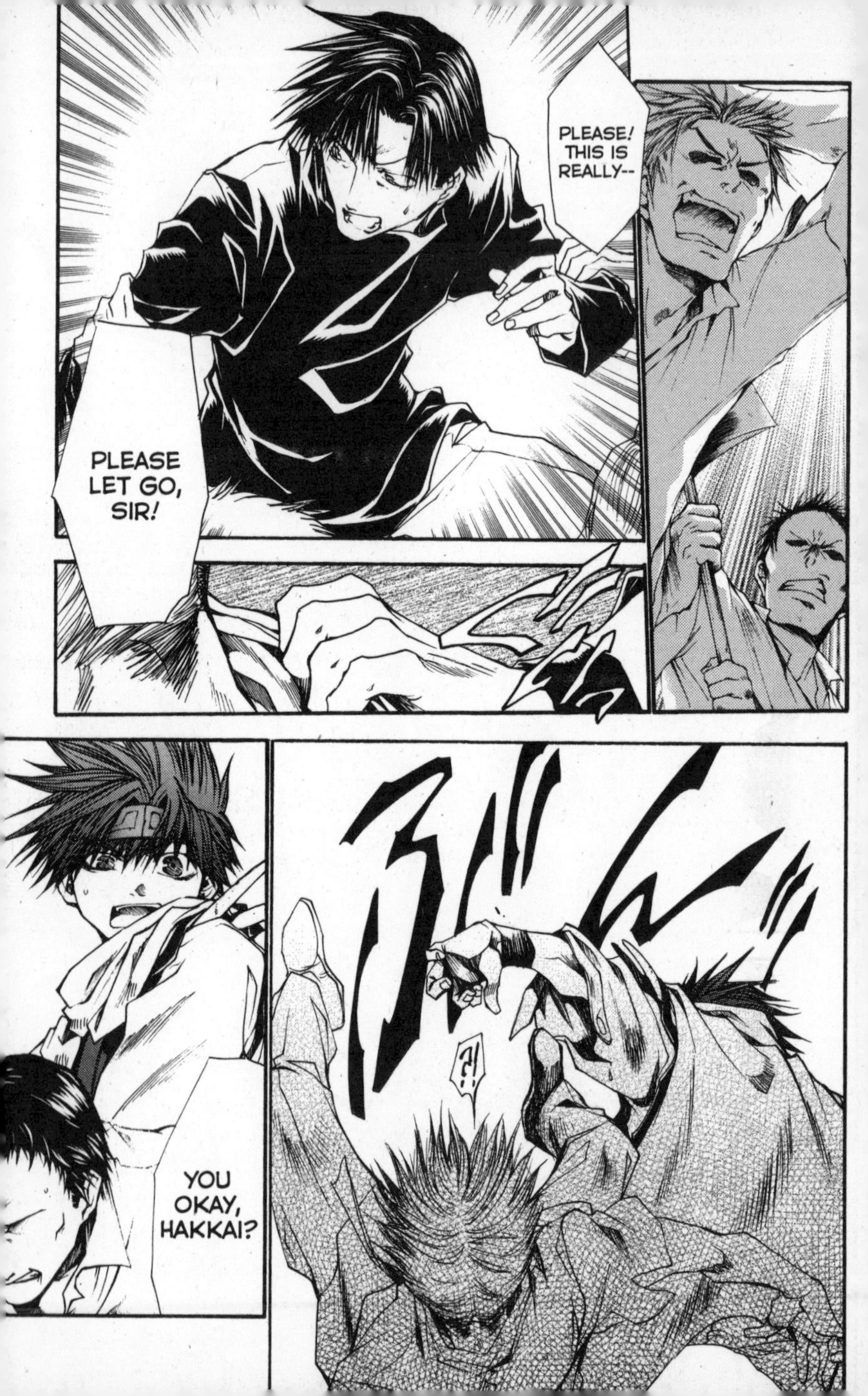
PLEASE! THIS IS REALLY--
PLEASE LET GO, SIR!
?!
YOU OKAY, HAKKAI?

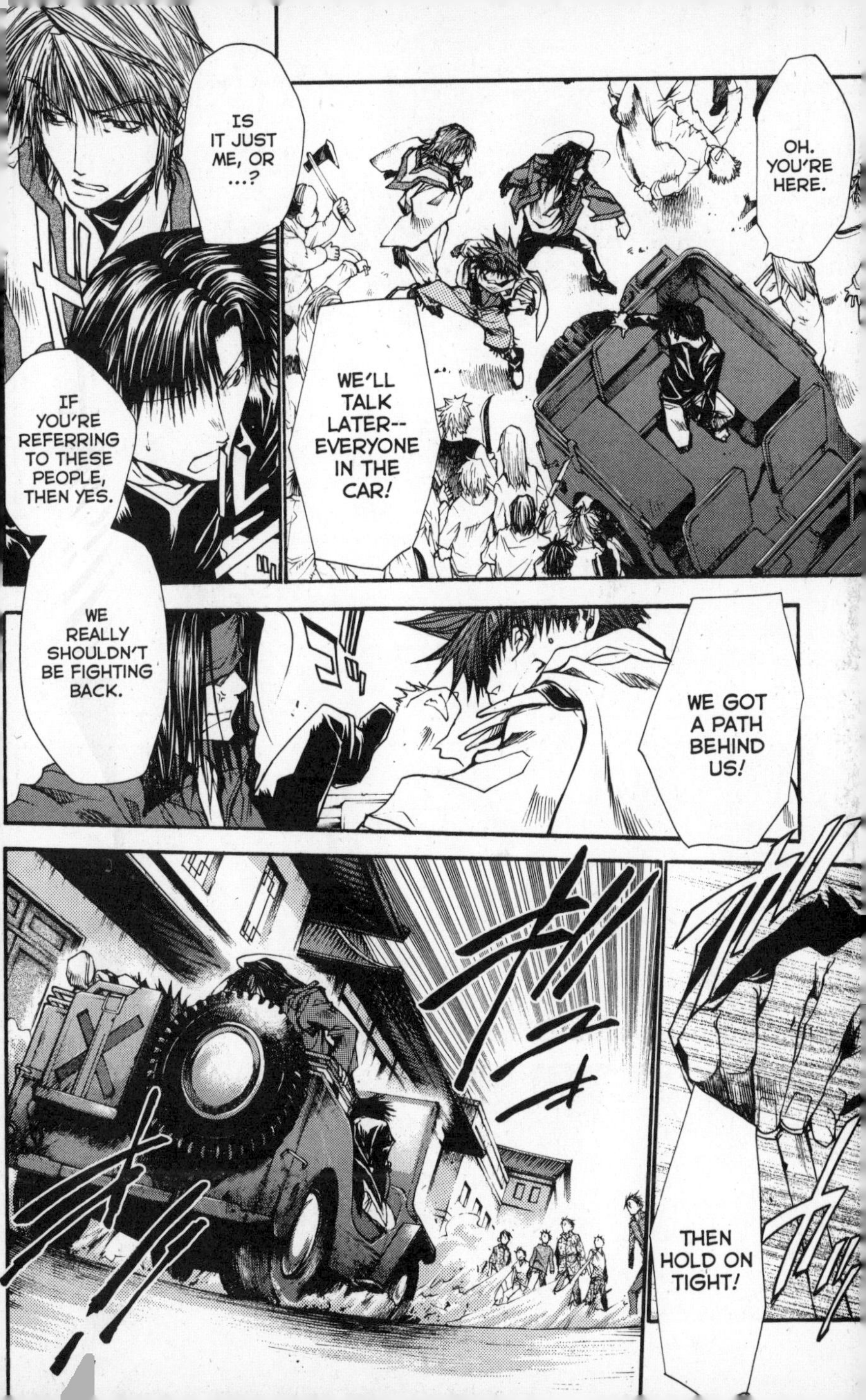
OH. YOU'RE HERE.
WE'LL TALK LATER-- EVERYONE IN THE CAR!
IS IT JUST ME, OR ...?
IF YOU'RE REFERRING TO THESE PEOPLE, THEN YES.
WE GOT A PATH BEHIND US!
WE REALLY SHOULDN'T BE FIGHTING BACK.
THEN HOLD ON TIGHT!

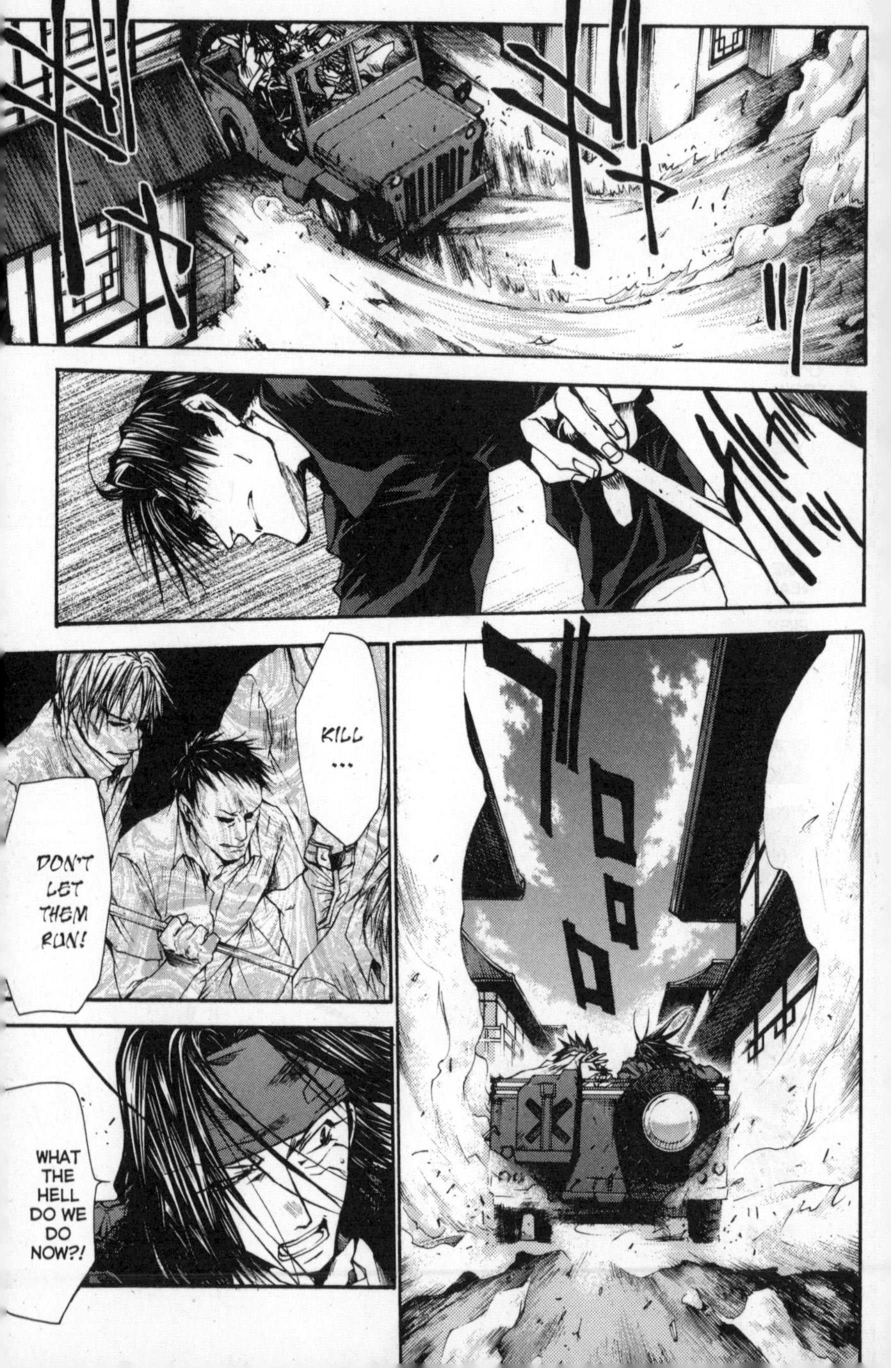
KILL ...
DON'T LET THEM RUN!
WHAT THE HELL DO WE DO NOW?!

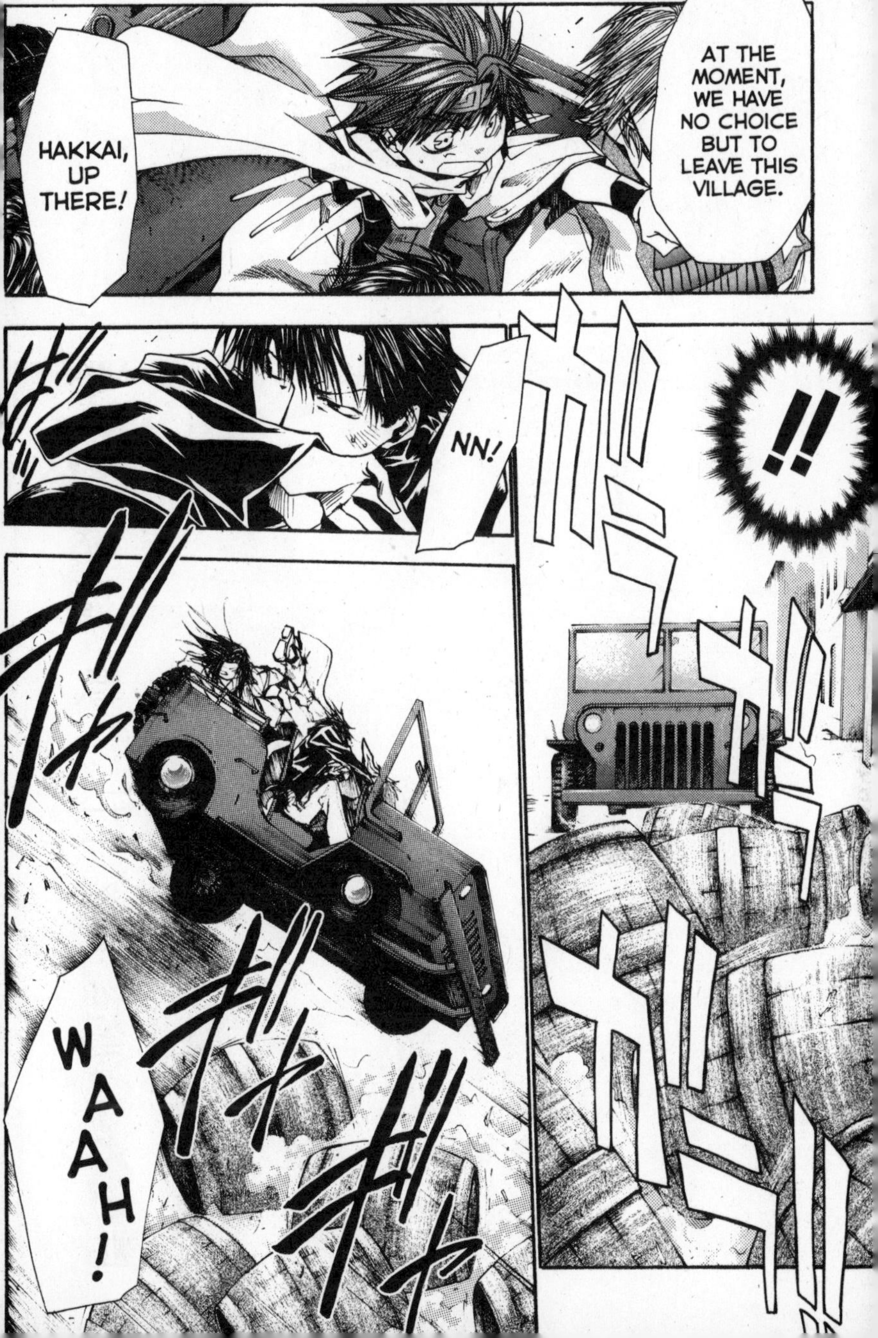
AT THE MOMENT, WE HAVE NO CHOICE BUT TO LEAVE THIS VILLAGE.
HAKKAI, UP THERE!
!!
NN!
WAAH!

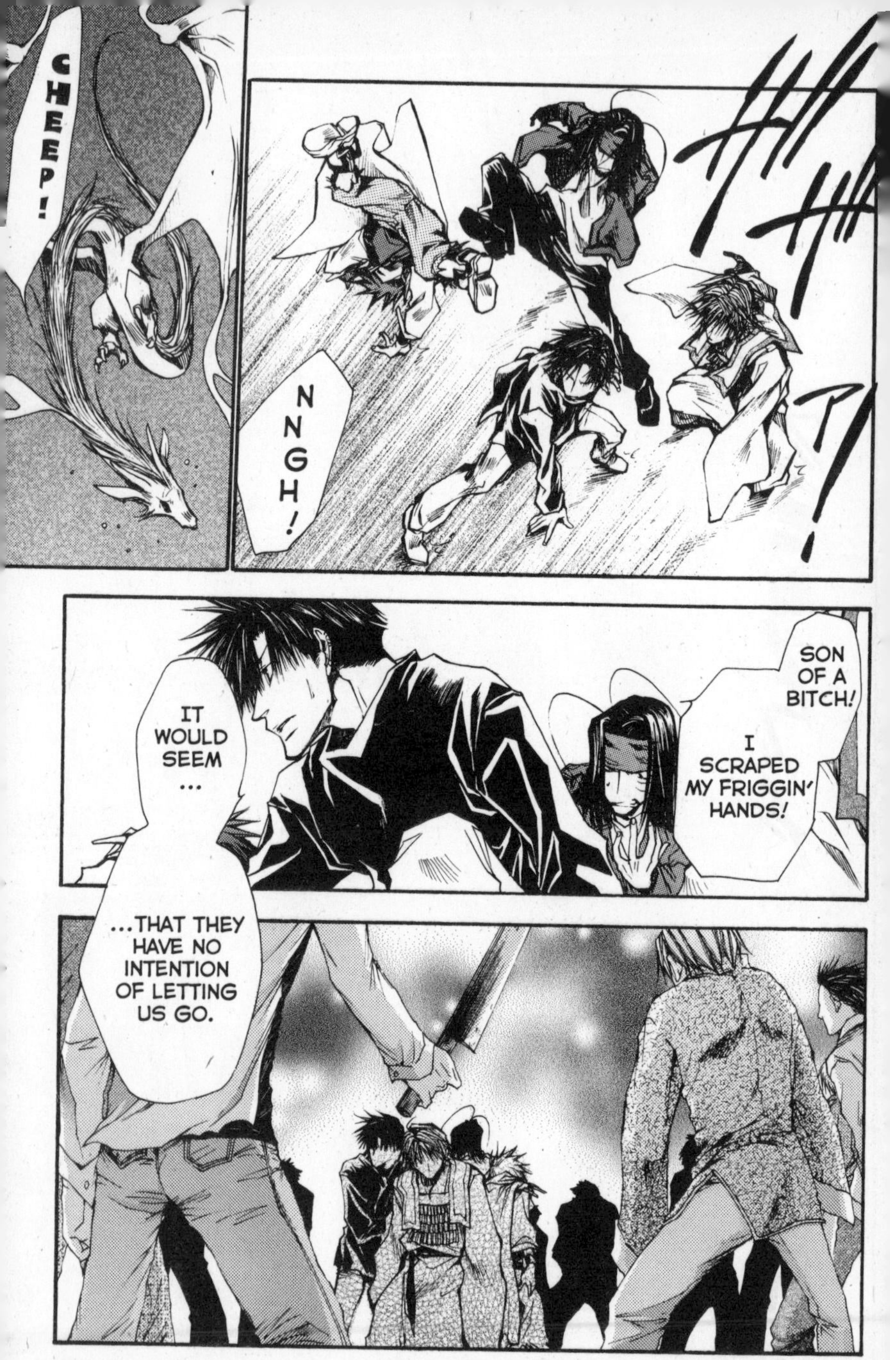
NNGH!
CHEEP!
SON OF A BITCH!
I SCRAPED MY FRIGGIN' HANDS!
IT WOULD SEEM ...
...THAT THEY HAVE NO INTENTION OF LETTING US GO.

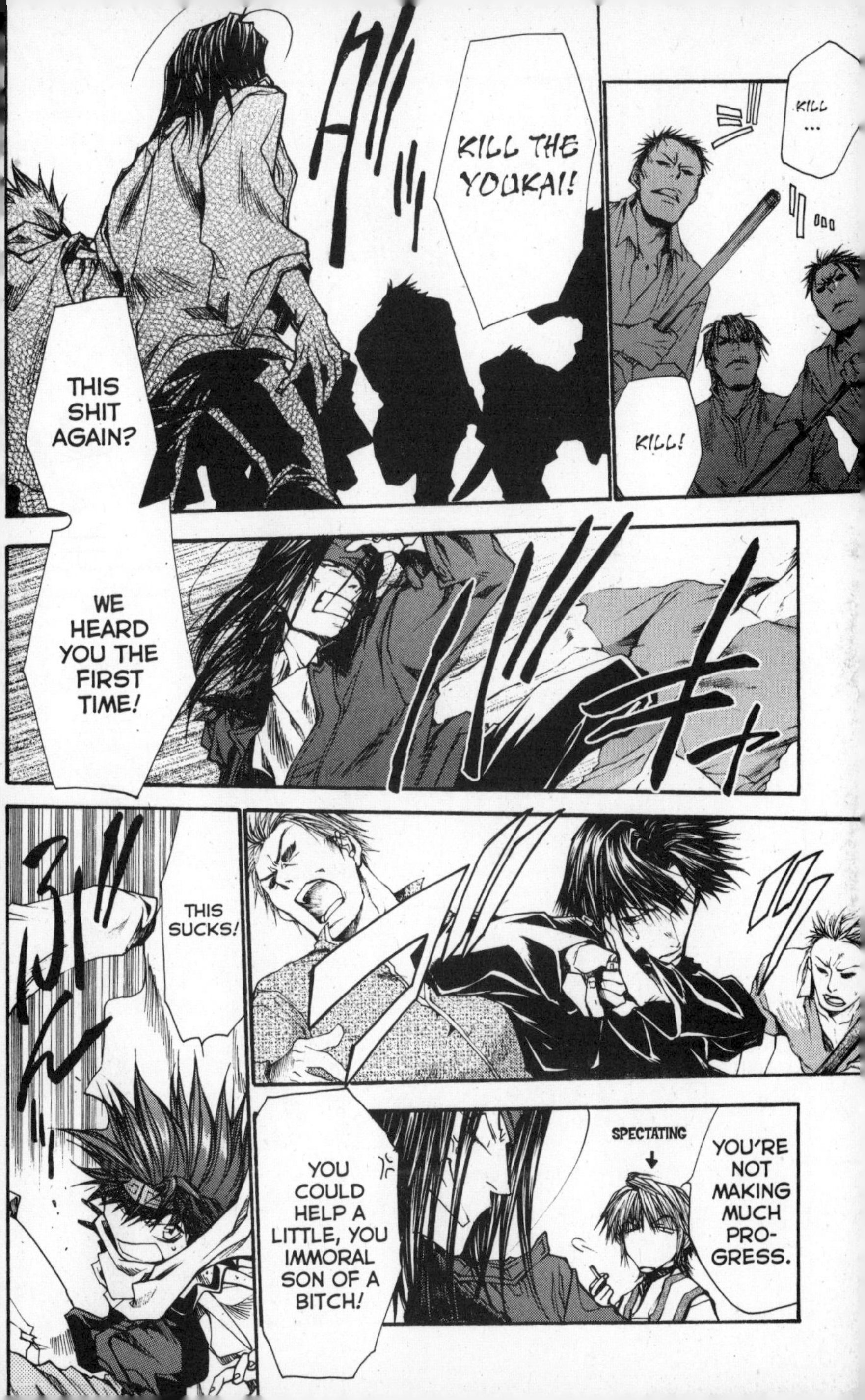
KILL ...
KILL!
KILL THE YOUKAI!
THIS SHIT AGAIN? WE HEARD YOU THE FIRST TIME!
SPECTATING
YOU'RE NOT MAKING MUCH PRO-GRESS.
YOU COULD HELP A LITTLE, YOU IMMORAL SON OF A BITCH!
THIS SUCKS!

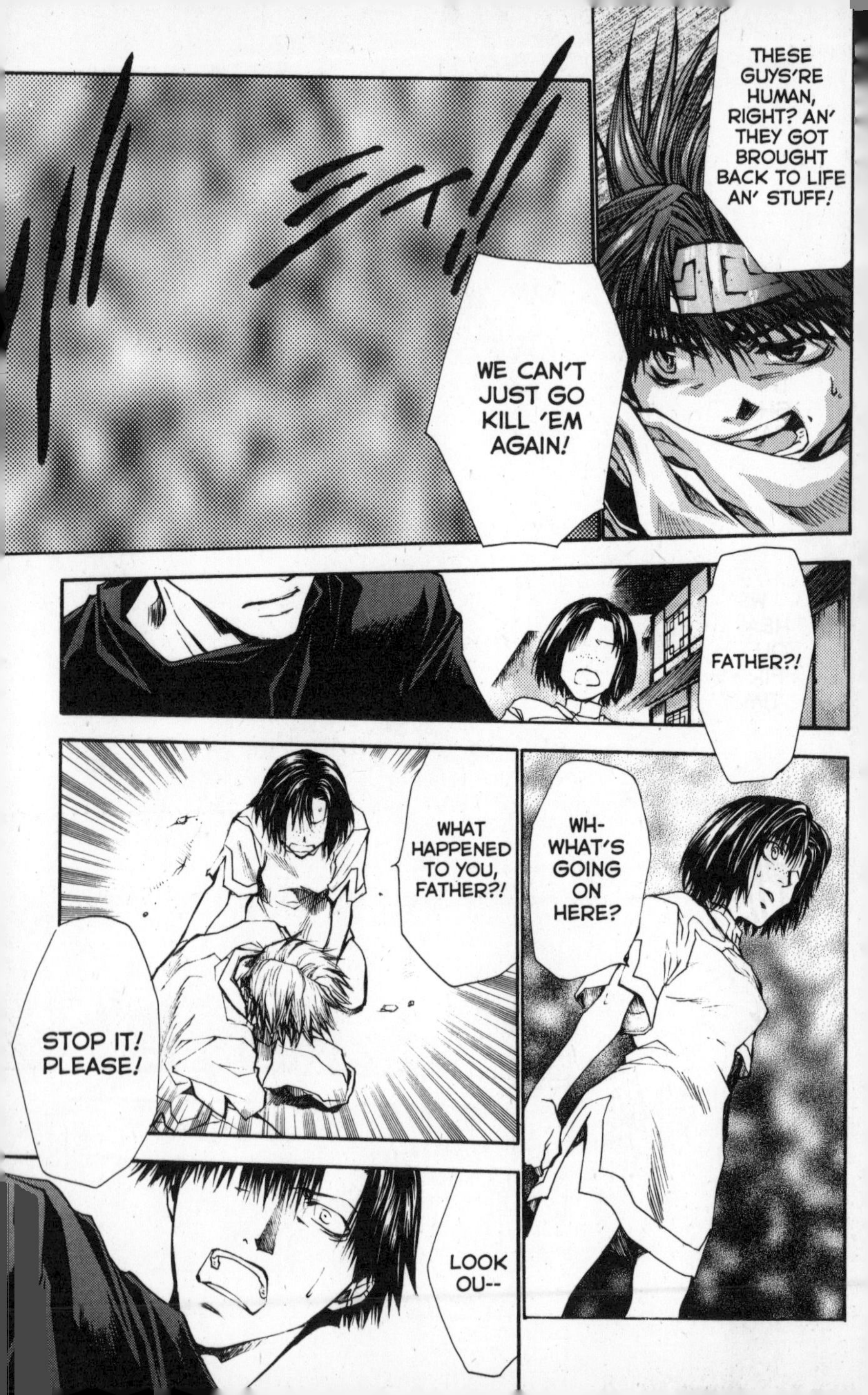
THESE GUYS'RE HUMAN, RIGHT? AN' THEY GOT BROUGHT BACK TO LIFE AN' STUFF!
WE CAN'T JUST GO KILL 'EM AGAIN!
FATHER?!
WH- WHAT'S GOING ON HERE?
WHAT HAPPENED TO YOU, FATHER?!
STOP IT! PLEASE!
LOOK OU--

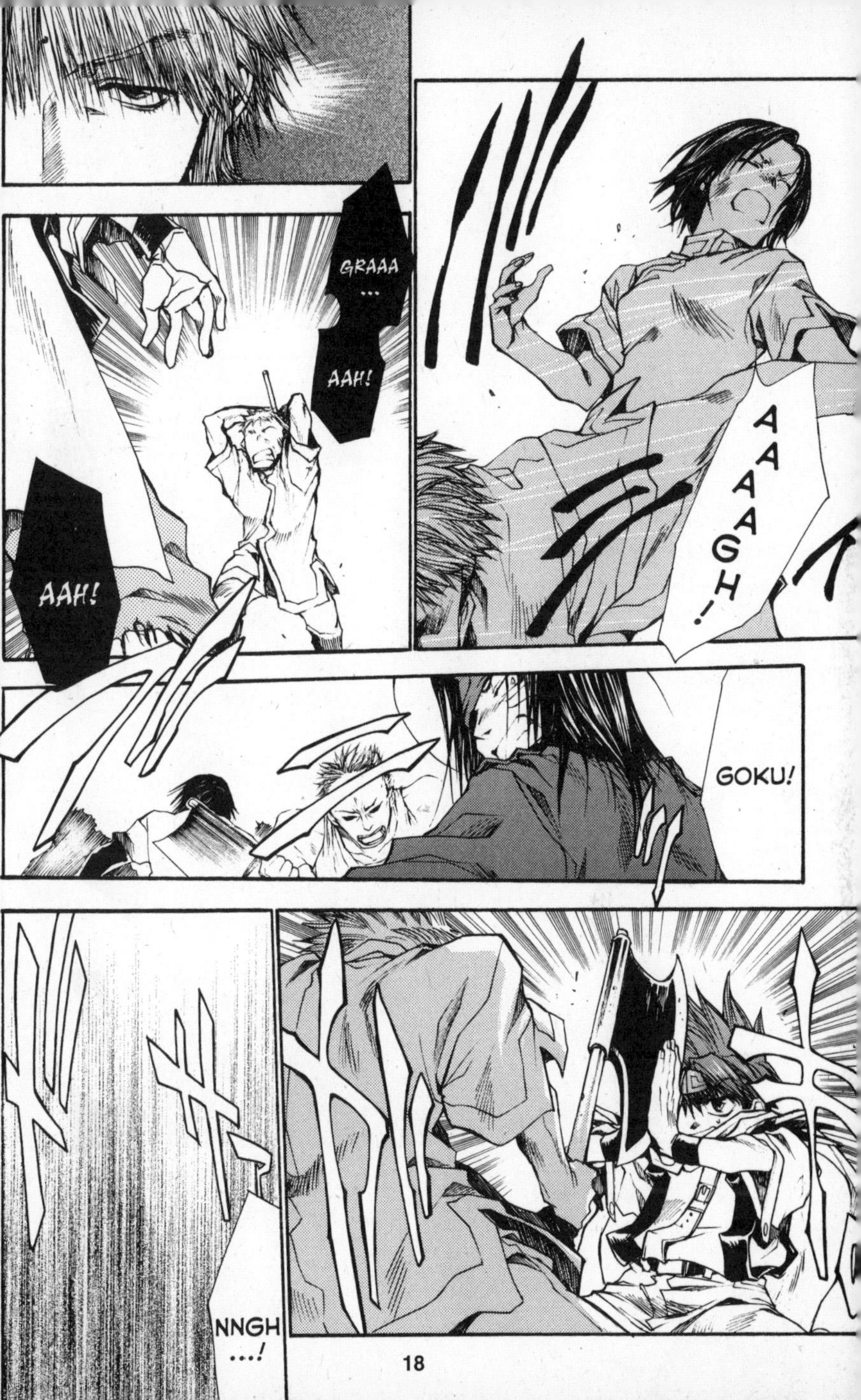
AAAAGH!
GRAAA...
AAH!
AAH!
GOKU!
NNGH...!

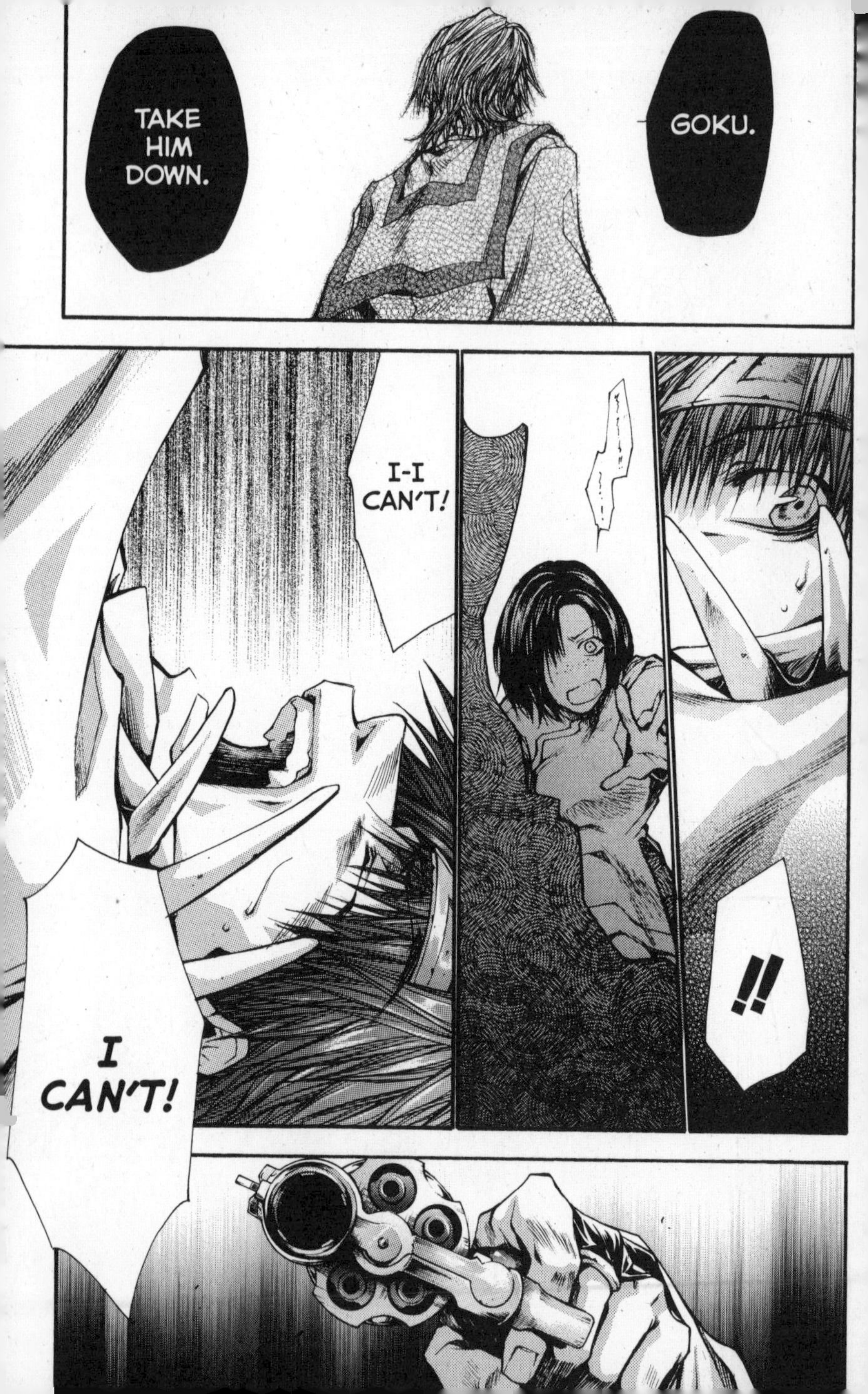
GOKU.
TAKE HIM DOWN.
!!
I-I CAN'T!
I CAN'T!

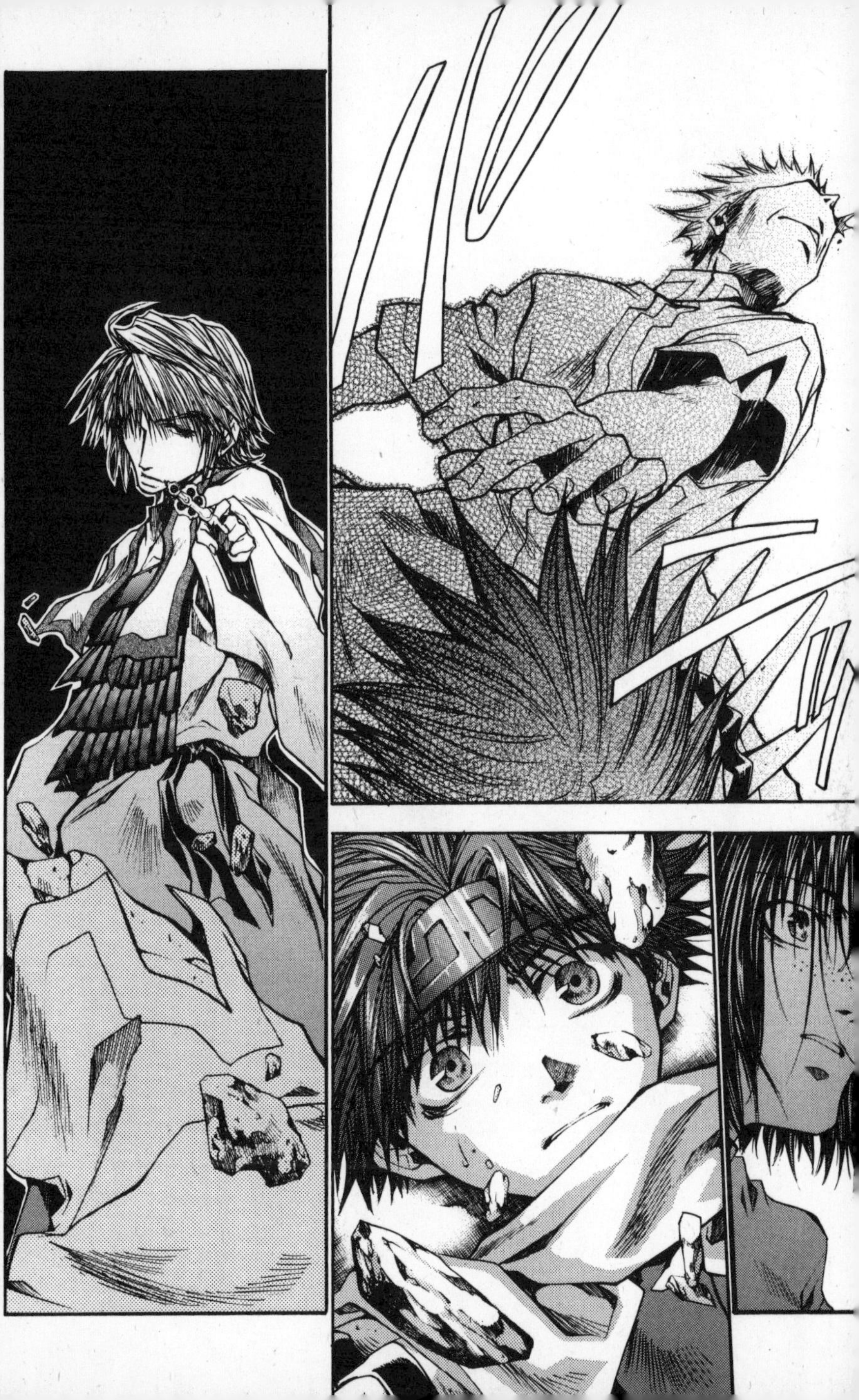

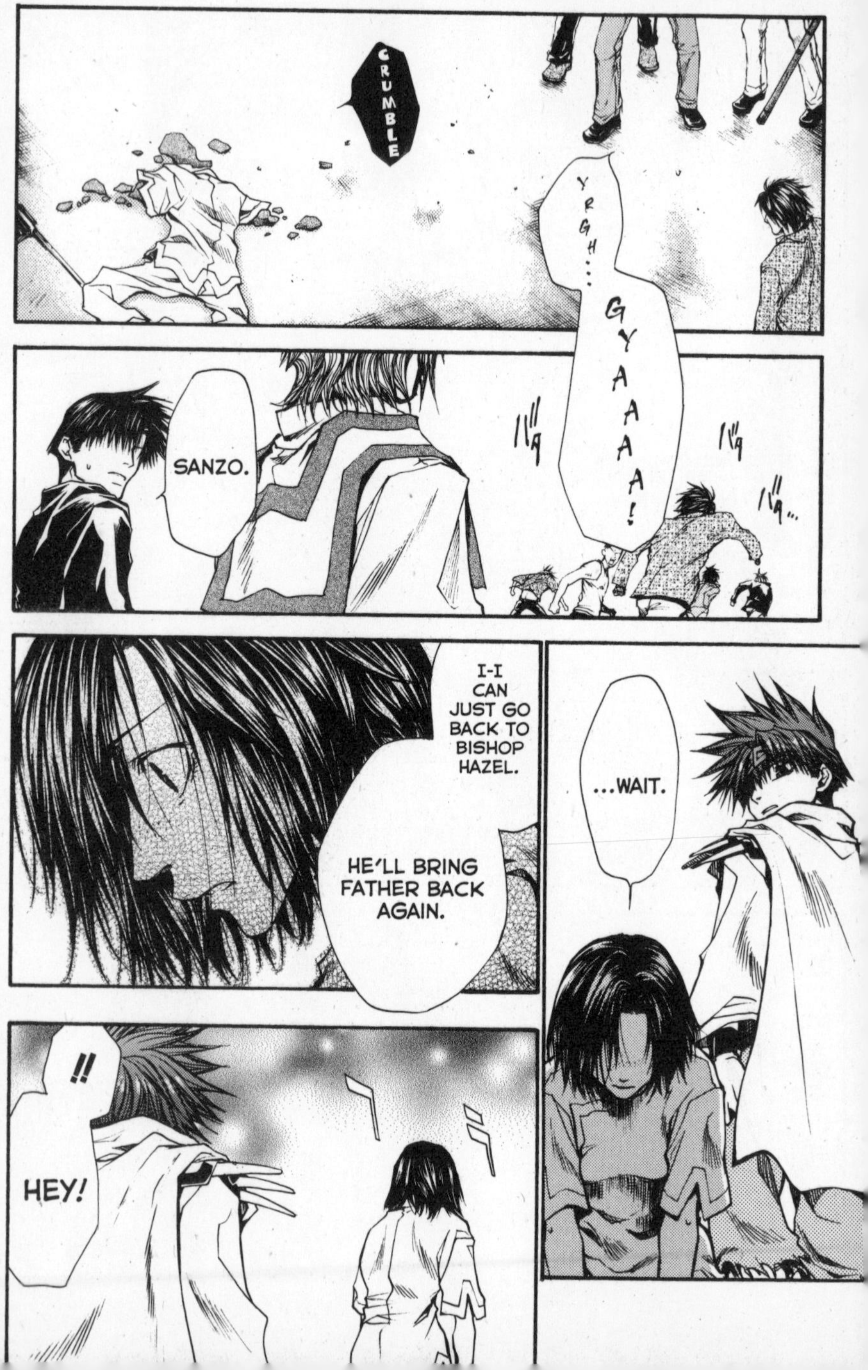
CRUMBLE
YRGH... GYAAAAA!
SANZO.
...WAIT.
I-I CAN JUST GO BACK TO BISHOP HAZEL.
HE'LL BRING FATHER BACK AGAIN.
!!
HEY!

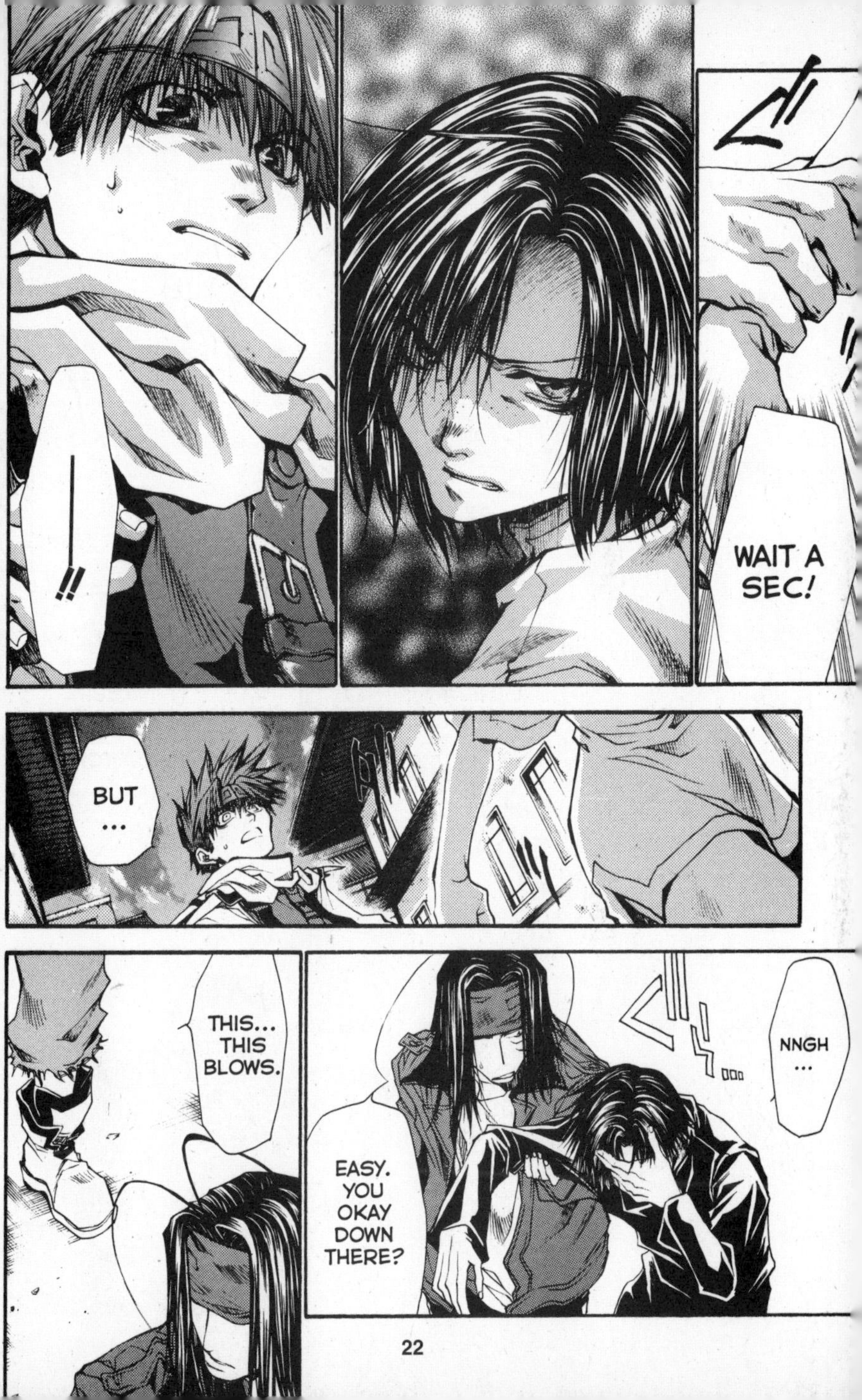
WAIT A SEC!
—!!
BUT ...
NNGH ...
EASY. YOU OKAY DOWN THERE?
THIS... THIS BLOWS.

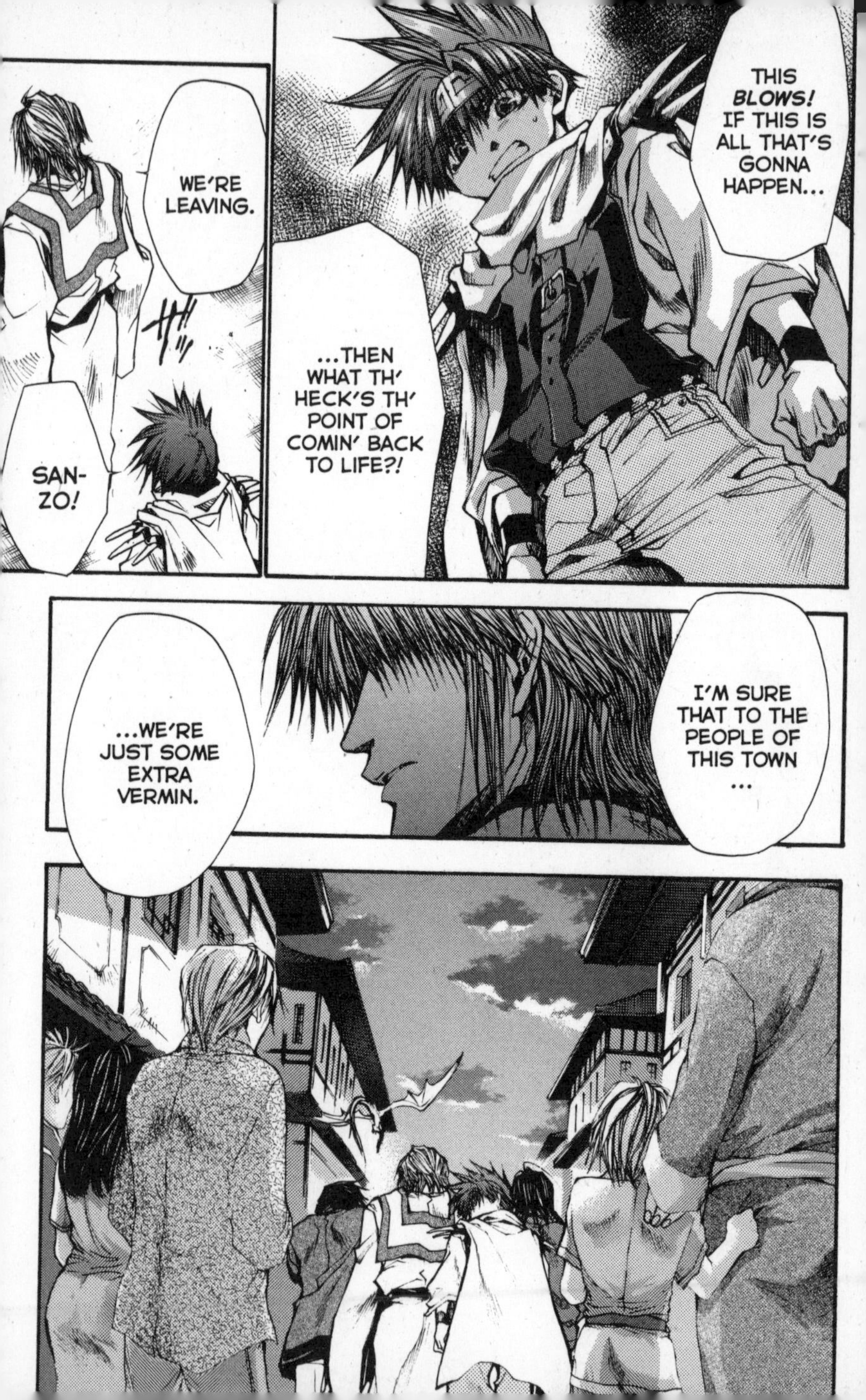
THIS BLOWS! IF THIS IS ALL THAT'S GONNA HAPPEN...
...THEN WHAT TH' HECK'S TH' POINT OF COMIN' BACK TO LIFE?!
WE'RE LEAVING.
SAN-ZO!
I'M SURE THAT TO THE PEOPLE OF THIS TOWN ...
...WE'RE JUST SOME EXTRA VERMIN.

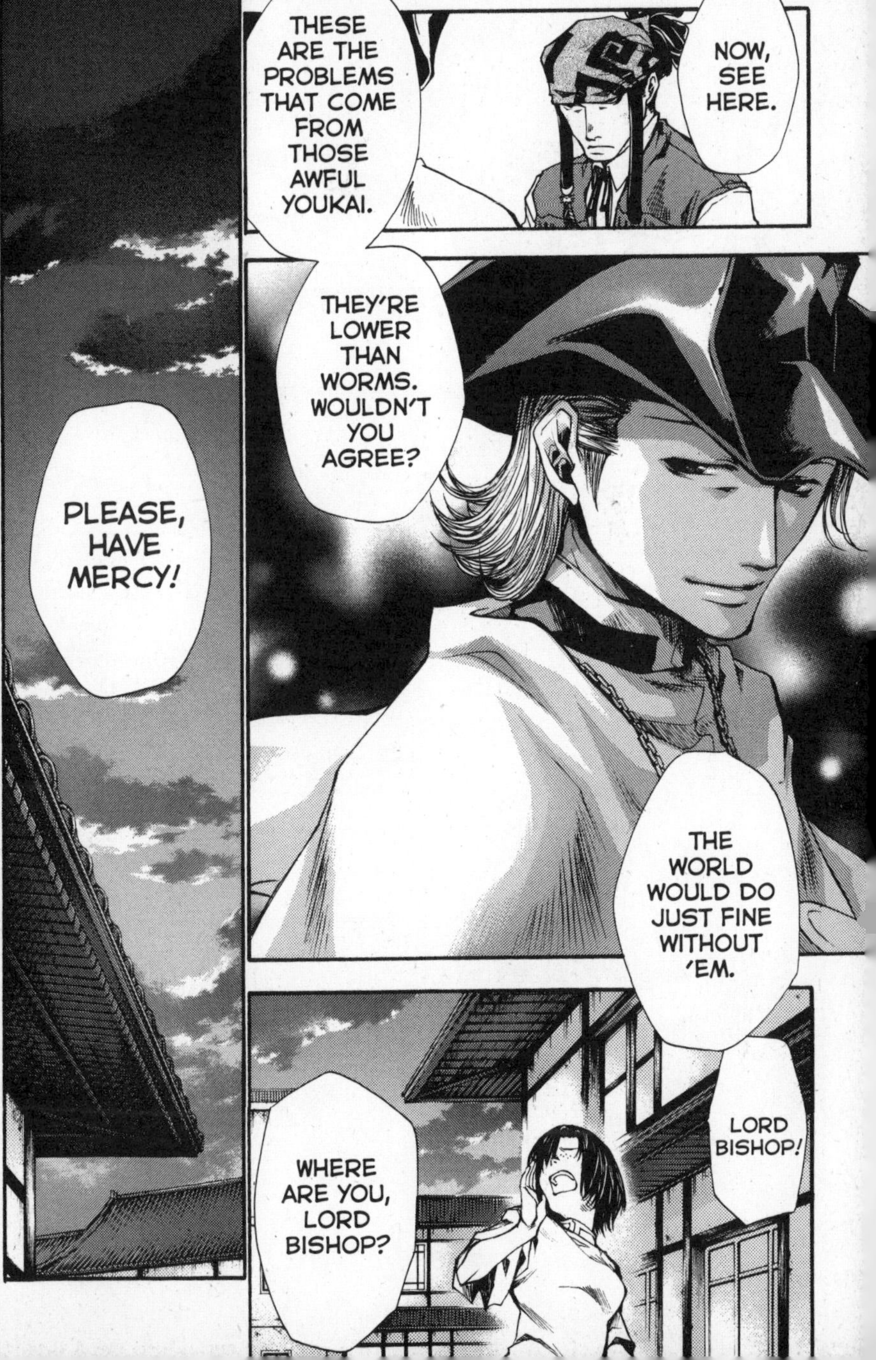
NOW, SEE HERE.
THESE ARE THE PROBLEMS THAT COME FROM THOSE AWFUL YOUKAI.
THEY'RE LOWER THAN WORMS. WOULDN'T YOU AGREE?
THE WORLD WOULD DO JUST FINE WITHOUT 'EM.
LORD BISHOP!
WHERE ARE YOU, LORD BISHOP?
PLEASE, HAVE MERCY!

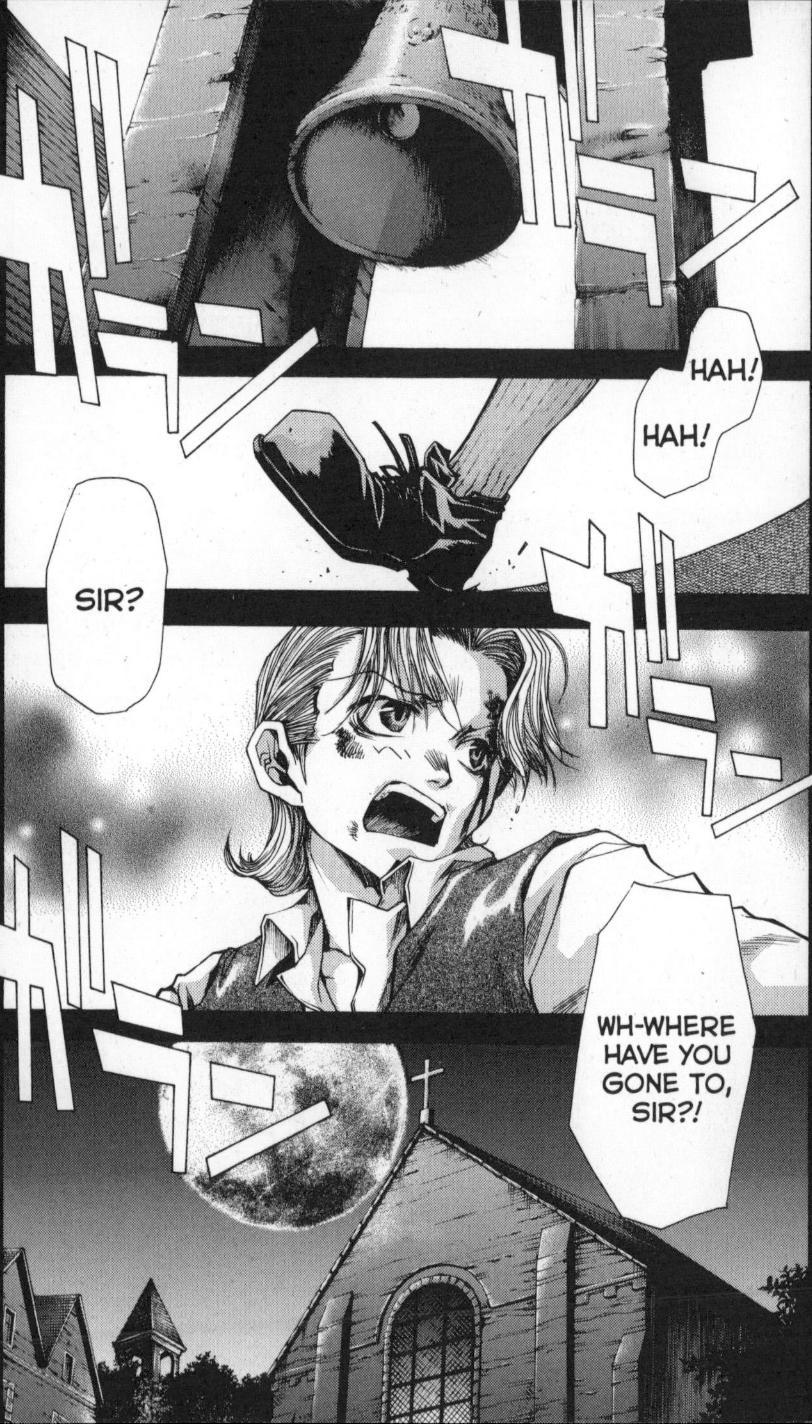
HAH!
HAH!
SIR?
WH-WHERE HAVE YOU GONE TO, SIR?!

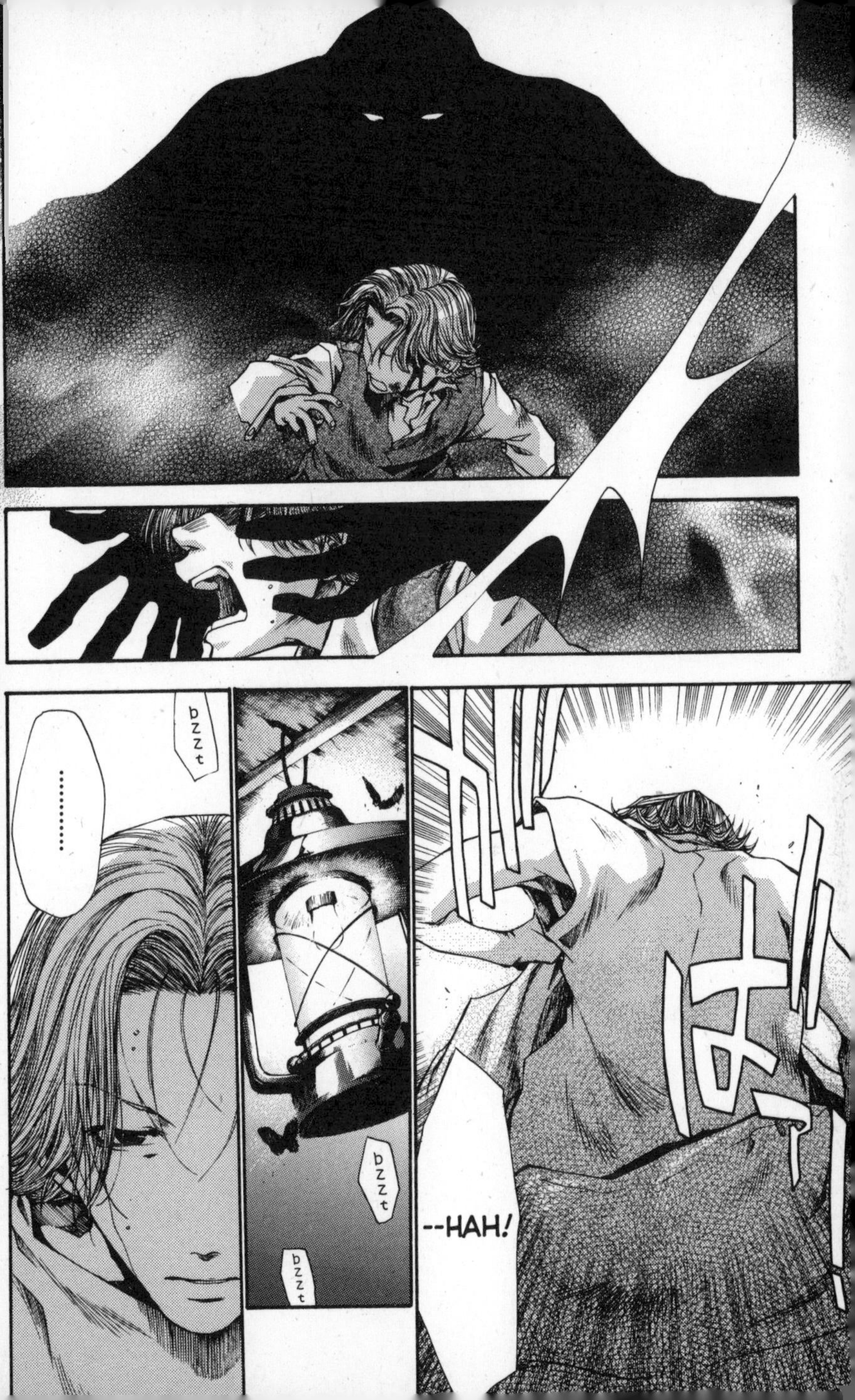
はっ
--HAH!
bzzt
bzzt
bzzt
....

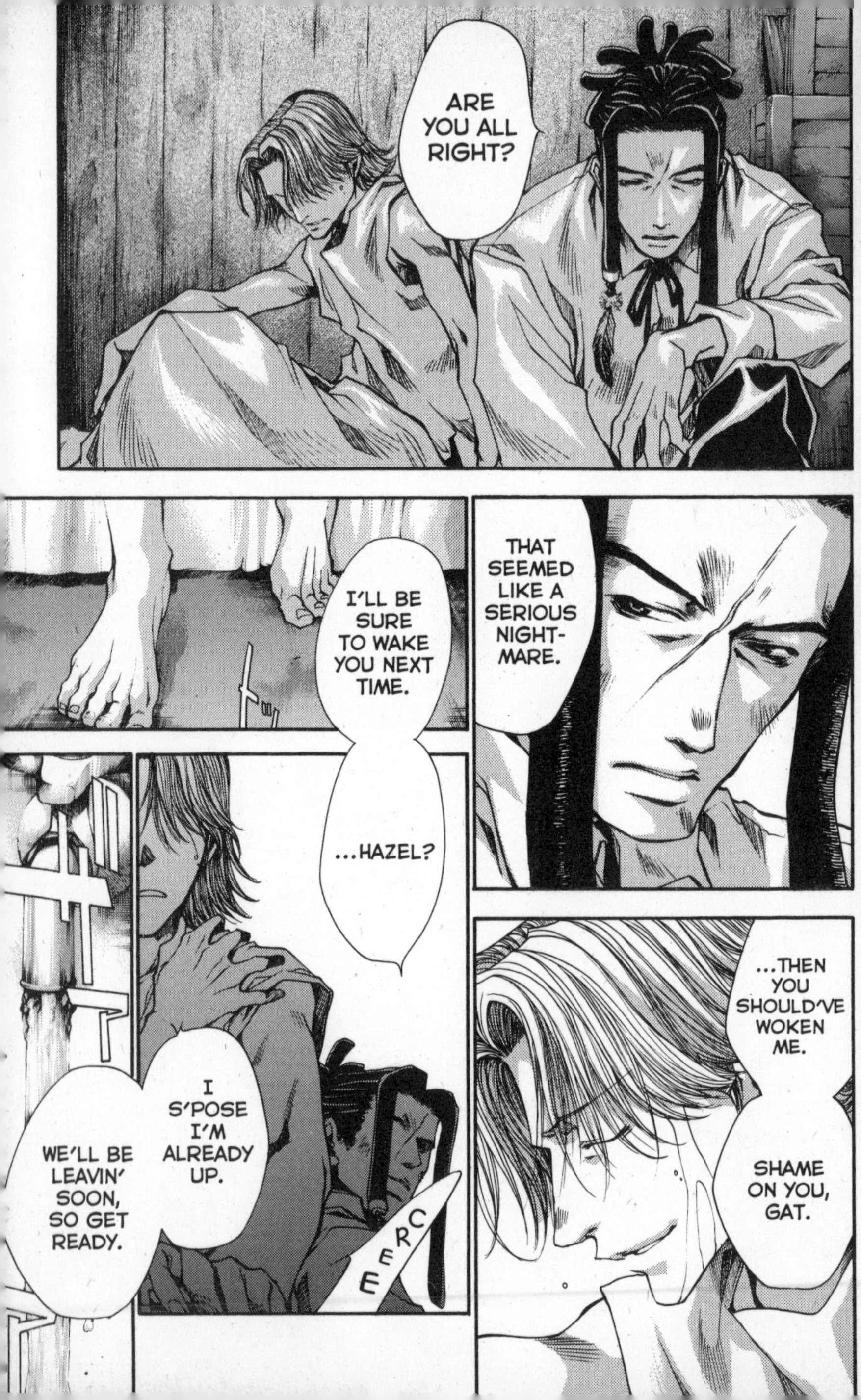
ARE YOU ALL RIGHT?
THAT SEEMED LIKE A SERIOUS NIGHT-MARE.
I'LL BE SURE TO WAKE YOU NEXT TIME.
...HAZEL?
...THEN YOU SHOULD'VE WOKEN ME.
SHAME ON YOU, GAT.
I S'POSE I'M ALREADY UP.
WE'LL BE LEAVIN' SOON, SO GET READY.
CREEE

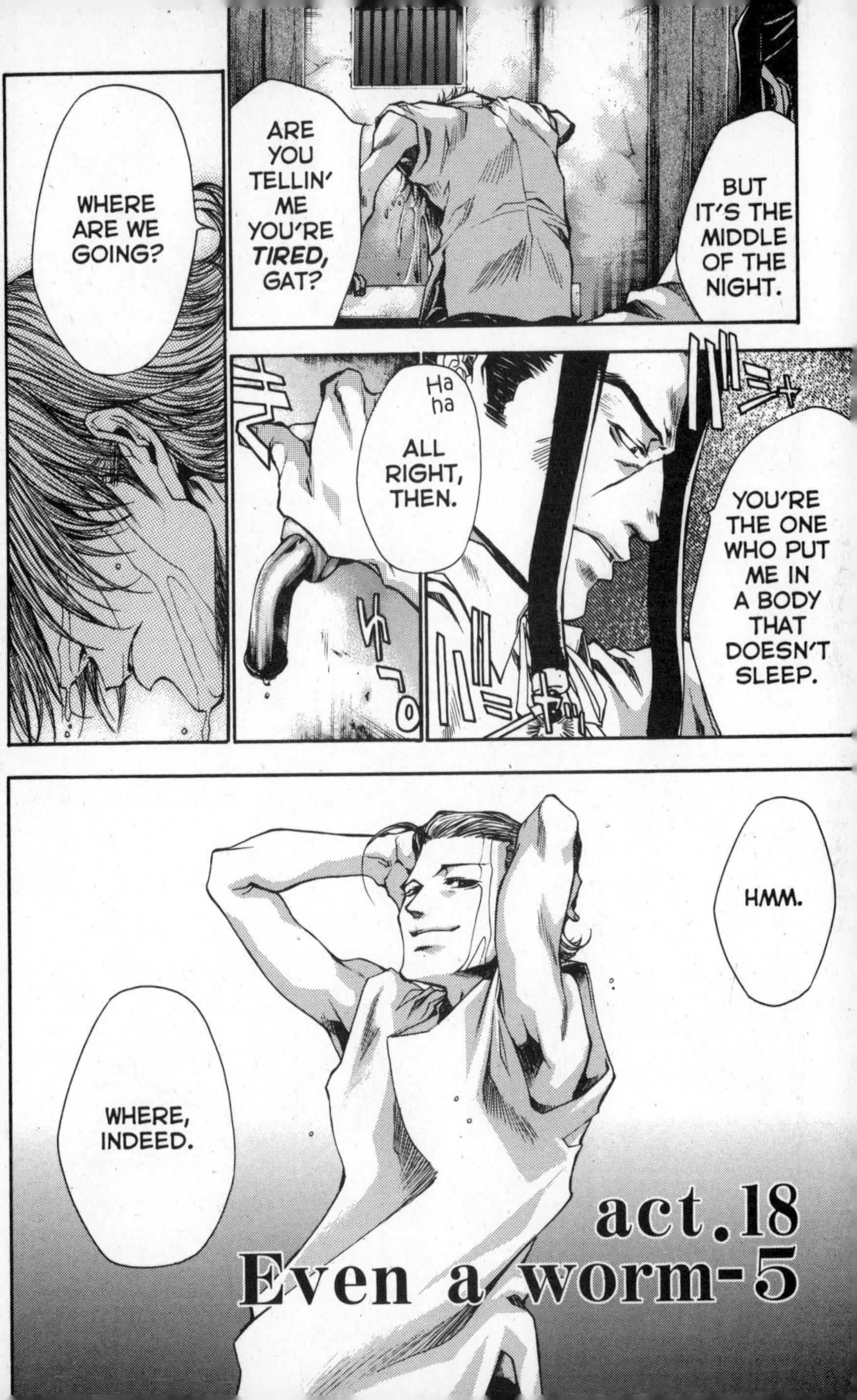
BUT IT'S THE MIDDLE OF THE NIGHT.
ARE YOU TELLIN' ME YOU'RE *TIRED*, GAT?
YOU'RE THE ONE WHO PUT ME IN A BODY THAT DOESN'T SLEEP.
Ha ha
ALL RIGHT, THEN.
WHERE ARE WE GOING?
HMM.
WHERE, INDEED.
act.18
Even a worm-5

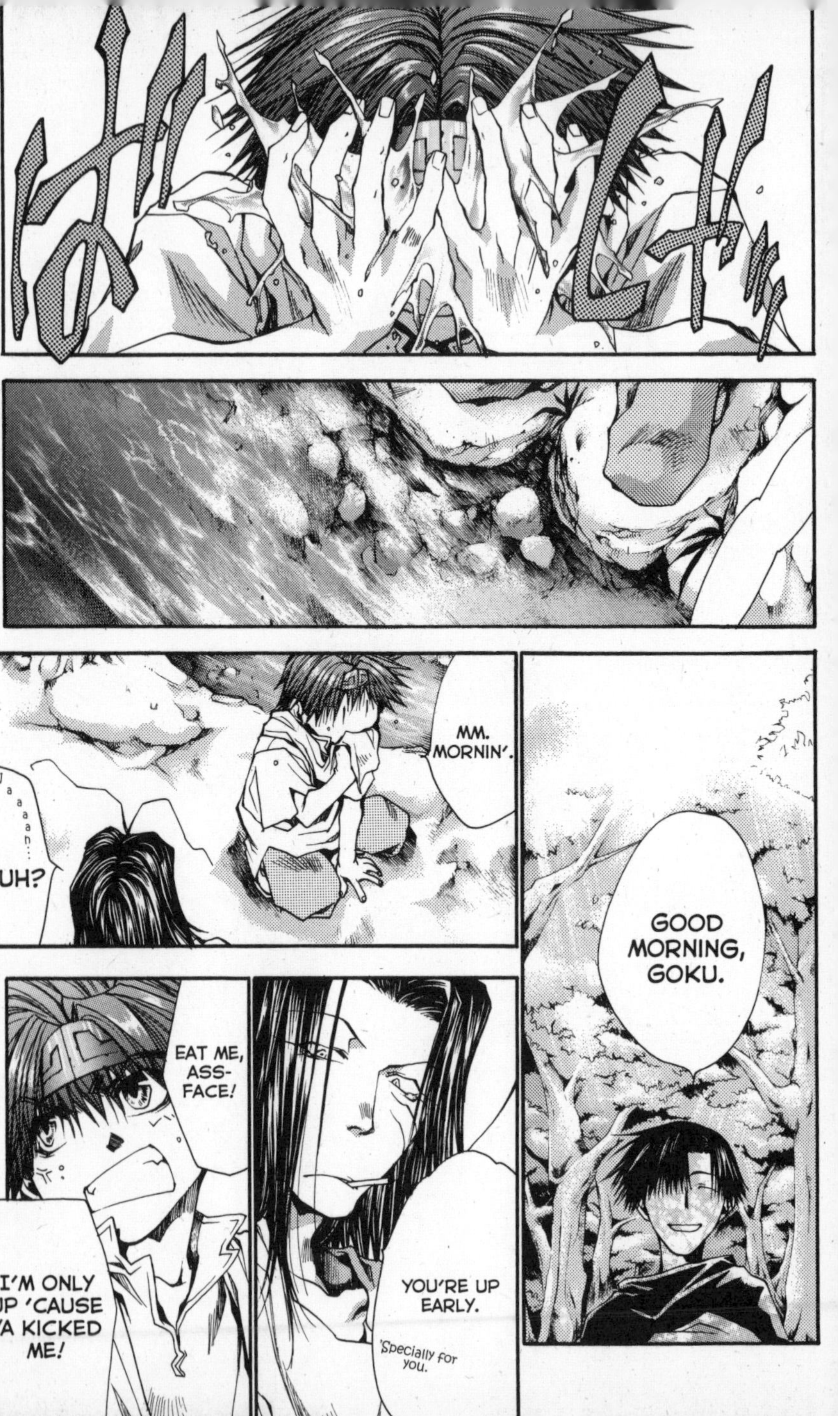
GOOD MORNING, GOKU.
MM. MORNIN'.
Waaaan...
HUH?
YOU'RE UP EARLY.
'Specially for you.
EAT ME, ASS-FACE!
I'M ONLY UP 'CAUSE YA KICKED ME!

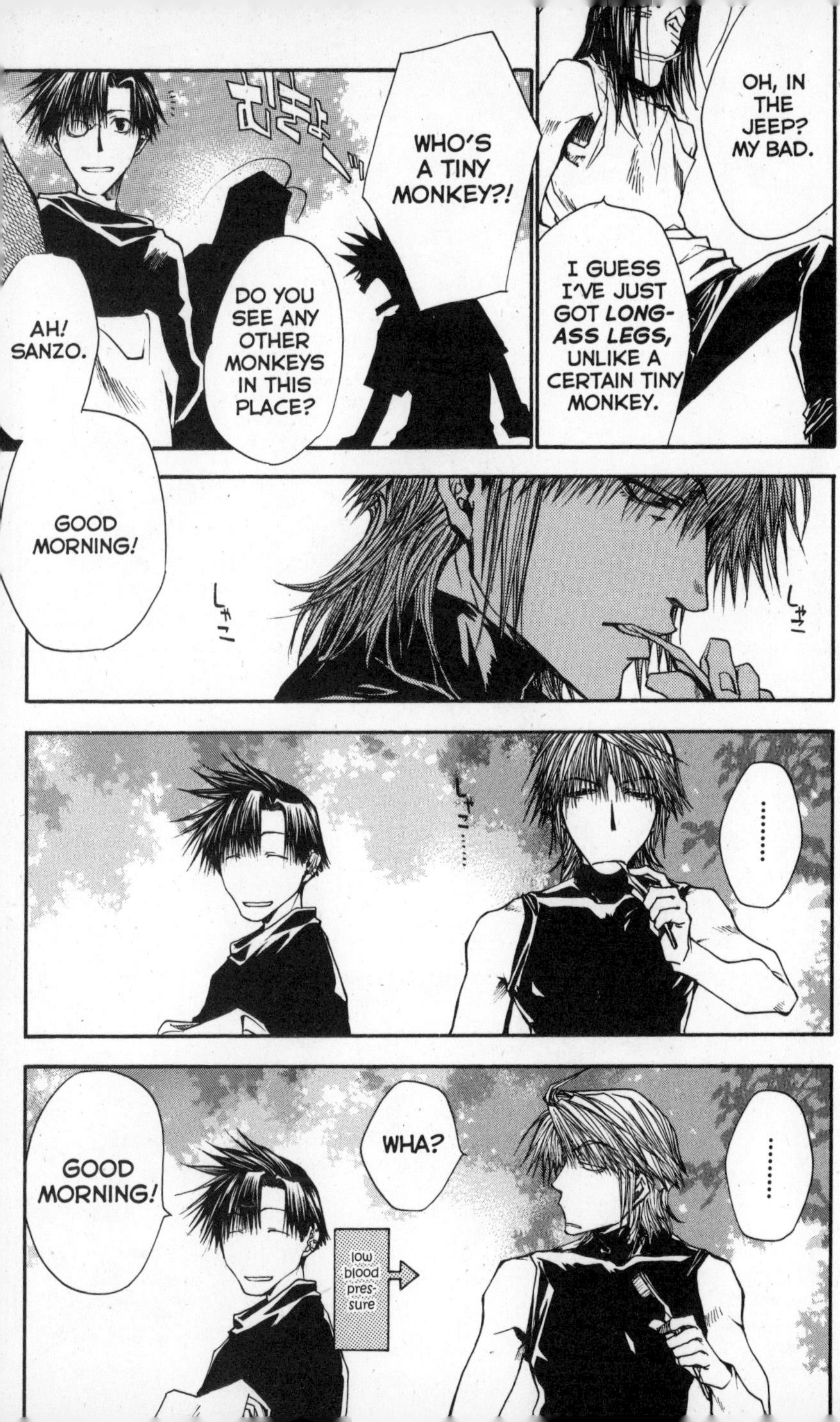
OH, IN THE JEEP? MY BAD.
I GUESS I'VE JUST GOT LONG-ASS LEGS, UNLIKE A CERTAIN TINY MONKEY.
WHO'S A TINY MONKEY?!
DO YOU SEE ANY OTHER MONKEYS IN THIS PLACE?
AH! SANZO.
GOOD MORNING!
....
....
WHA?
GOOD MORNING!
low blood pres-sure

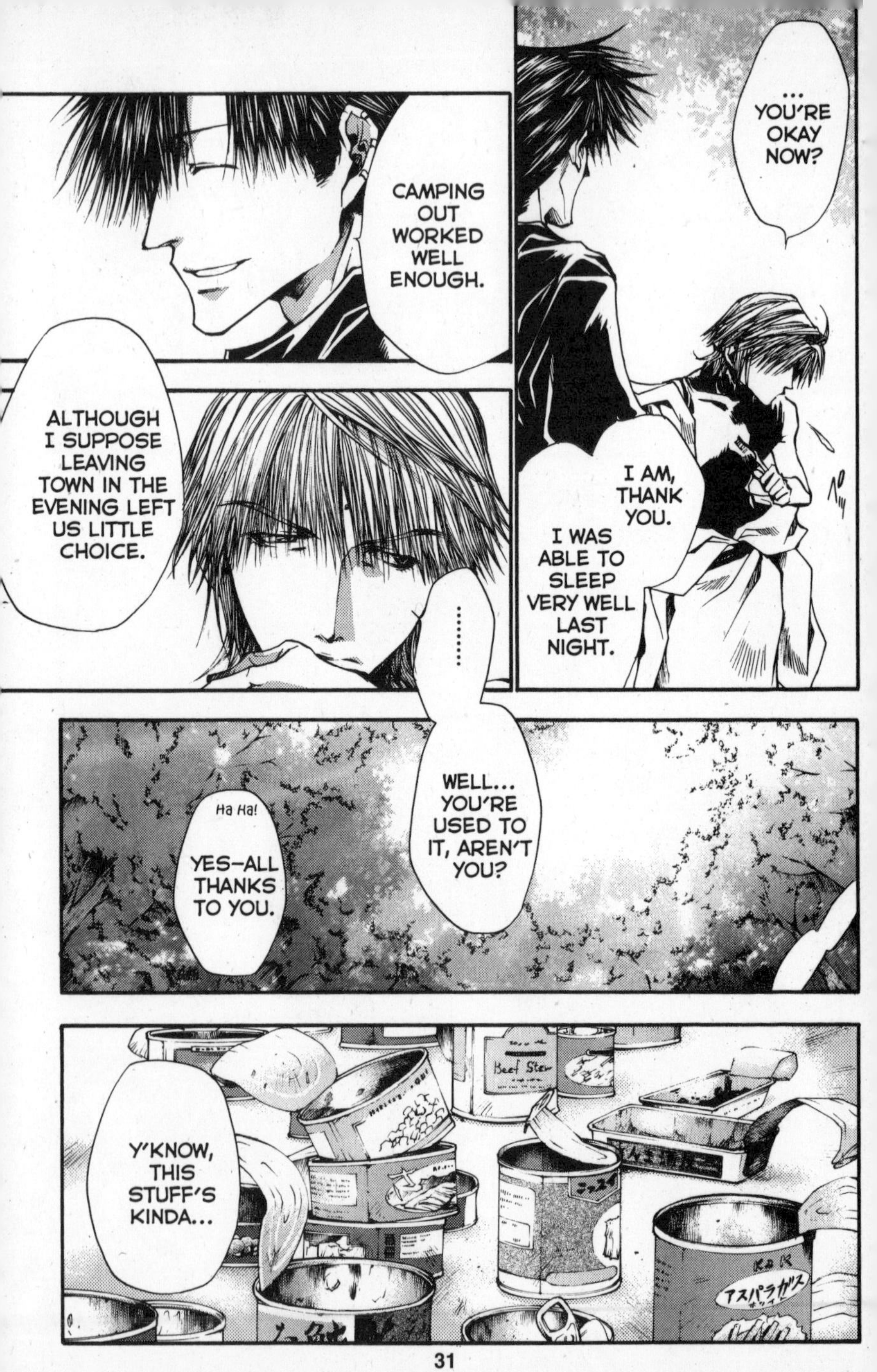
...YOU'RE OKAY NOW?
I AM, THANK YOU.
I WAS ABLE TO SLEEP VERY WELL LAST NIGHT.
CAMPING OUT WORKED WELL ENOUGH.
ALTHOUGH I SUPPOSE LEAVING TOWN IN THE EVENING LEFT US LITTLE CHOICE.
....
WELL... YOU'RE USED TO IT, AREN'T YOU?
Ha Ha!
YES—ALL THANKS TO YOU.
Y'KNOW, THIS STUFF'S KINDA...
アスパラガス

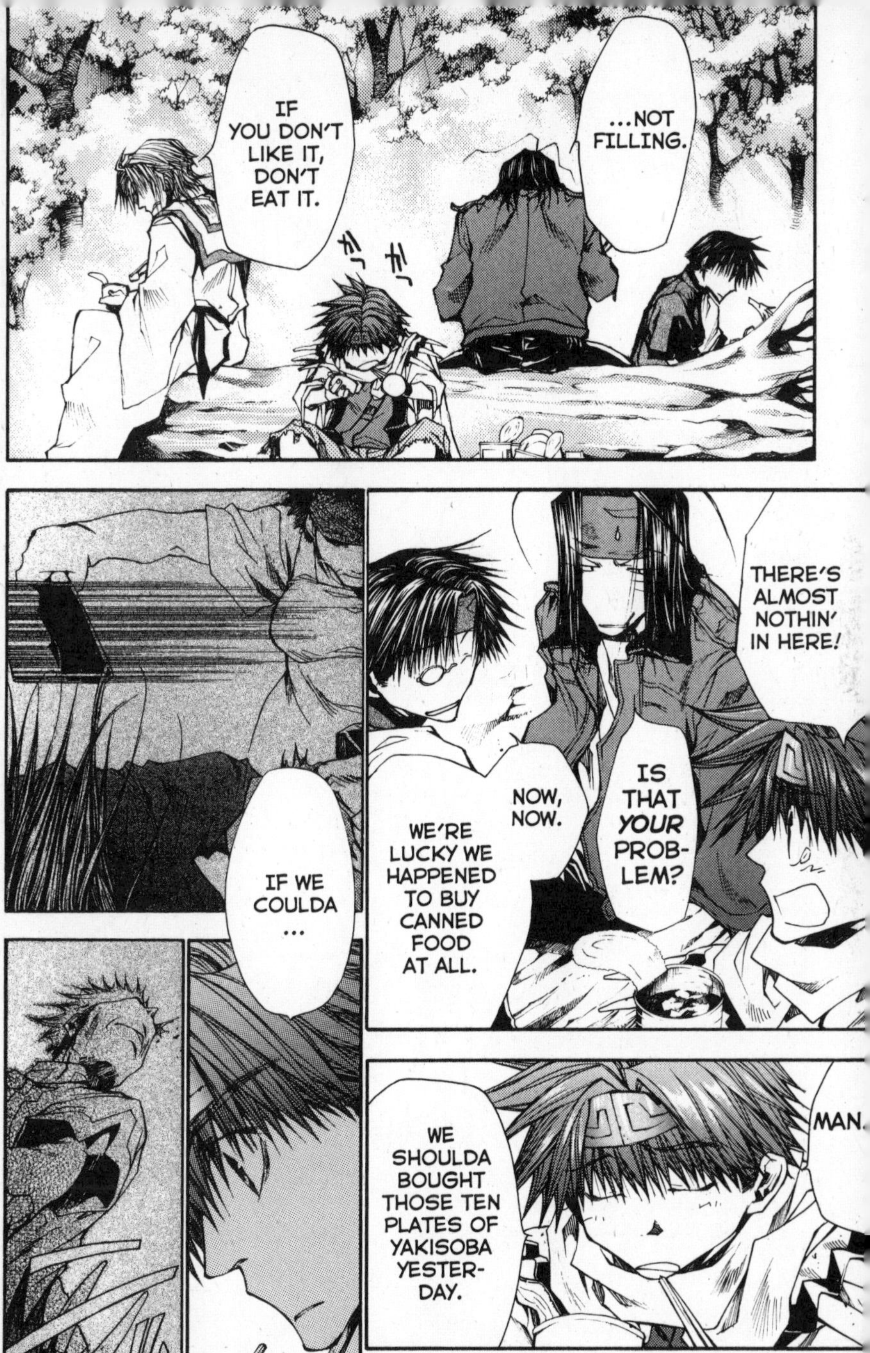
...NOT FILLING.
IF YOU DON'T LIKE IT, DON'T EAT IT.
THERE'S ALMOST NOTHIN' IN HERE!
IS THAT *YOUR* PROB-LEM?
NOW, NOW.
WE'RE LUCKY WE HAPPENED TO BUY CANNED FOOD AT ALL.
MAN.
WE SHOULDA BOUGHT THOSE TEN PLATES OF YAKISOBA YESTER-DAY.
IF WE COULDA ...

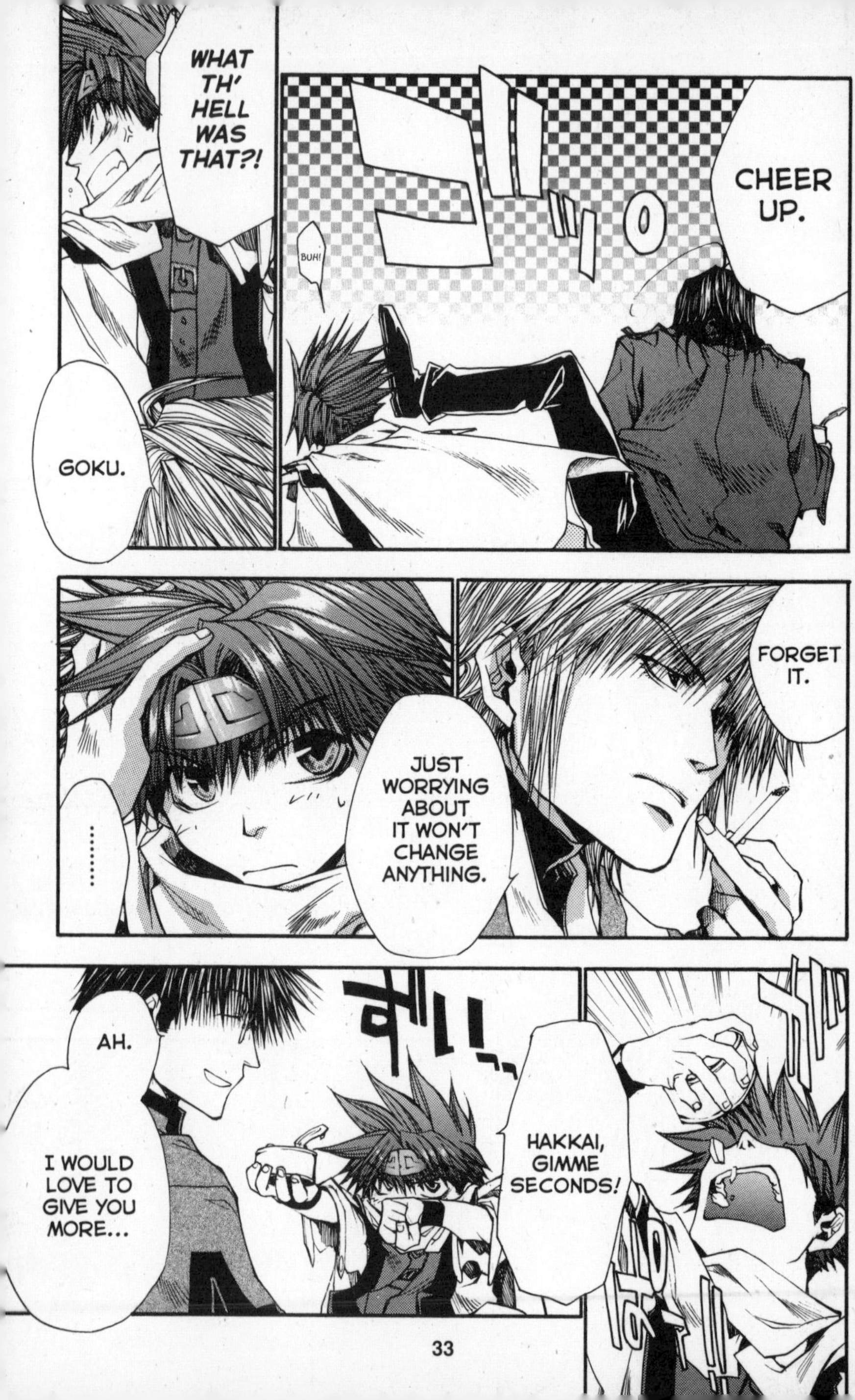
CHEER UP.
BUH!
WHAT TH' HELL WAS THAT?!
GOKU.
FORGET IT.
JUST WORRYING ABOUT IT WON'T CHANGE ANYTHING.
......
HAKKAI, GIMME SECONDS!
AH.
I WOULD LOVE TO GIVE YOU MORE...

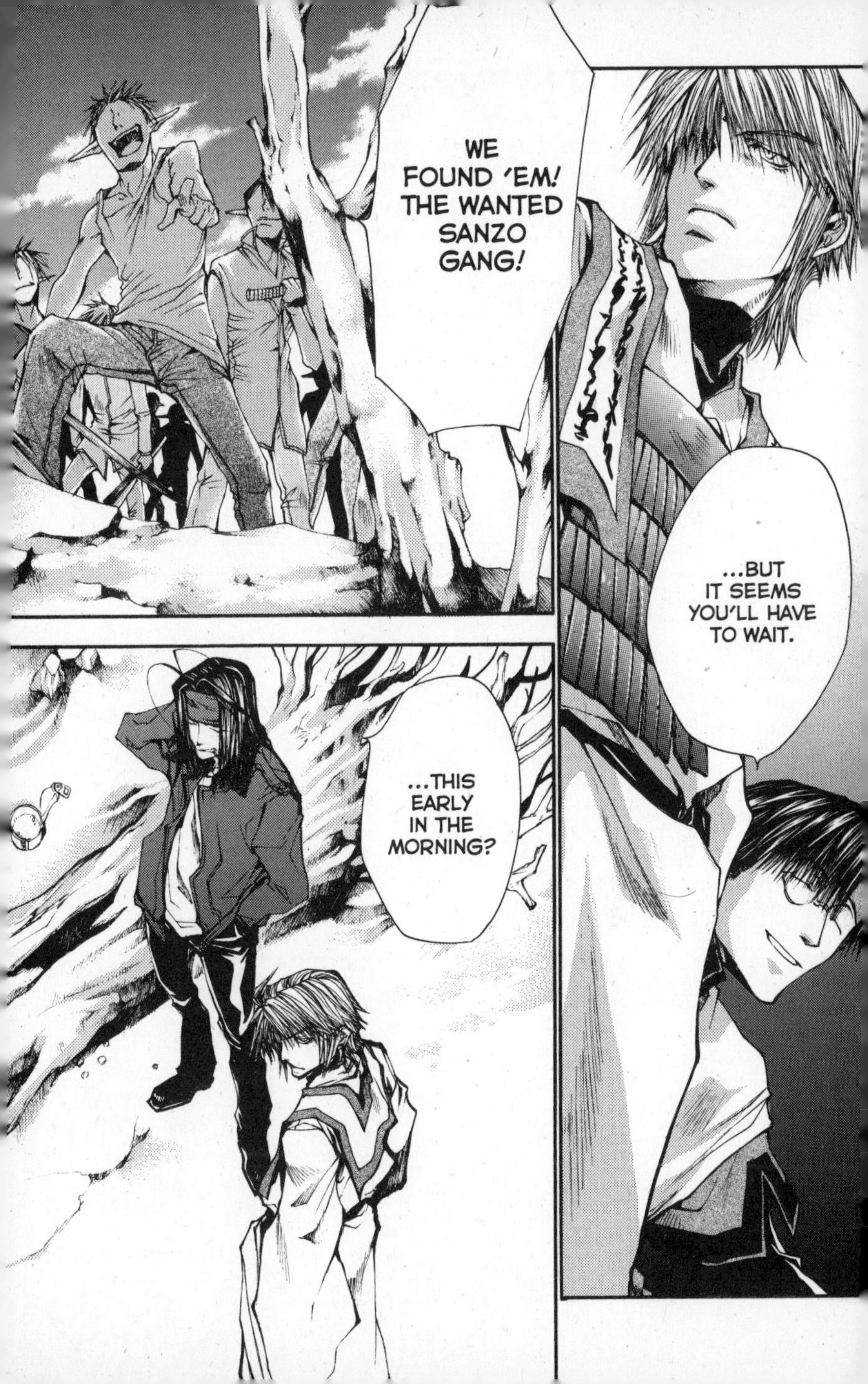
WE FOUND 'EM! THE WANTED SANZO GANG!
...THIS EARLY IN THE MORNING?
...BUT IT SEEMS YOU'LL HAVE TO WAIT.

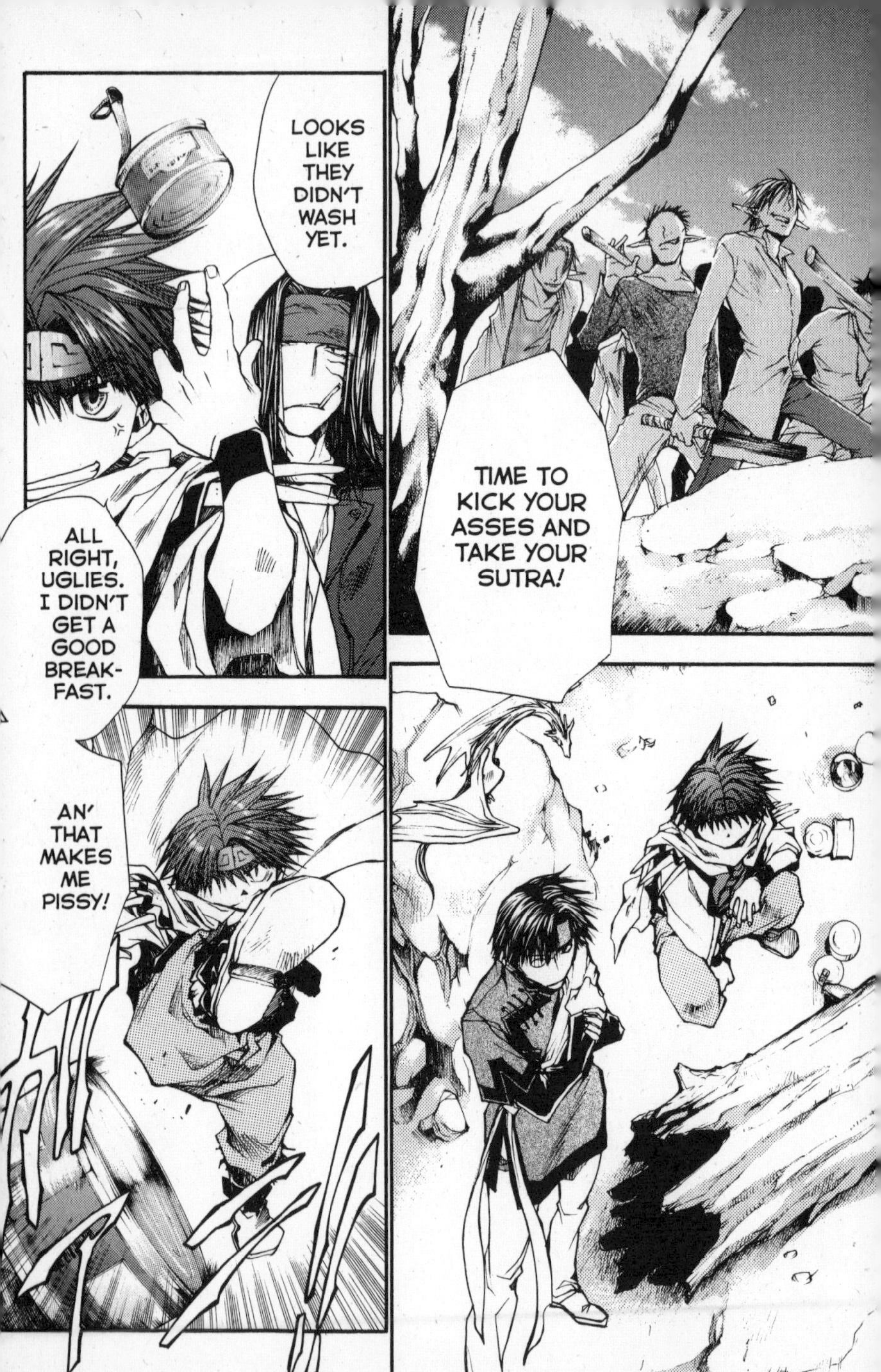
TIME TO KICK YOUR ASSES AND TAKE YOUR SUTRA!
LOOKS LIKE THEY DIDN'T WASH YET.
ALL RIGHT, UGLIES. I DIDN'T GET A GOOD BREAK-FAST.
AN' THAT MAKES ME PISSY!

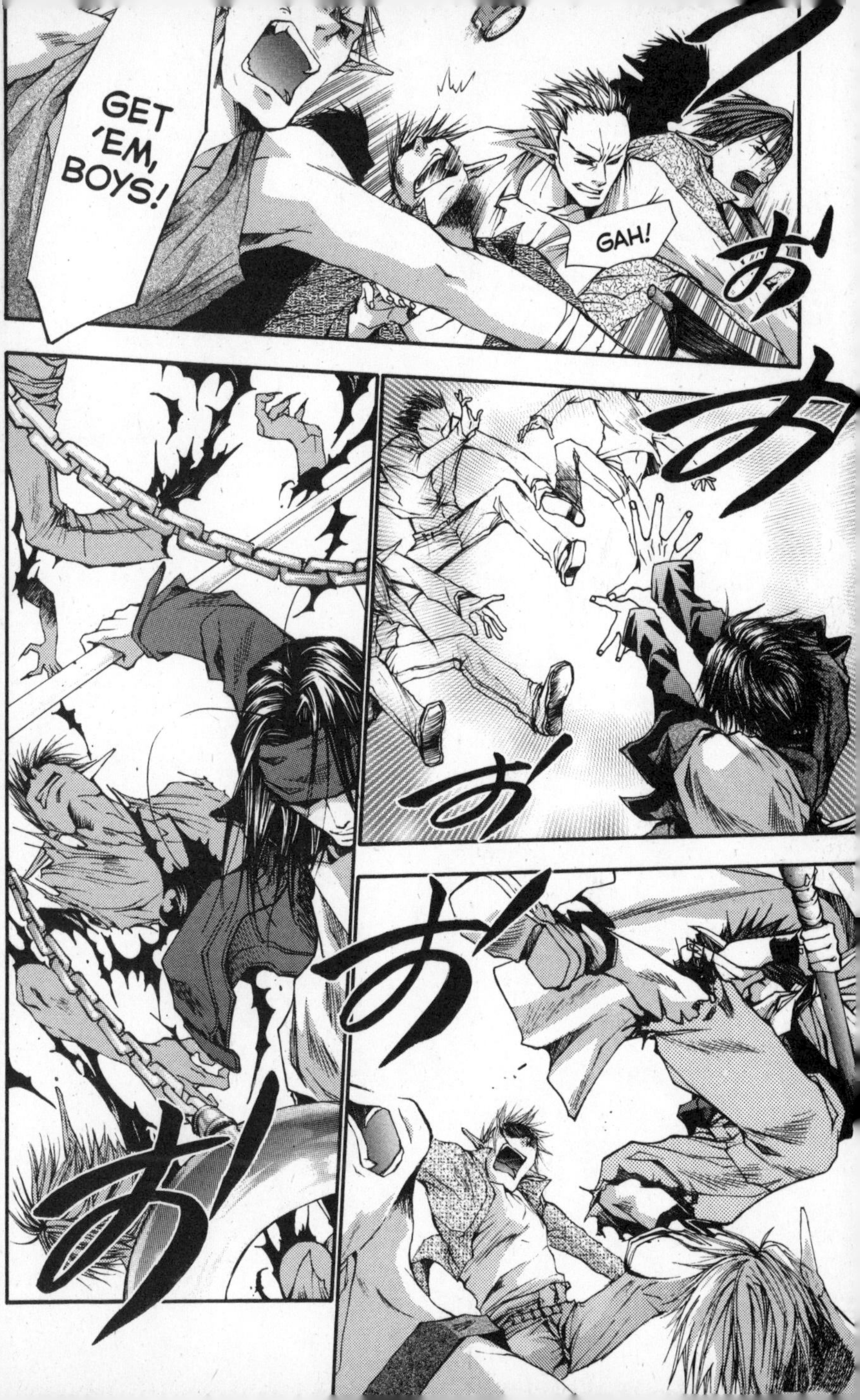
GET 'EM, BOYS!
GAH!
お
お
お
お
お

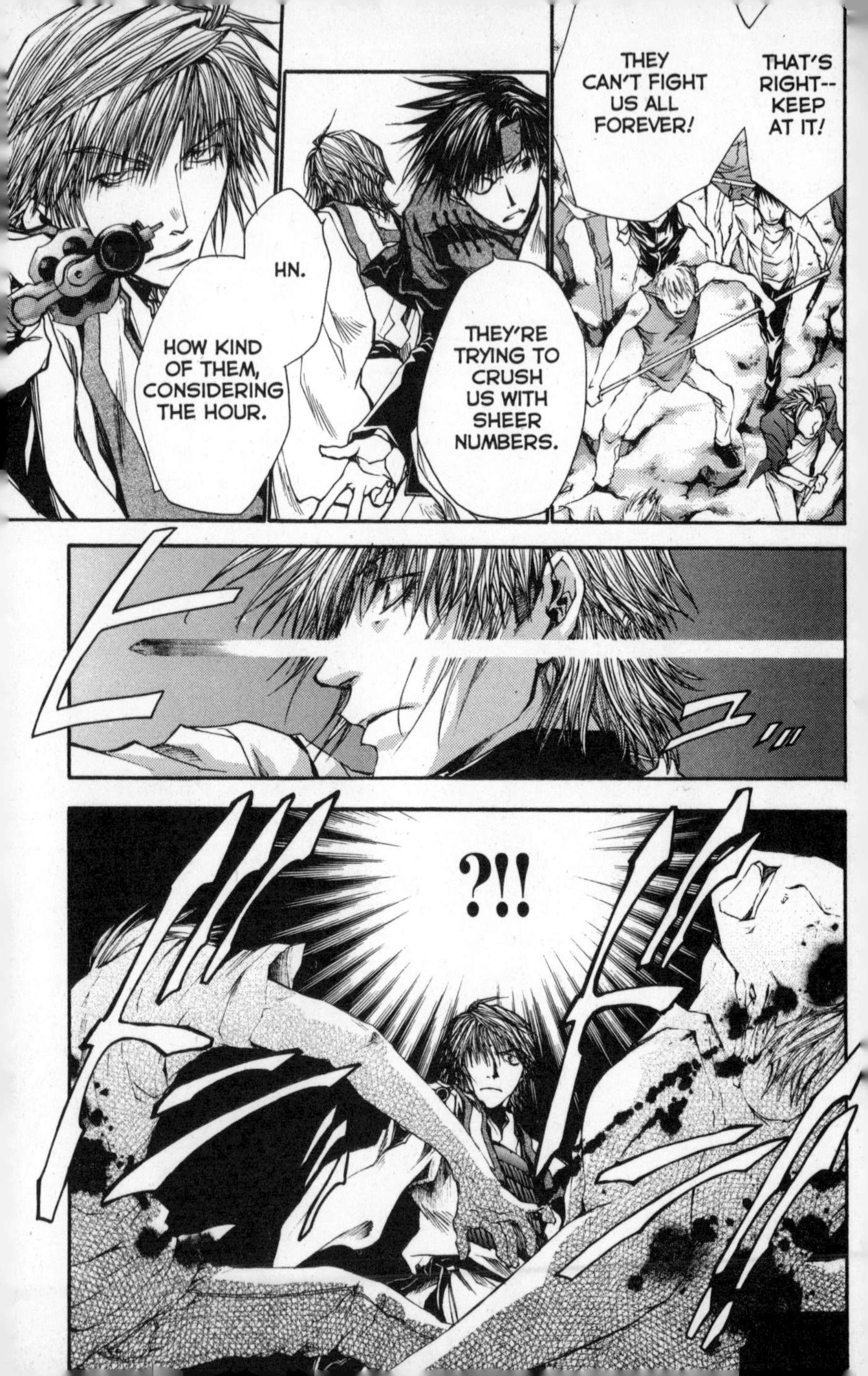
THAT'S RIGHT-- KEEP AT IT!
THEY CAN'T FIGHT US ALL FOREVER!
THEY'RE TRYING TO CRUSH US WITH SHEER NUMBERS.
HN.
HOW KIND OF THEM, CONSIDERING THE HOUR.
?!!

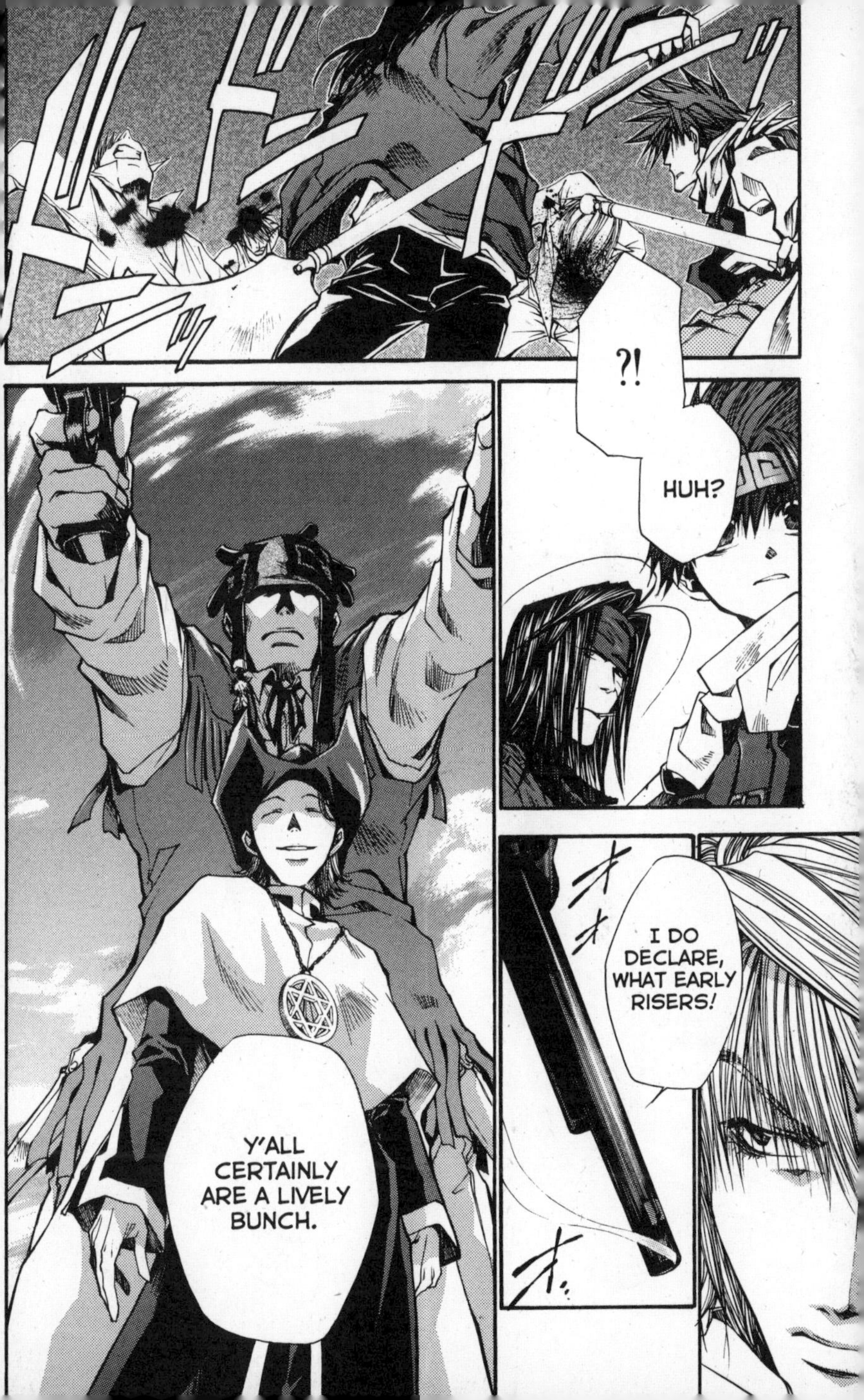
?!
HUH?
I DO DECLARE, WHAT EARLY RISERS!
Y'ALL CERTAINLY ARE A LIVELY BUNCH.

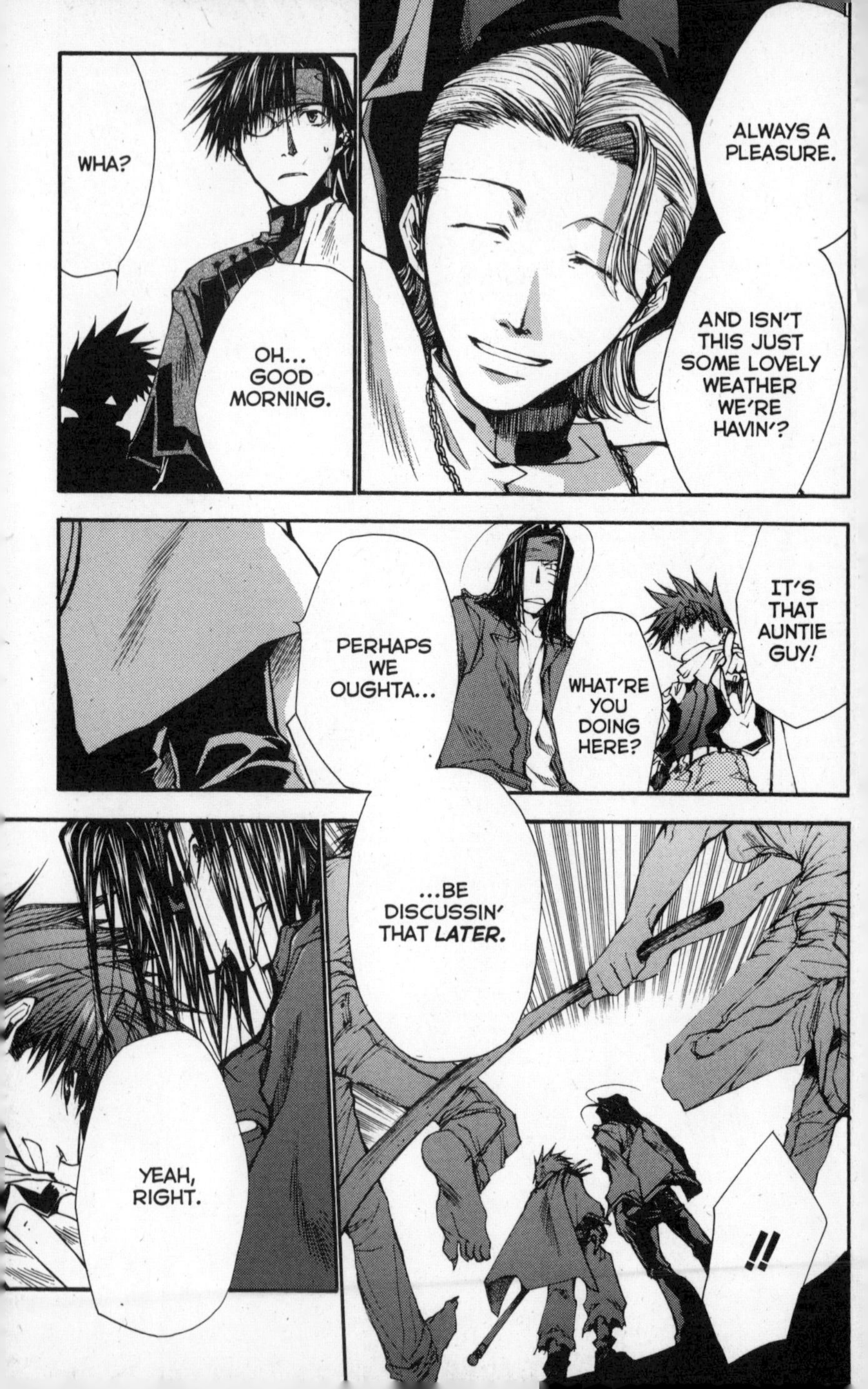
ALWAYS A PLEASURE.
AND ISN'T THIS JUST SOME LOVELY WEATHER WE'RE HAVIN'?
WHA?
OH... GOOD MORNING.
IT'S THAT AUNTIE GUY!
WHAT'RE YOU DOING HERE?
PERHAPS WE OUGHTA...
...BE DISCUSSIN' THAT *LATER.*
!!
YEAH, RIGHT.

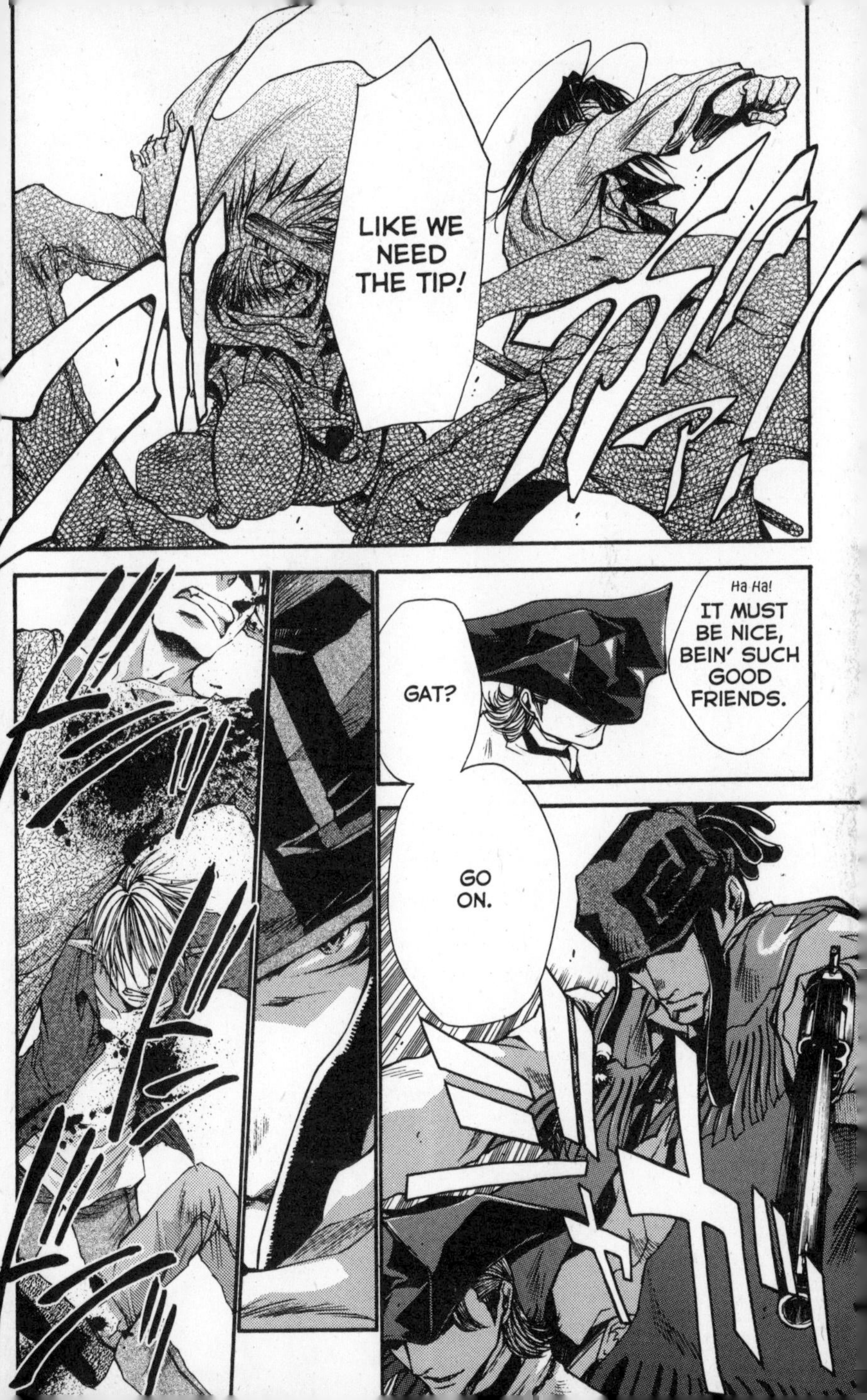
LIKE WE NEED THE TIP!
Ha Ha!
IT MUST BE NICE, BEIN' SUCH GOOD FRIENDS.
GAT?
GO ON.

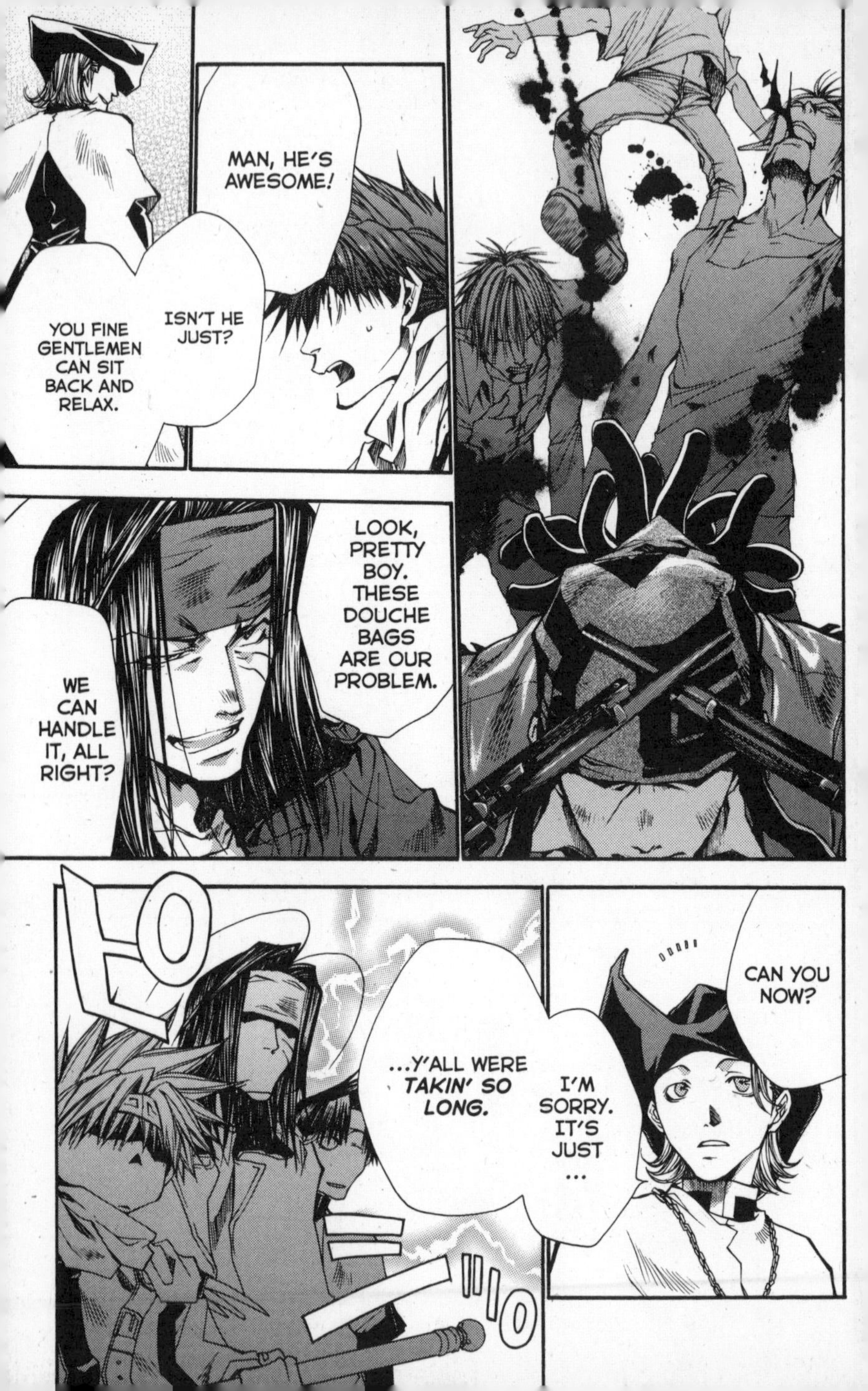
MAN, HE'S AWESOME!
ISN'T HE JUST?
YOU FINE GENTLEMEN CAN SIT BACK AND RELAX.
LOOK, PRETTY BOY. THESE DOUCHE BAGS ARE OUR PROBLEM.
WE CAN HANDLE IT, ALL RIGHT?
CAN YOU NOW?
I'M SORRY. IT'S JUST ...
...Y'ALL WERE *TAKIN'* SO LONG.

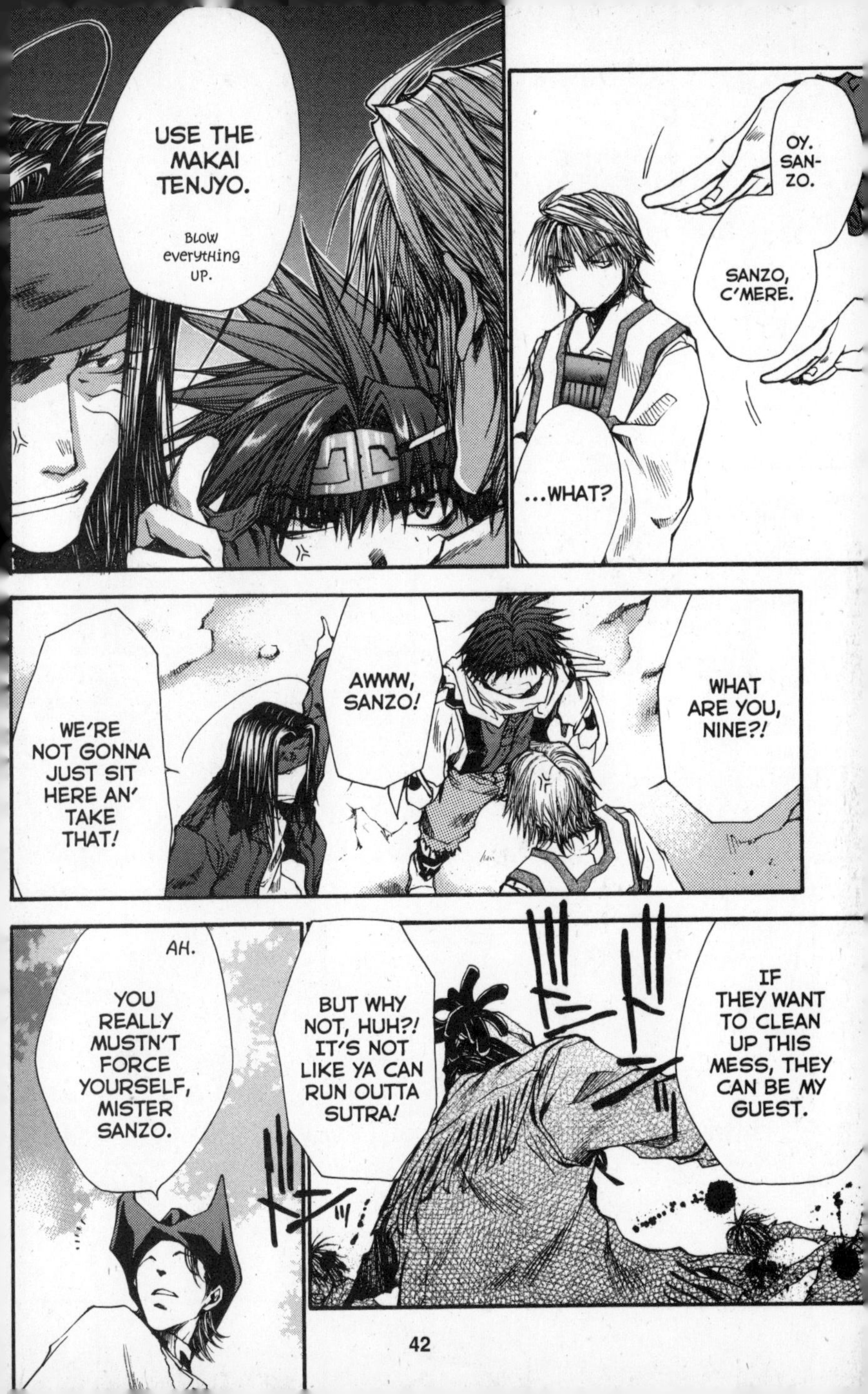
OY. SANZO.
SANZO, C'MERE.
...WHAT?
USE THE MAKAI TENJYO.
BLOW everything UP.
WHAT ARE YOU, NINE?!
AWWW, SANZO!
WE'RE NOT GONNA JUST SIT HERE AN' TAKE THAT!
IF THEY WANT TO CLEAN UP THIS MESS, THEY CAN BE MY GUEST.
BUT WHY NOT, HUH?! IT'S NOT LIKE YA CAN RUN OUTTA SUTRA!
AH.
YOU REALLY MUSTN'T FORCE YOURSELF, MISTER SANZO.

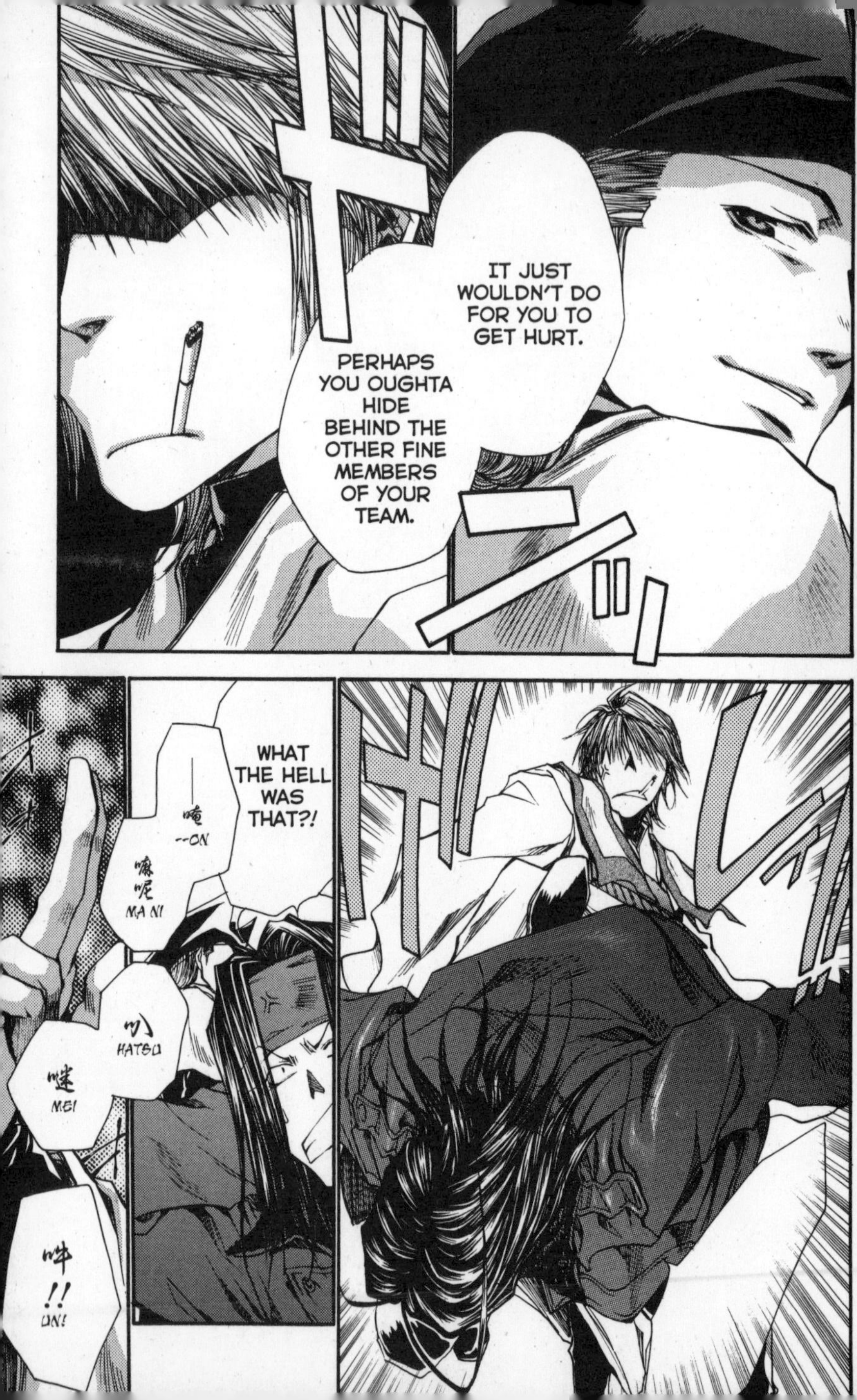
IT JUST WOULDN'T DO FOR YOU TO GET HURT.
PERHAPS YOU OUGHTA HIDE BEHIND THE OTHER FINE MEMBERS OF YOUR TEAM.
WHAT THE HELL WAS THAT?!
唵
--ON
嘛呢
MA NI
叭
HATSU
咪
MEI
吽!!
UN!

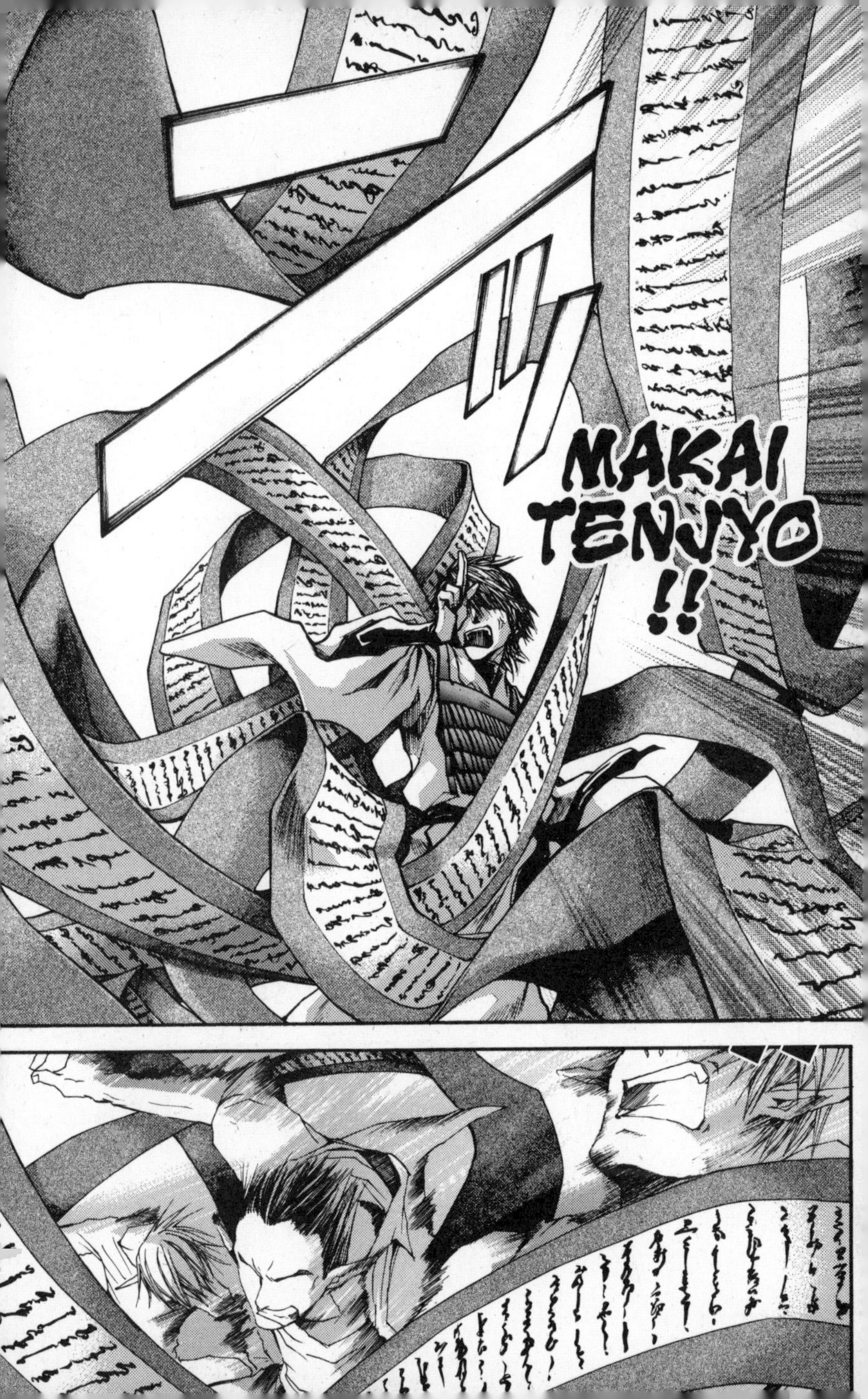
MAKAI TENJYO!!

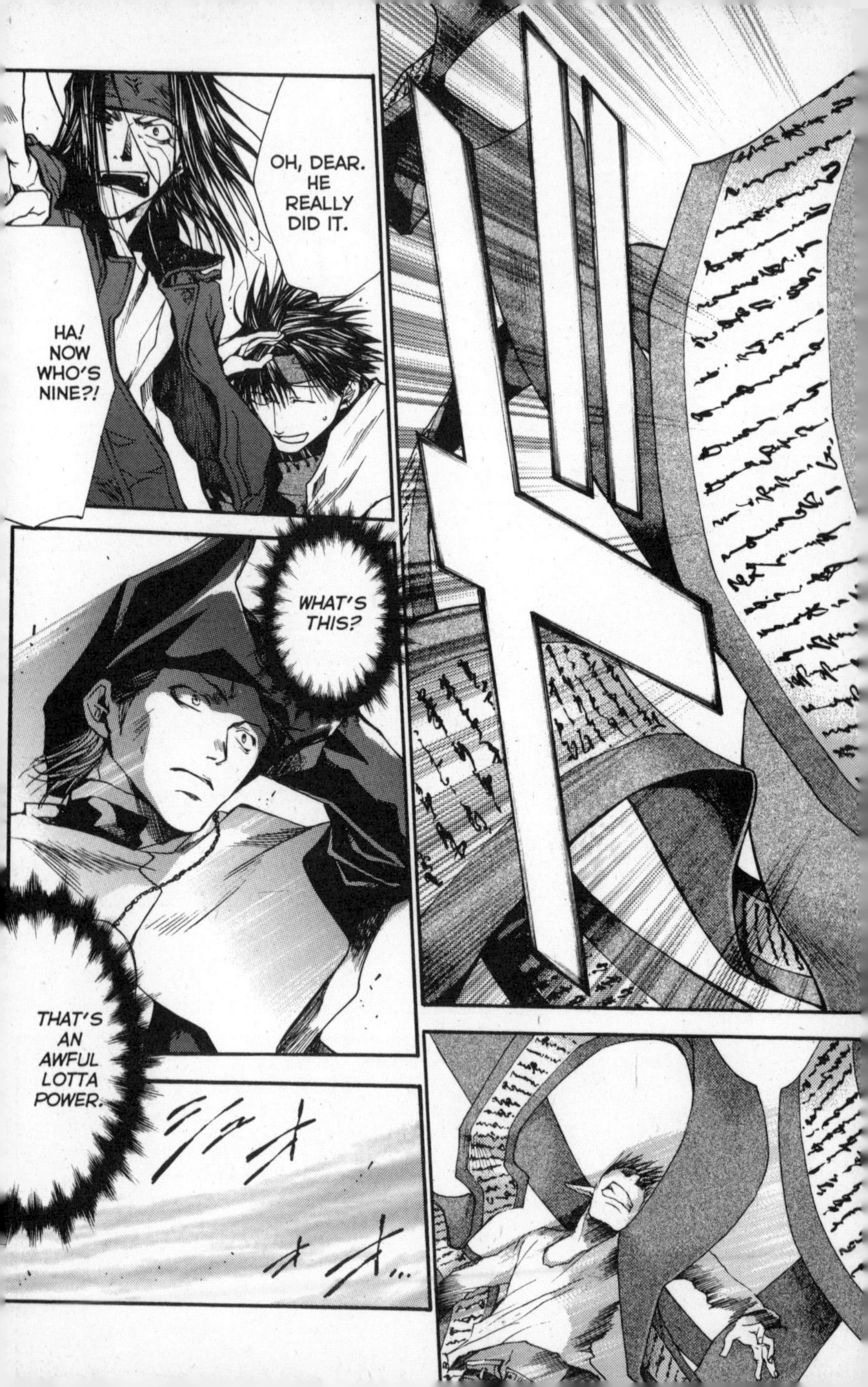
OH, DEAR. HE REALLY DID IT.
HA! NOW WHO'S NINE?!
WHAT'S THIS?
THAT'S AN AWFUL LOTTA POWER.

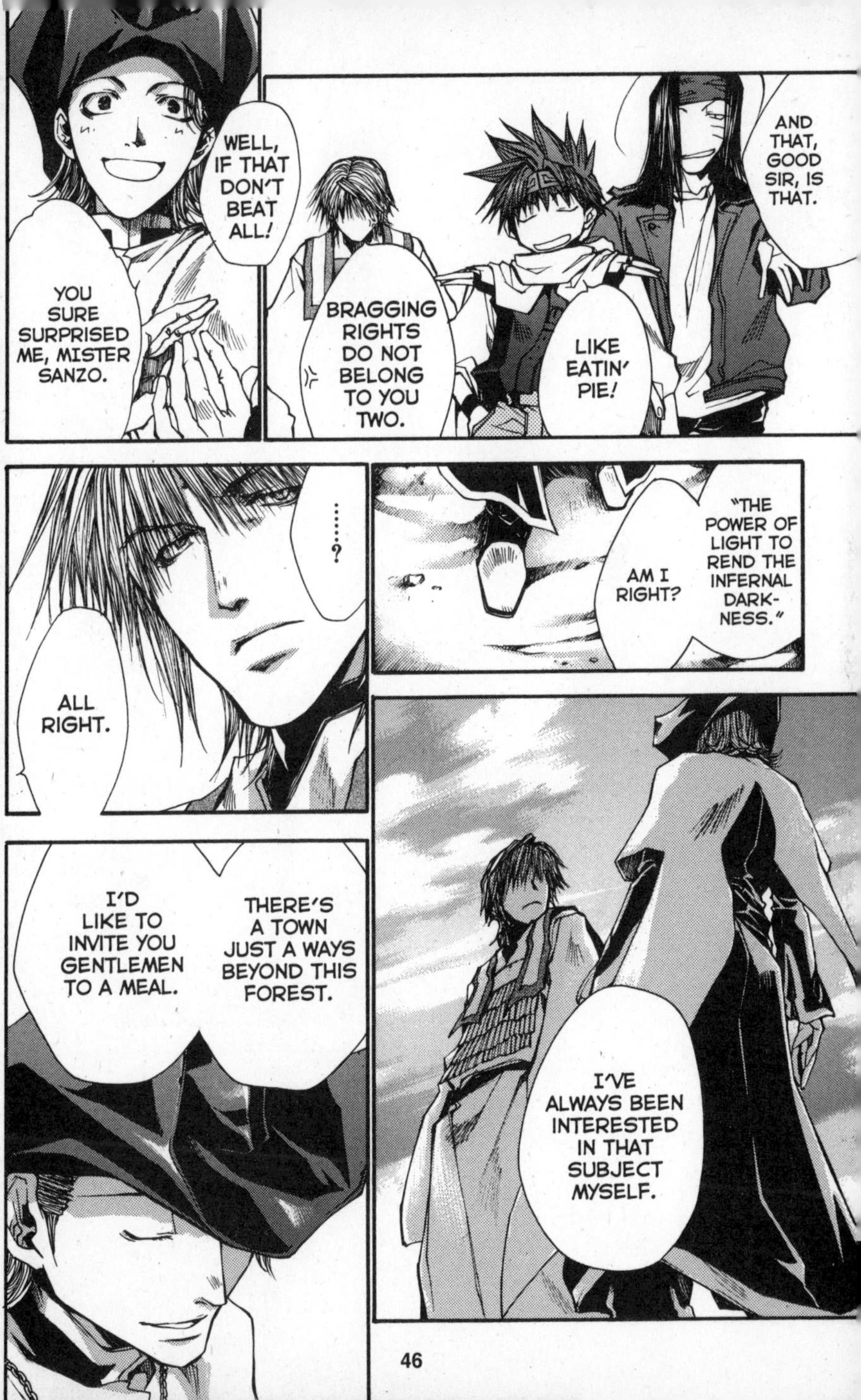
AND THAT, GOOD SIR, IS THAT.
LIKE EATIN' PIE!
BRAGGING RIGHTS DO NOT BELONG TO YOU TWO.
WELL, IF THAT DON'T BEAT ALL!
YOU SURE SURPRISED ME, MISTER SANZO.
"THE POWER OF LIGHT TO REND THE INFERNAL DARK-NESS."
AM I RIGHT?
......?
ALL RIGHT.
I'VE ALWAYS BEEN INTERESTED IN THAT SUBJECT MYSELF.
THERE'S A TOWN JUST A WAYS BEYOND THIS FOREST.
I'D LIKE TO INVITE YOU GENTLEMEN TO A MEAL.

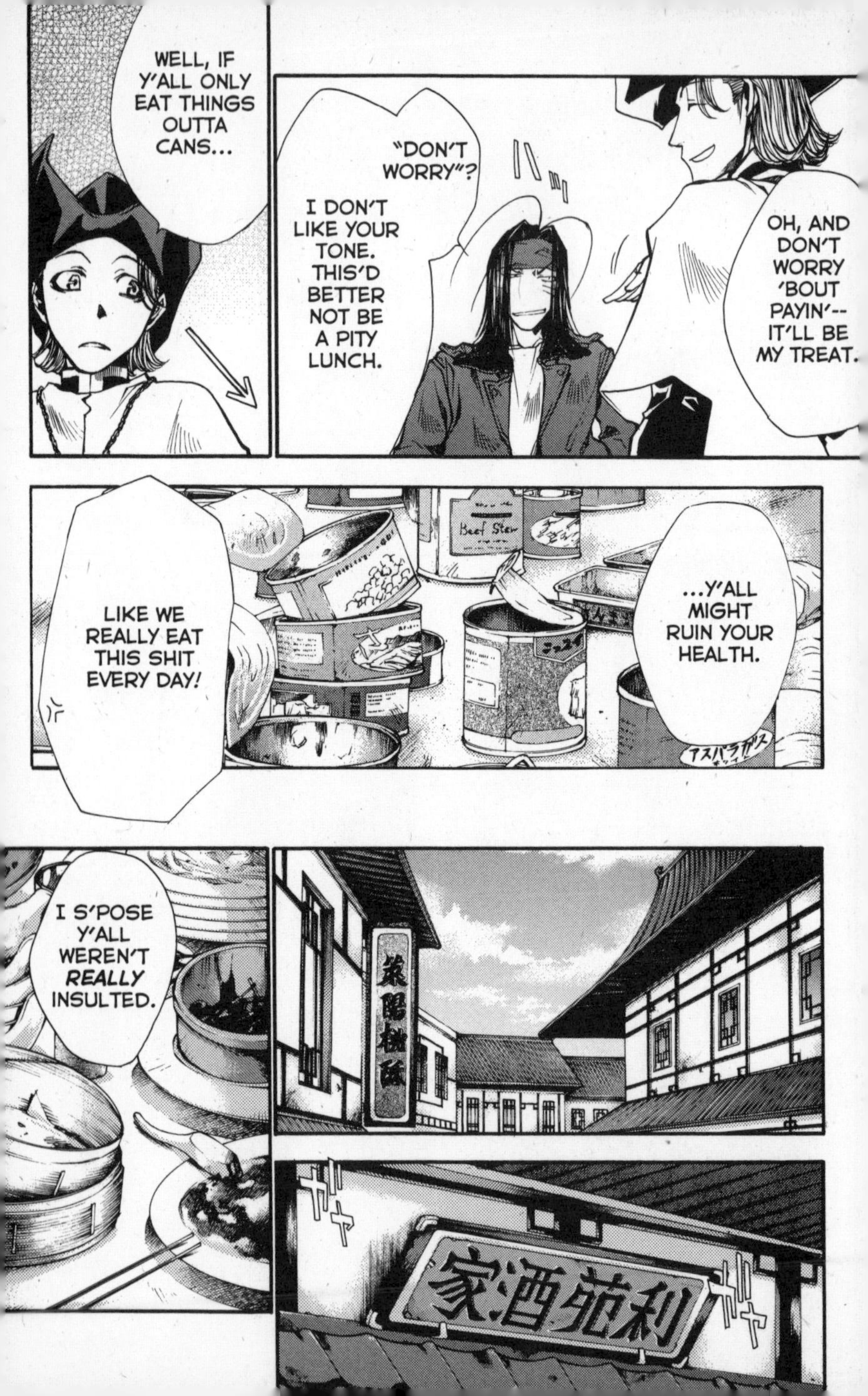
OH, AND DON'T WORRY 'BOUT PAYIN'-- IT'LL BE MY TREAT.
"DON'T WORRY"?
I DON'T LIKE YOUR TONE. THIS'D BETTER NOT BE A PITY LUNCH.
WELL, IF Y'ALL ONLY EAT THINGS OUTTA CANS...
...Y'ALL MIGHT RUIN YOUR HEALTH.
アスパラガス
Beef Stew
LIKE WE REALLY EAT THIS SHIT EVERY DAY!
利苑酒家
ガヤ
ガヤ
I S'POSE Y'ALL WEREN'T *REALLY* INSULTED.

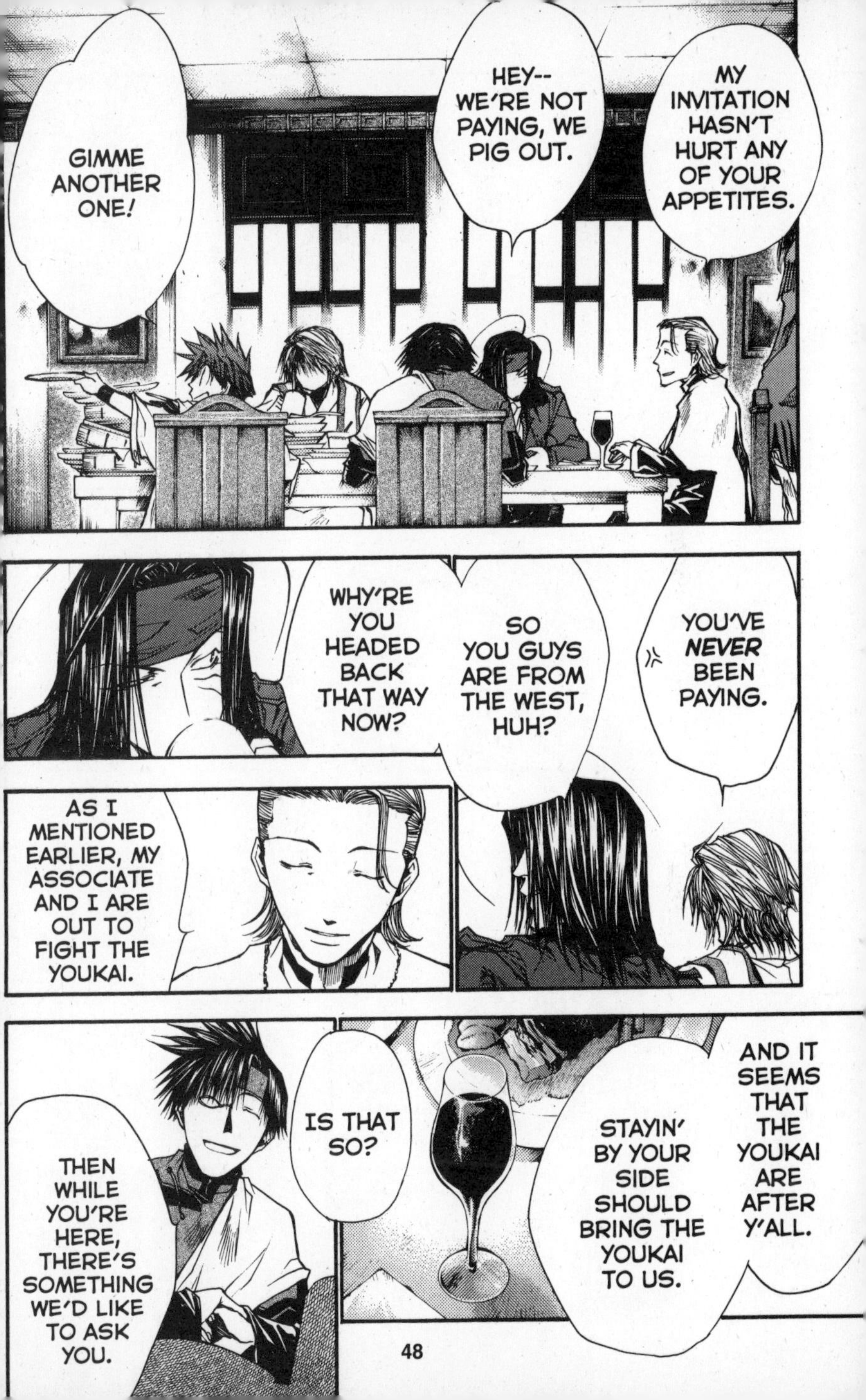
MY INVITATION HASN'T HURT ANY OF YOUR APPETITES.
HEY-- WE'RE NOT PAYING, WE PIG OUT.
GIMME ANOTHER ONE!
YOU'VE *NEVER* BEEN PAYING.
SO YOU GUYS ARE FROM THE WEST, HUH?
WHY'RE YOU HEADED BACK THAT WAY NOW?
AS I MENTIONED EARLIER, MY ASSOCIATE AND I ARE OUT TO FIGHT THE YOUKAI.
AND IT SEEMS THAT THE YOUKAI ARE AFTER Y'ALL.
STAYIN' BY YOUR SIDE SHOULD BRING THE YOUKAI TO US.
IS THAT SO?
THEN WHILE YOU'RE HERE, THERE'S SOMETHING WE'D LIKE TO ASK YOU.

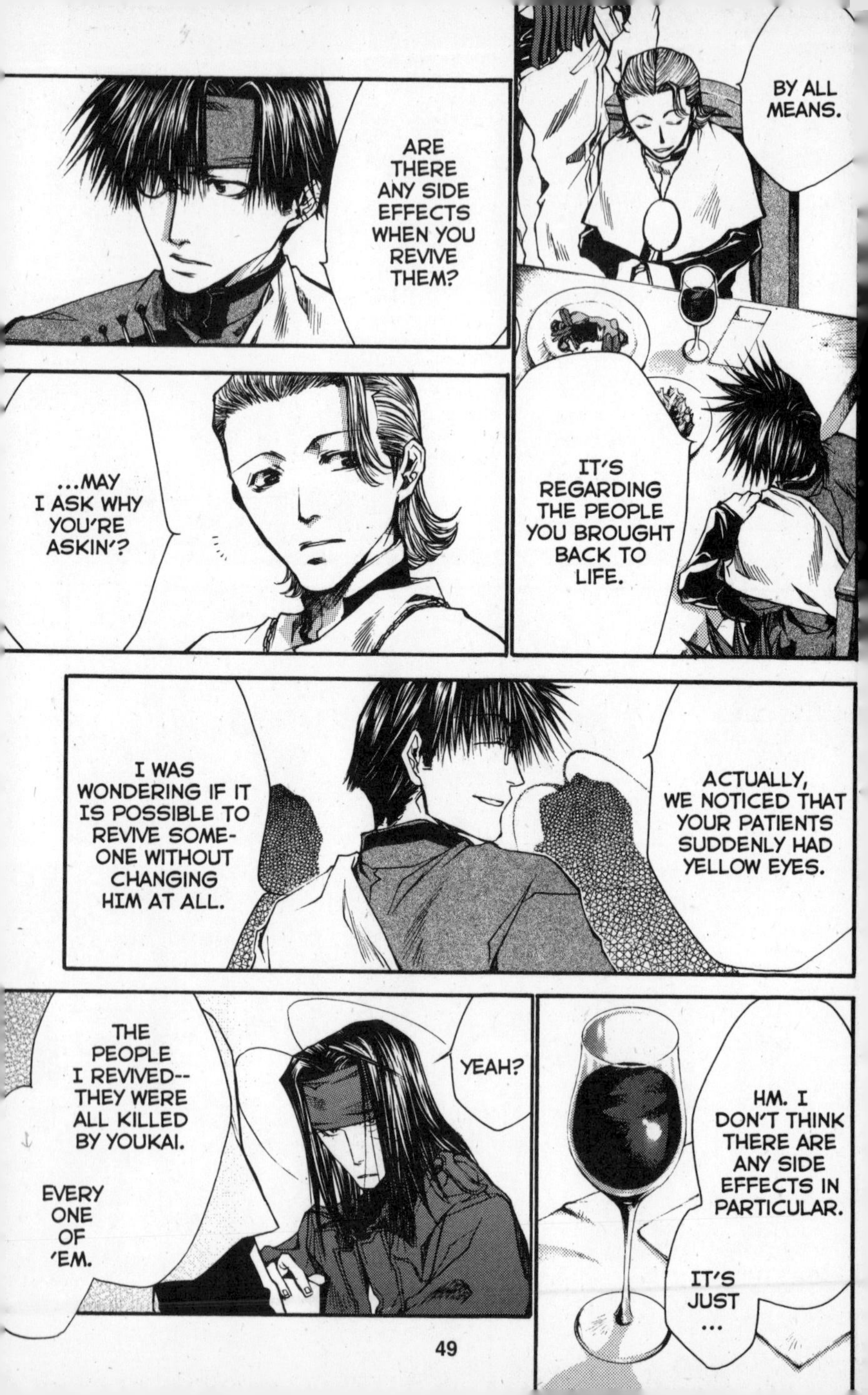
BY ALL MEANS.
ARE THERE ANY SIDE EFFECTS WHEN YOU REVIVE THEM?
IT'S REGARDING THE PEOPLE YOU BROUGHT BACK TO LIFE.
...MAY I ASK WHY YOU'RE ASKIN'?
ACTUALLY, WE NOTICED THAT YOUR PATIENTS SUDDENLY HAD YELLOW EYES.
I WAS WONDERING IF IT IS POSSIBLE TO REVIVE SOME-ONE WITHOUT CHANGING HIM AT ALL.
HM. I DON'T THINK THERE ARE ANY SIDE EFFECTS IN PARTICULAR.
IT'S JUST ...
YEAH?
THE PEOPLE I REVIVED-- THEY WERE ALL KILLED BY YOUKAI.
EVERY ONE OF 'EM.

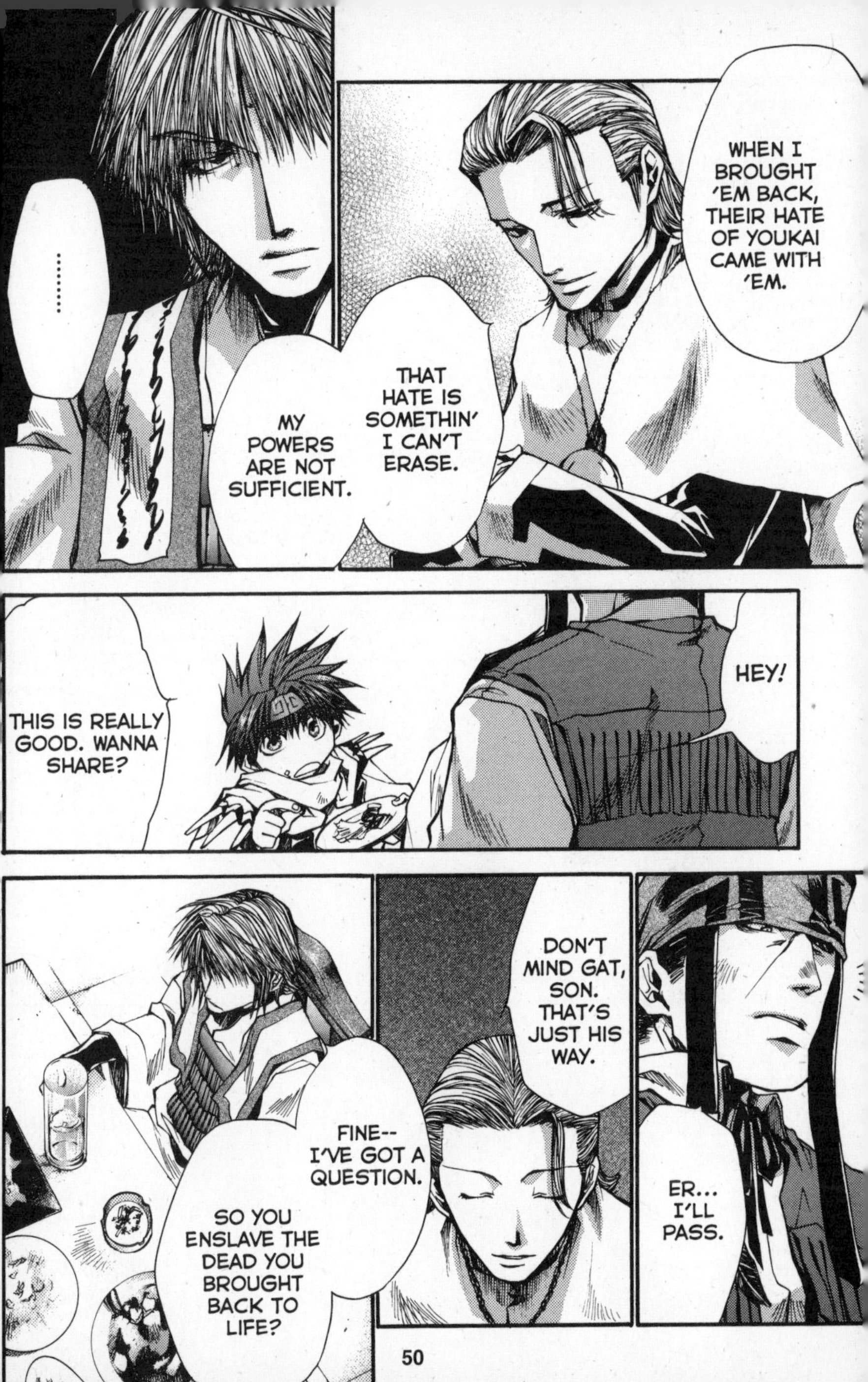
WHEN I BROUGHT 'EM BACK, THEIR HATE OF YOUKAI CAME WITH 'EM.
THAT HATE IS SOMETHIN' I CAN'T ERASE.
......
MY POWERS ARE NOT SUFFICIENT.
HEY!
THIS IS REALLY GOOD. WANNA SHARE?
ER... I'LL PASS.
DON'T MIND GAT, SON. THAT'S JUST HIS WAY.
FINE-- I'VE GOT A QUESTION.
SO YOU ENSLAVE THE DEAD YOU BROUGHT BACK TO LIFE?

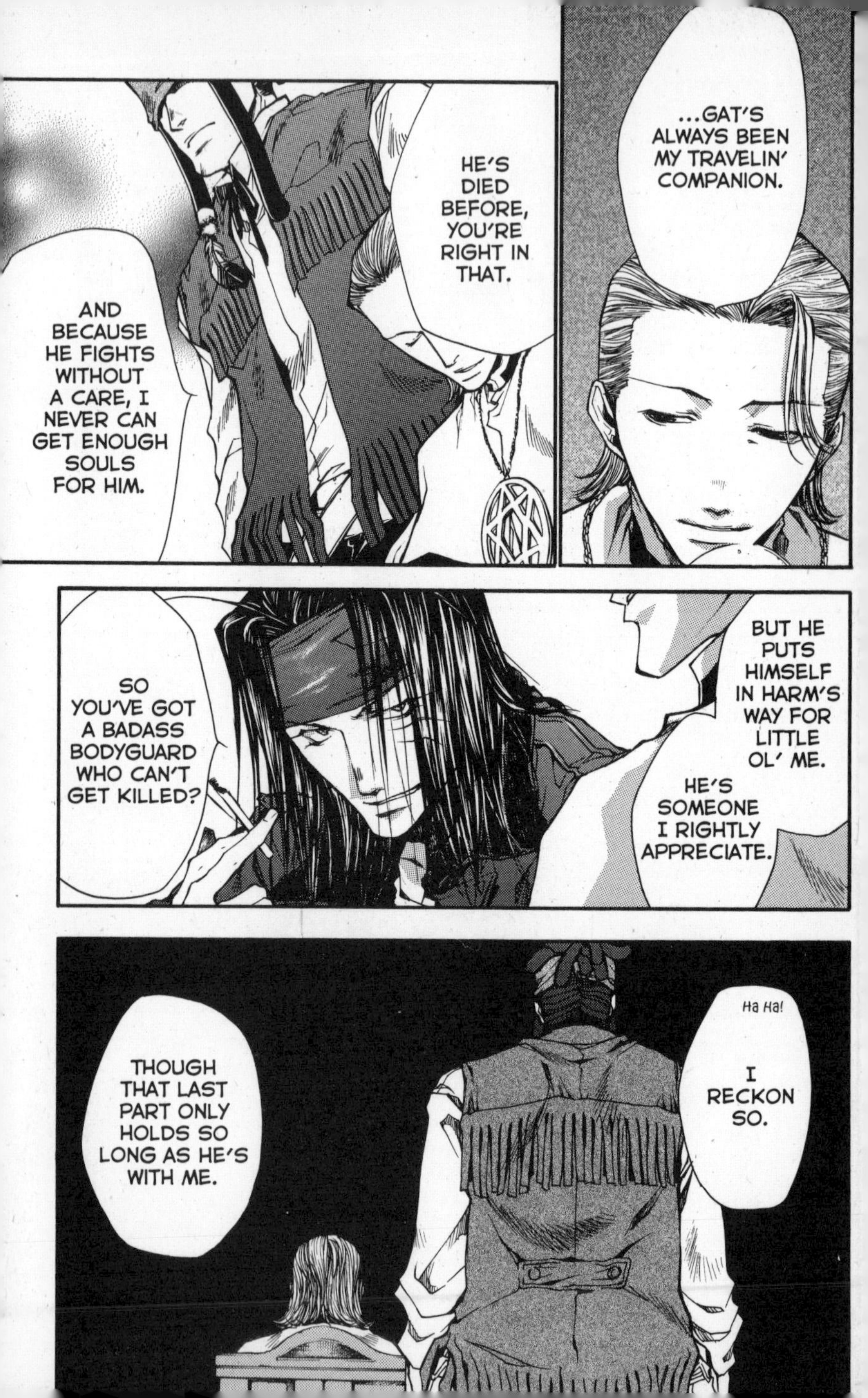
...GAT'S ALWAYS BEEN MY TRAVELIN' COMPANION.
HE'S DIED BEFORE, YOU'RE RIGHT IN THAT.
AND BECAUSE HE FIGHTS WITHOUT A CARE, I NEVER CAN GET ENOUGH SOULS FOR HIM.
BUT HE PUTS HIMSELF IN HARM'S WAY FOR LITTLE OL' ME.
HE'S SOMEONE I RIGHTLY APPRECIATE.
SO YOU'VE GOT A BADASS BODYGUARD WHO CAN'T GET KILLED?
Ha Ha!
I RECKON SO.
THOUGH THAT LAST PART ONLY HOLDS SO LONG AS HE'S WITH ME.

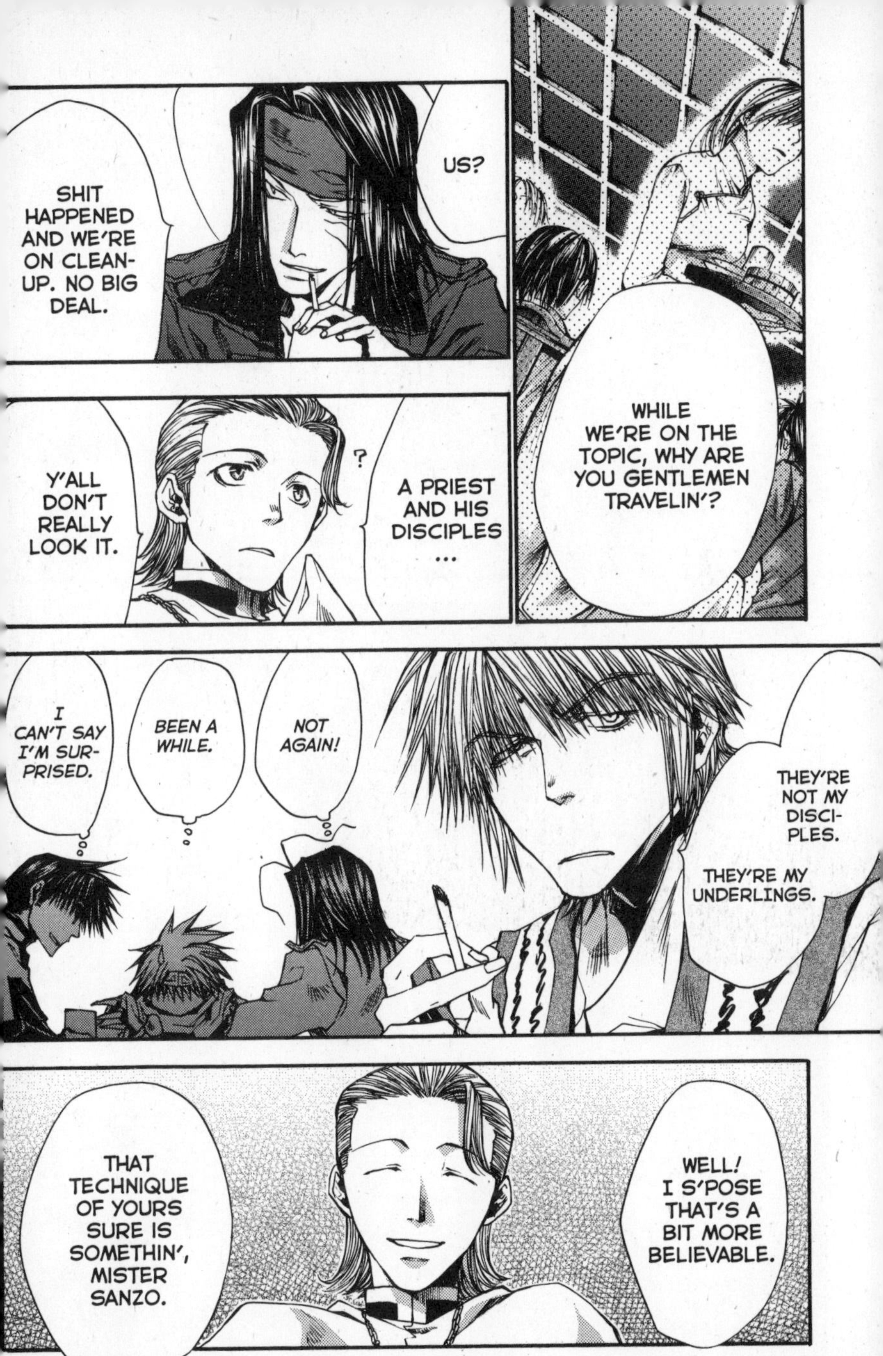
WHILE WE'RE ON THE TOPIC, WHY ARE YOU GENTLEMEN TRAVELIN'?
US?
SHIT HAPPENED AND WE'RE ON CLEAN-UP. NO BIG DEAL.
A PRIEST AND HIS DISCIPLES ...
?
Y'ALL DON'T REALLY LOOK IT.
THEY'RE NOT MY DISCIPLES.
THEY'RE MY UNDERLINGS.
NOT AGAIN!
BEEN A WHILE.
I CAN'T SAY I'M SURPRISED.
WELL! I S'POSE THAT'S A BIT MORE BELIEVABLE.
THAT TECHNIQUE OF YOURS SURE IS SOMETHIN', MISTER SANZO.

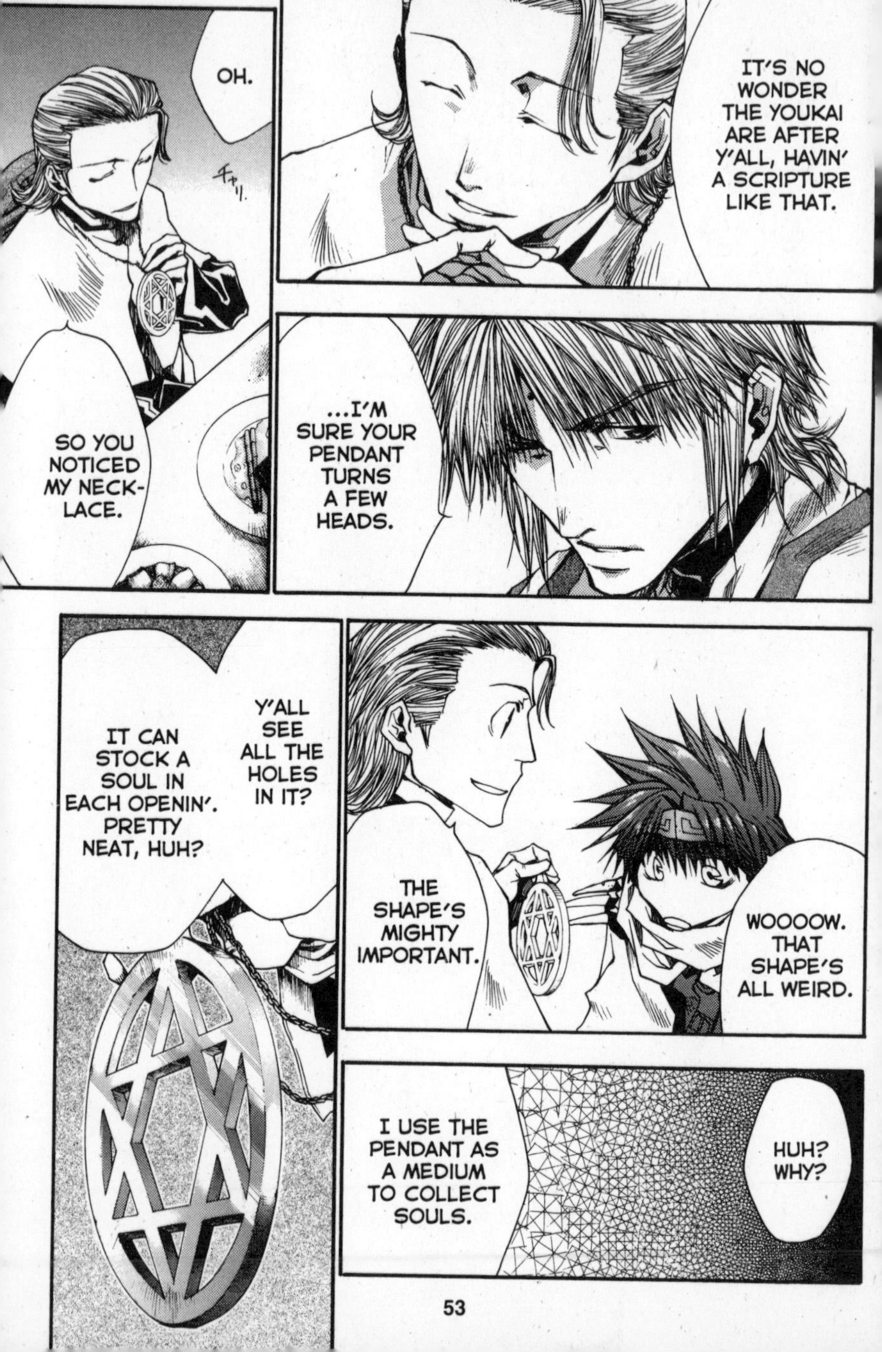

IT'S NO WONDER THE YOUKAI ARE AFTER Y'ALL, HAVIN' A SCRIPTURE LIKE THAT.
...I'M SURE YOUR PENDANT TURNS A FEW HEADS.
OH.
チャリ
SO YOU NOTICED MY NECK-LACE.
WOOOOW. THAT SHAPE'S ALL WEIRD.
THE SHAPE'S MIGHTY IMPORTANT.
HUH? WHY?
I USE THE PENDANT AS A MEDIUM TO COLLECT SOULS.
Y'ALL SEE ALL THE HOLES IN IT?
IT CAN STOCK A SOUL IN EACH OPENIN'. PRETTY NEAT, HUH?

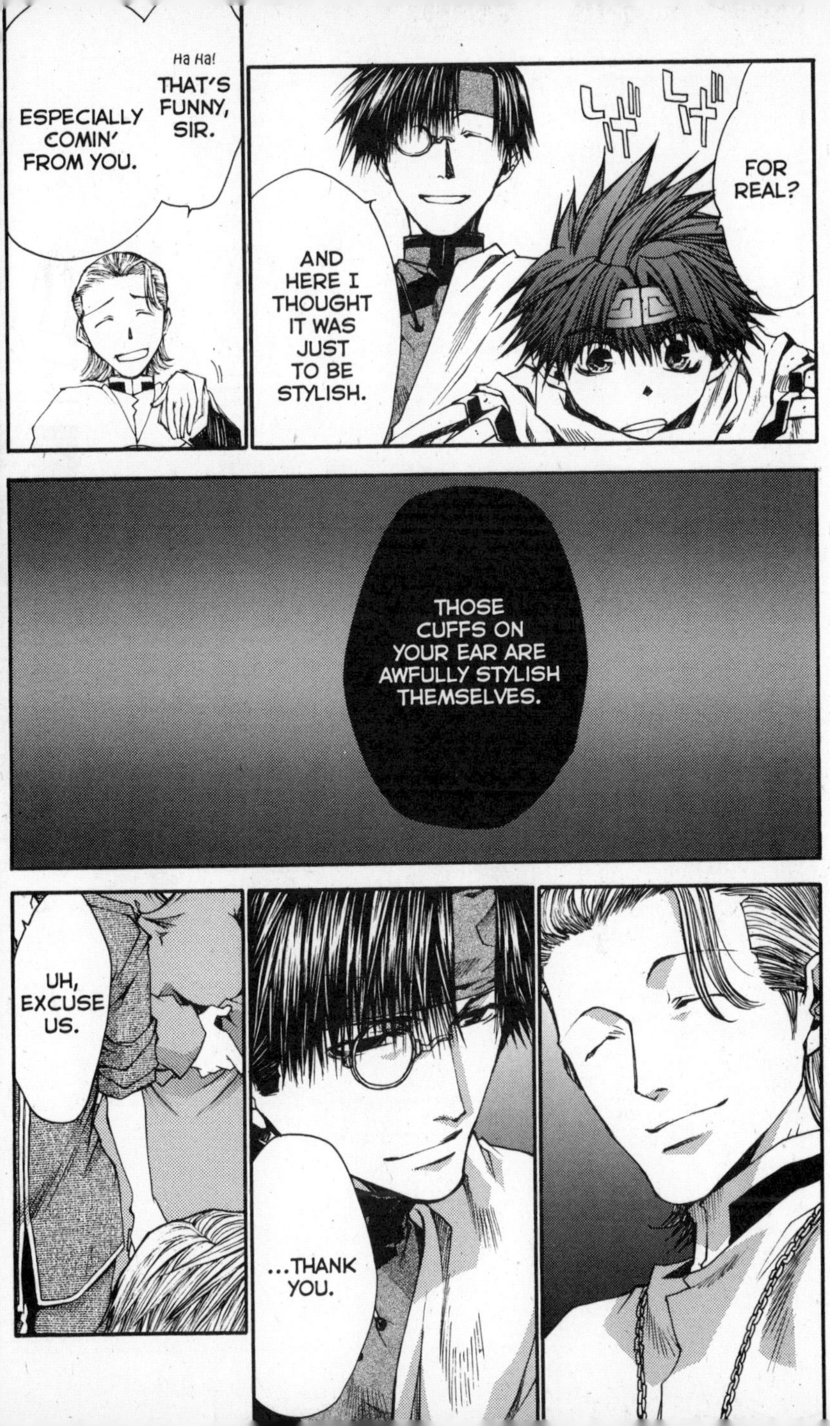
FOR REAL?
AND HERE I THOUGHT IT WAS JUST TO BE STYLISH.
Ha Ha!
THAT'S FUNNY, SIR.
ESPECIALLY COMIN' FROM YOU.
THOSE CUFFS ON YOUR EAR ARE AWFULLY STYLISH THEMSELVES.
...THANK YOU.
UH, EXCUSE US.

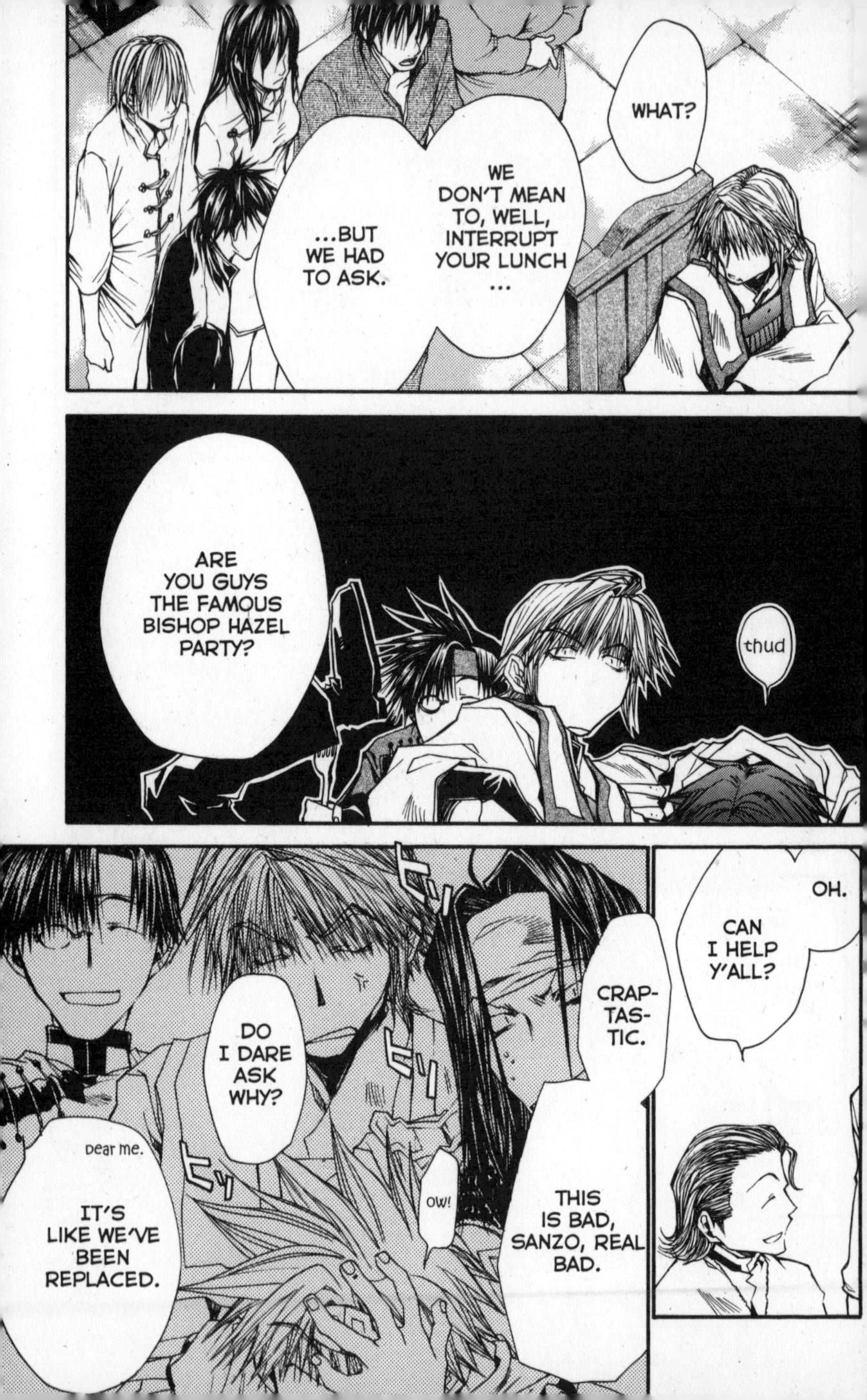
WHAT?
WE DON'T MEAN TO, WELL, INTERRUPT YOUR LUNCH ...
...BUT WE HAD TO ASK.
thud
ARE YOU GUYS THE FAMOUS BISHOP HAZEL PARTY?
OH.
CAN I HELP Y'ALL?
CRAP-TAS-TIC.
THIS IS BAD, SANZO, REAL BAD.
DO I DARE ASK WHY?
OW!
Dear me.
IT'S LIKE WE'VE BEEN REPLACED.

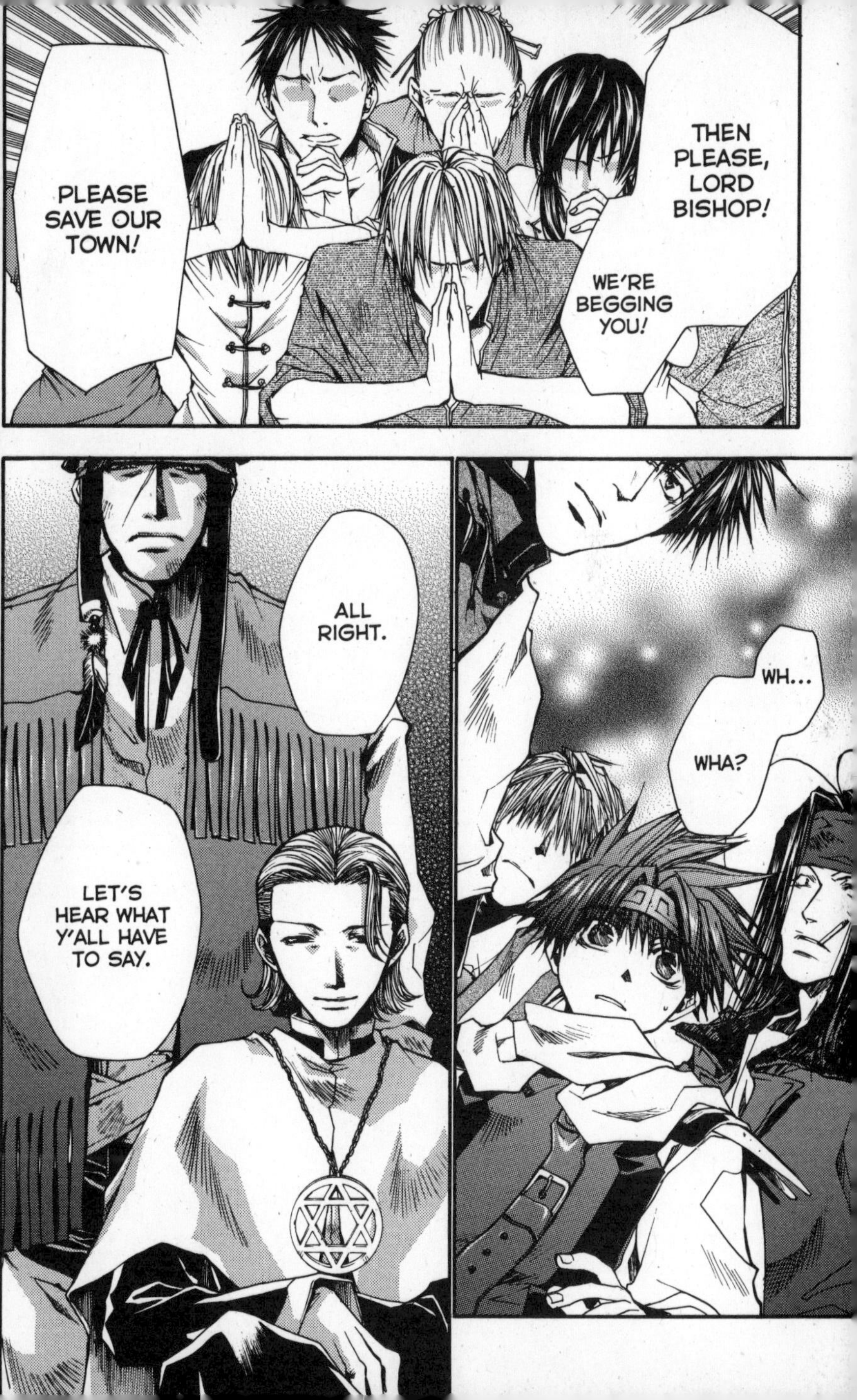
THEN PLEASE, LORD BISHOP!
WE'RE BEGGING YOU!
PLEASE SAVE OUR TOWN!
WH...
WHA?
ALL RIGHT.
LET'S HEAR WHAT Y'ALL HAVE TO SAY.

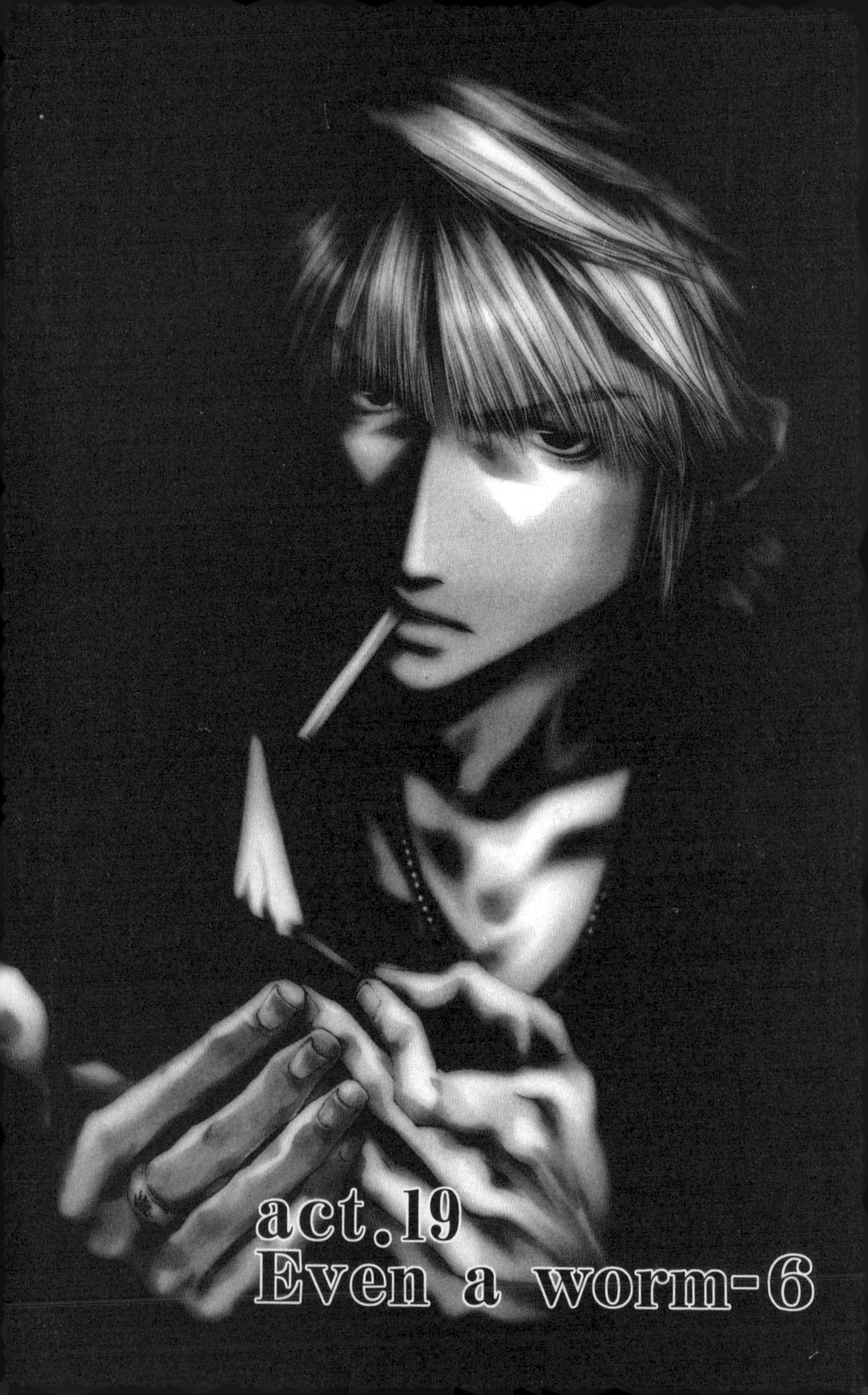
act.19
Even a worm-6

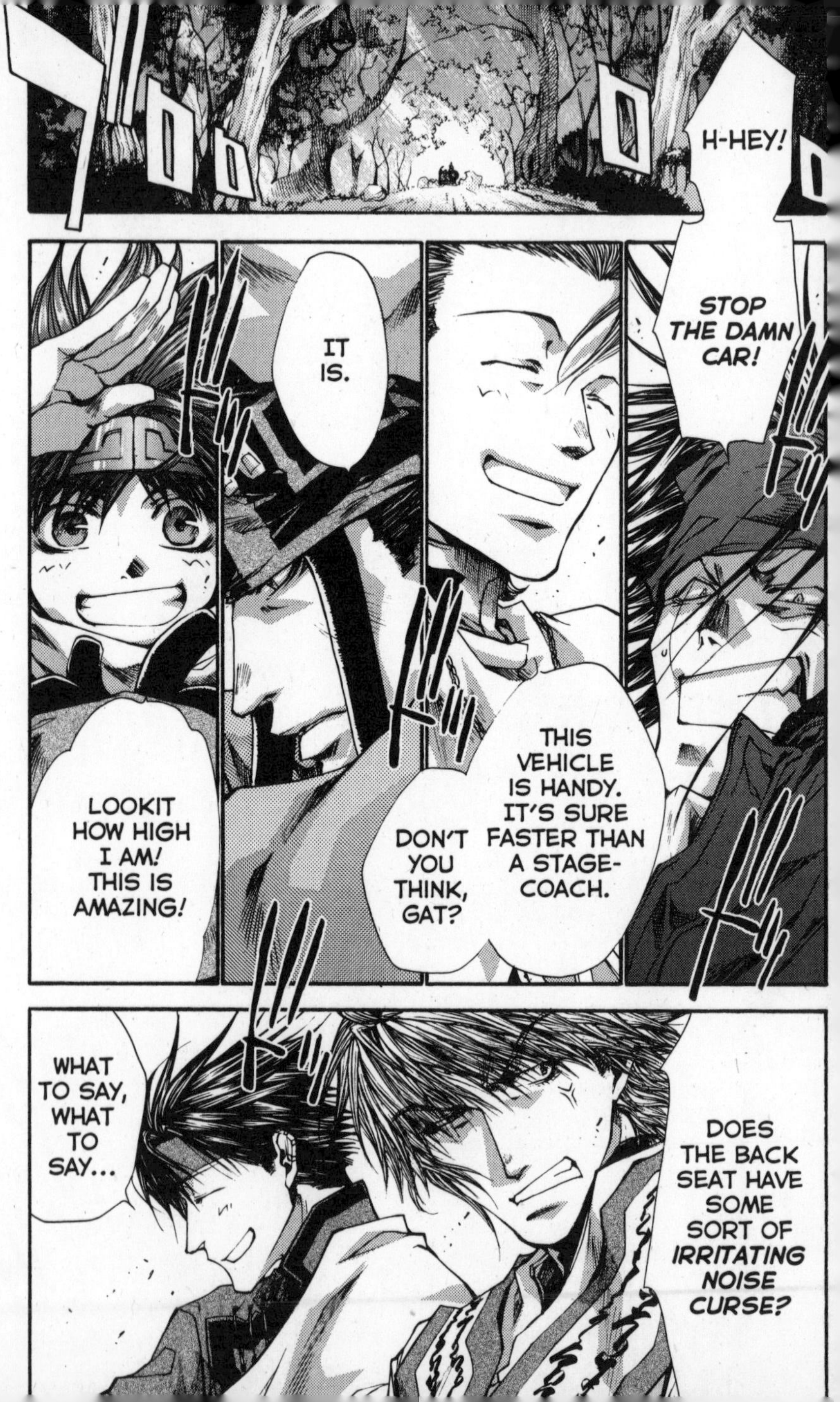
H-HEY!
STOP THE DAMN CAR!
THIS VEHICLE IS HANDY. IT'S SURE FASTER THAN A STAGE-COACH.
DON'T YOU THINK, GAT?
IT IS.
LOOKIT HOW HIGH I AM! THIS IS AMAZING!
DOES THE BACK SEAT HAVE SOME SORT OF IRRITATING NOISE CURSE?
WHAT TO SAY, WHAT TO SAY...

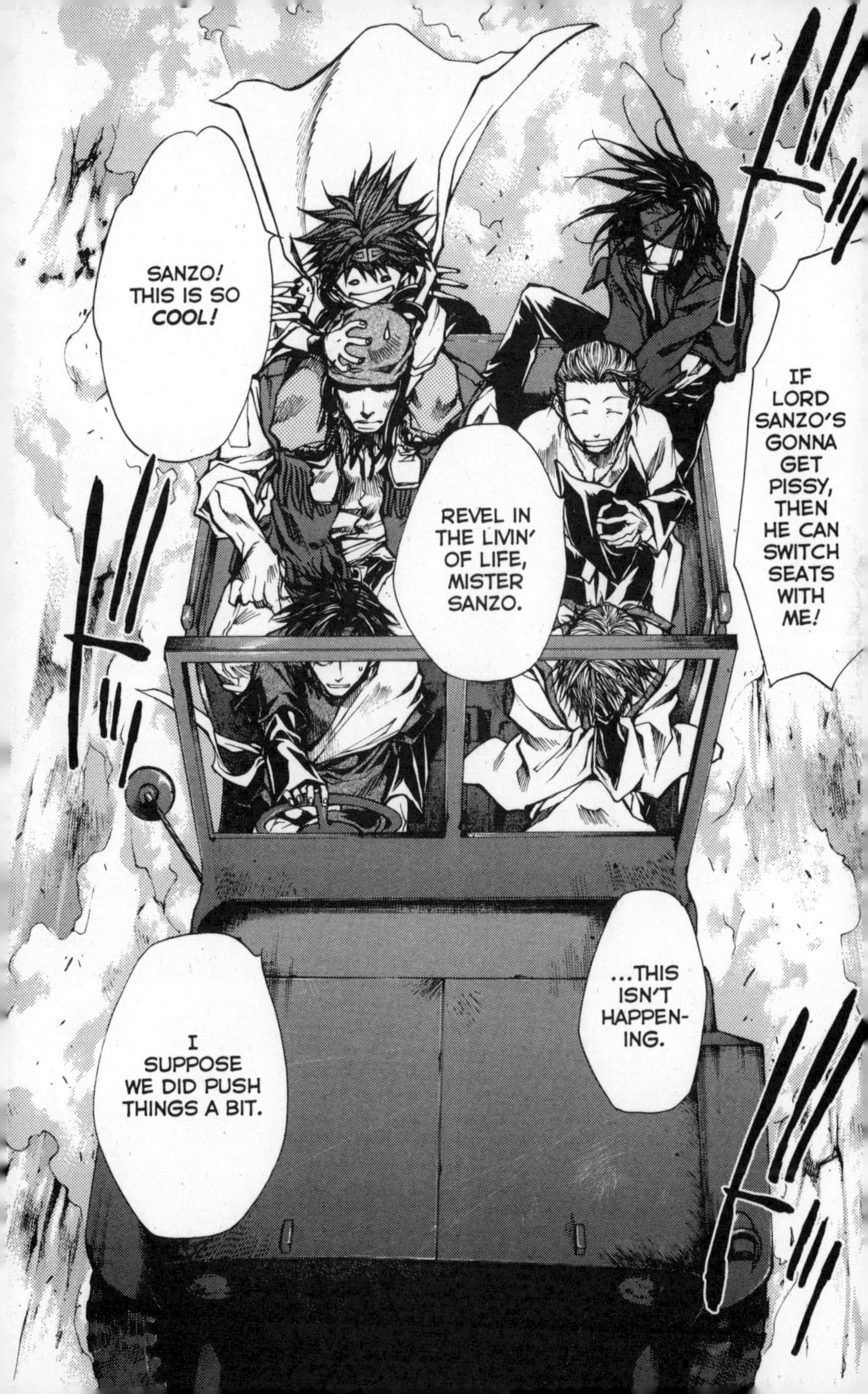
SANZO! THIS IS SO COOL!
IF LORD SANZO'S GONNA GET PISSY, THEN HE CAN SWITCH SEATS WITH ME!
REVEL IN THE LIVIN' OF LIFE, MISTER SANZO.
...THIS ISN'T HAPPEN-ING.
I SUPPOSE WE DID PUSH THINGS A BIT.

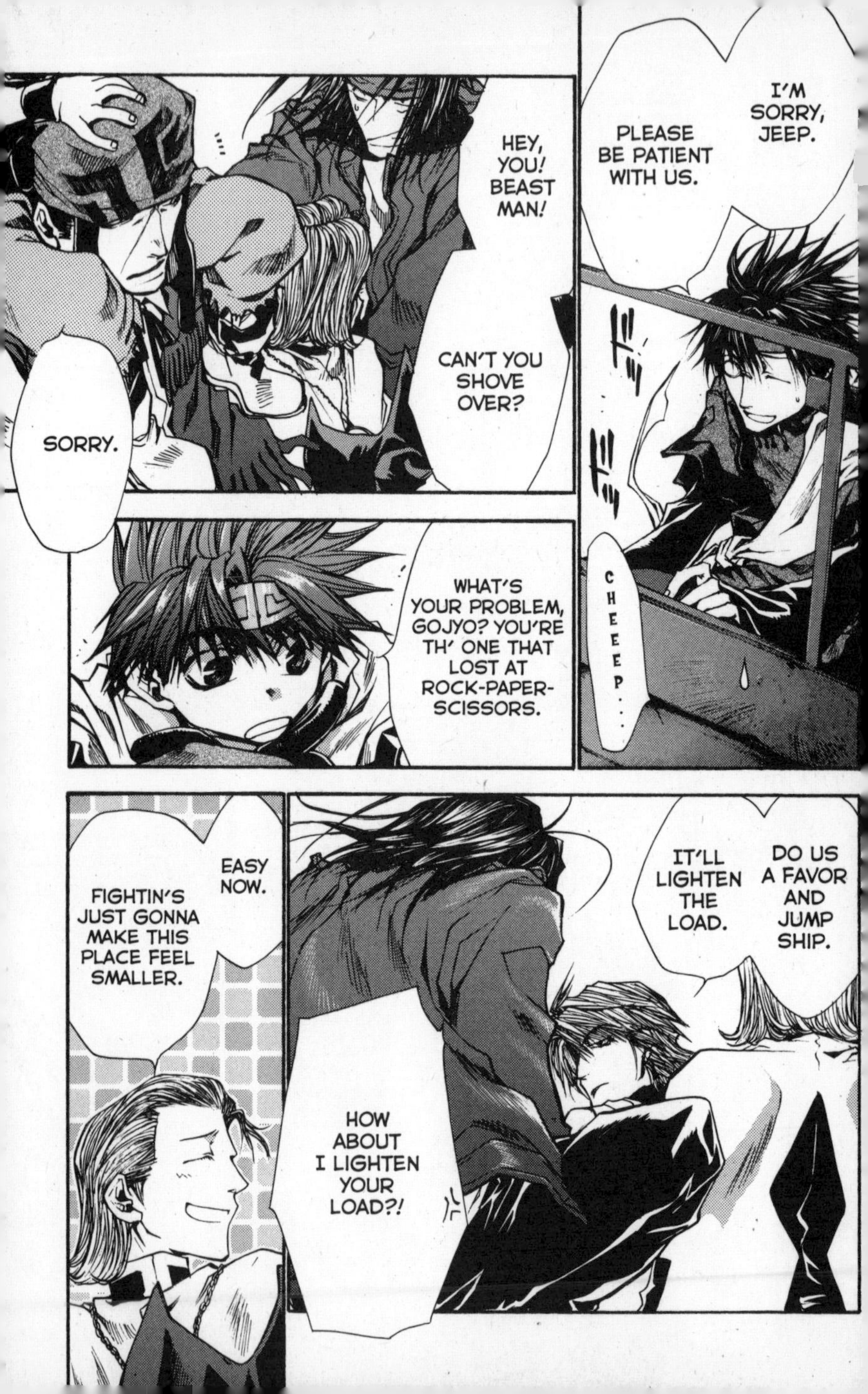
I'M SORRY, JEEP.
PLEASE BE PATIENT WITH US.
CHEEEP...
HEY, YOU! BEAST MAN!
CAN'T YOU SHOVE OVER?
SORRY.
WHAT'S YOUR PROBLEM, GOJYO? YOU'RE TH' ONE THAT LOST AT ROCK-PAPER-SCISSORS.
DO US A FAVOR AND JUMP SHIP.
IT'LL LIGHTEN THE LOAD.
HOW ABOUT I LIGHTEN YOUR LOAD?!
EASY NOW.
FIGHTIN'S JUST GONNA MAKE THIS PLACE FEEL SMALLER.

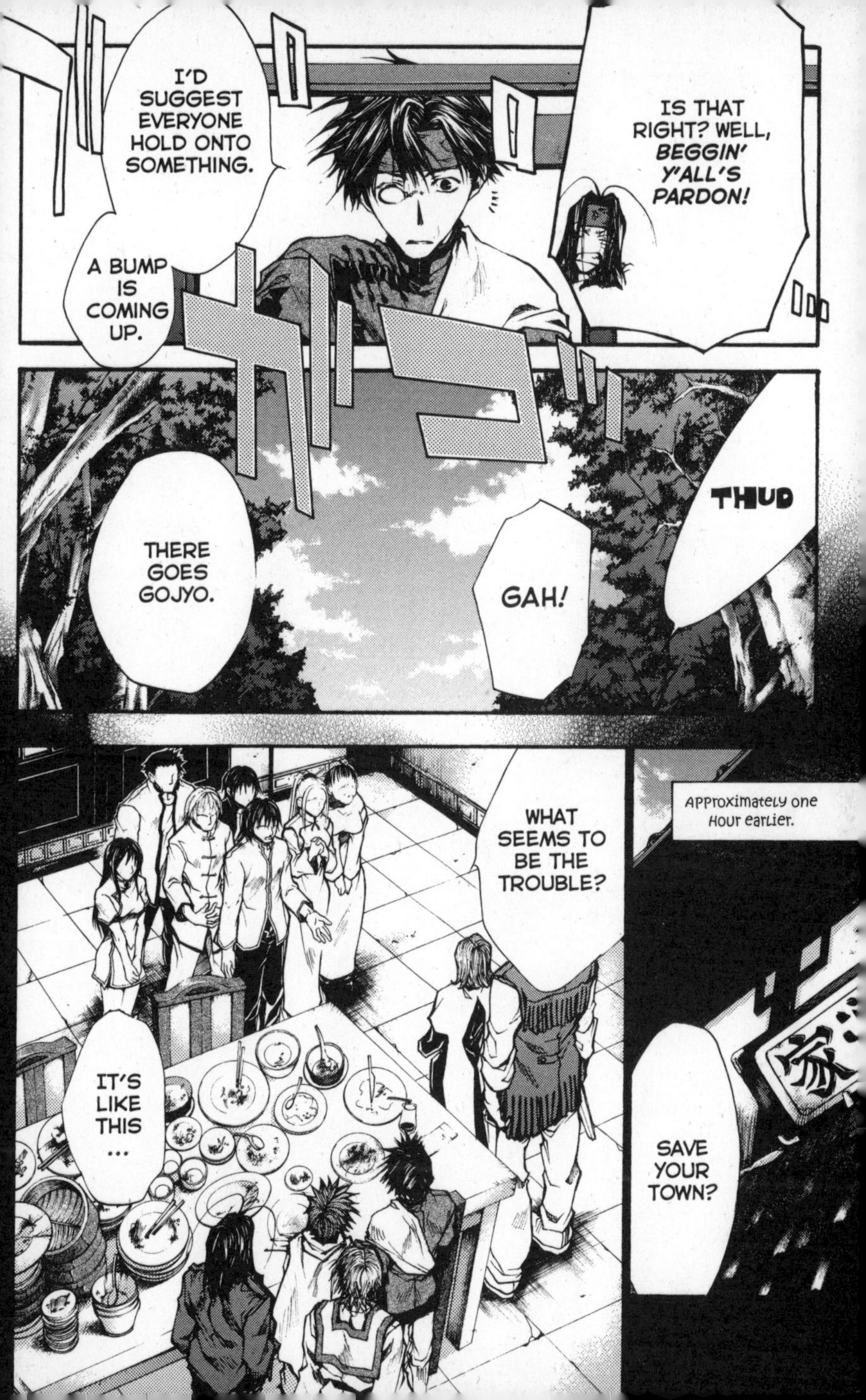
IS THAT RIGHT? WELL, BEGGIN' Y'ALL'S PARDON!
I'D SUGGEST EVERYONE HOLD ONTO SOMETHING.
A BUMP IS COMING UP.
THUD
GAH!
THERE GOES GOJYO.
Approximately one Hour earlier.
SAVE YOUR TOWN?
WHAT SEEMS TO BE THE TROUBLE?
IT'S LIKE THIS...

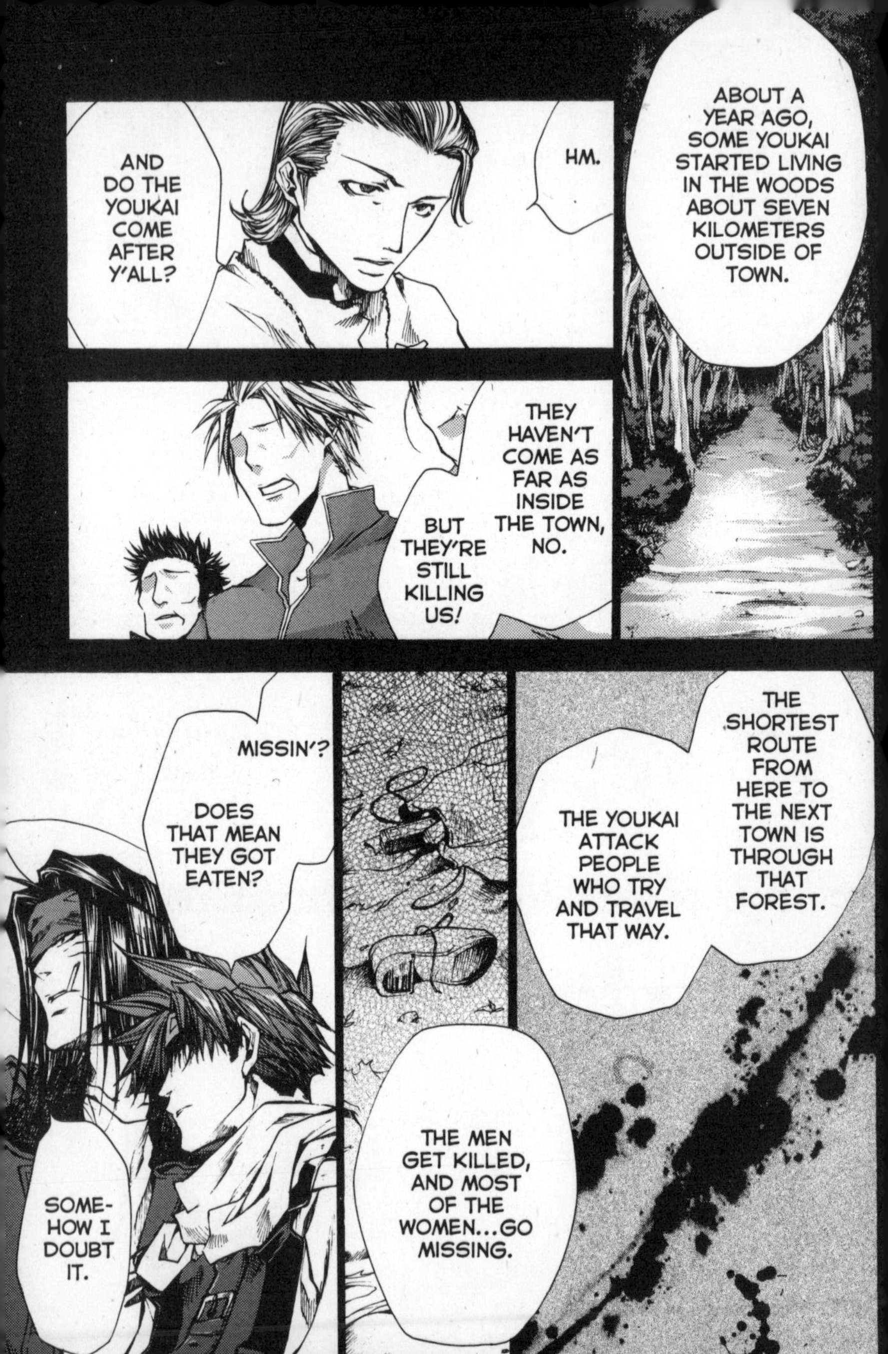
ABOUT A YEAR AGO, SOME YOUKAI STARTED LIVING IN THE WOODS ABOUT SEVEN KILOMETERS OUTSIDE OF TOWN.
HM.
AND DO THE YOUKAI COME AFTER Y'ALL?
THEY HAVEN'T COME AS FAR AS INSIDE THE TOWN, NO.
BUT THEY'RE STILL KILLING US!
THE SHORTEST ROUTE FROM HERE TO THE NEXT TOWN IS THROUGH THAT FOREST.
THE YOUKAI ATTACK PEOPLE WHO TRY AND TRAVEL THAT WAY.
THE MEN GET KILLED, AND MOST OF THE WOMEN...GO MISSING.
MISSIN'?
DOES THAT MEAN THEY GOT EATEN?
SOME-HOW I DOUBT IT.

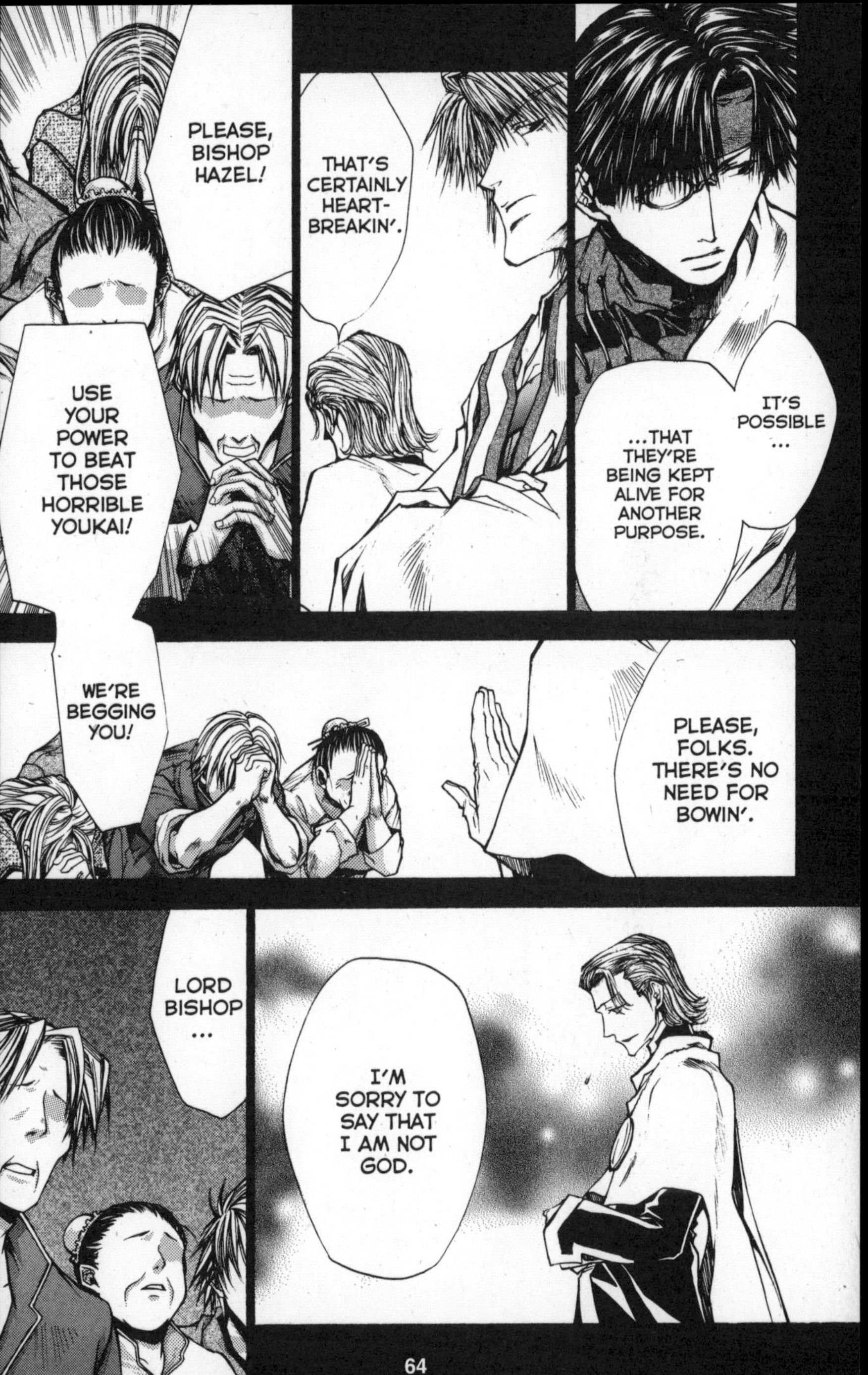
IT'S POSSIBLE ...
...THAT THEY'RE BEING KEPT ALIVE FOR ANOTHER PURPOSE.
THAT'S CERTAINLY HEART-BREAKIN'.
PLEASE, BISHOP HAZEL!
USE YOUR POWER TO BEAT THOSE HORRIBLE YOUKAI!
WE'RE BEGGING YOU!
PLEASE, FOLKS. THERE'S NO NEED FOR BOWIN'.
I'M SORRY TO SAY THAT I AM NOT GOD.
LORD BISHOP ...

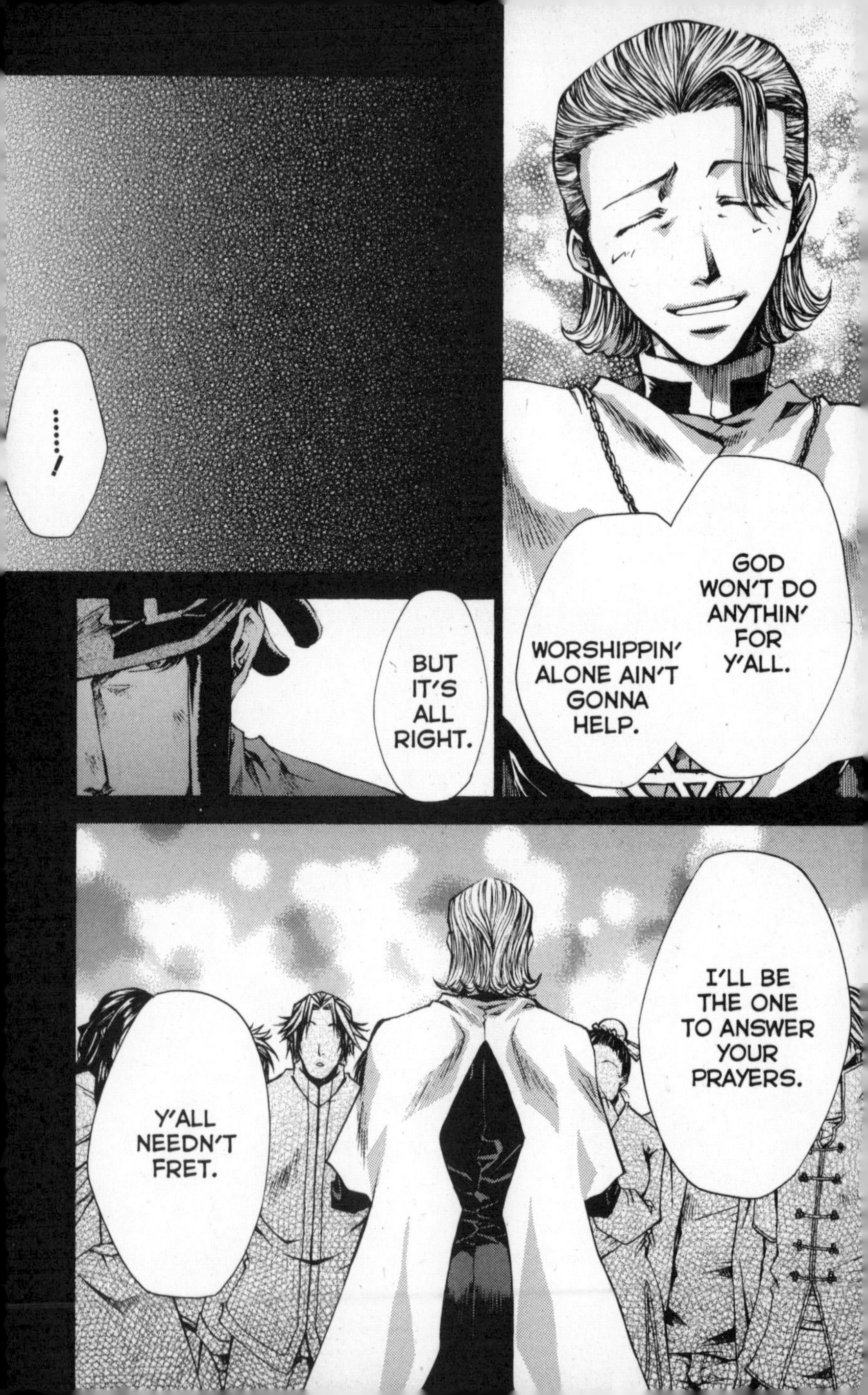
GOD WON'T DO ANYTHIN' FOR Y'ALL.
WORSHIPPIN' ALONE AIN'T GONNA HELP.
......!
BUT IT'S ALL RIGHT.
I'LL BE THE ONE TO ANSWER YOUR PRAYERS.
Y'ALL NEEDN'T FRET.

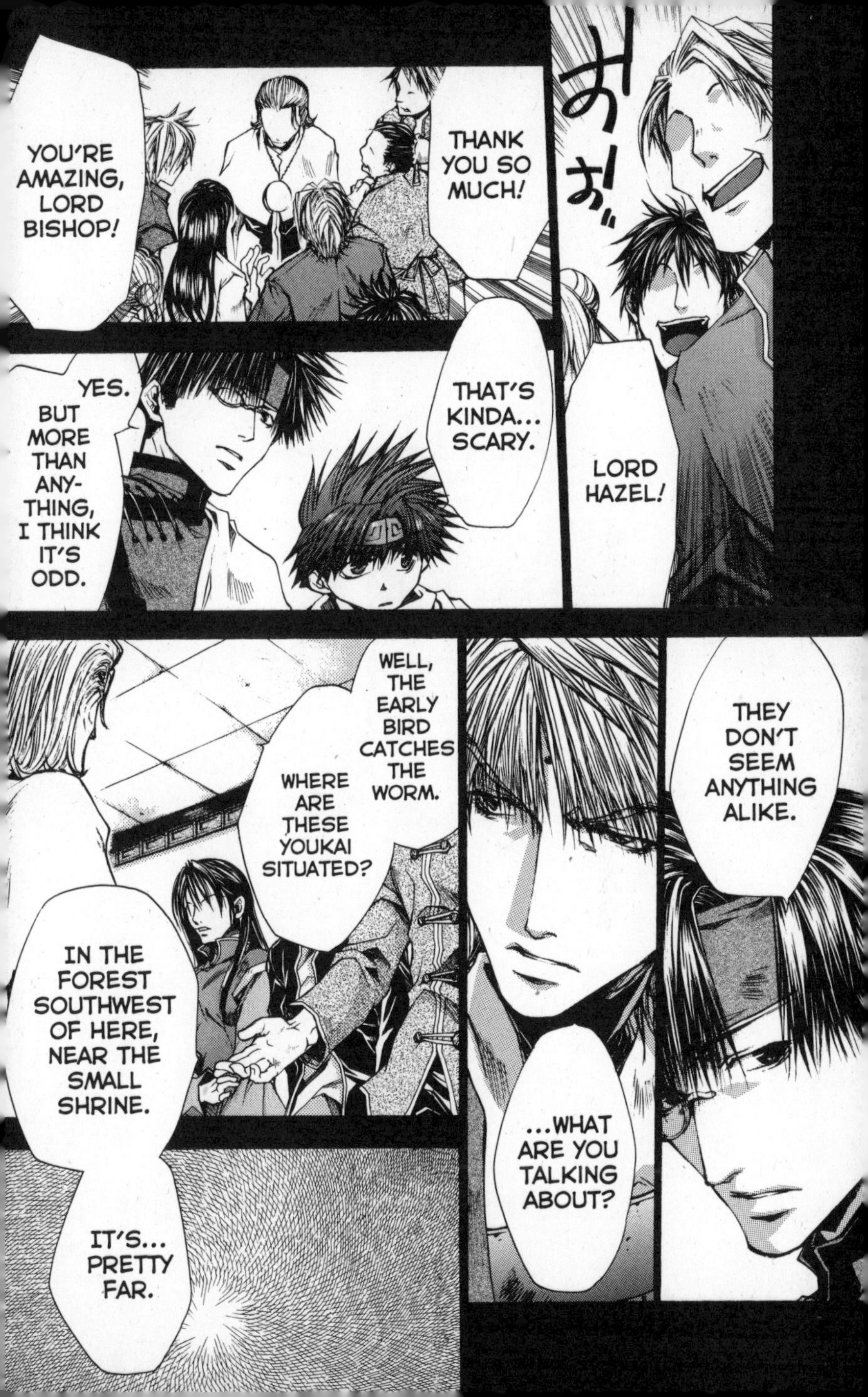
LORD HAZEL!
THANK YOU SO MUCH!
YOU'RE AMAZING, LORD BISHOP!
THAT'S KINDA... SCARY.
YES. BUT MORE THAN ANYTHING, I THINK IT'S ODD.
THEY DON'T SEEM ANYTHING ALIKE.
...WHAT ARE YOU TALKING ABOUT?
WELL, THE EARLY BIRD CATCHES THE WORM.
WHERE ARE THESE YOUKAI SITUATED?
IN THE FOREST SOUTHWEST OF HERE, NEAR THE SMALL SHRINE.
IT'S... PRETTY FAR.

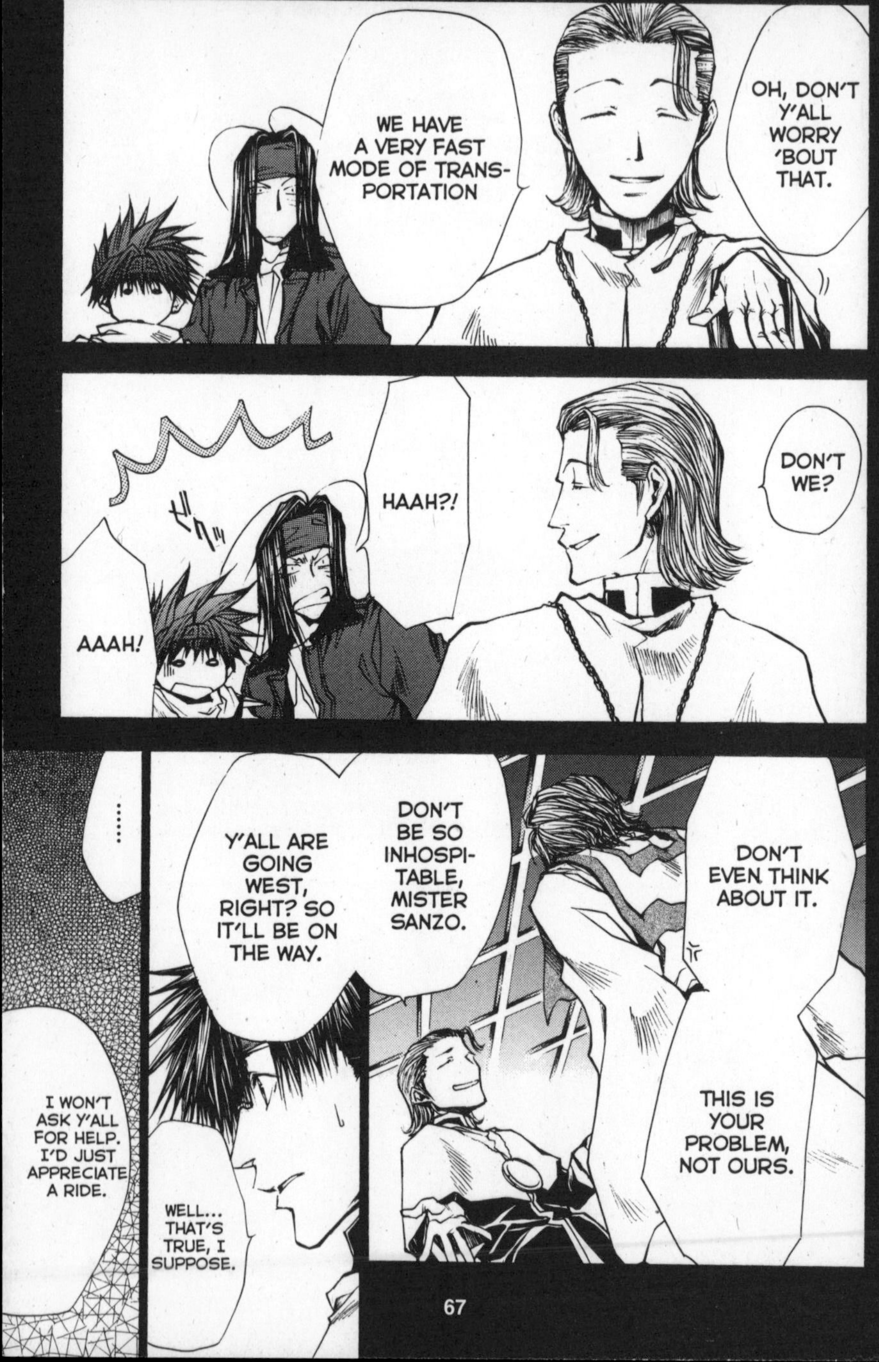
OH, DON'T Y'ALL WORRY 'BOUT THAT.
WE HAVE A VERY FAST MODE OF TRANS-PORTATION
DON'T WE?
HAAH?!
AAAH!
DON'T EVEN THINK ABOUT IT.
DON'T BE SO INHOSPI-TABLE, MISTER SANZO.
Y'ALL ARE GOING WEST, RIGHT? SO IT'LL BE ON THE WAY.
THIS IS YOUR PROBLEM, NOT OURS.
WELL... THAT'S TRUE, I SUPPOSE.
......
I WON'T ASK Y'ALL FOR HELP. I'D JUST APPRECIATE A RIDE.

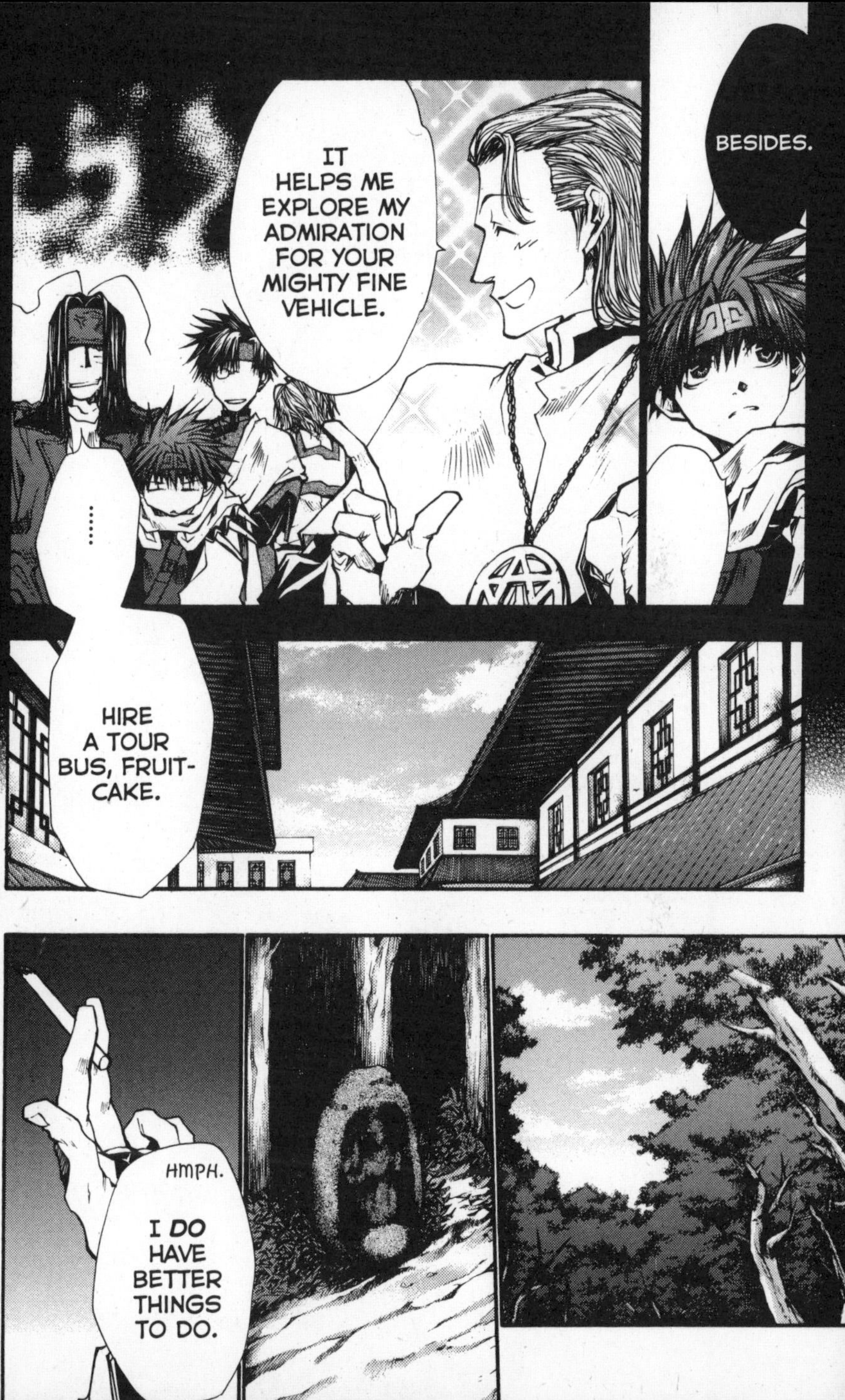
BESIDES.
IT HELPS ME EXPLORE MY ADMIRATION FOR YOUR MIGHTY FINE VEHICLE.
......
HIRE A TOUR BUS, FRUIT-CAKE.
HMPH.
I *DO* HAVE BETTER THINGS TO DO.

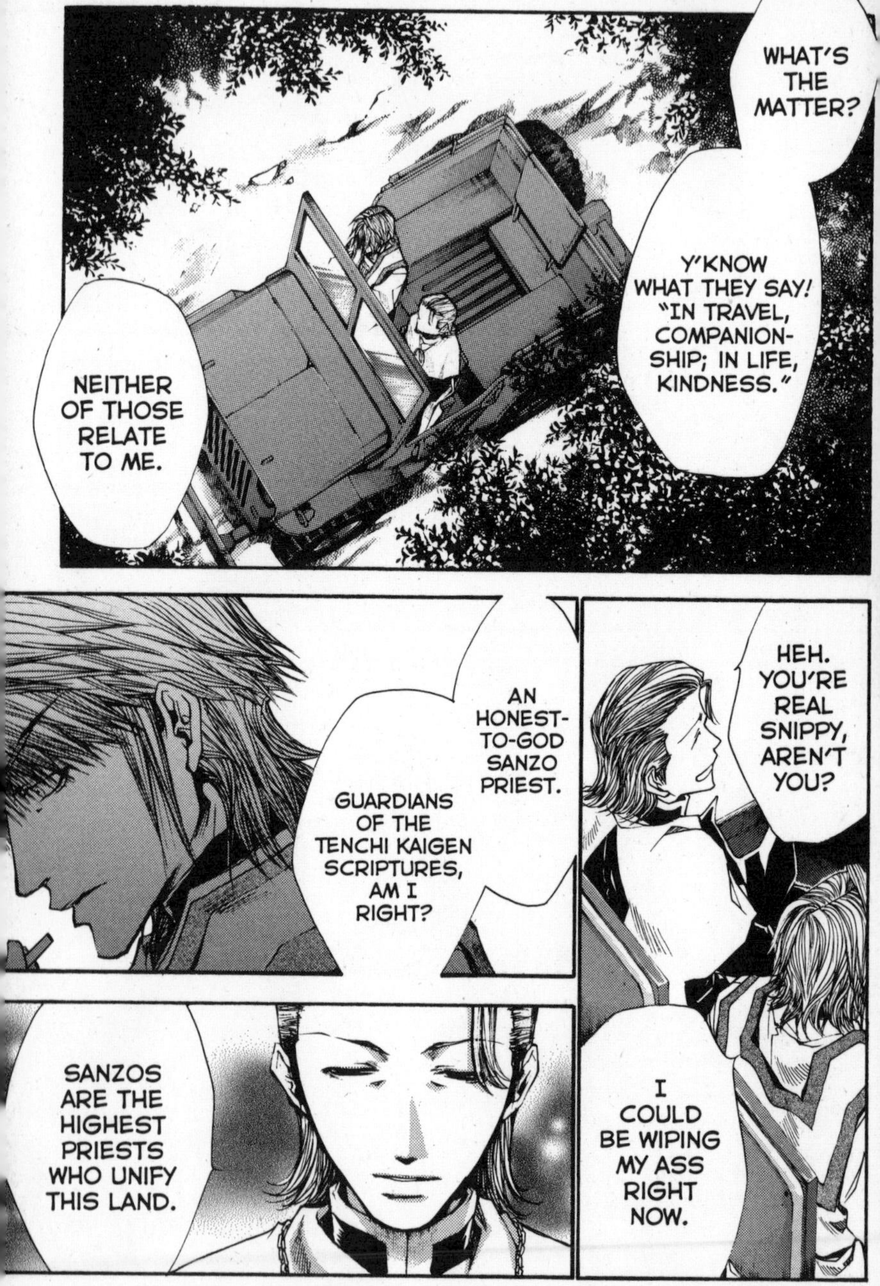
WHAT'S THE MATTER?
Y'KNOW WHAT THEY SAY! "IN TRAVEL, COMPANIONSHIP; IN LIFE, KINDNESS."
NEITHER OF THOSE RELATE TO ME.
HEH. YOU'RE REAL SNIPPY, AREN'T YOU?
I COULD BE WIPING MY ASS RIGHT NOW.
AN HONEST-TO-GOD SANZO PRIEST.
GUARDIANS OF THE TENCHI KAIGEN SCRIPTURES, AM I RIGHT?
SANZOS ARE THE HIGHEST PRIESTS WHO UNIFY THIS LAND.

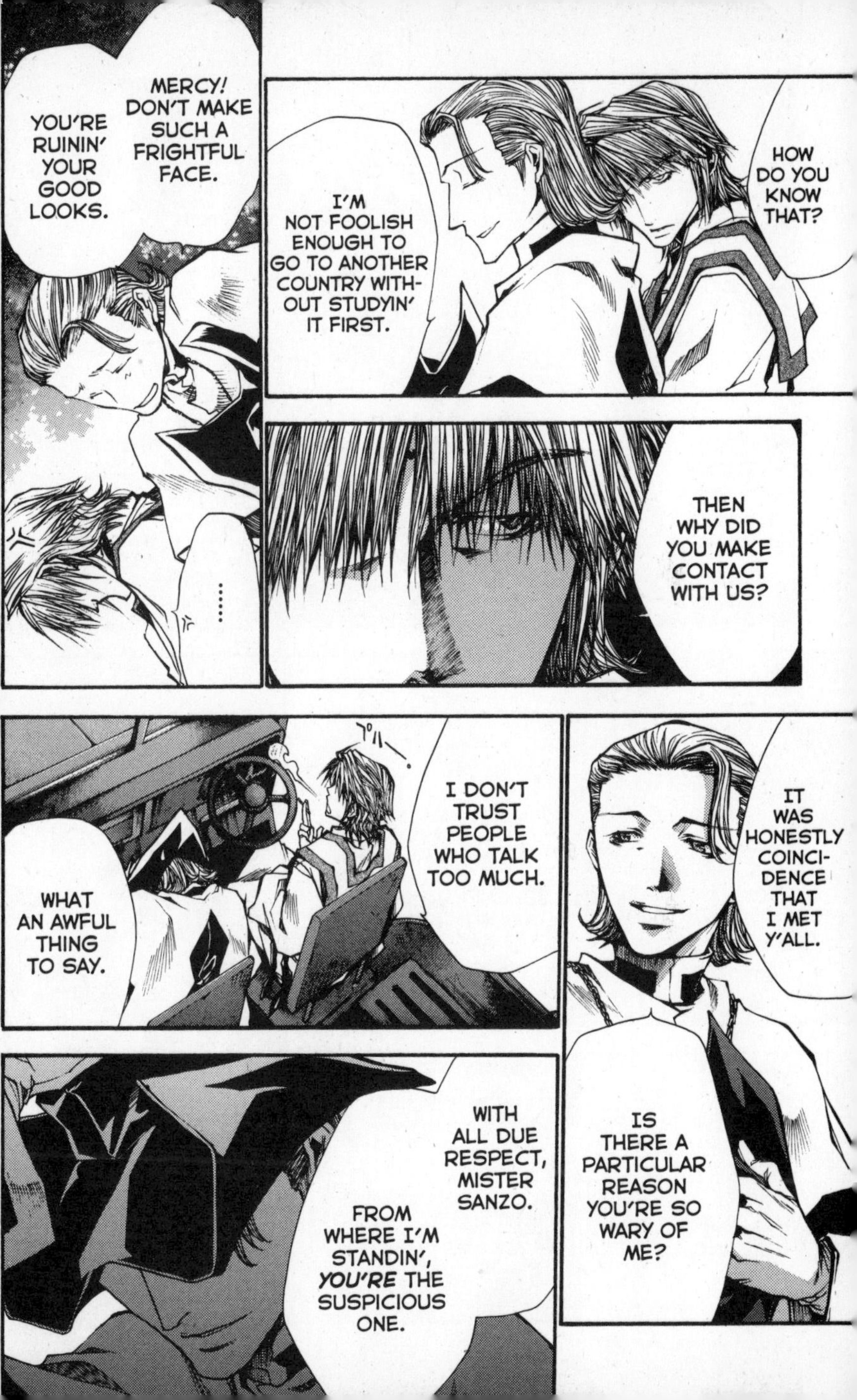
HOW DO YOU KNOW THAT?
I'M NOT FOOLISH ENOUGH TO GO TO ANOTHER COUNTRY WITH-OUT STUDYIN' IT FIRST.
THEN WHY DID YOU MAKE CONTACT WITH US?
MERCY! DON'T MAKE SUCH A FRIGHTFUL FACE.
YOU'RE RUININ' YOUR GOOD LOOKS.
......
IT WAS HONESTLY COINCI-DENCE THAT I MET Y'ALL.
I DON'T TRUST PEOPLE WHO TALK TOO MUCH.
WHAT AN AWFUL THING TO SAY.
IS THERE A PARTICULAR REASON YOU'RE SO WARY OF ME?
WITH ALL DUE RESPECT, MISTER SANZO.
FROM WHERE I'M STANDIN', *YOU'RE* THE SUSPICIOUS ONE.

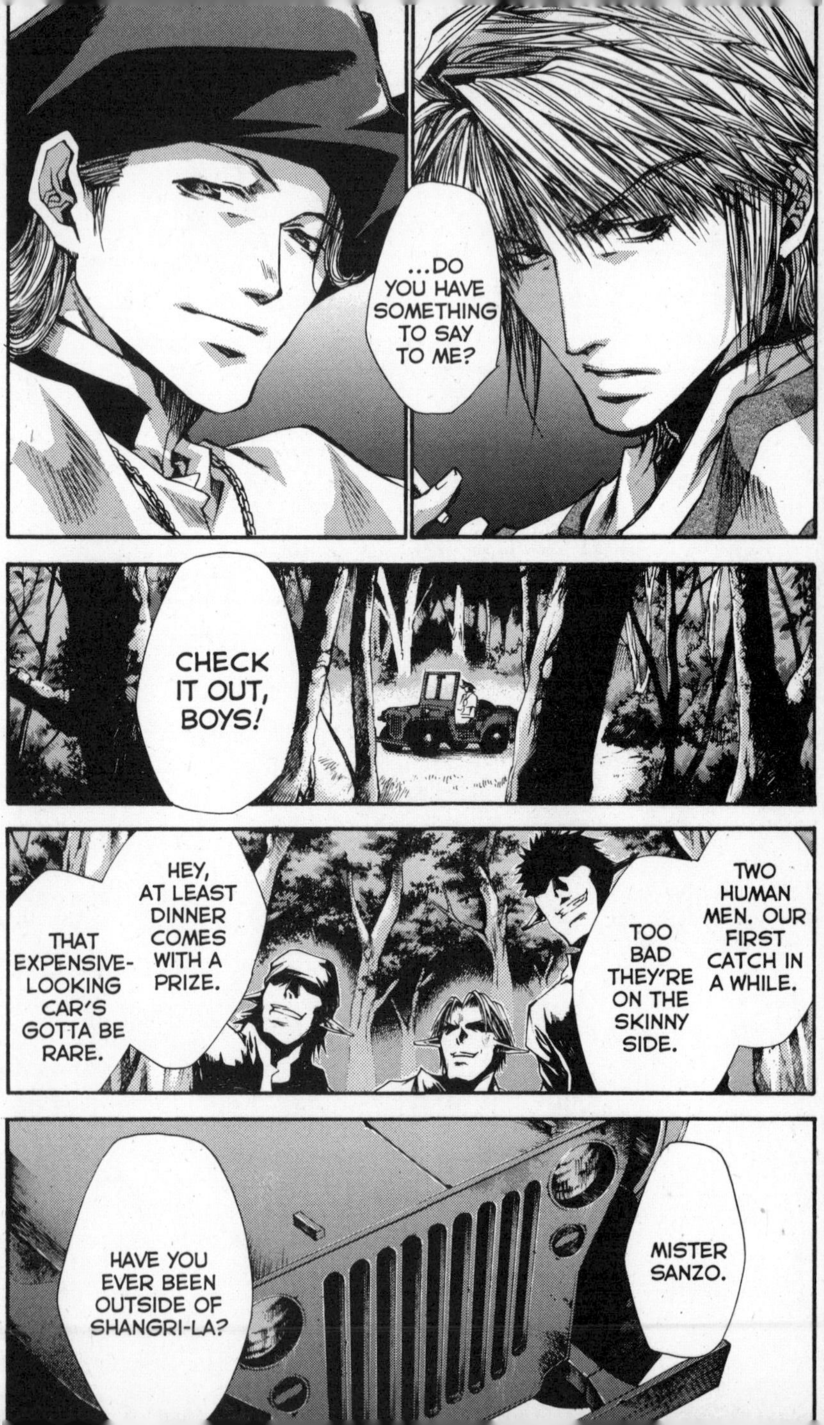
...DO YOU HAVE SOMETHING TO SAY TO ME?
CHECK IT OUT, BOYS!
TWO HUMAN MEN. OUR FIRST CATCH IN A WHILE.
TOO BAD THEY'RE ON THE SKINNY SIDE.
HEY, AT LEAST DINNER COMES WITH A PRIZE.
THAT EXPENSIVE-LOOKING CAR'S GOTTA BE RARE.
MISTER SANZO.
HAVE YOU EVER BEEN OUTSIDE OF SHANGRI-LA?

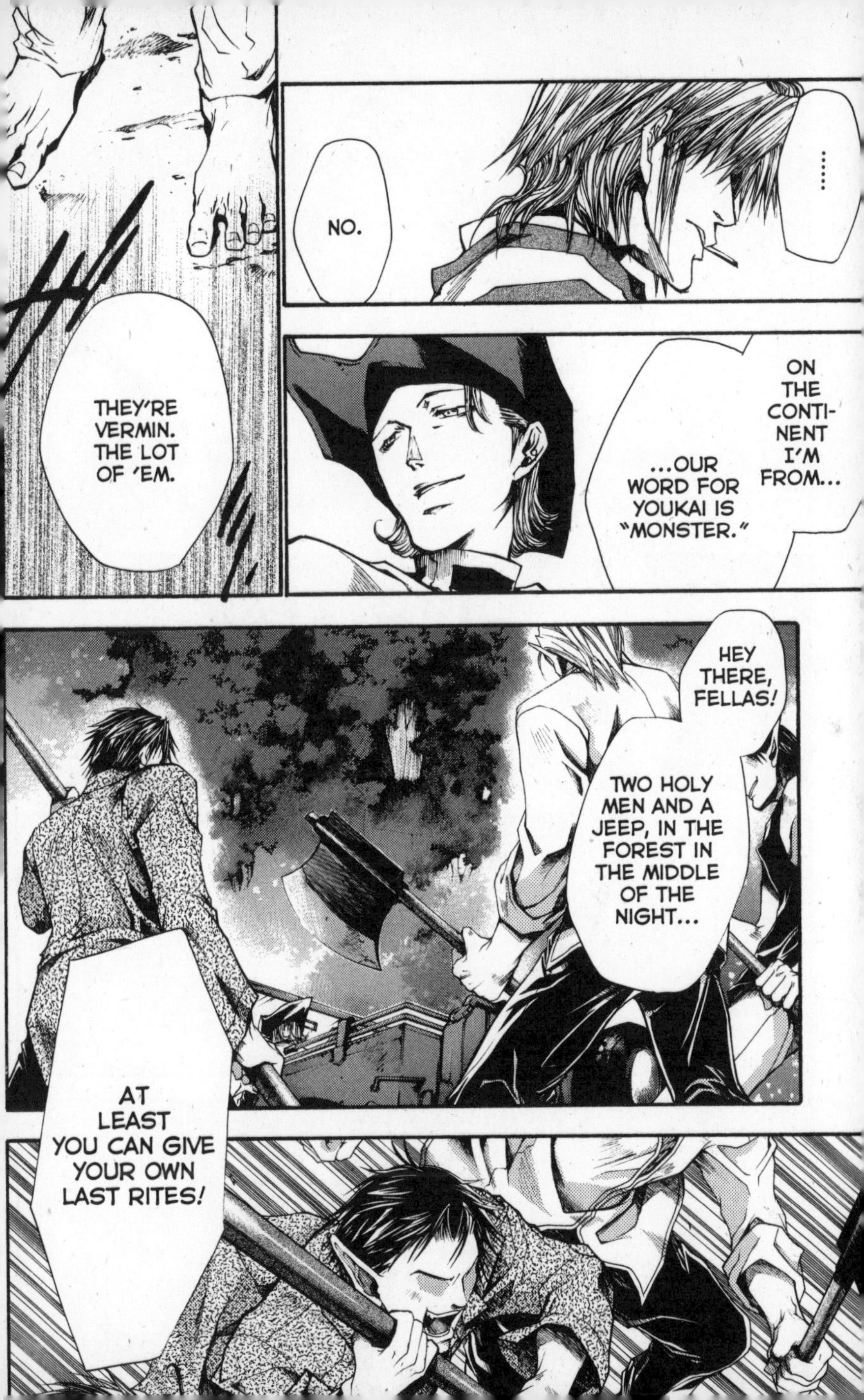
......
NO.
ON THE CONTINENT I'M FROM...
...OUR WORD FOR YOUKAI IS "MONSTER."
THEY'RE VERMIN. THE LOT OF 'EM.
HEY THERE, FELLAS!
TWO HOLY MEN AND A JEEP, IN THE FOREST IN THE MIDDLE OF THE NIGHT...
AT LEAST YOU CAN GIVE YOUR OWN LAST RITES!

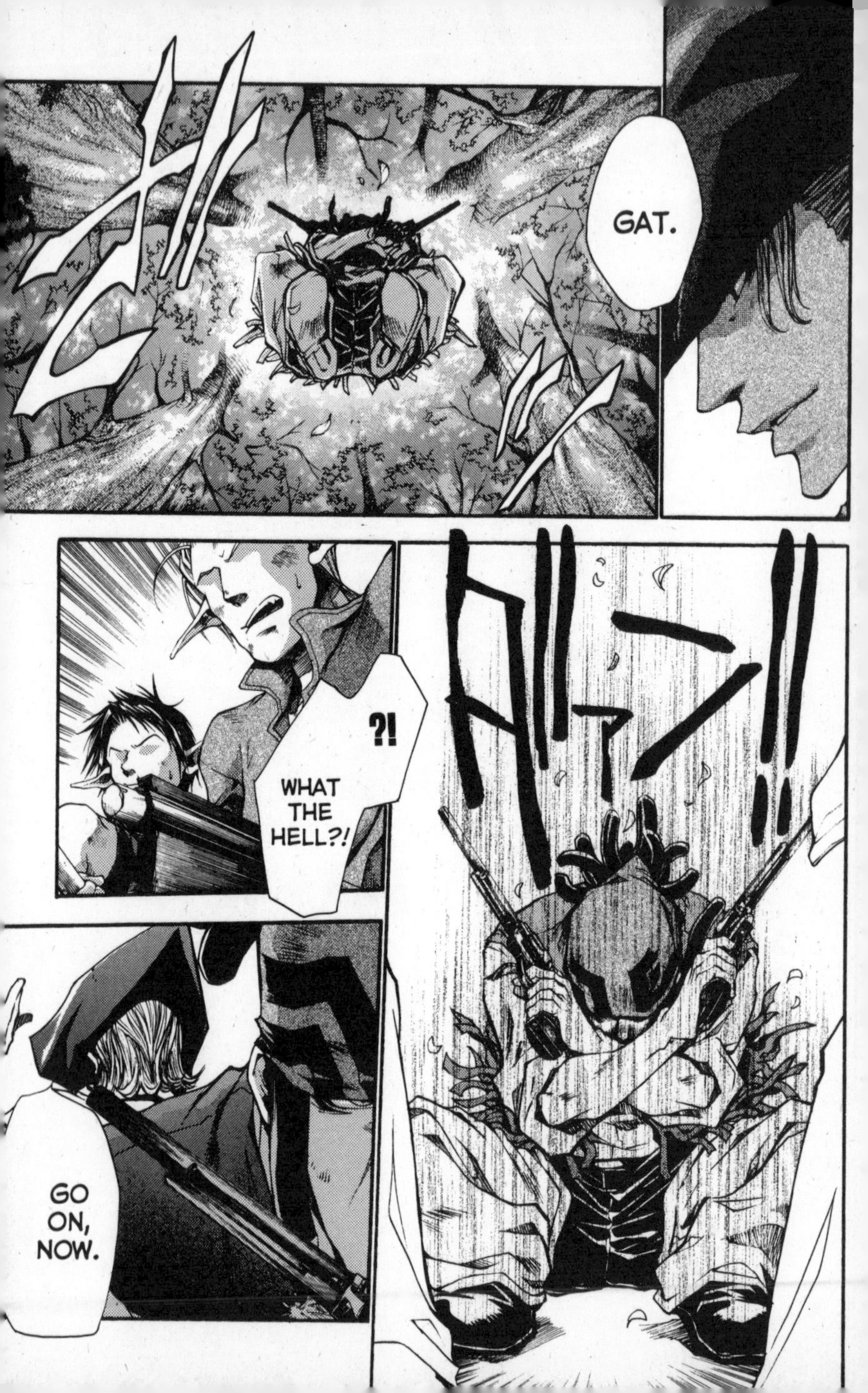
GAT.
?!
WHAT THE HELL?!
GO ON, NOW.

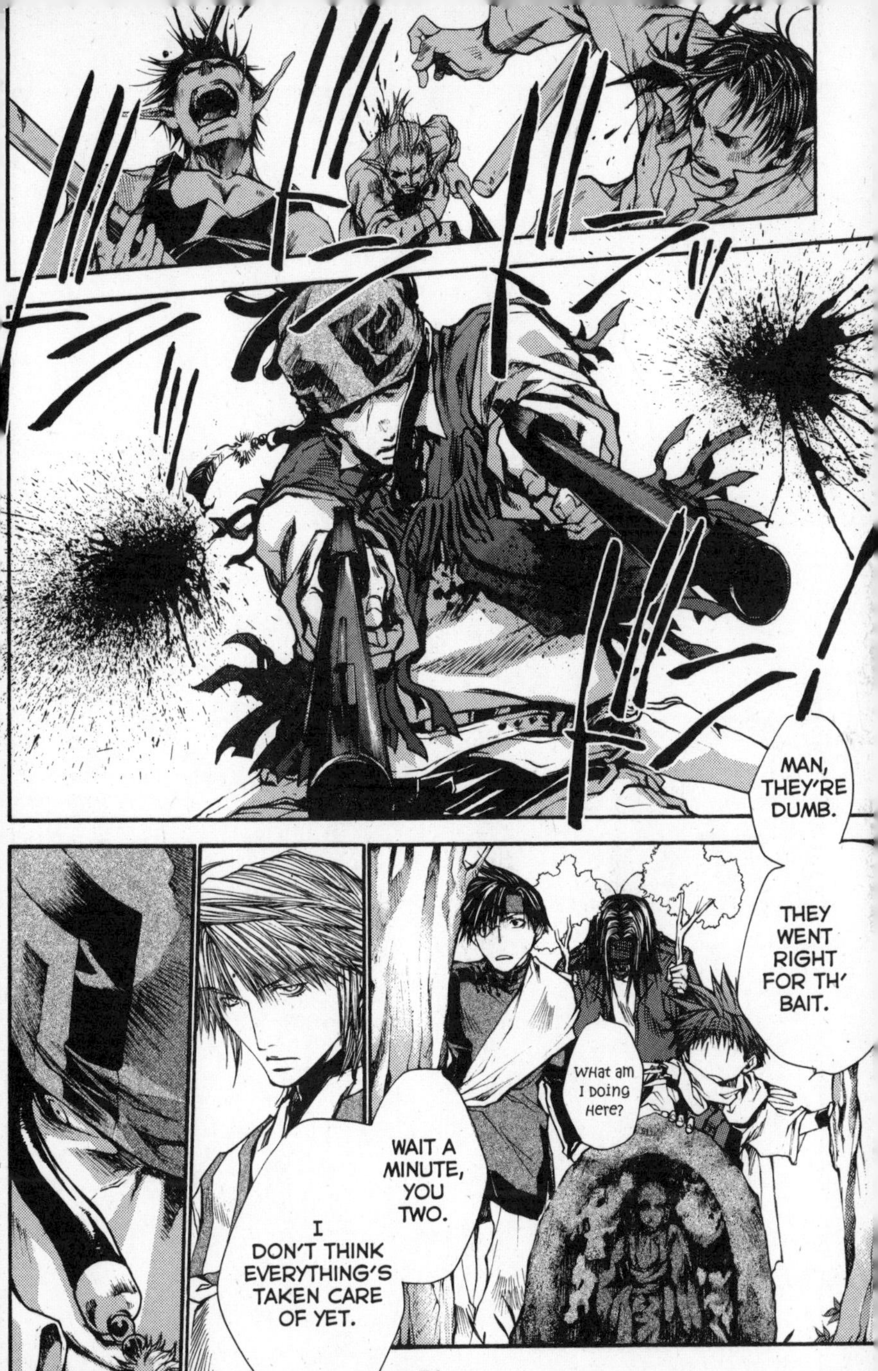
MAN, THEY'RE DUMB.
THEY WENT RIGHT FOR TH' BAIT.
What am I doing Here?
WAIT A MINUTE, YOU TWO.
I DON'T THINK EVERYTHING'S TAKEN CARE OF YET.

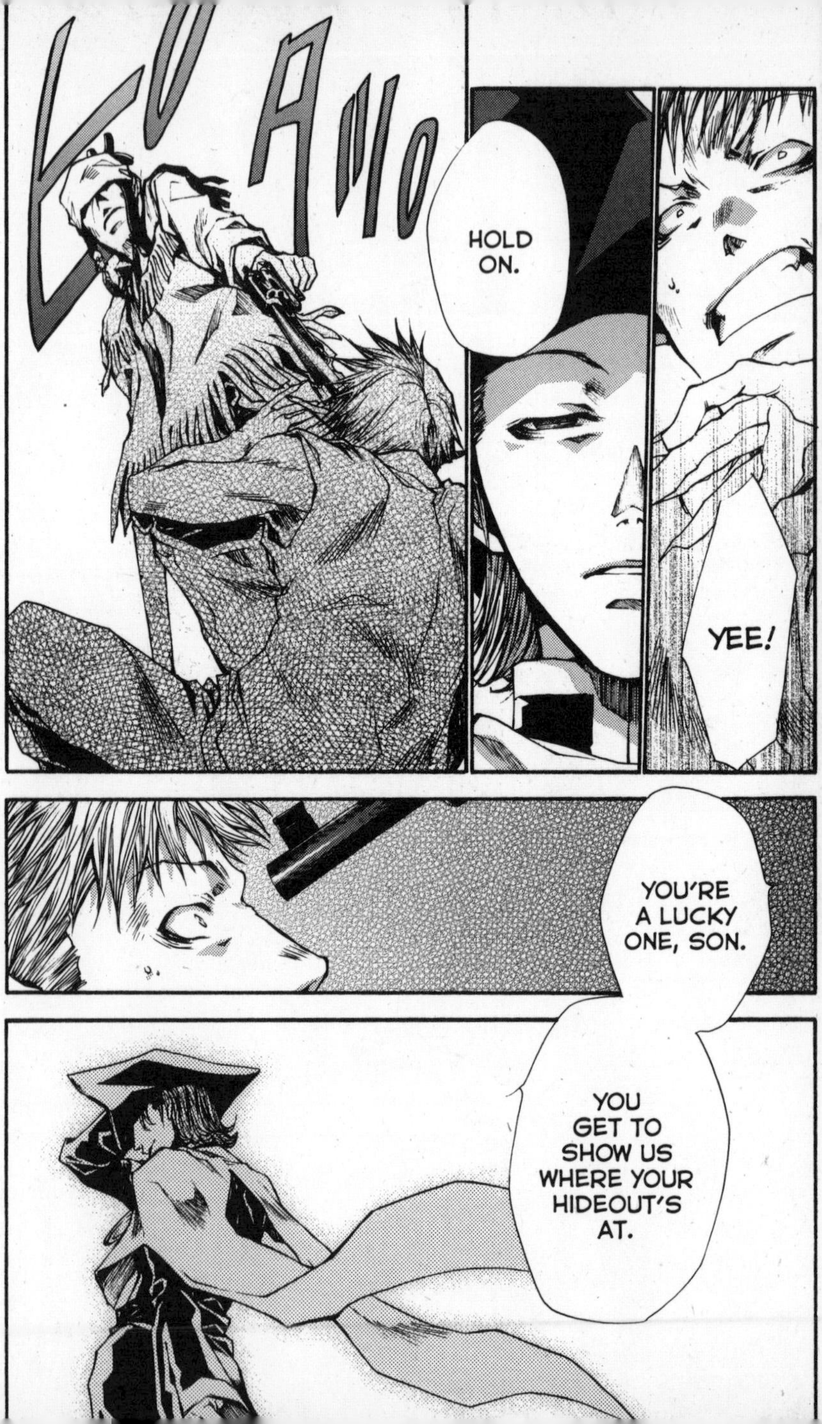
YEE!
HOLD ON.
YOU'RE A LUCKY ONE, SON.
YOU GET TO SHOW US WHERE YOUR HIDEOUT'S AT.

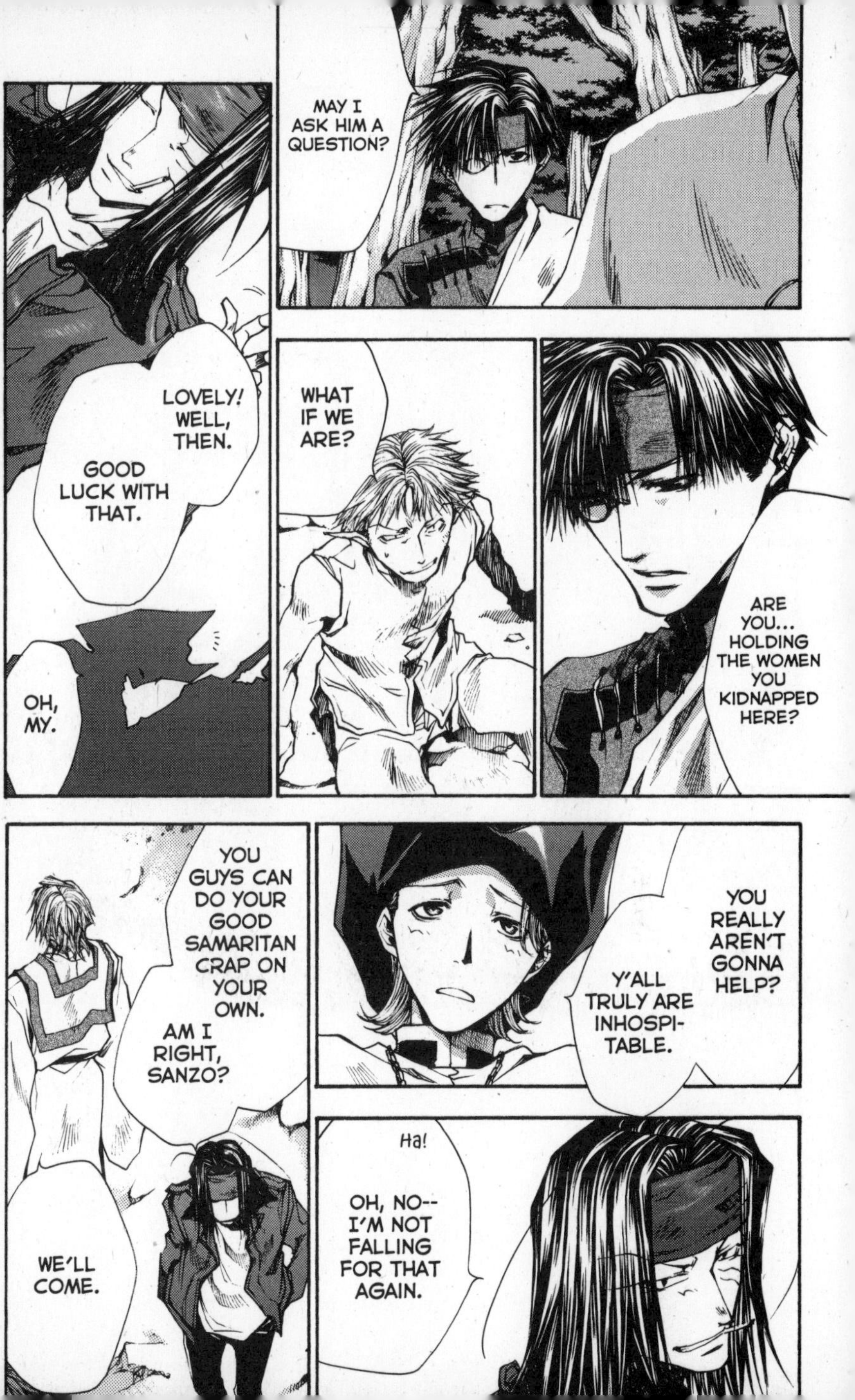
MAY I ASK HIM A QUESTION?
ARE YOU... HOLDING THE WOMEN YOU KIDNAPPED HERE?
WHAT IF WE ARE?
LOVELY! WELL, THEN.
GOOD LUCK WITH THAT.
OH, MY.
YOU REALLY AREN'T GONNA HELP?
Y'ALL TRULY ARE INHOSPI-TABLE.
Ha!
OH, NO-- I'M NOT FALLING FOR THAT AGAIN.
YOU GUYS CAN DO YOUR GOOD SAMARITAN CRAP ON YOUR OWN.
AM I RIGHT, SANZO?
WE'LL COME.

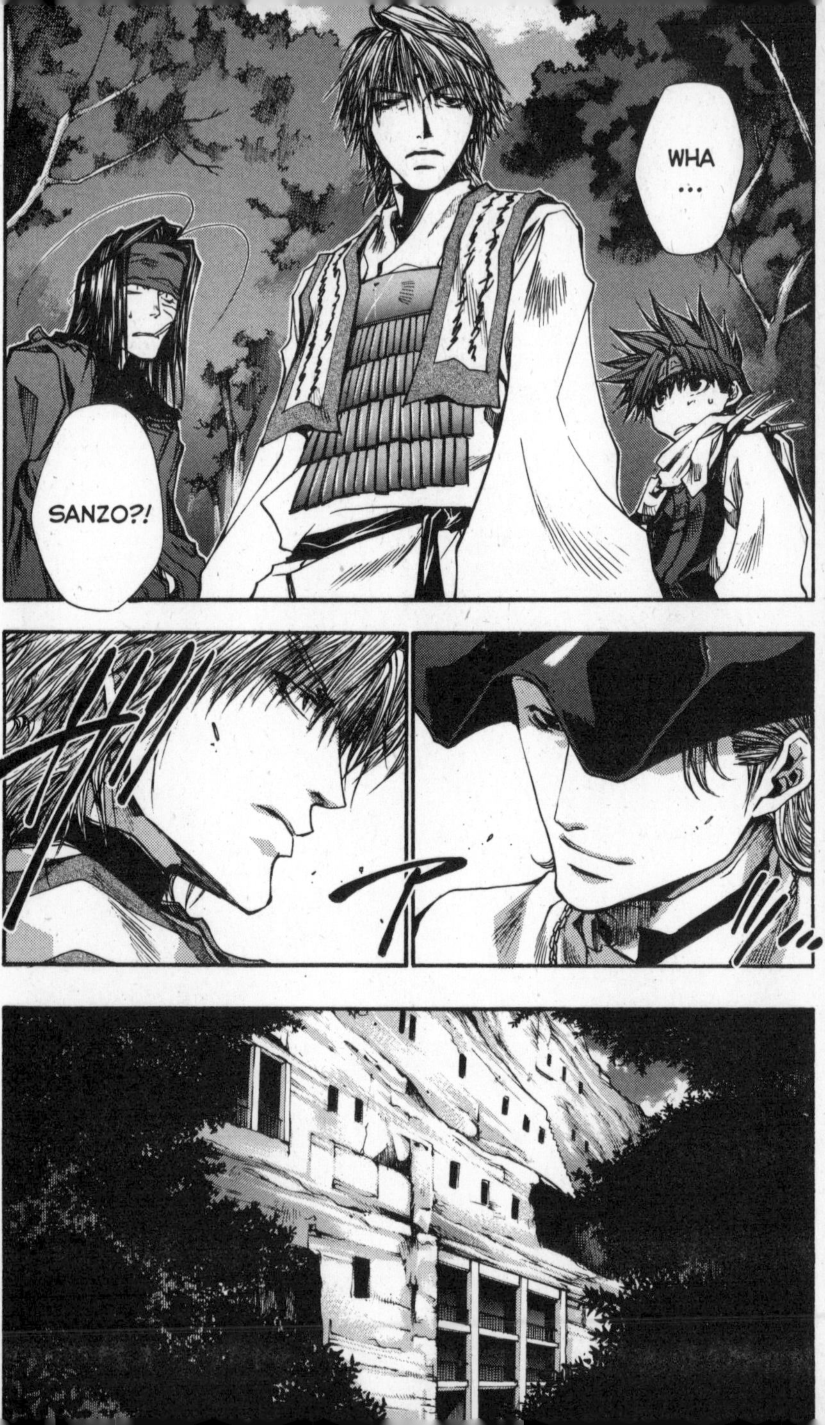
WHA ...
SANZO?!

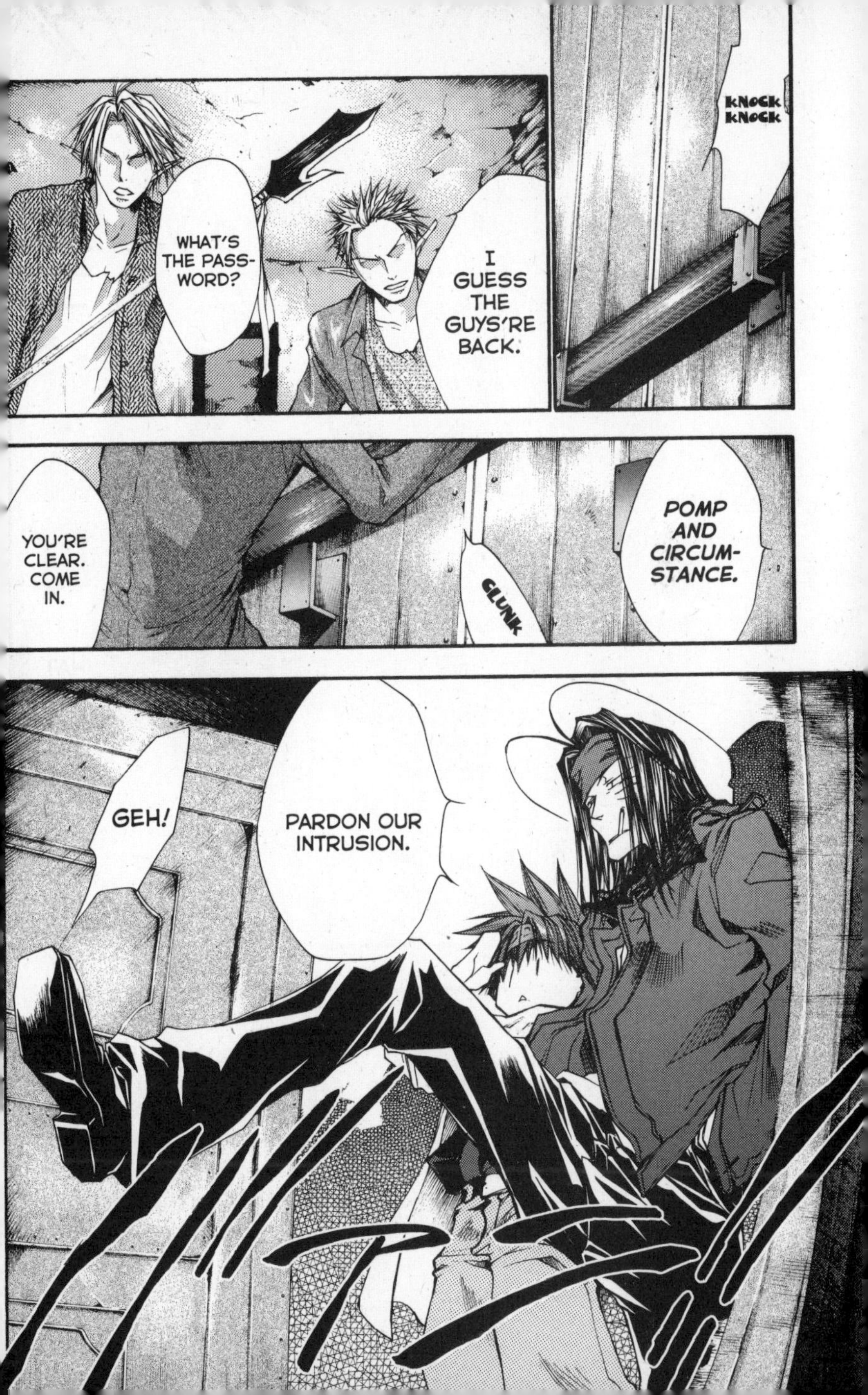
KNOCK KNOCK
I GUESS THE GUYS'RE BACK.
WHAT'S THE PASS-WORD?
POMP AND CIRCUM-STANCE.
CLUNK
YOU'RE CLEAR. COME IN.
PARDON OUR INTRUSION.
GEH!

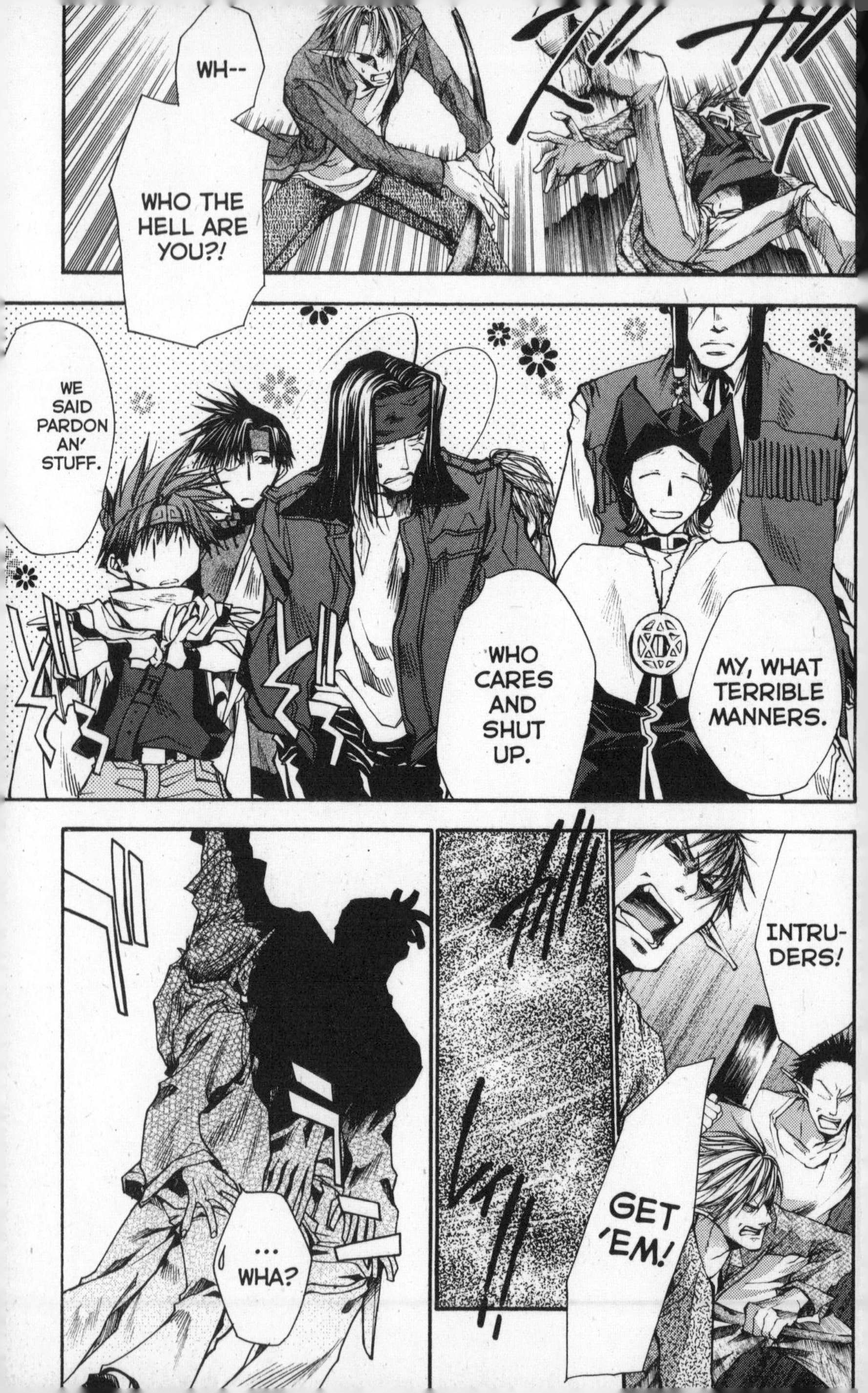
WH--
WHO THE HELL ARE YOU?!
MY, WHAT TERRIBLE MANNERS.
WHO CARES AND SHUT UP.
WE SAID PARDON AN' STUFF.
INTRU-DERS!
GET 'EM!
...WHA?

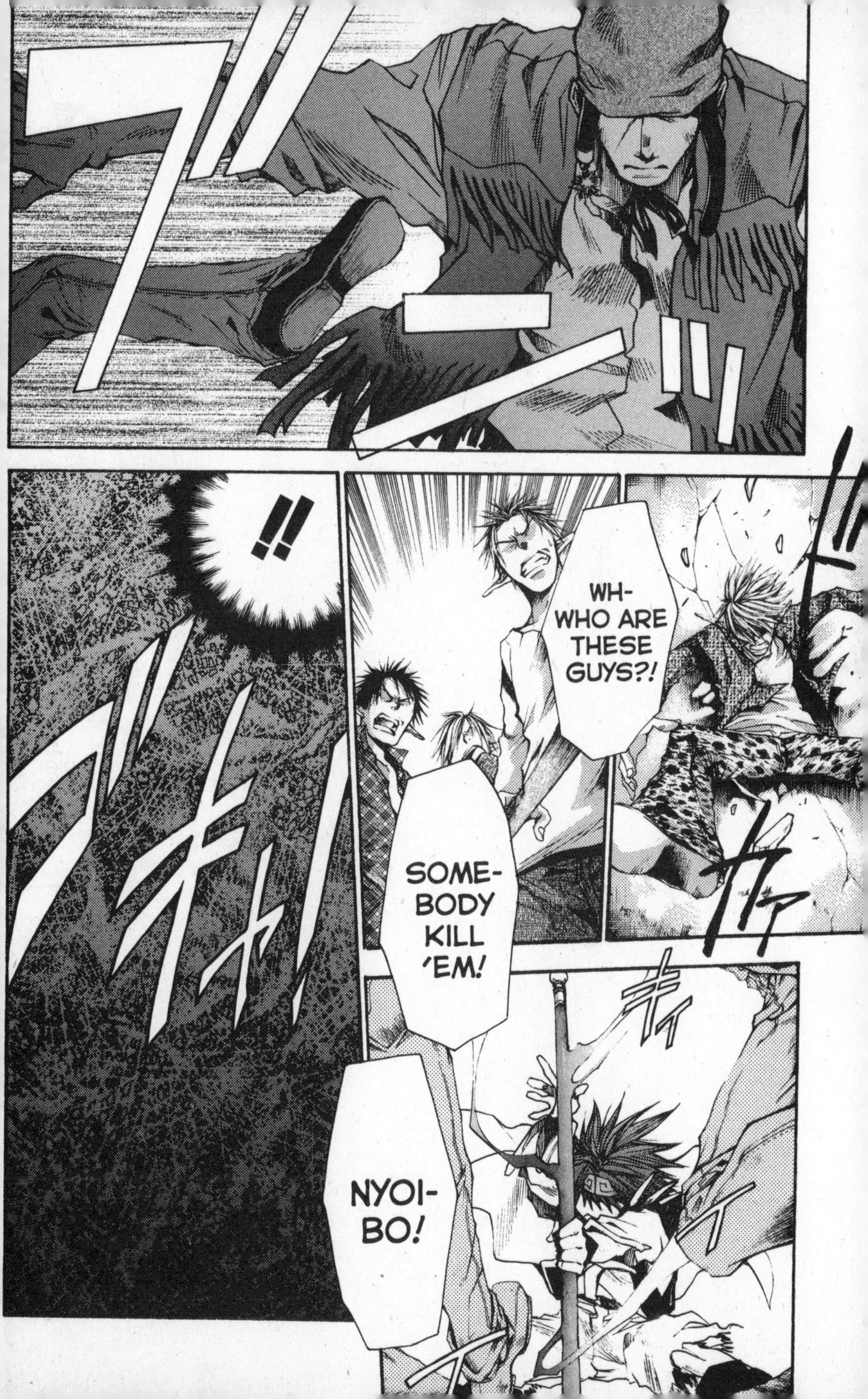
WH-WHO ARE THESE GUYS?!
SOMEBODY KILL 'EM!
NYOI-BO!
!!

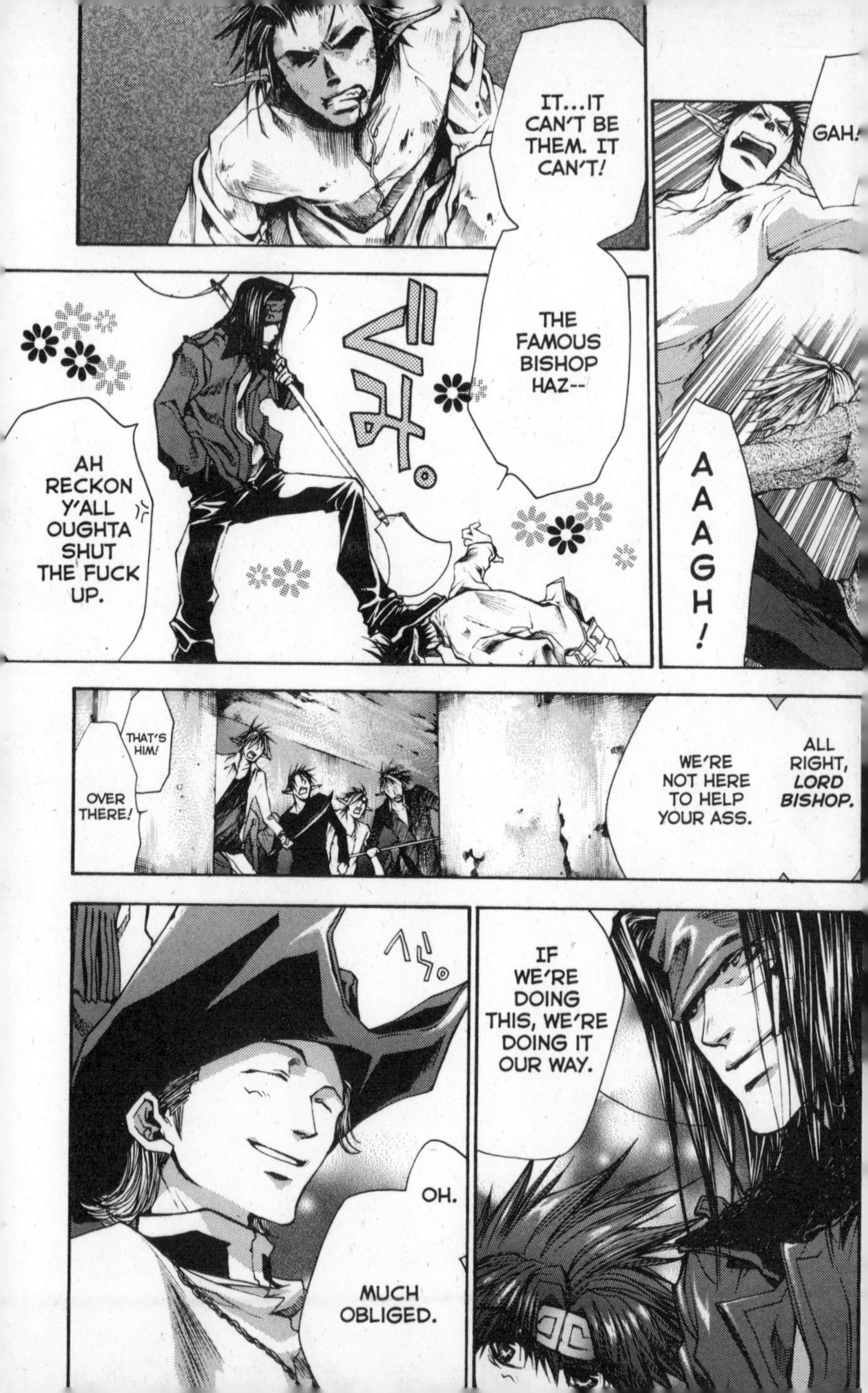
GAH!
AAAGH!
IT...IT CAN'T BE THEM. IT CAN'T!
THE FAMOUS BISHOP HAZ--
AH RECKON Y'ALL OUGHTA SHUT THE FUCK UP.
ALL RIGHT, *LORD BISHOP.*
WE'RE NOT HERE TO HELP YOUR ASS.
THAT'S HIM!
OVER THERE!
IF WE'RE DOING THIS, WE'RE DOING IT OUR WAY.
へら。
OH.
MUCH OBLIGED.

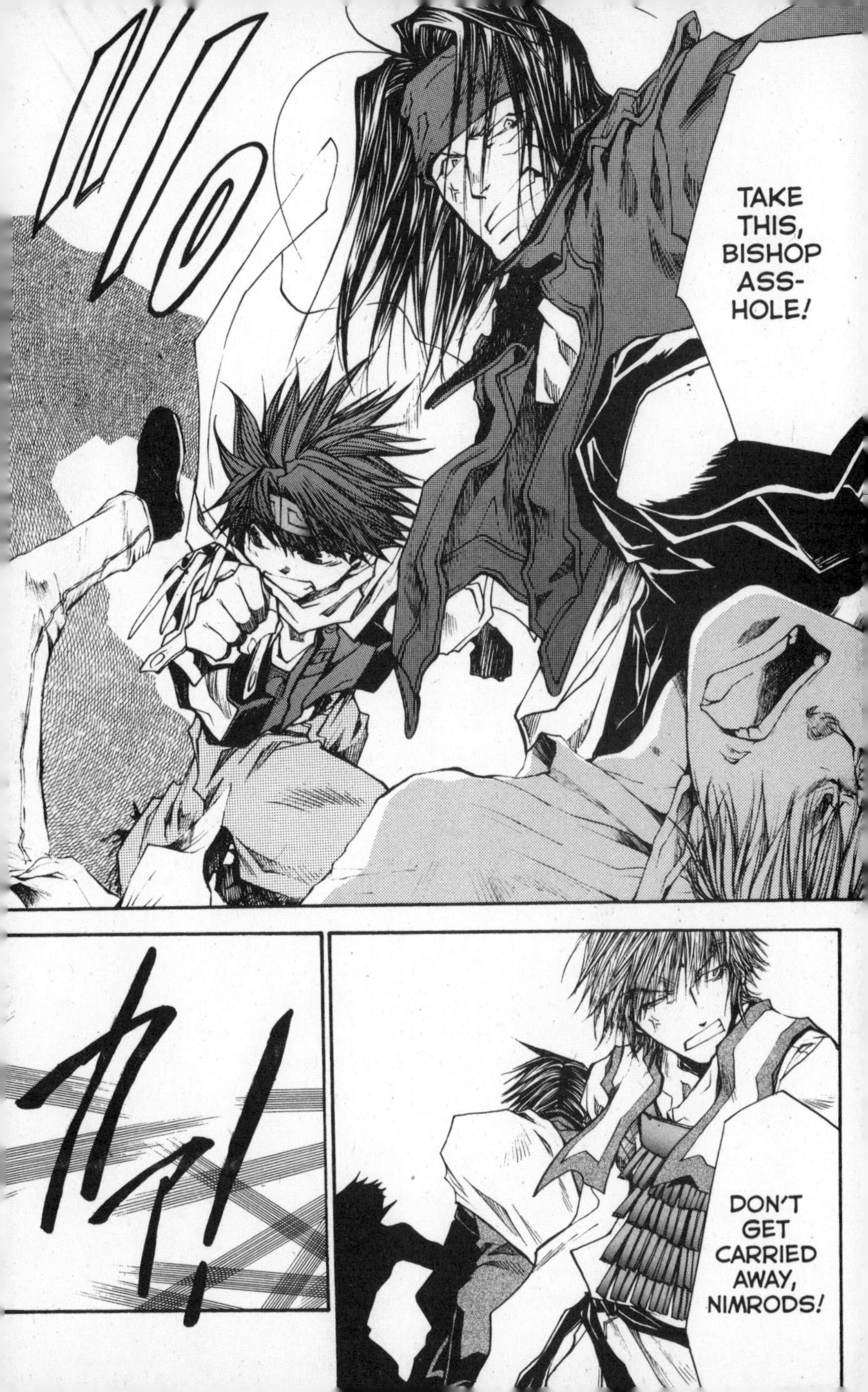
TAKE THIS, BISHOP ASS-HOLE!
DON'T GET CARRIED AWAY, NIMRODS!

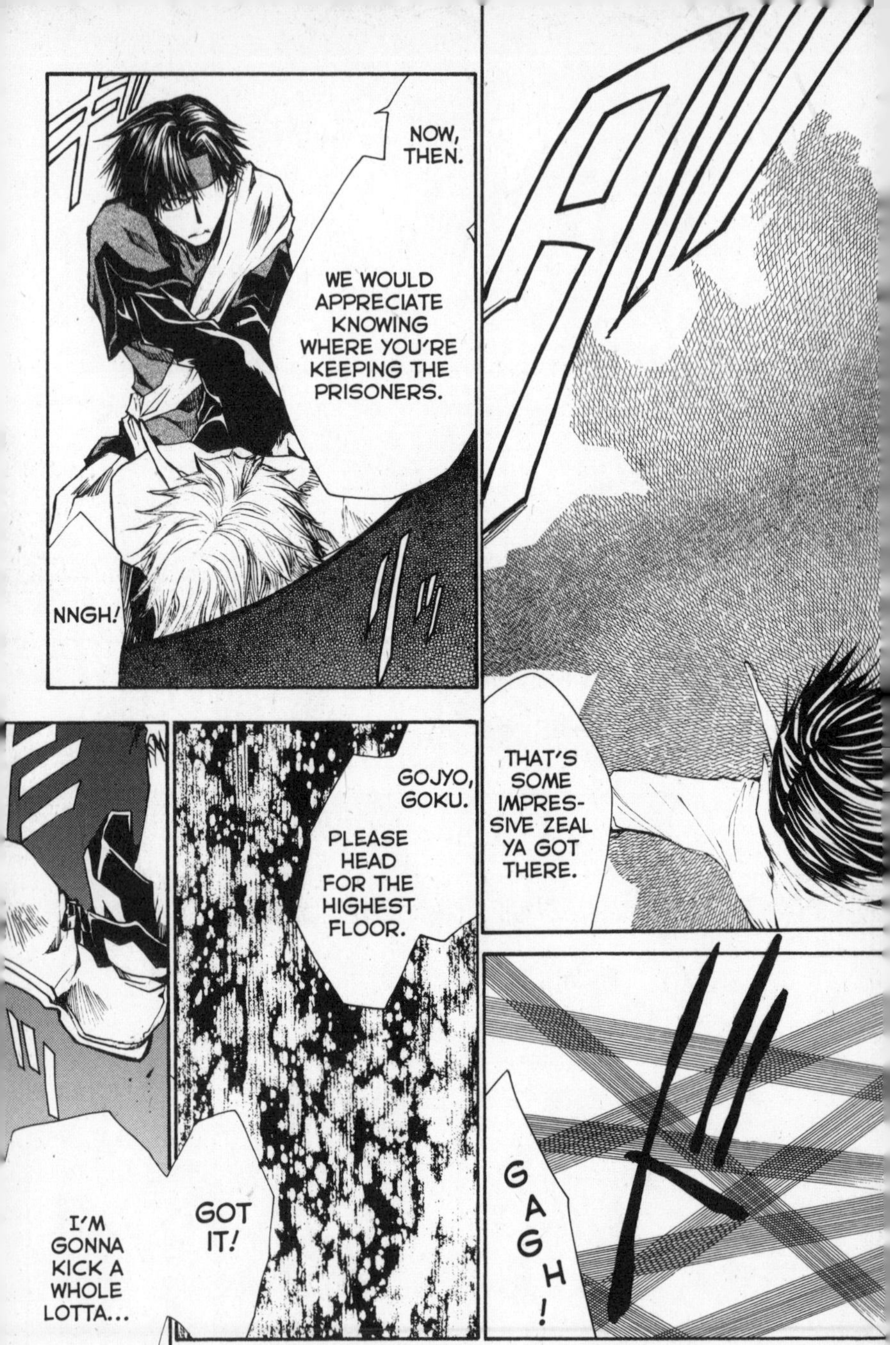

THAT'S SOME IMPRESSIVE ZEAL YA GOT THERE.
GAGH!
NOW, THEN.
WE WOULD APPRECIATE KNOWING WHERE YOU'RE KEEPING THE PRISONERS.
NNGH!
GOJYO, GOKU.
PLEASE HEAD FOR THE HIGHEST FLOOR.
GOT IT!
I'M GONNA KICK A WHOLE LOTTA...

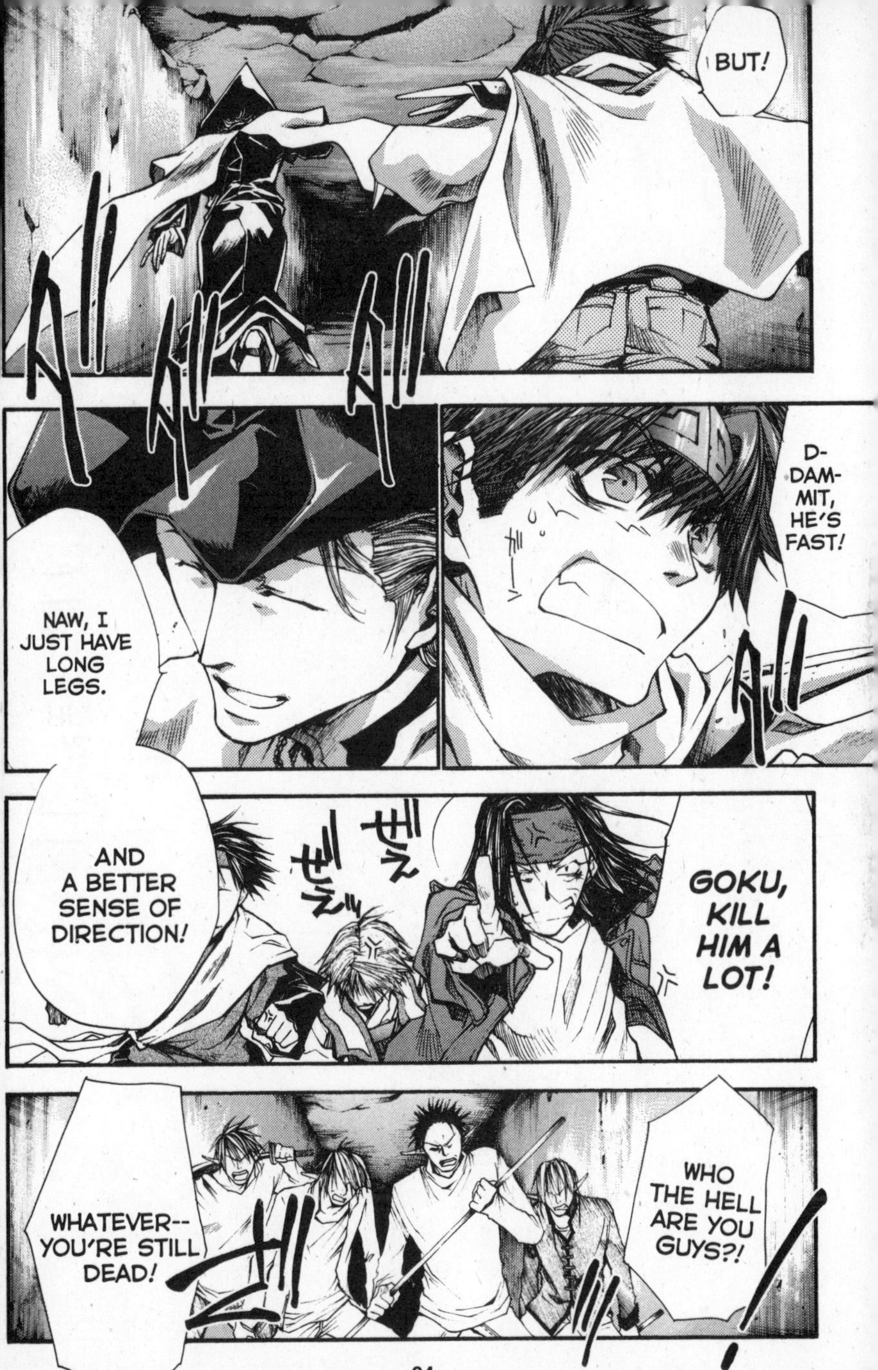
BUT!
D-DAM-MIT, HE'S FAST!
NAW, I JUST HAVE LONG LEGS.
AND A BETTER SENSE OF DIRECTION!
GOKU, KILL HIM A LOT!
WHO THE HELL ARE YOU GUYS?!
WHATEVER-- YOU'RE STILL DEAD!

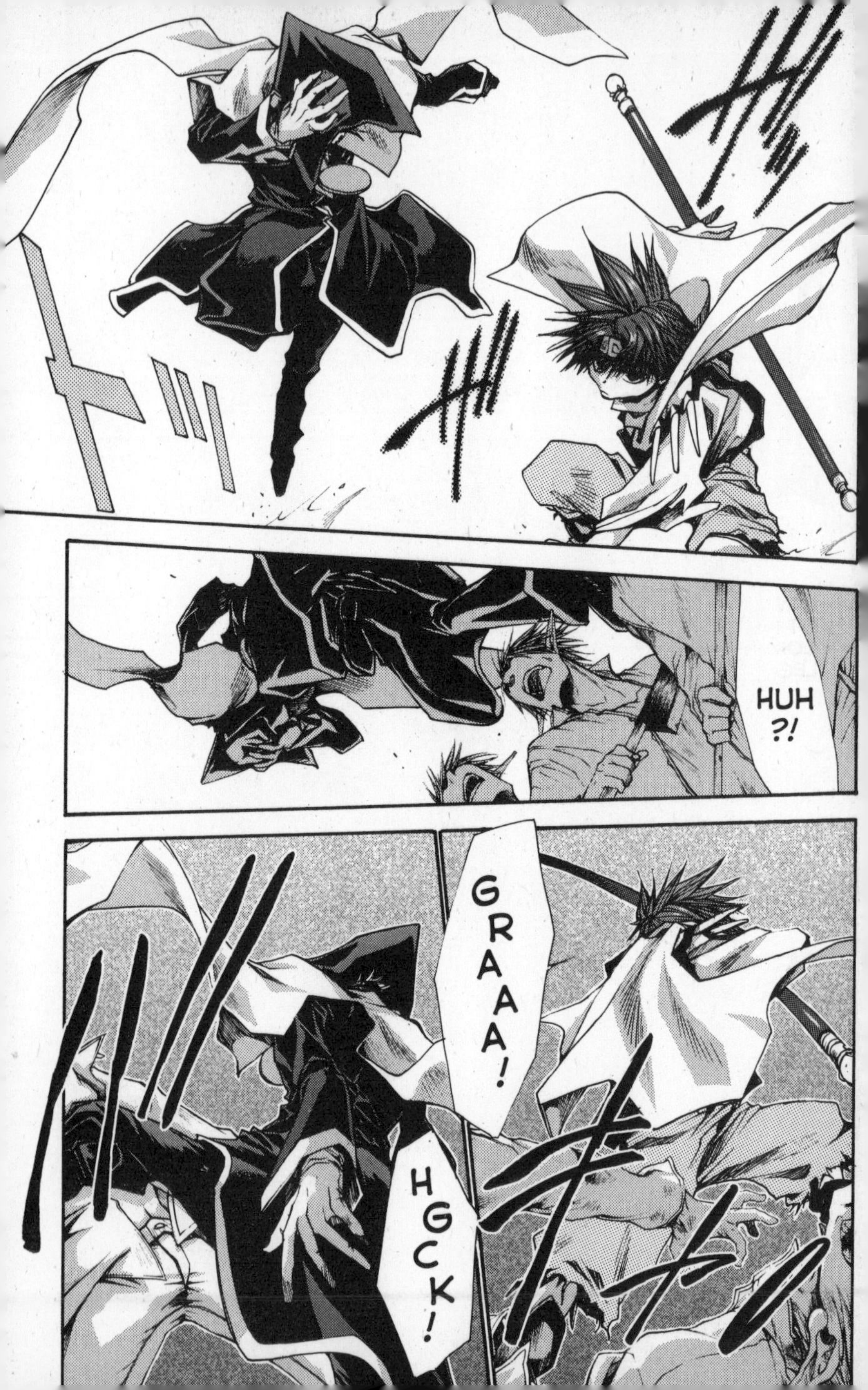
HUH ?!
GRAAA!
HGCK!

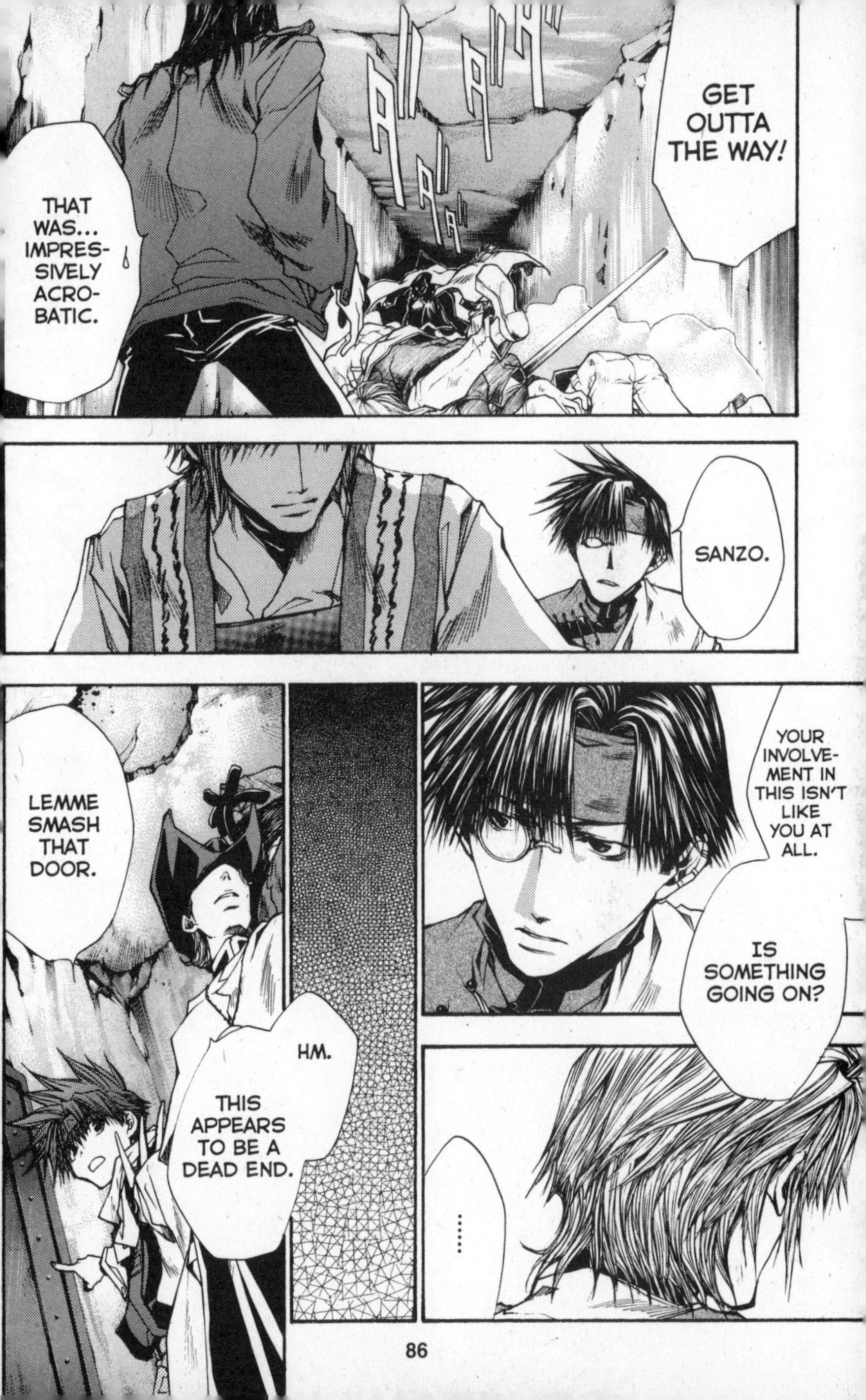
GET OUTTA THE WAY!
THAT WAS... IMPRESSIVELY ACROBATIC.
SANZO.
YOUR INVOLVEMENT IN THIS ISN'T LIKE YOU AT ALL.
IS SOMETHING GOING ON?
......
LEMME SMASH THAT DOOR.
HM.
THIS APPEARS TO BE A DEAD END.

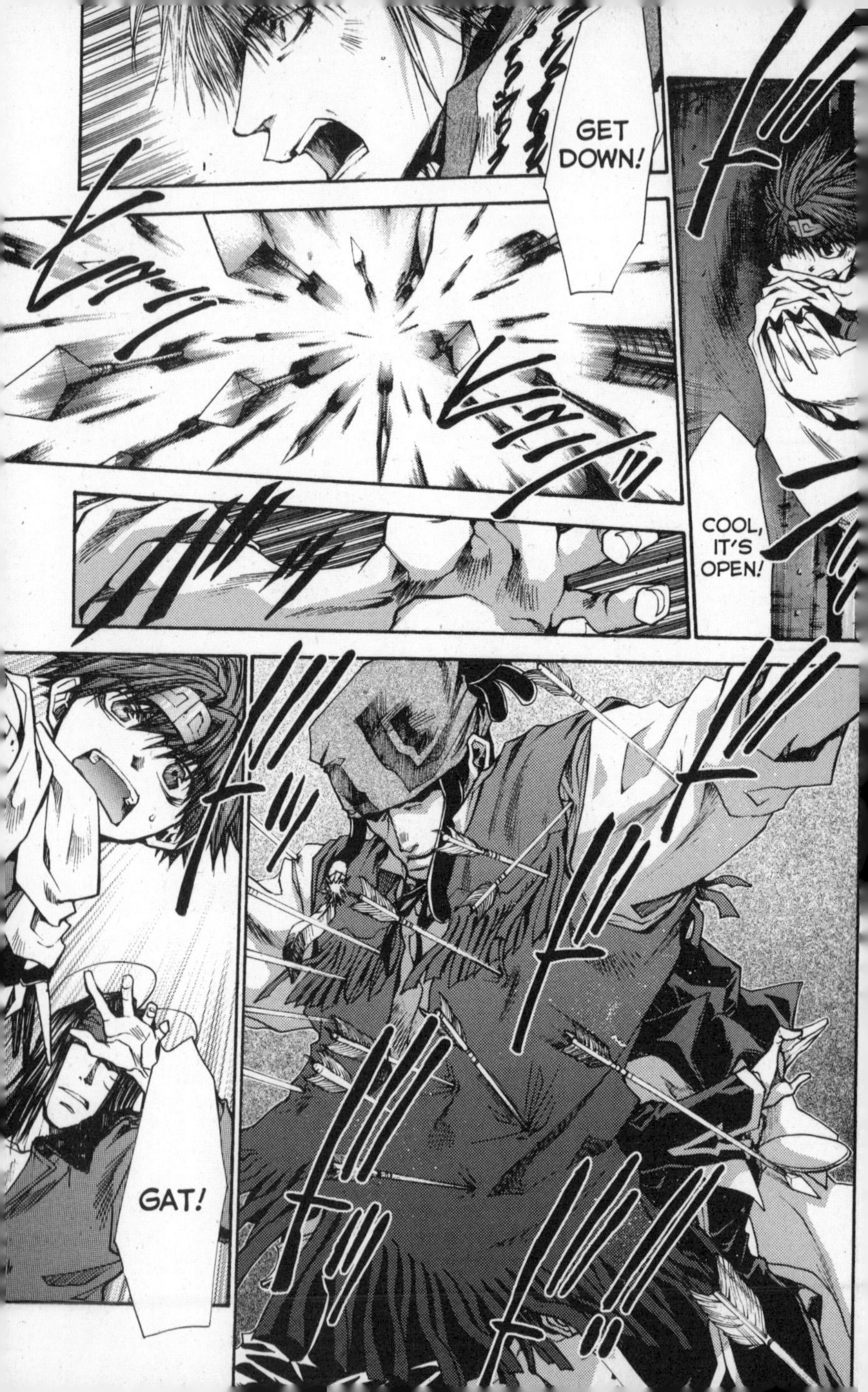
COOL, IT'S OPEN!
GET DOWN!
GAT!

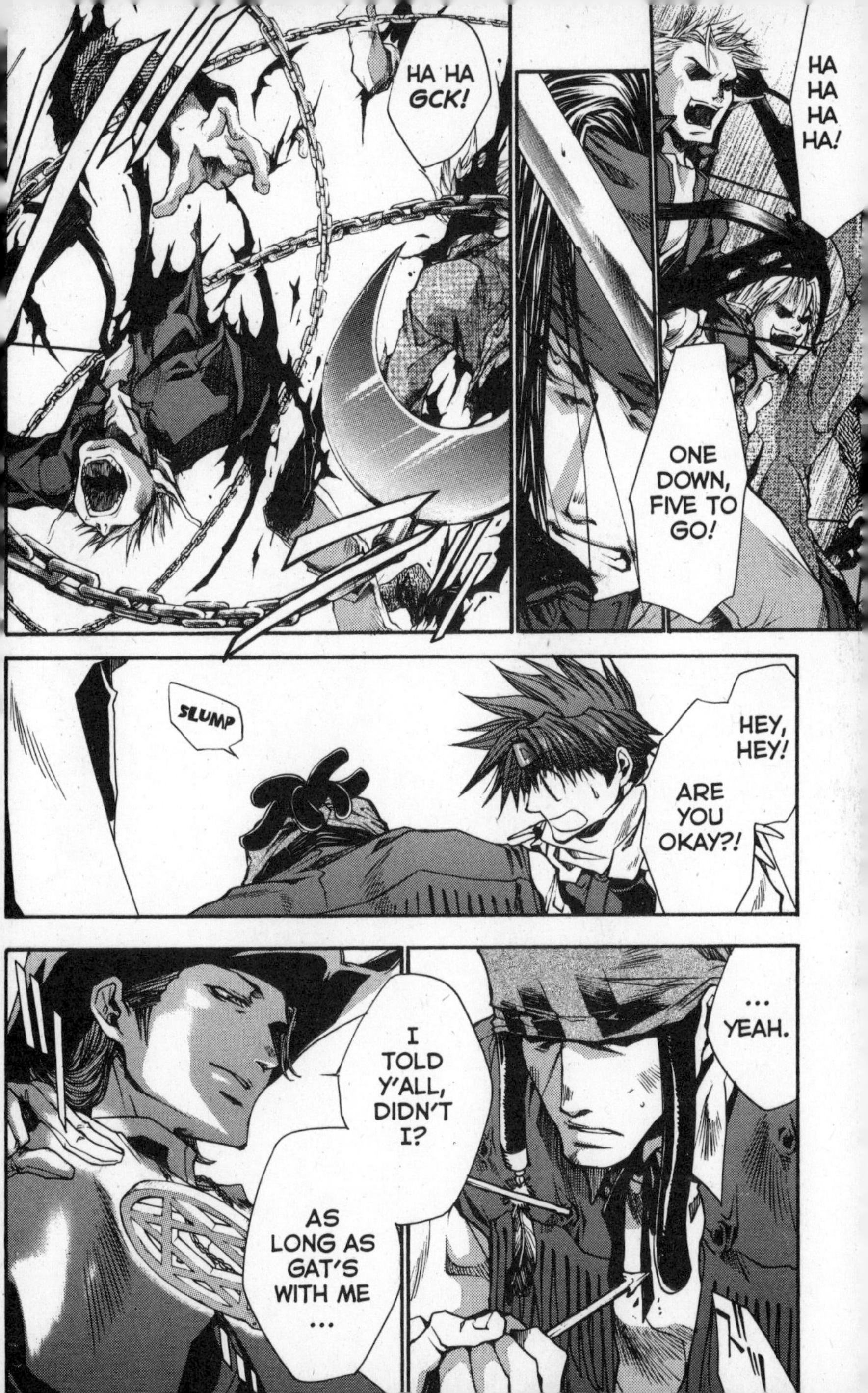
HA HA HA HA!
ONE DOWN, FIVE TO GO!
HA HA GCK!
HEY, HEY!
ARE YOU OKAY?!
SLUMP
... YEAH.
I TOLD Y'ALL, DIDN'T I?
AS LONG AS GAT'S WITH ME ...

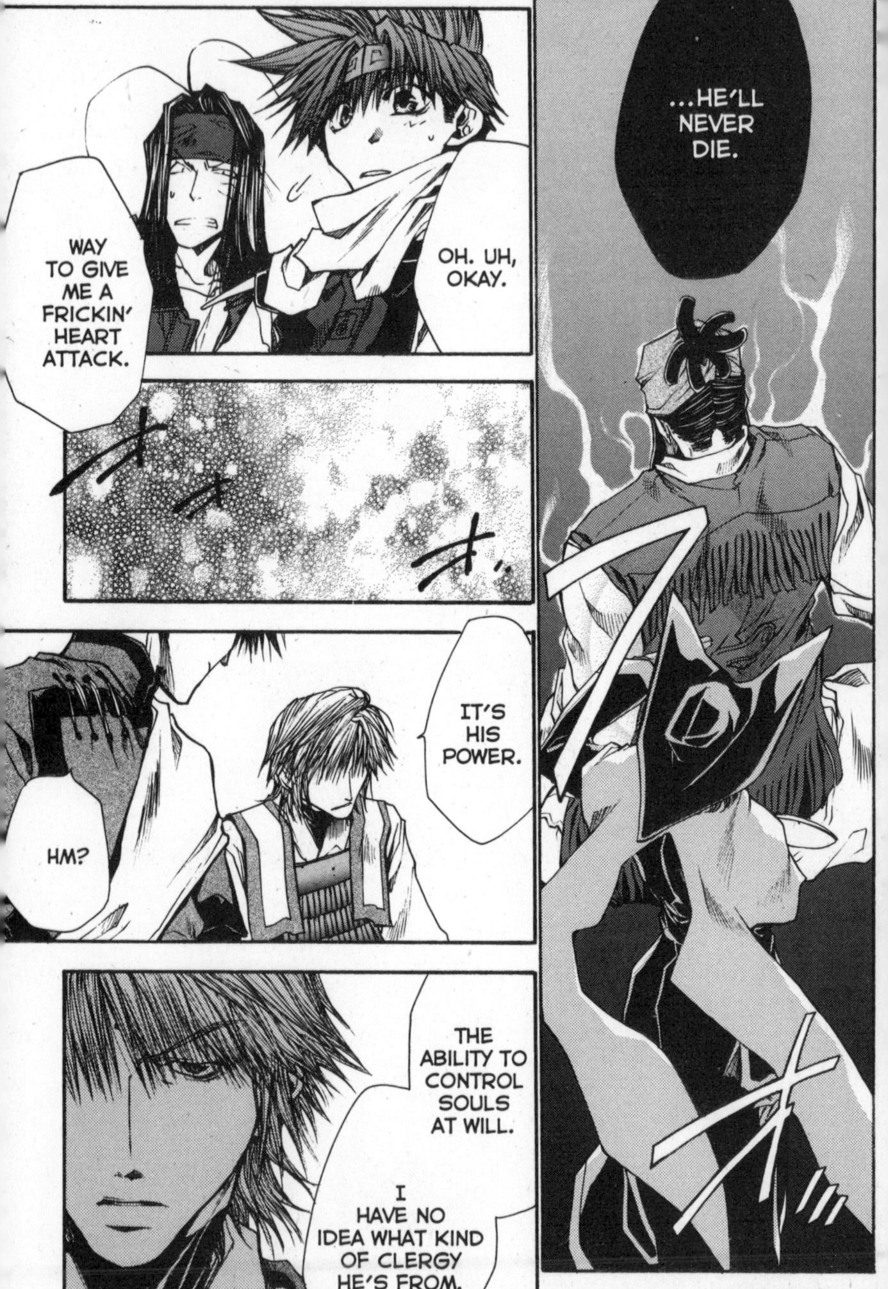
...HE'LL NEVER DIE.
OH. UH, OKAY.
WAY TO GIVE ME A FRICKIN' HEART ATTACK.
IT'S HIS POWER.
HM?
THE ABILITY TO CONTROL SOULS AT WILL.
I HAVE NO IDEA WHAT KIND OF CLERGY HE'S FROM.

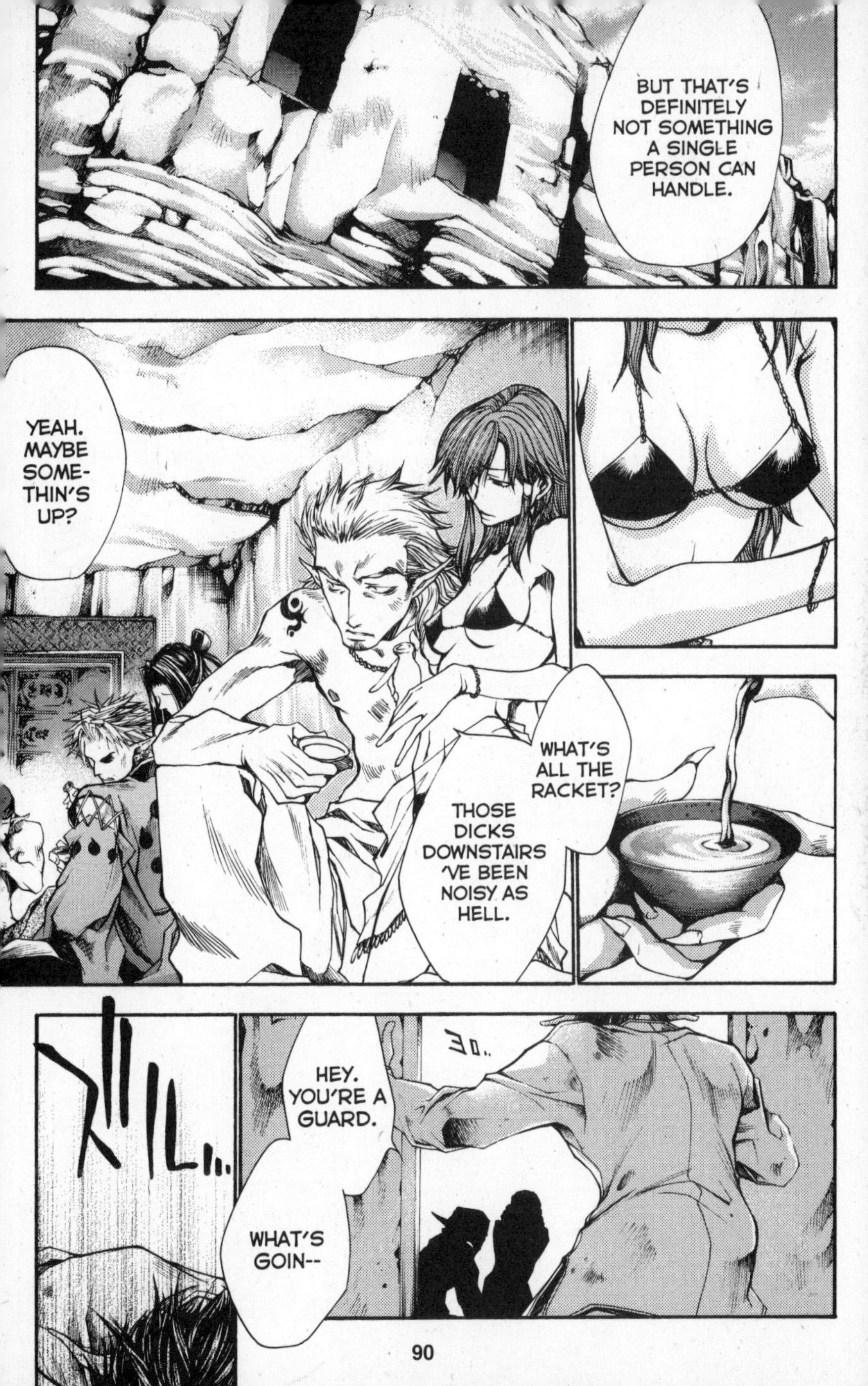

BUT THAT'S DEFINITELY NOT SOMETHING A SINGLE PERSON CAN HANDLE.
WHAT'S ALL THE RACKET?
THOSE DICKS DOWNSTAIRS 'VE BEEN NOISY AS HELL.
YEAH. MAYBE SOME-THIN'S UP?
HEY. YOU'RE A GUARD.
WHAT'S GOIN--

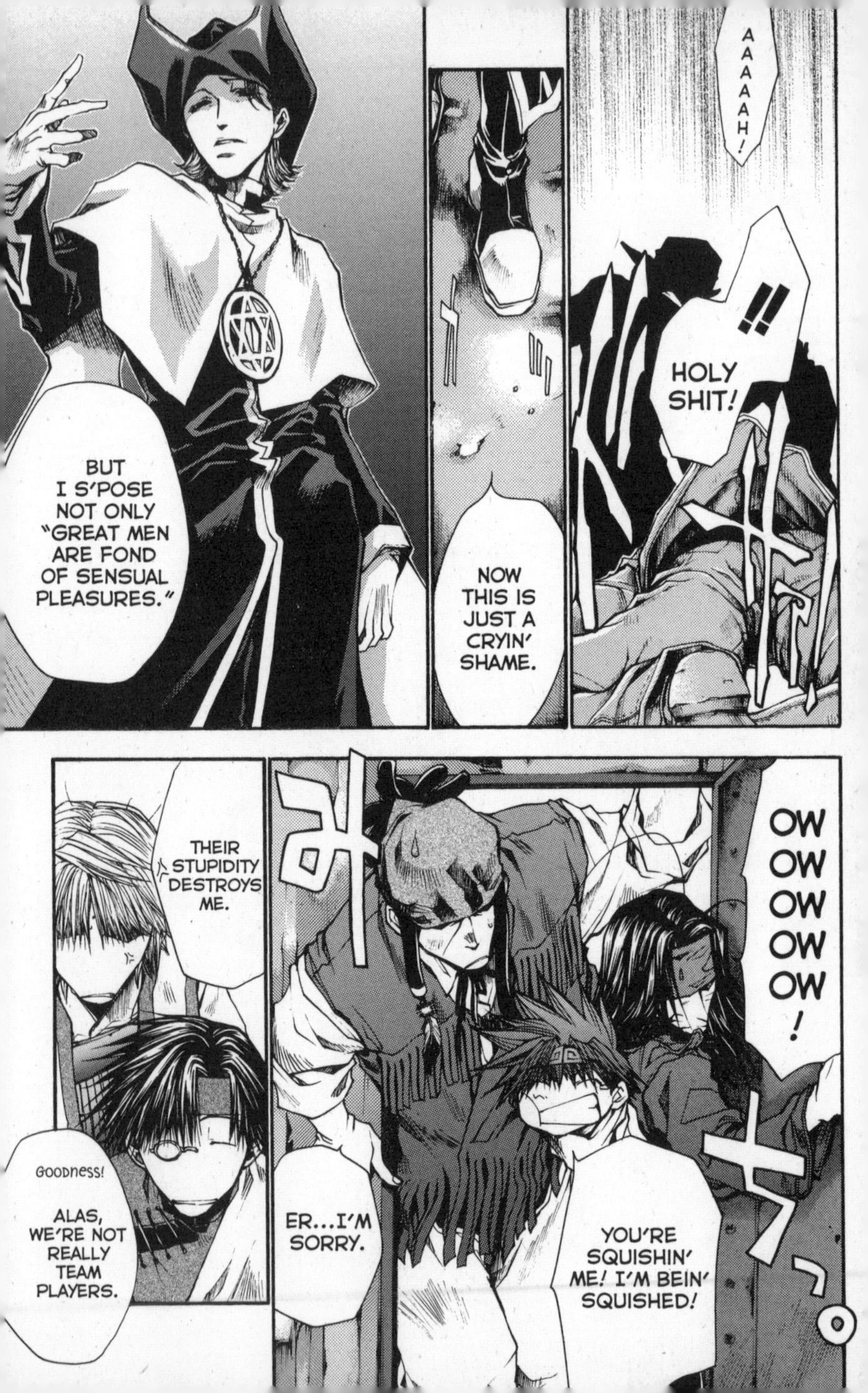
AAAAAH!
!!
HOLY SHIT!
NOW THIS IS JUST A CRYIN' SHAME.
BUT I S'POSE NOT ONLY "GREAT MEN ARE FOND OF SENSUAL PLEASURES."
OW OW OW OW OW!
YOU'RE SQUISHIN' ME! I'M BEIN' SQUISHED!
ER...I'M SORRY.
THEIR STUPIDITY DESTROYS ME.
Goodness!
ALAS, WE'RE NOT REALLY TEAM PLAYERS.

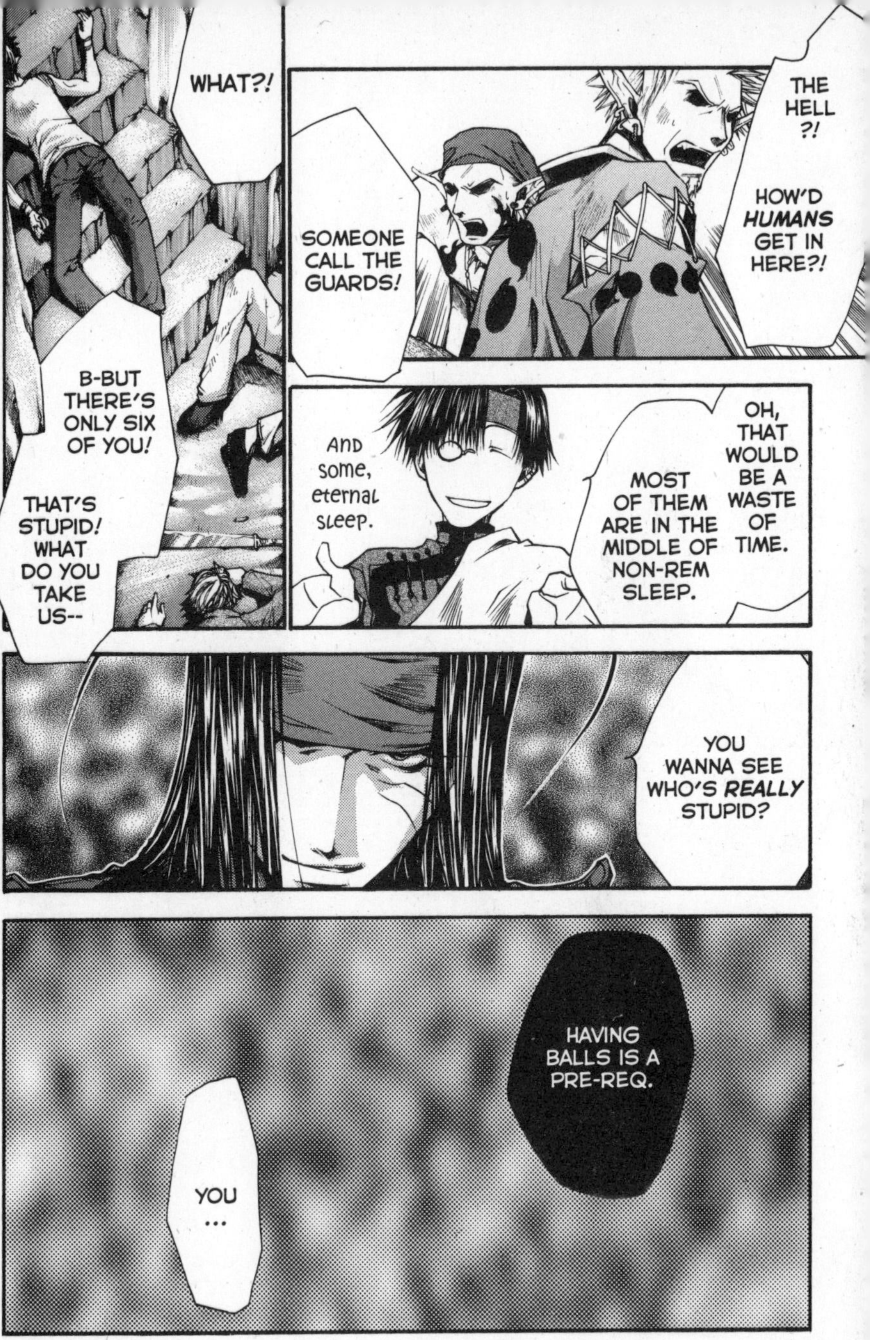
THE HELL ?!
HOW'D *HUMANS* GET IN HERE?!
SOMEONE CALL THE GUARDS!
OH, THAT WOULD BE A WASTE OF TIME.
MOST OF THEM ARE IN THE MIDDLE OF NON-REM SLEEP.
And some, eternal sleep.
WHAT?!
B-BUT THERE'S ONLY SIX OF YOU!
THAT'S STUPID! WHAT DO YOU TAKE US--
YOU WANNA SEE WHO'S *REALLY* STUPID?
HAVING BALLS IS A PRE-REQ.
YOU ...

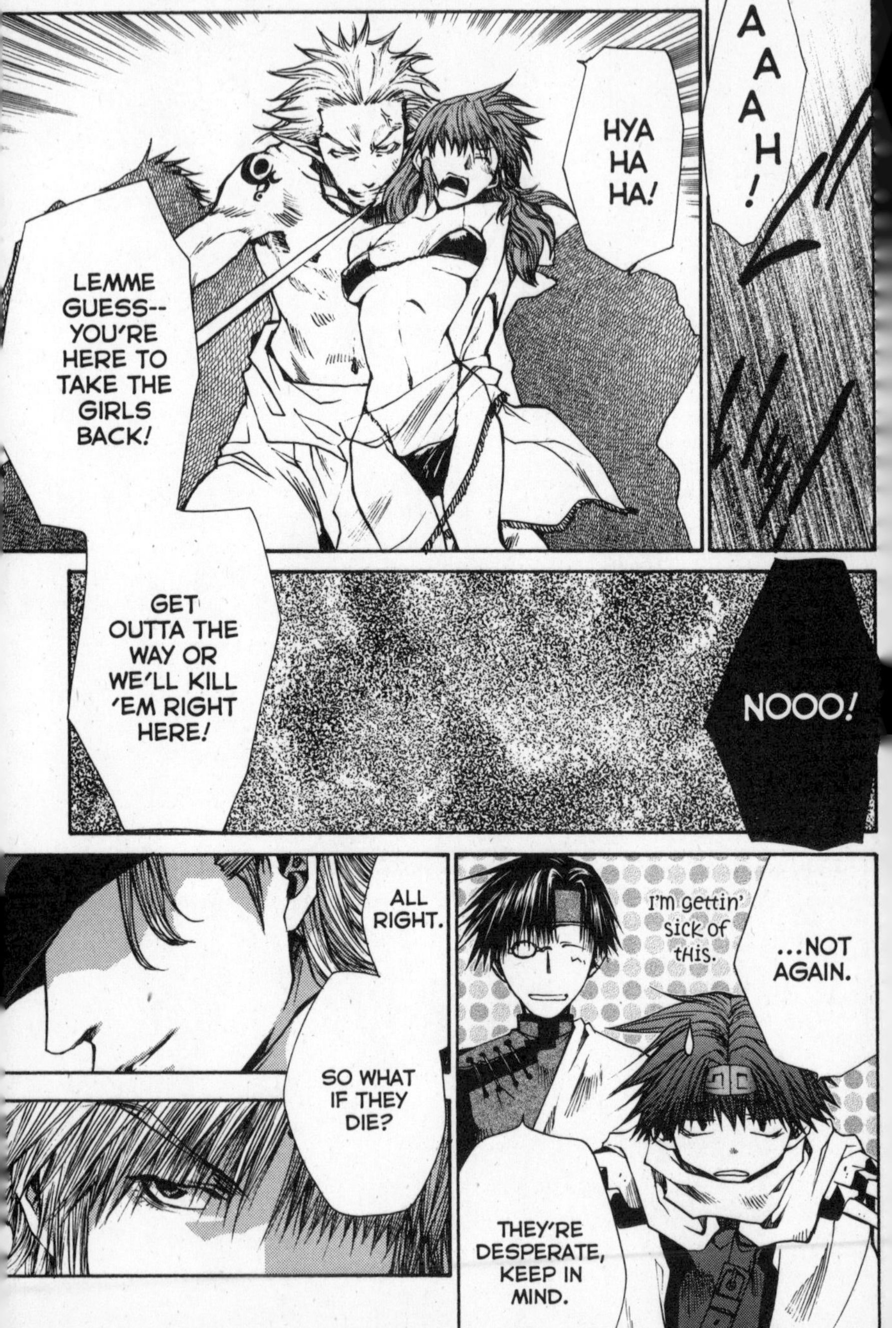
AAAH!
HYA HA HA!
LEMME GUESS-- YOU'RE HERE TO TAKE THE GIRLS BACK!
NOOO!
GET OUTTA THE WAY OR WE'LL KILL 'EM RIGHT HERE!
...NOT AGAIN.
I'm gettin' sick of this.
THEY'RE DESPERATE, KEEP IN MIND.
ALL RIGHT.
SO WHAT IF THEY DIE?

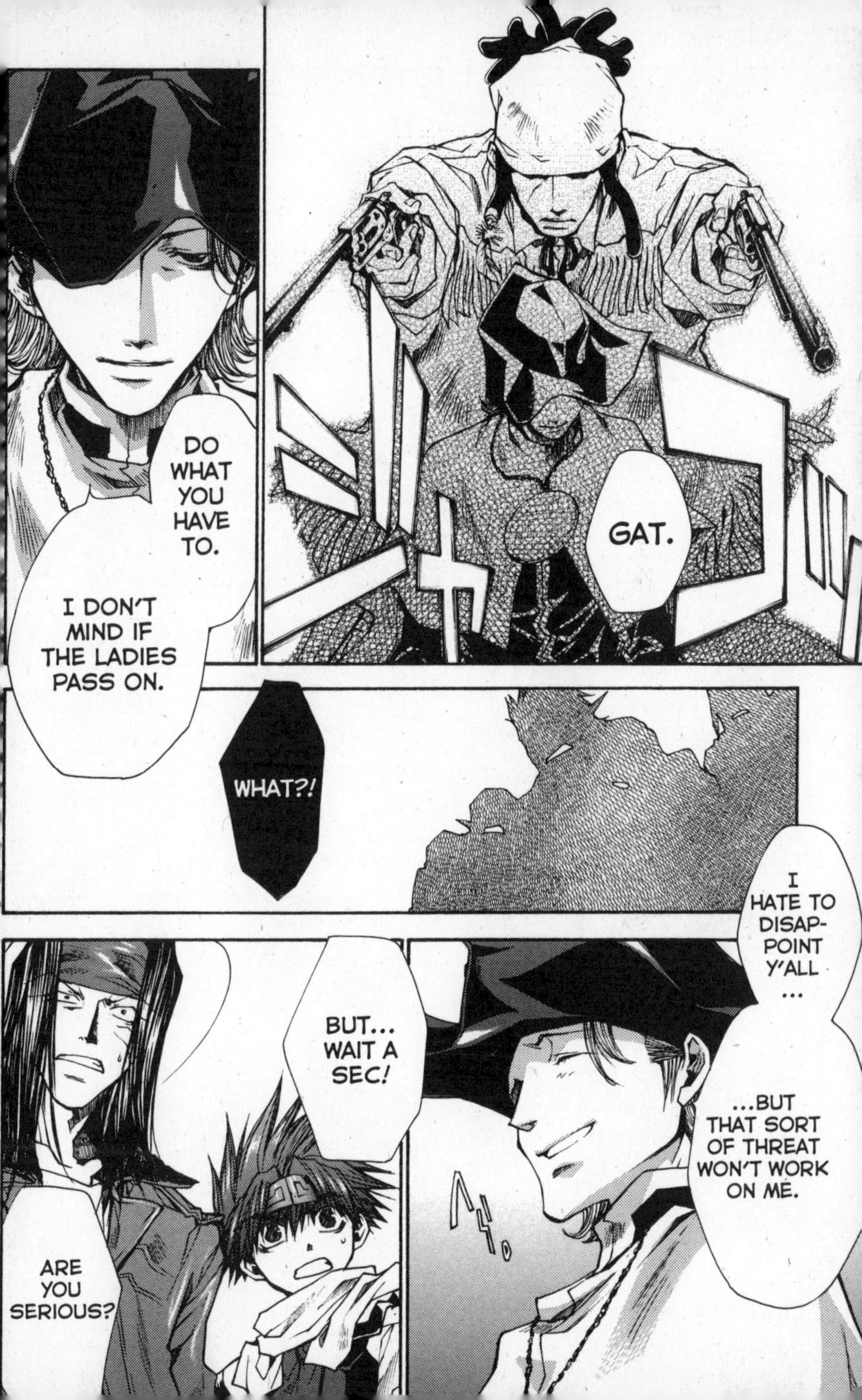
GAT.
DO WHAT YOU HAVE TO.
I DON'T MIND IF THE LADIES PASS ON.
WHAT?!
I HATE TO DISAP-POINT Y'ALL...
...BUT THAT SORT OF THREAT WON'T WORK ON ME.
BUT... WAIT A SEC!
ARE YOU SERIOUS?

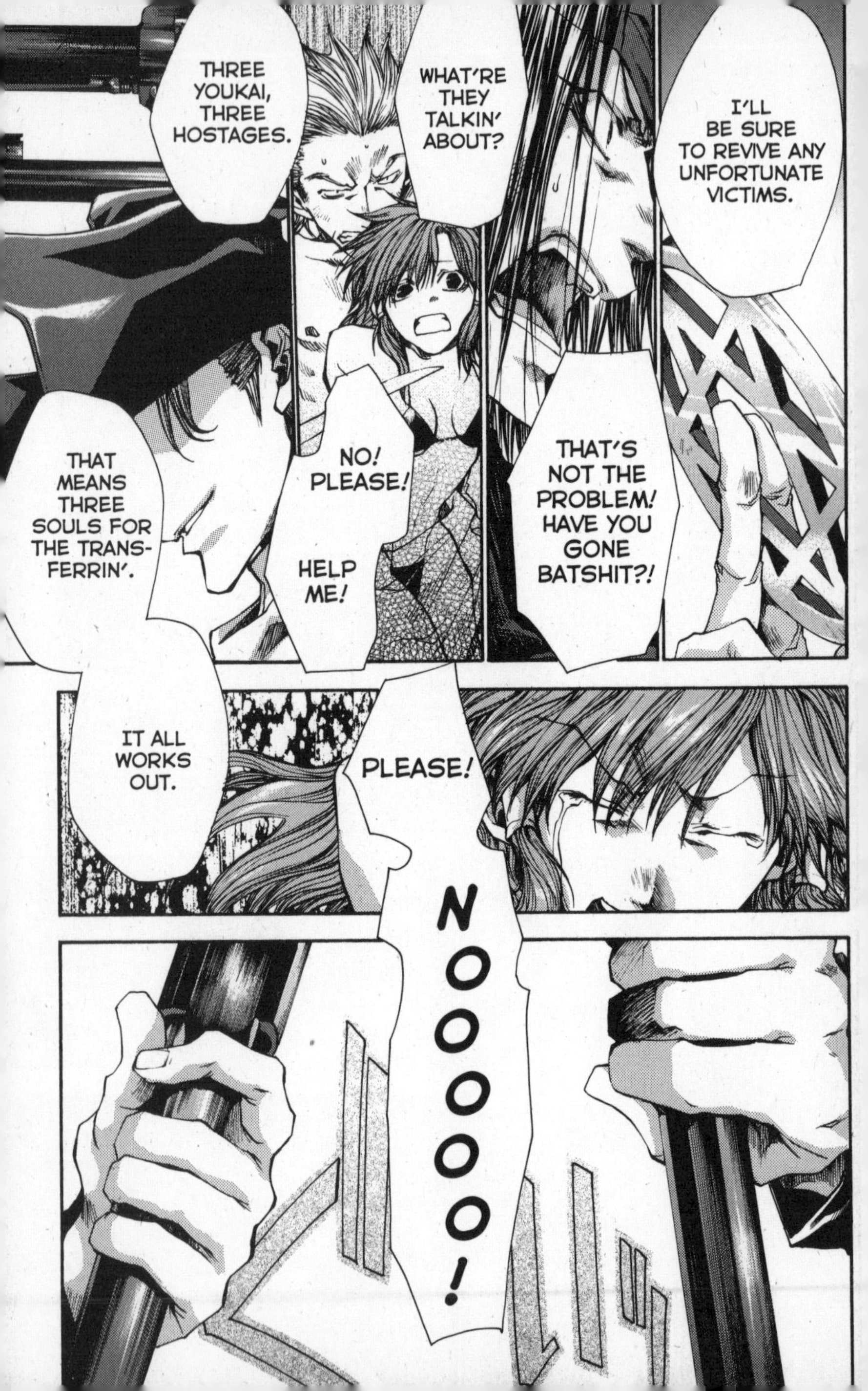
I'LL BE SURE TO REVIVE ANY UNFORTUNATE VICTIMS.
THAT'S NOT THE PROBLEM! HAVE YOU GONE BATSHIT?!
WHAT'RE THEY TALKIN' ABOUT?
NO! PLEASE!
HELP ME!
THREE YOUKAI, THREE HOSTAGES.
THAT MEANS THREE SOULS FOR THE TRANS-FERRIN'.
PLEASE!
IT ALL WORKS OUT.
NOOOOO!

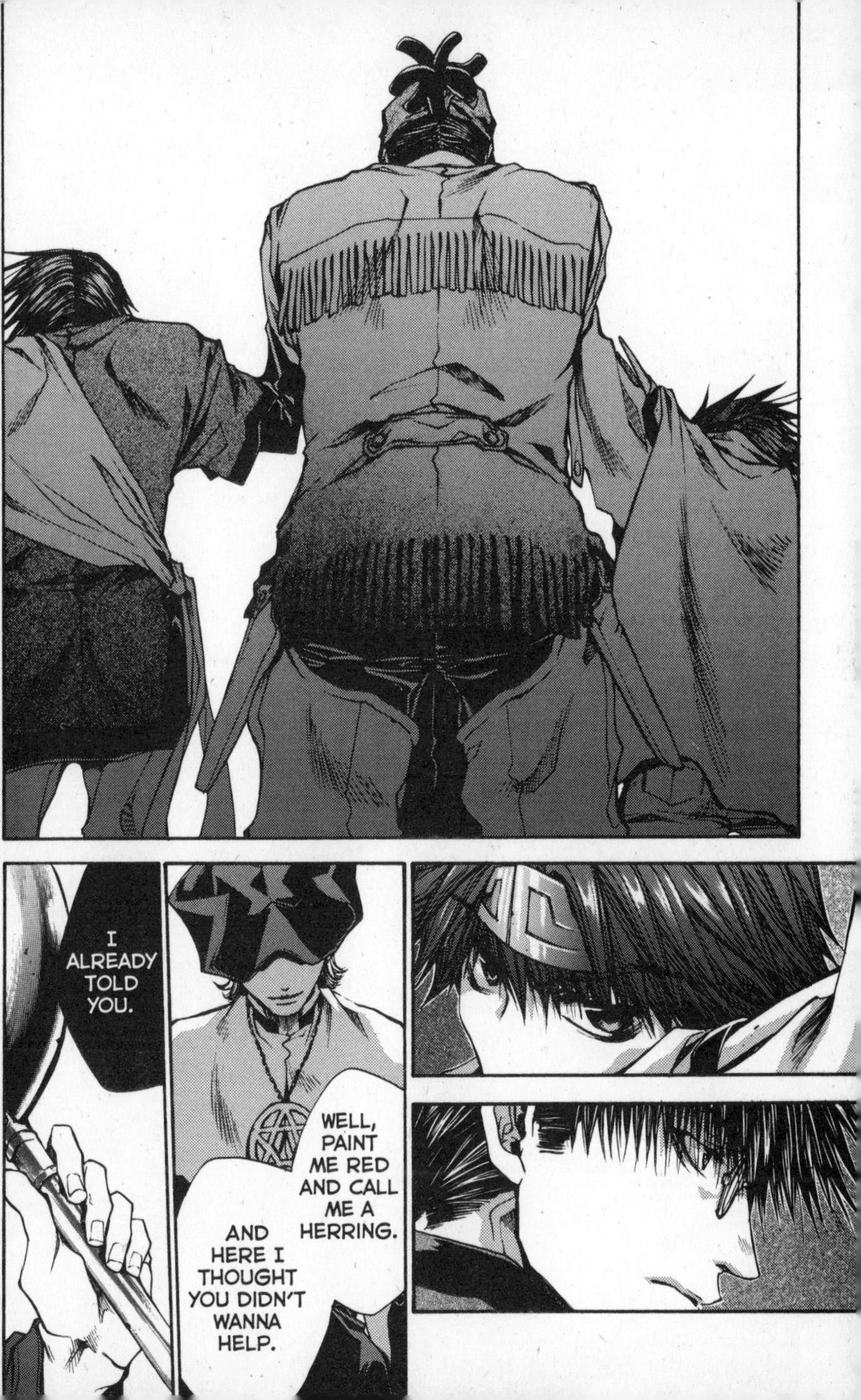
WELL, PAINT ME RED AND CALL ME A HERRING.
AND HERE I THOUGHT YOU DIDN'T WANNA HELP.
I ALREADY TOLD YOU.

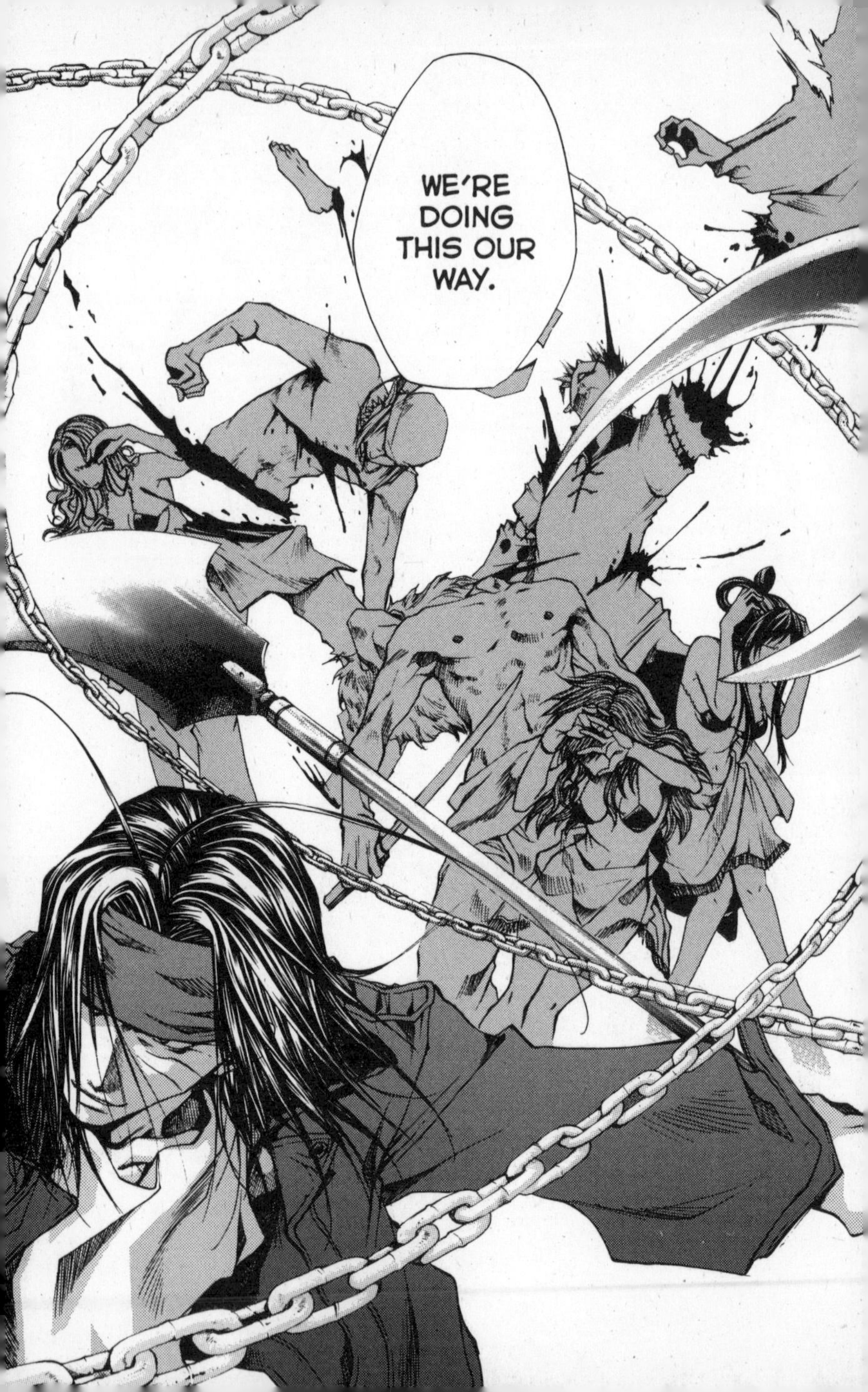
WE'RE DOING THIS OUR WAY.

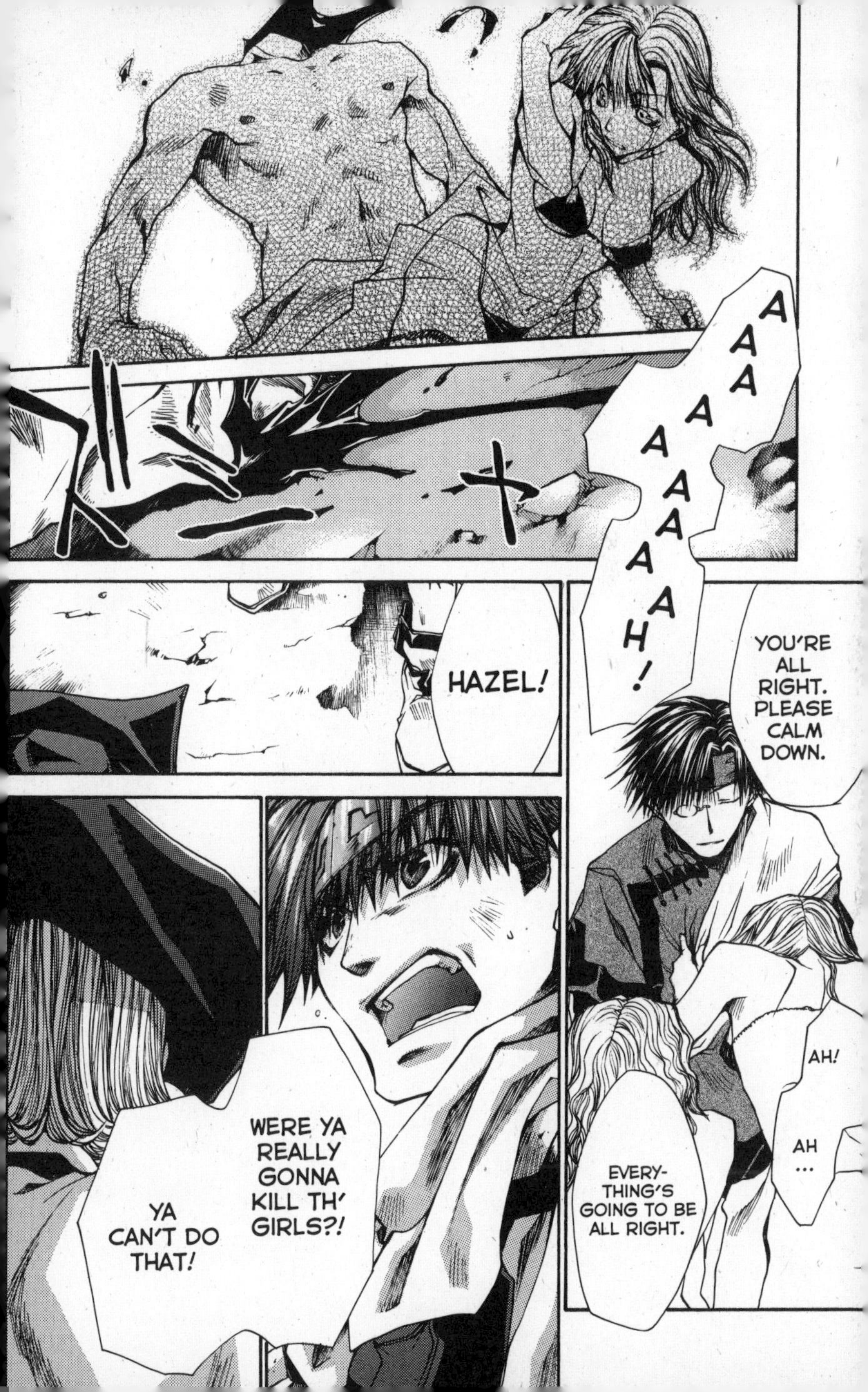
AAAAAAAAAH!
YOU'RE ALL RIGHT. PLEASE CALM DOWN.
AH!
AH...
EVERY-THING'S GOING TO BE ALL RIGHT.
HAZEL!
WERE YA REALLY GONNA KILL TH' GIRLS?!
YA CAN'T DO THAT!

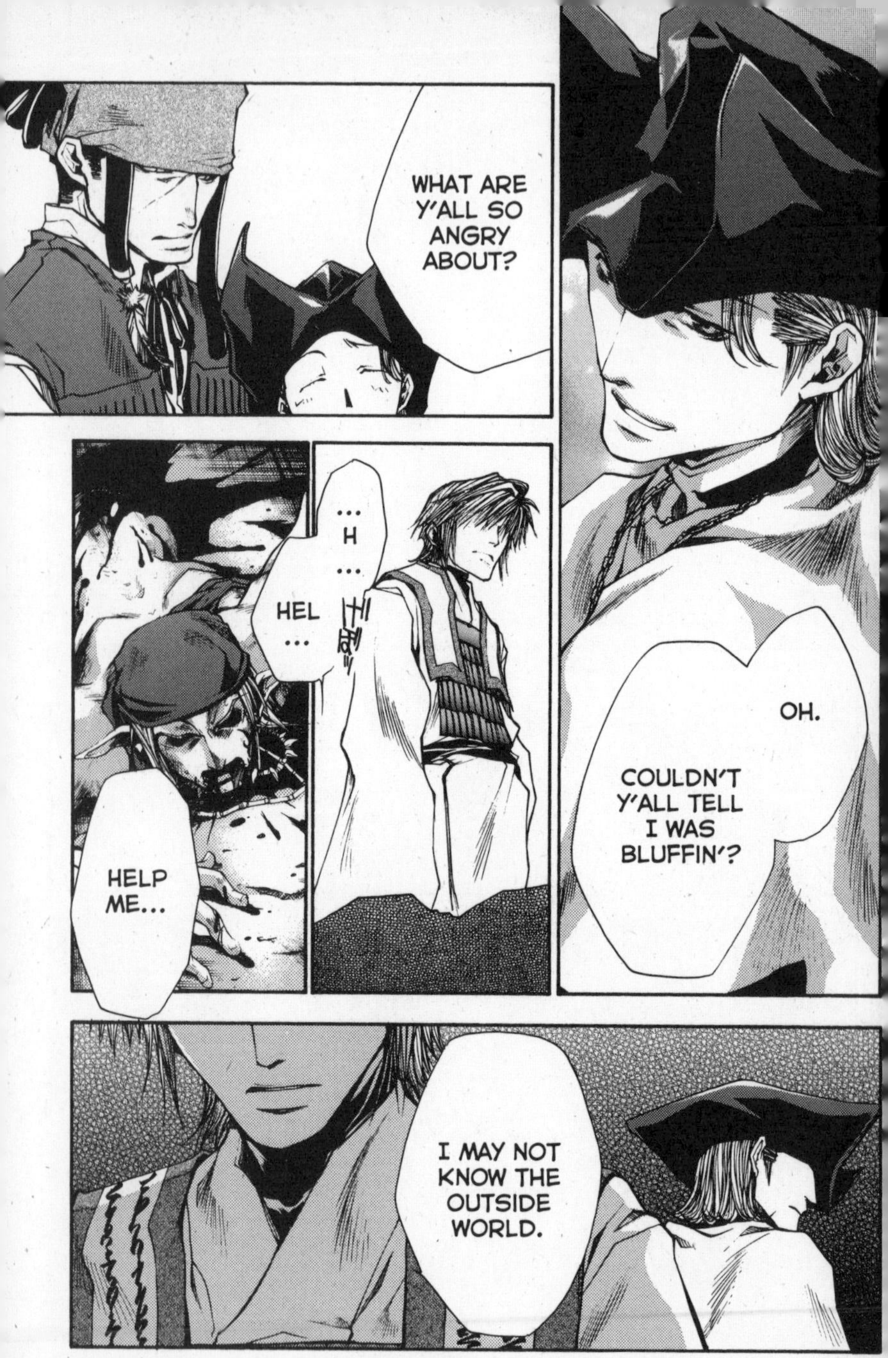
OH.
COULDN'T Y'ALL TELL I WAS BLUFFIN'?
WHAT ARE Y'ALL SO ANGRY ABOUT?
...H...
HEL...
HELP ME...
I MAY NOT KNOW THE OUTSIDE WORLD.

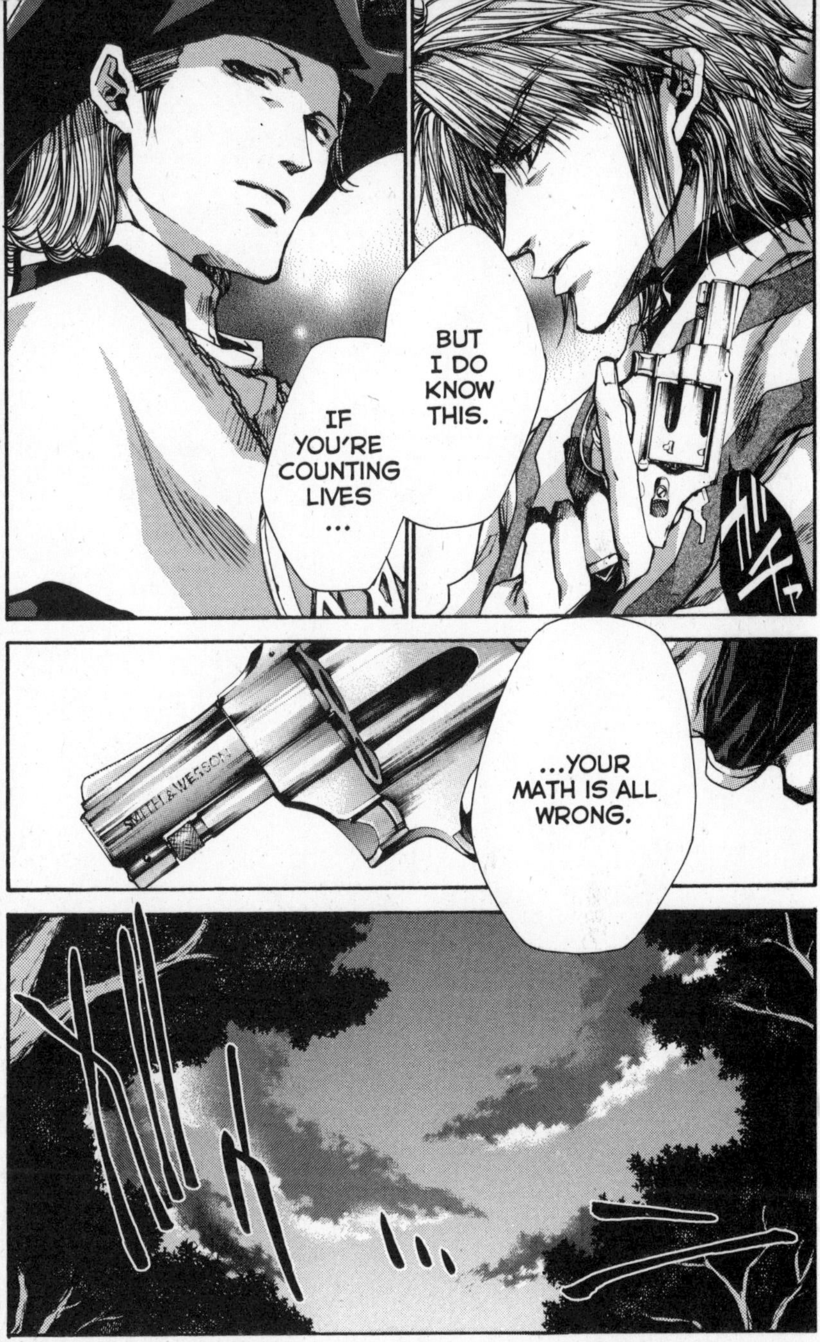
BUT I DO KNOW THIS.
IF YOU'RE COUNTING LIVES ...
SMITH & WESSON
...YOUR MATH IS ALL WRONG.

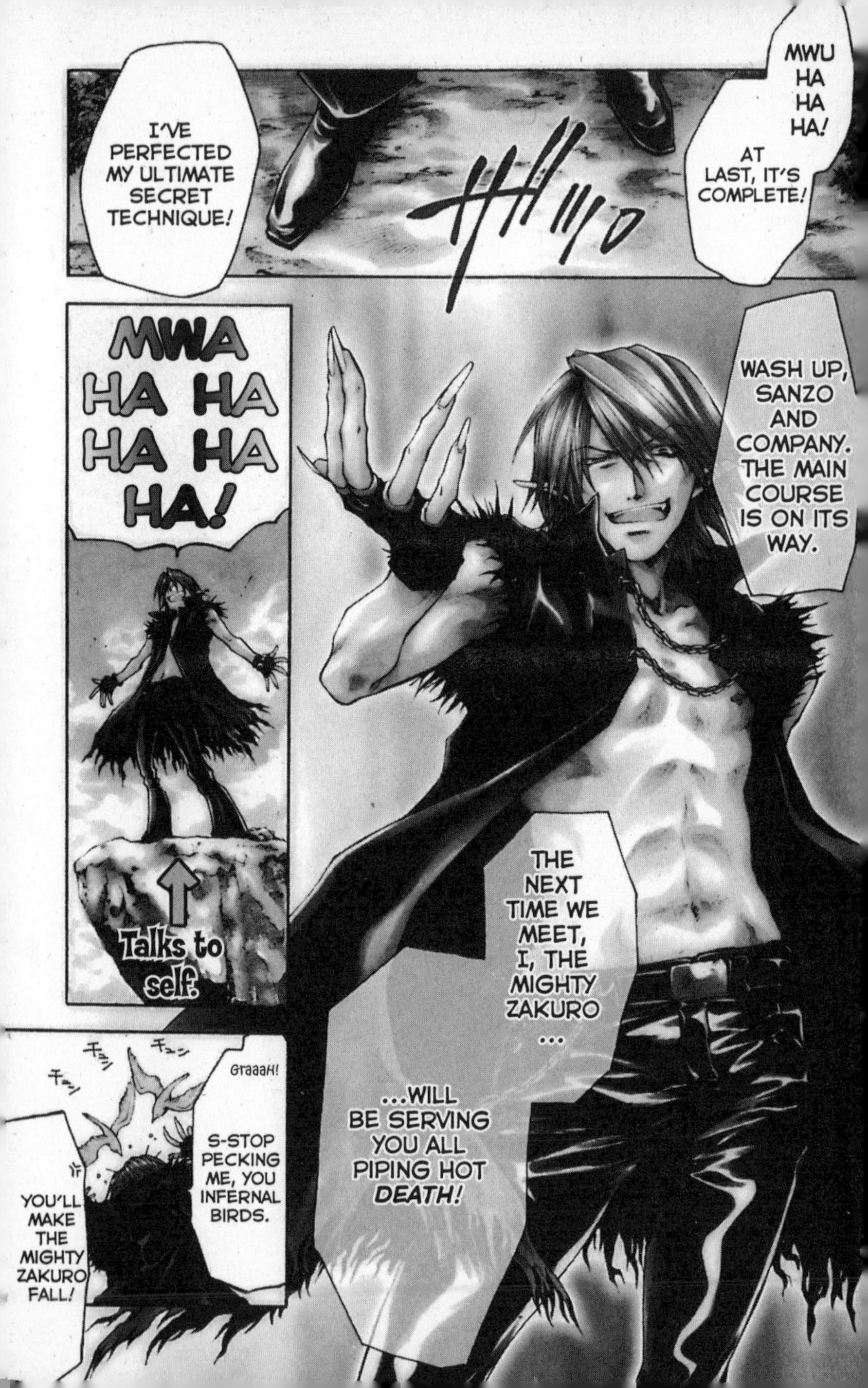

MWU HA HA HA! AT LAST, IT'S COMPLETE!
I'VE PERFECTED MY ULTIMATE SECRET TECHNIQUE!
WASH UP, SANZO AND COMPANY. THE MAIN COURSE IS ON ITS WAY.
THE NEXT TIME WE MEET, I, THE MIGHTY ZAKURO ...
...WILL BE SERVING YOU ALL PIPING HOT DEATH!
MWA HA HA HA HA HA!
Talks to self.
チュン
チュン
チュン
GraaaH!
S-STOP PECKING ME, YOU INFERNAL BIRDS.
YOU'LL MAKE THE MIGHTY ZAKURO FALL!

act.20
Even a worm-7

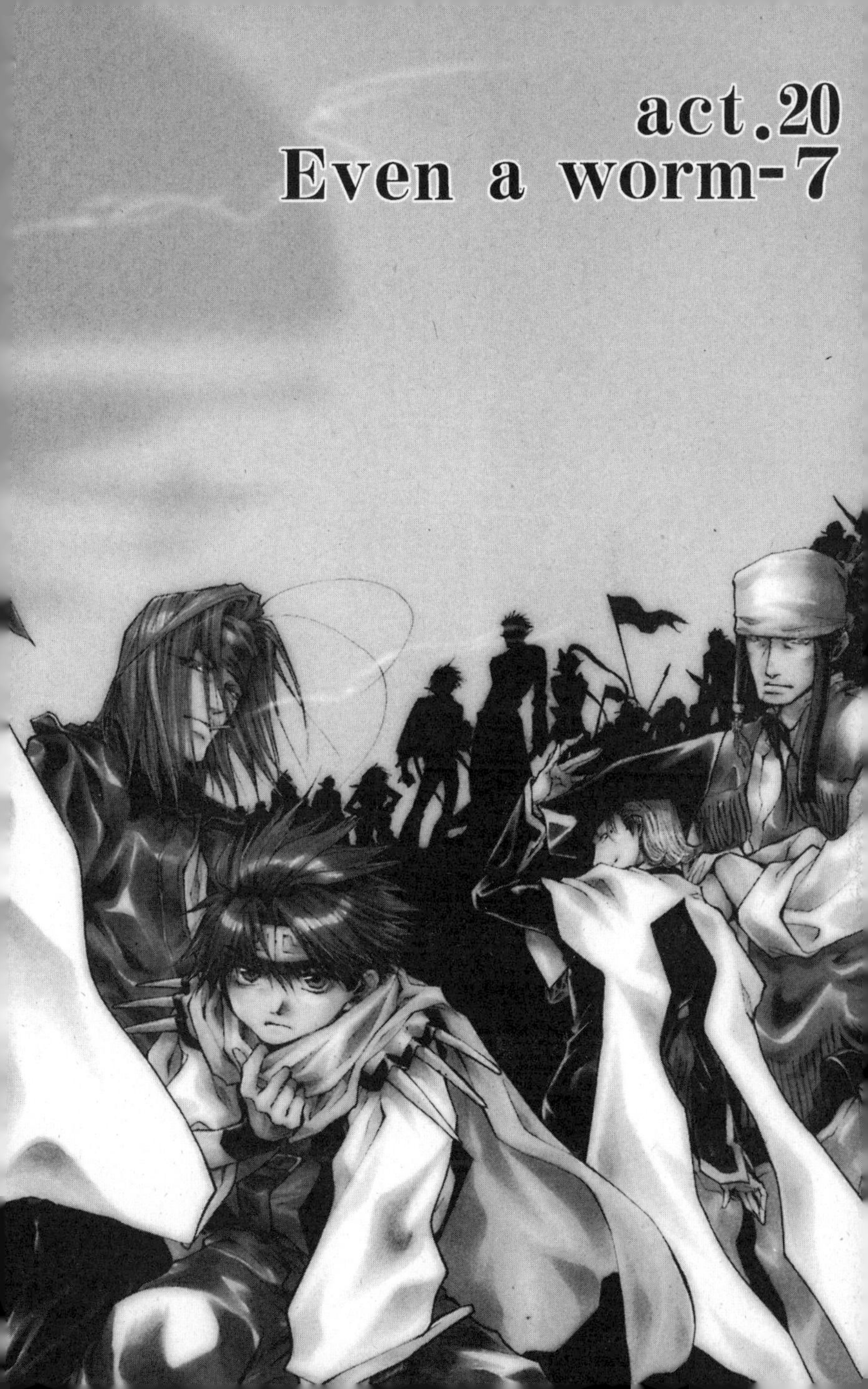

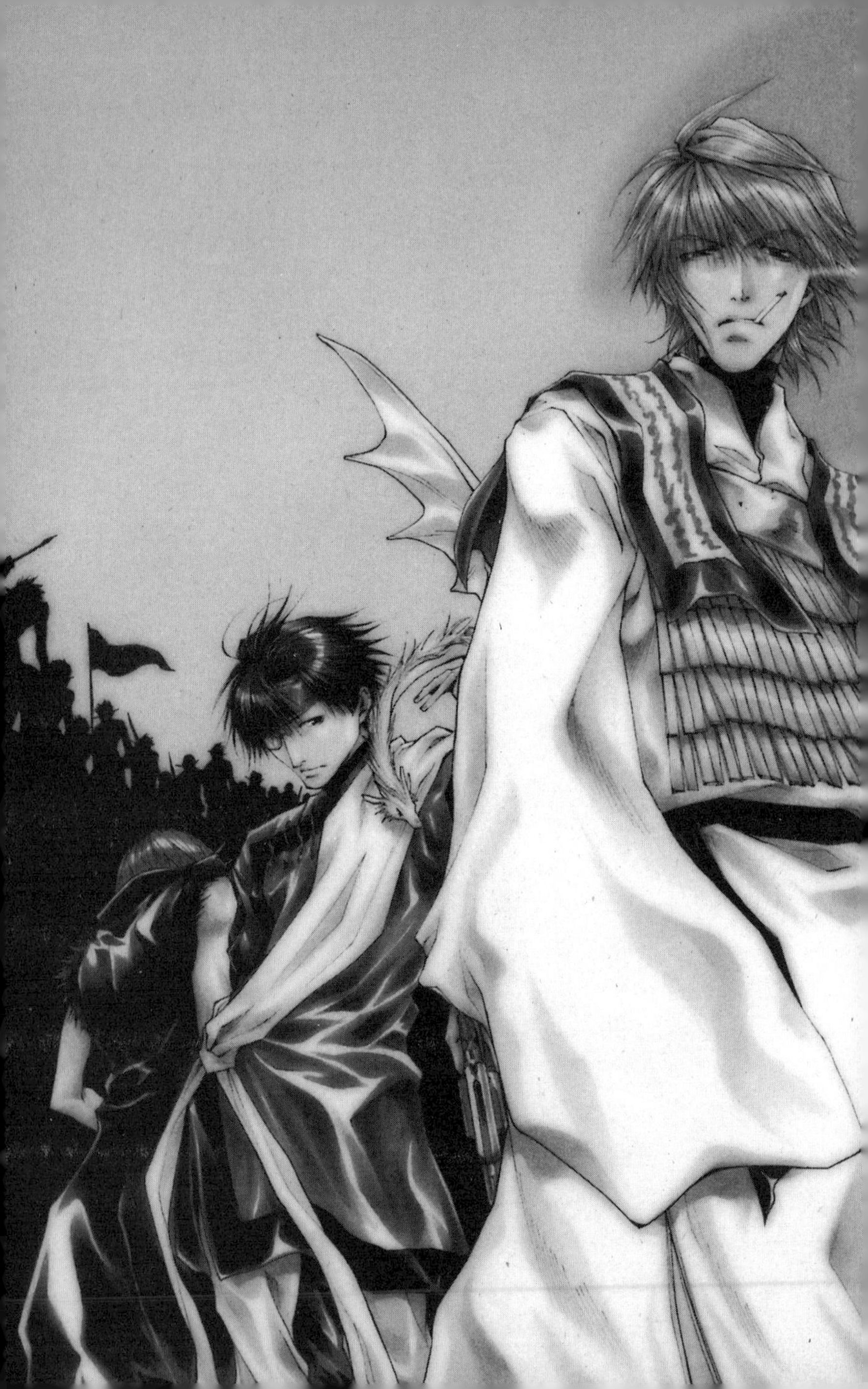

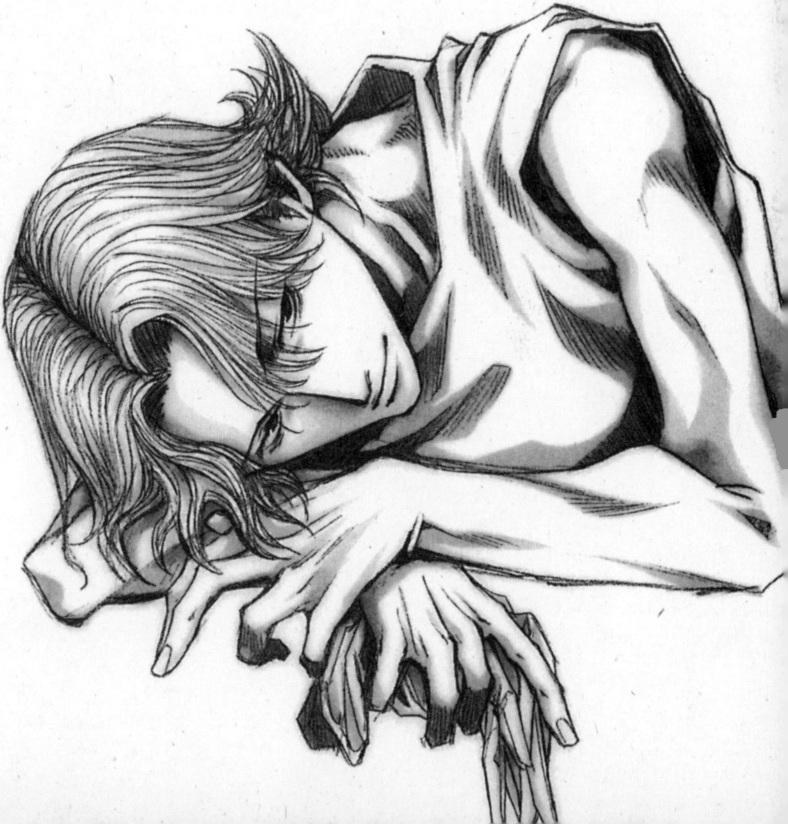

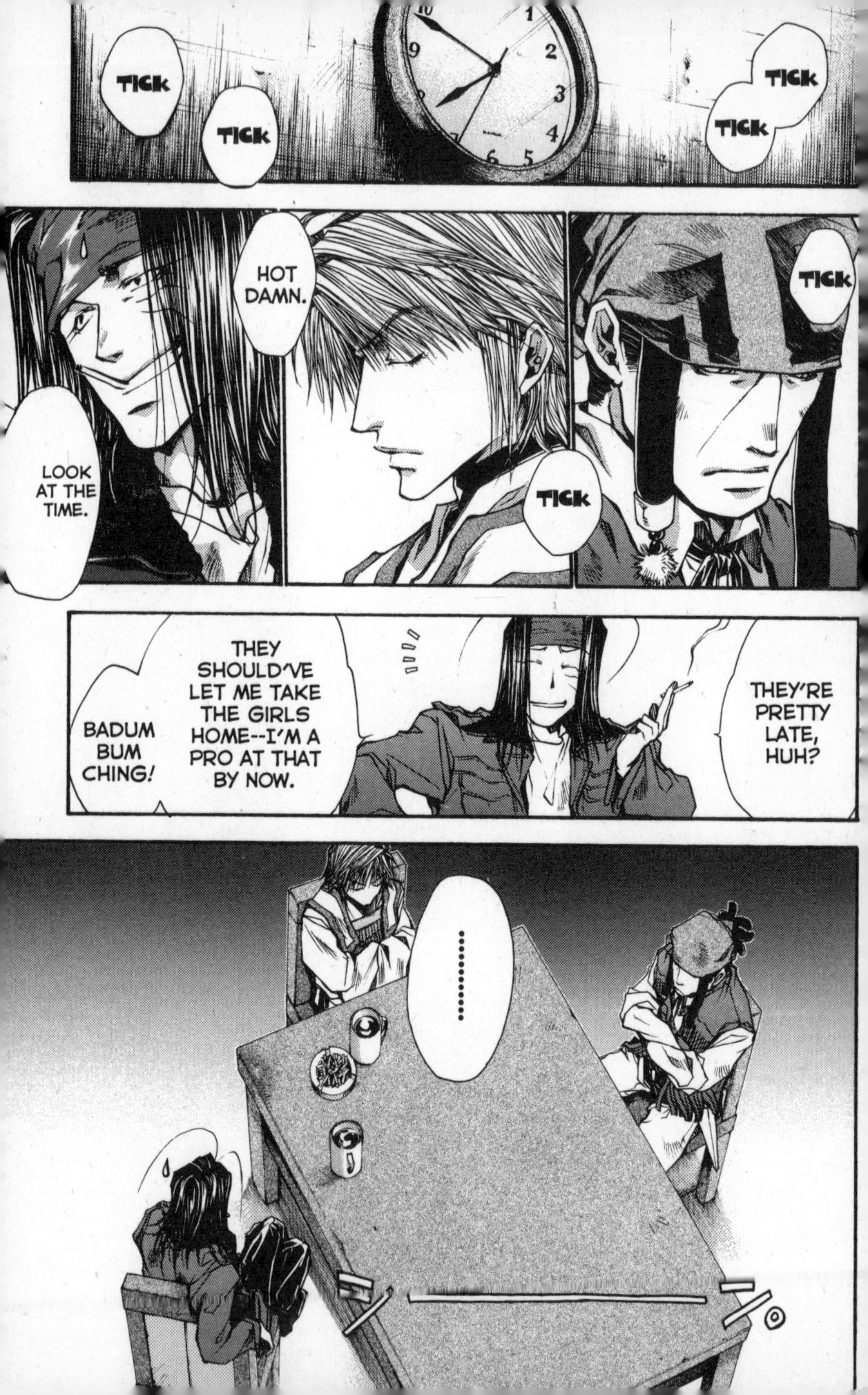
TICK
TICK
TICK
TICK
TICK
HOT DAMN.
TICK
LOOK AT THE TIME.
THEY'RE PRETTY LATE, HUH?
THEY SHOULD'VE LET ME TAKE THE GIRLS HOME--I'M A PRO AT THAT BY NOW.
BADUM BUM CHING!
....

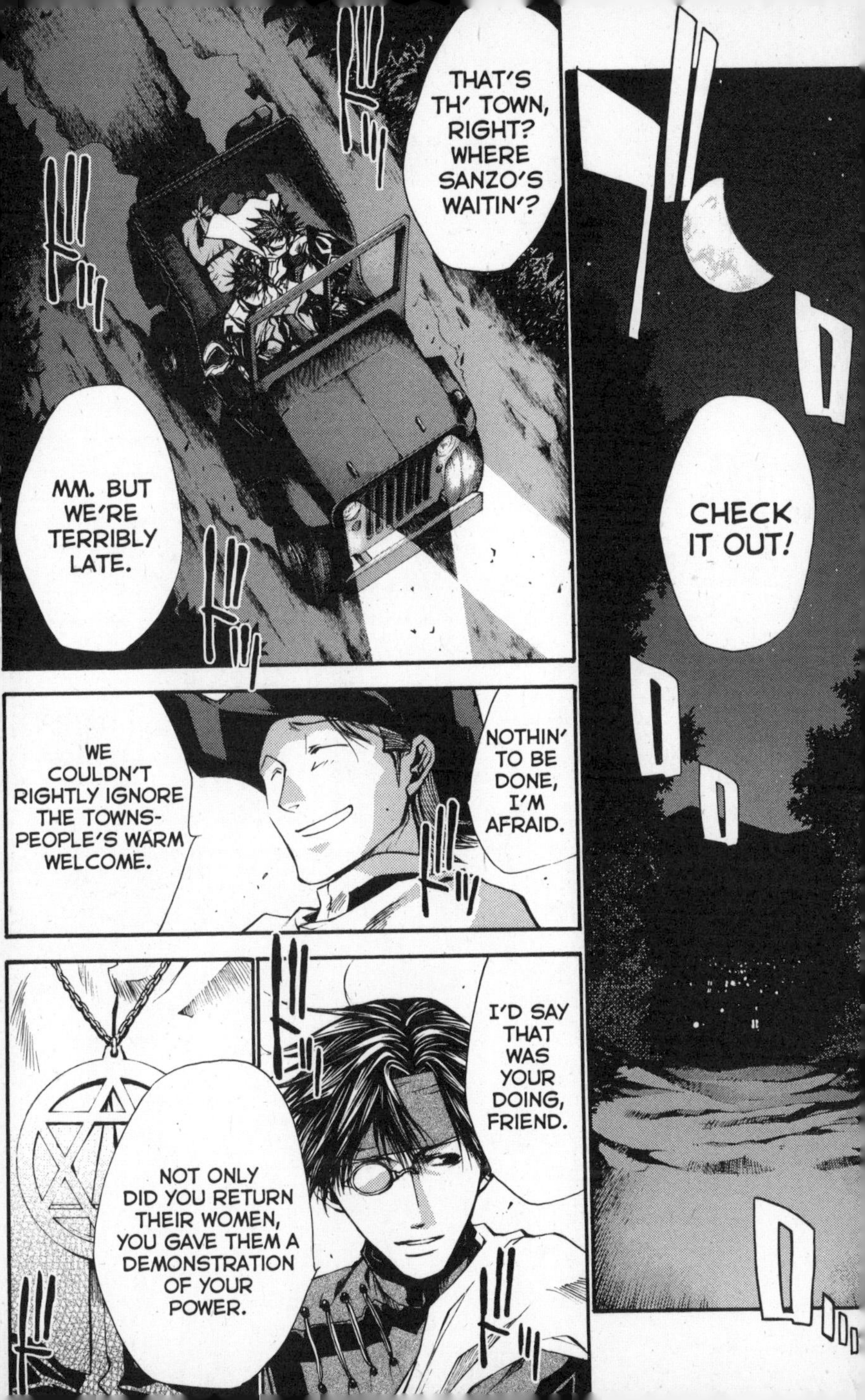
CHECK IT OUT!
THAT'S TH' TOWN, RIGHT? WHERE SANZO'S WAITIN'?
MM. BUT WE'RE TERRIBLY LATE.
NOTHIN' TO BE DONE, I'M AFRAID.
WE COULDN'T RIGHTLY IGNORE THE TOWNS-PEOPLE'S WARM WELCOME.
I'D SAY THAT WAS YOUR DOING, FRIEND.
NOT ONLY DID YOU RETURN THEIR WOMEN, YOU GAVE THEM A DEMONSTRATION OF YOUR POWER.

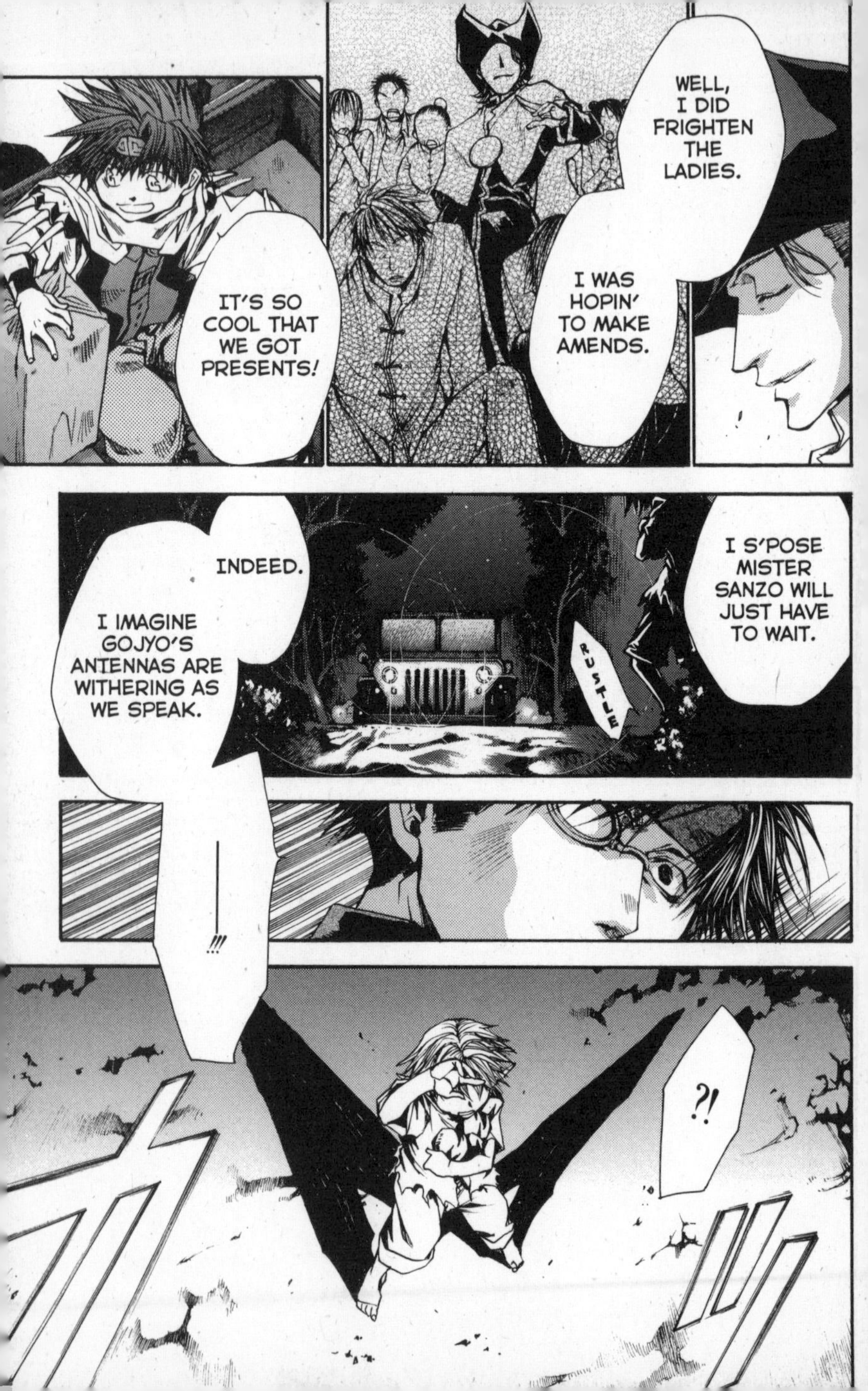
WELL, I DID FRIGHTEN THE LADIES.
I WAS HOPIN' TO MAKE AMENDS.
IT'S SO COOL THAT WE GOT PRESENTS!
I S'POSE MISTER SANZO WILL JUST HAVE TO WAIT.
RUSTLE
INDEED.
I IMAGINE GOJYO'S ANTENNAS ARE WITHERING AS WE SPEAK.
!!!
?!

...HUH?

WHOA. WHAT'S TH' MATTER, HAKKAI?

HEY!

!!

NN!
...

...I'M SORRY. DID WE SCARE YOU?

NN.

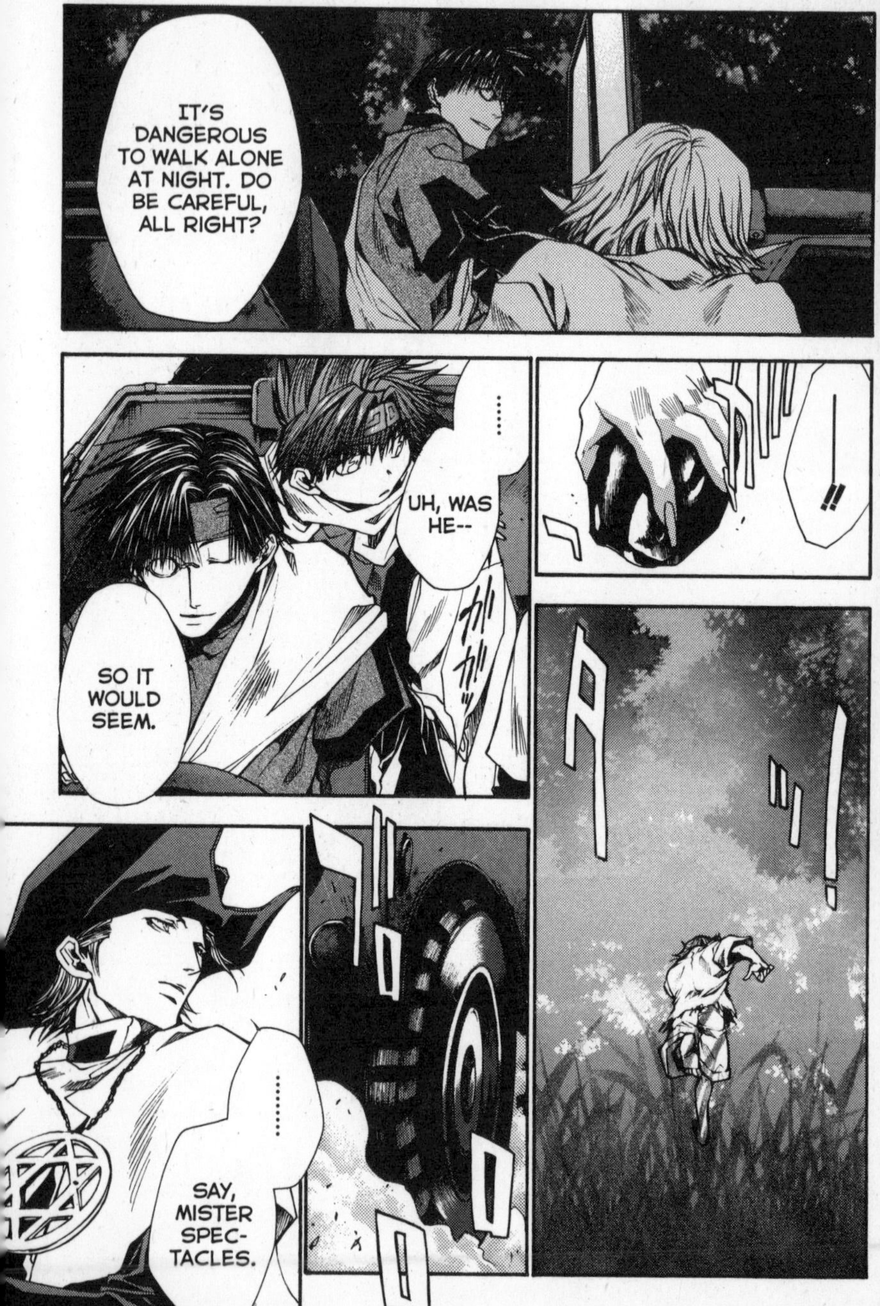

IT'S DANGEROUS TO WALK ALONE AT NIGHT. DO BE CAREFUL, ALL RIGHT?
!!
......
UH, WAS HE--
SO IT WOULD SEEM.
......
SAY, MISTER SPEC-TACLES.

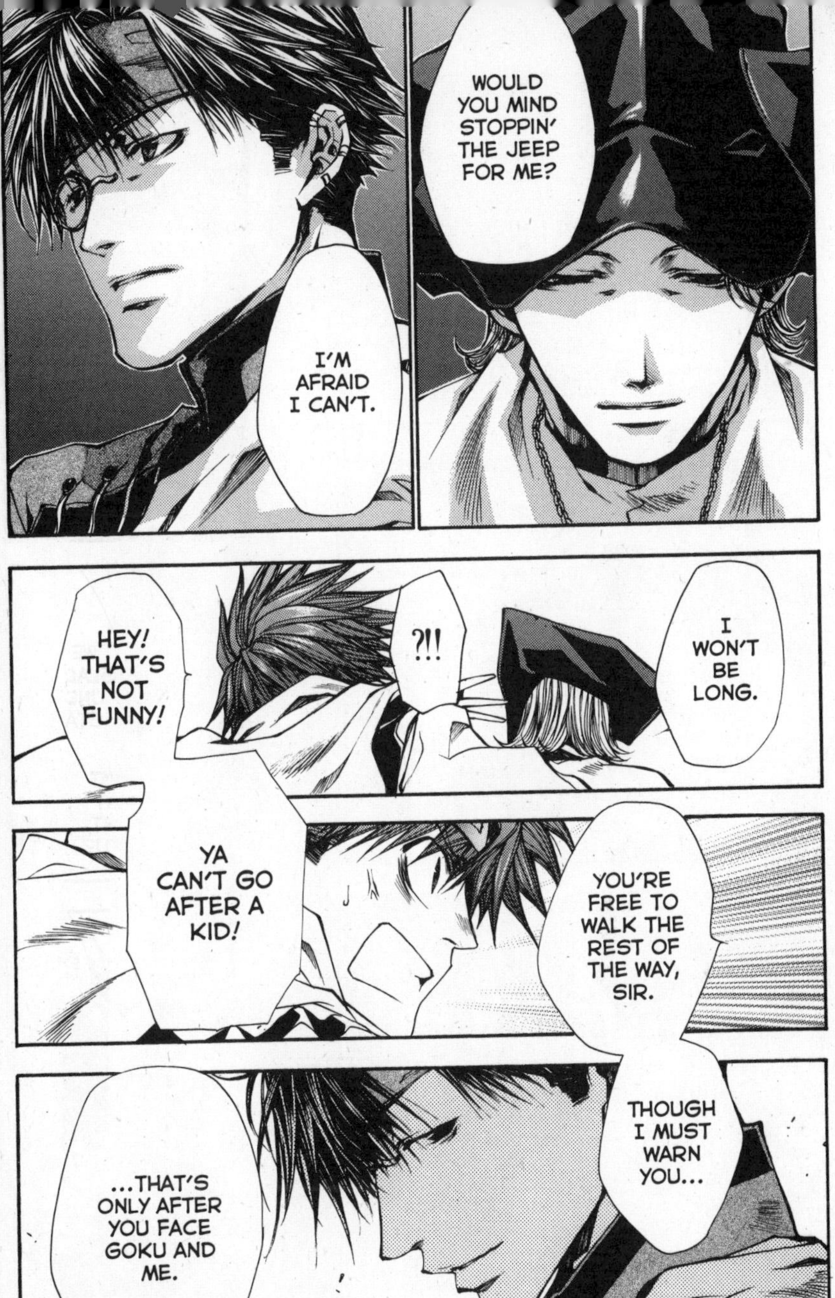
WOULD YOU MIND STOPPIN' THE JEEP FOR ME?
I'M AFRAID I CAN'T.
I WON'T BE LONG.
?!!
HEY! THAT'S NOT FUNNY!
YA CAN'T GO AFTER A KID!
YOU'RE FREE TO WALK THE REST OF THE WAY, SIR.
THOUGH I MUST WARN YOU...
...THAT'S ONLY AFTER YOU FACE GOKU AND ME.

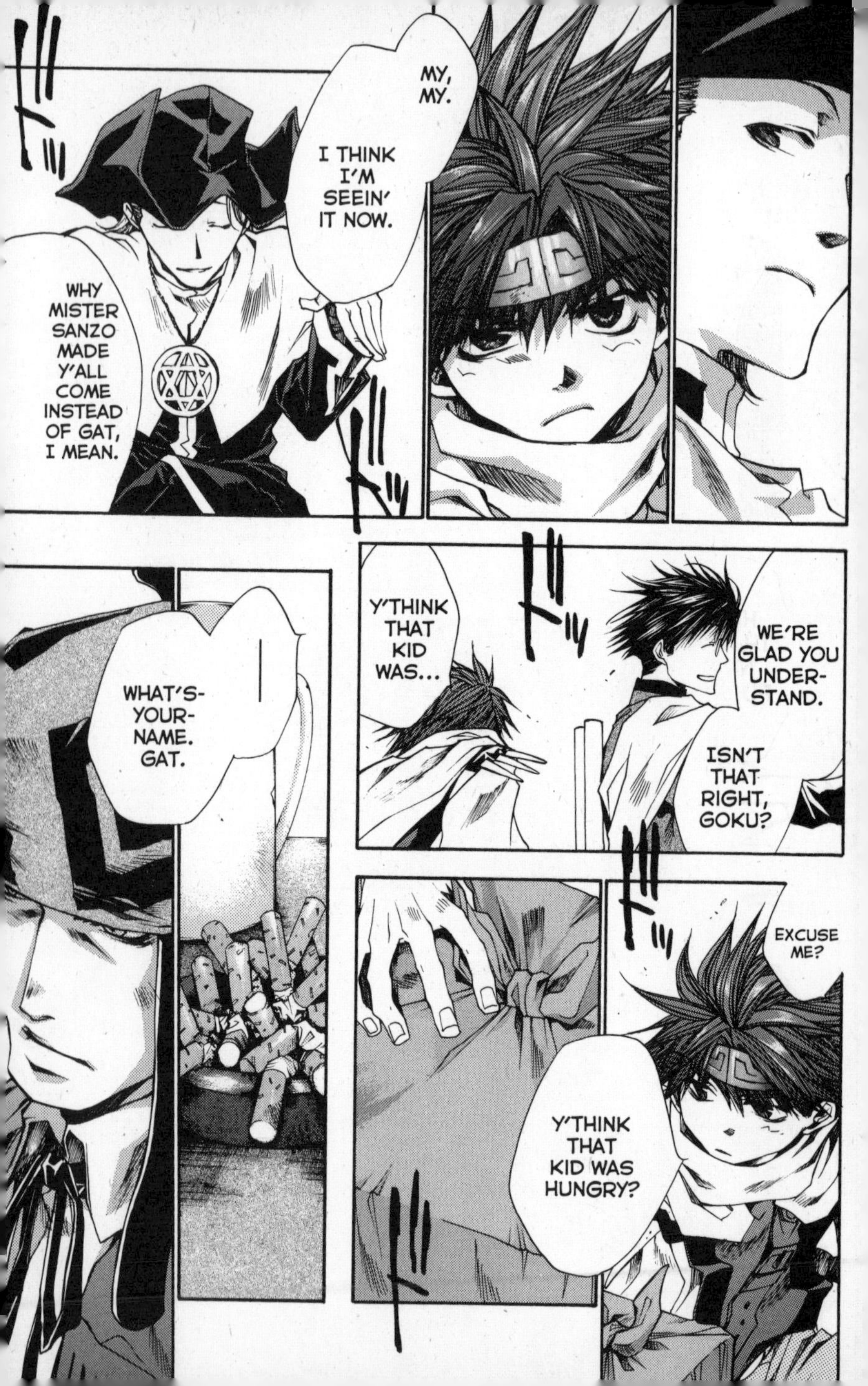
MY, MY.
I THINK I'M SEEIN' IT NOW.
WHY MISTER SANZO MADE Y'ALL COME INSTEAD OF GAT, I MEAN.
WE'RE GLAD YOU UNDER-STAND.
ISN'T THAT RIGHT, GOKU?
Y'THINK THAT KID WAS...
EXCUSE ME?
Y'THINK THAT KID WAS HUNGRY?
WHAT'S-YOUR-NAME. GAT.

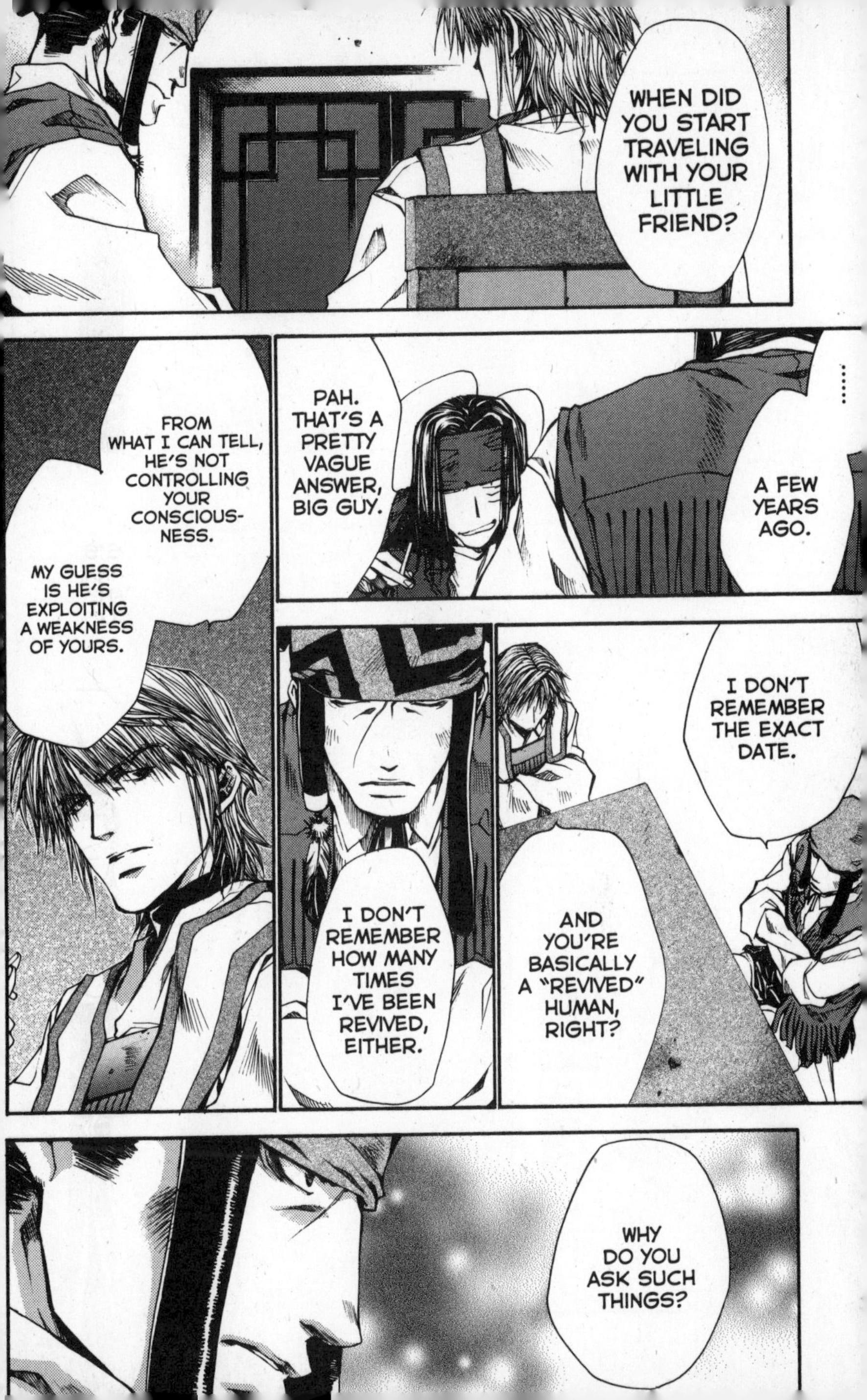
WHEN DID YOU START TRAVELING WITH YOUR LITTLE FRIEND?
......
A FEW YEARS AGO.
PAH. THAT'S A PRETTY VAGUE ANSWER, BIG GUY.
I DON'T REMEMBER THE EXACT DATE.
AND YOU'RE BASICALLY A "REVIVED" HUMAN, RIGHT?
I DON'T REMEMBER HOW MANY TIMES I'VE BEEN REVIVED, EITHER.
FROM WHAT I CAN TELL, HE'S NOT CONTROLLING YOUR CONSCIOUS-NESS.
MY GUESS IS HE'S EXPLOITING A WEAKNESS OF YOURS.
WHY DO YOU ASK SUCH THINGS?

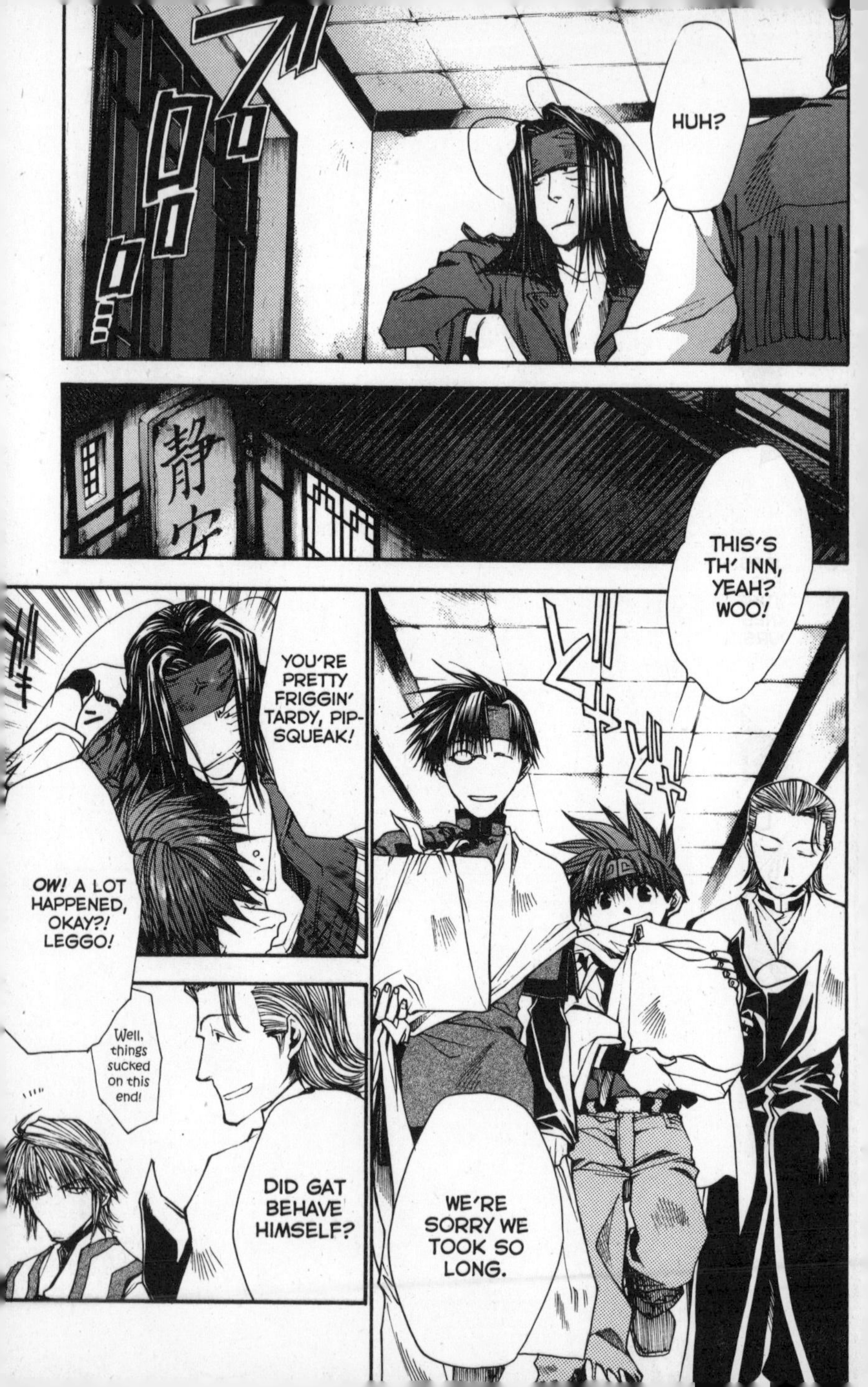
HUH?
THIS'S TH' INN, YEAH? WOO!
WE'RE SORRY WE TOOK SO LONG.
YOU'RE PRETTY FRIGGIN' TARDY, PIP-SQUEAK!
OW! A LOT HAPPENED, OKAY?! LEGGO!
Well, things sucked on this end!
DID GAT BEHAVE HIMSELF?

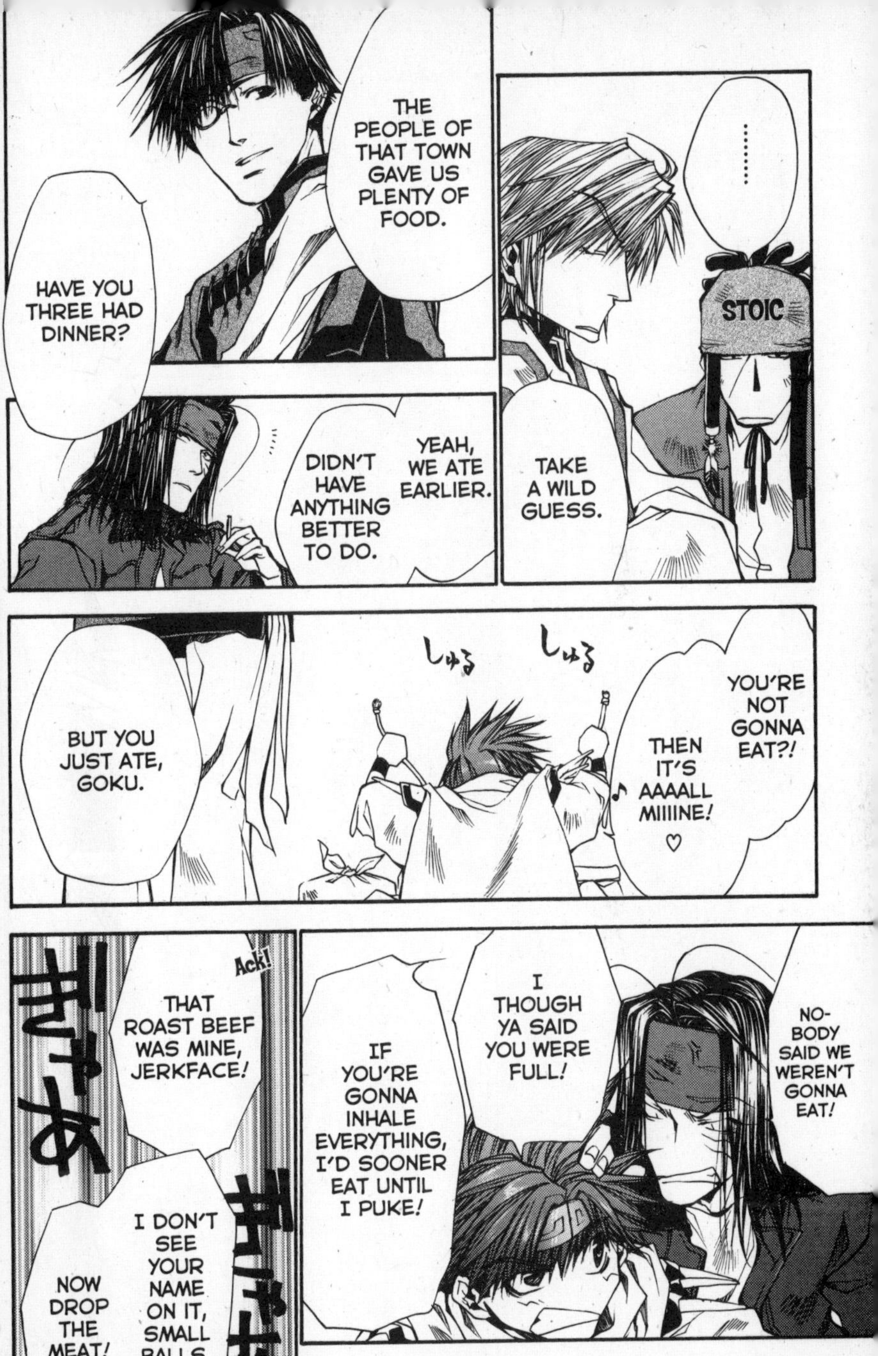
THE PEOPLE OF THAT TOWN GAVE US PLENTY OF FOOD.
HAVE YOU THREE HAD DINNER?
......
STOIC
TAKE A WILD GUESS.
YEAH, WE ATE EARLIER.
DIDN'T HAVE ANYTHING BETTER TO DO.
YOU'RE NOT GONNA EAT?!
THEN IT'S AAAALL MIIIINE! ♪ ♡
しゅる
しゅる
BUT YOU JUST ATE, GOKU.
NO-BODY SAID WE WEREN'T GONNA EAT!
I THOUGH YA SAID YOU WERE FULL!
IF YOU'RE GONNA INHALE EVERYTHING, I'D SOONER EAT UNTIL I PUKE!
Ack!
THAT ROAST BEEF WAS MINE, JERKFACE!
ぎゃあ
I DON'T SEE YOUR NAME ON IT, SMALL BALLS.
ぎゃあ
NOW DROP THE MEAT!

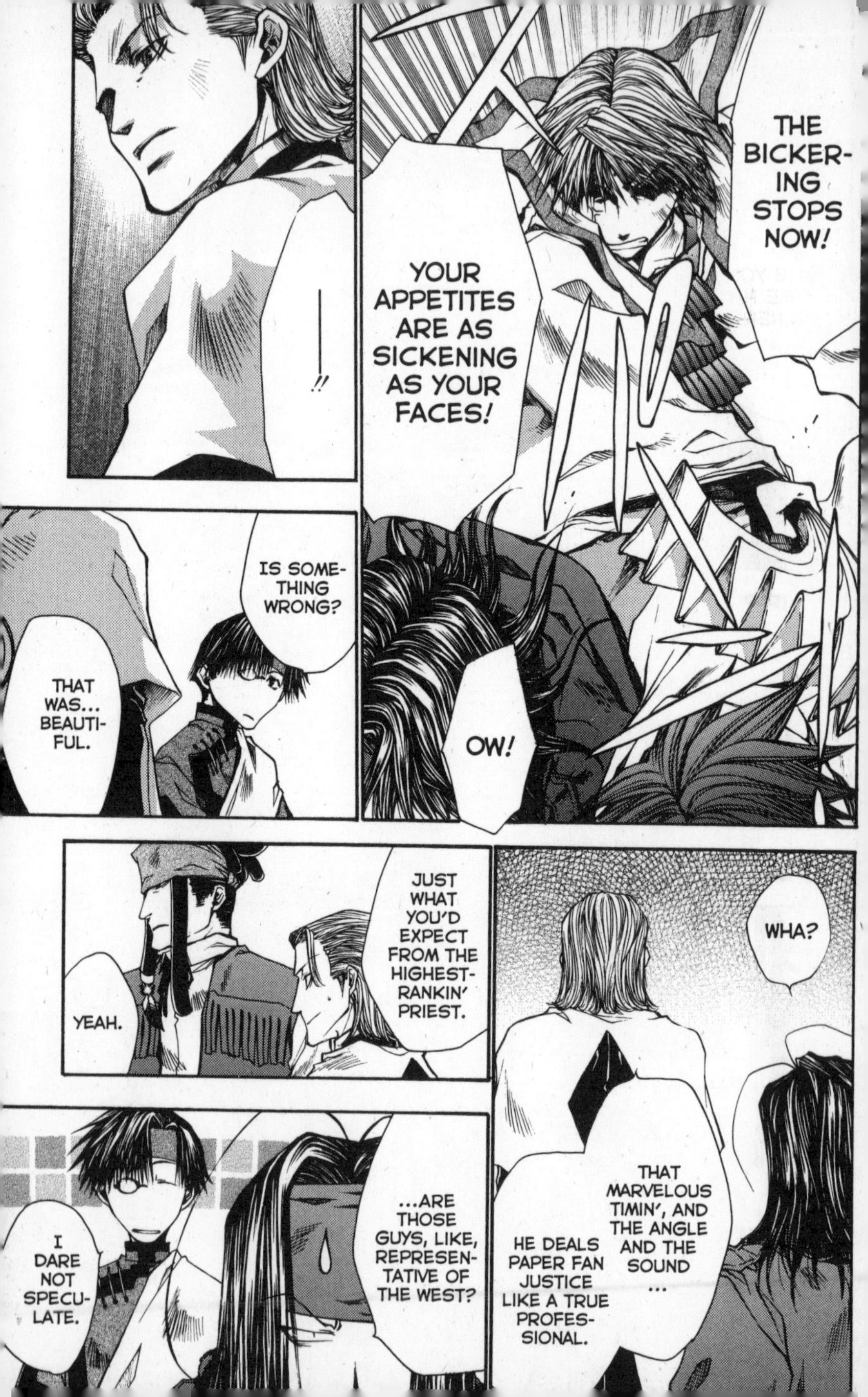
THE BICKERING STOPS NOW!
YOUR APPETITES ARE AS SICKENING AS YOUR FACES!
OW!
——!!
IS SOMETHING WRONG?
THAT WAS... BEAUTIFUL.
WHA?
THAT MARVELOUS TIMIN', AND THE ANGLE AND THE SOUND ...
HE DEALS PAPER FAN JUSTICE LIKE A TRUE PROFESSIONAL.
JUST WHAT YOU'D EXPECT FROM THE HIGHEST-RANKIN' PRIEST.
YEAH.
...ARE THOSE GUYS, LIKE, REPRESENTATIVE OF THE WEST?
I DARE NOT SPECULATE.

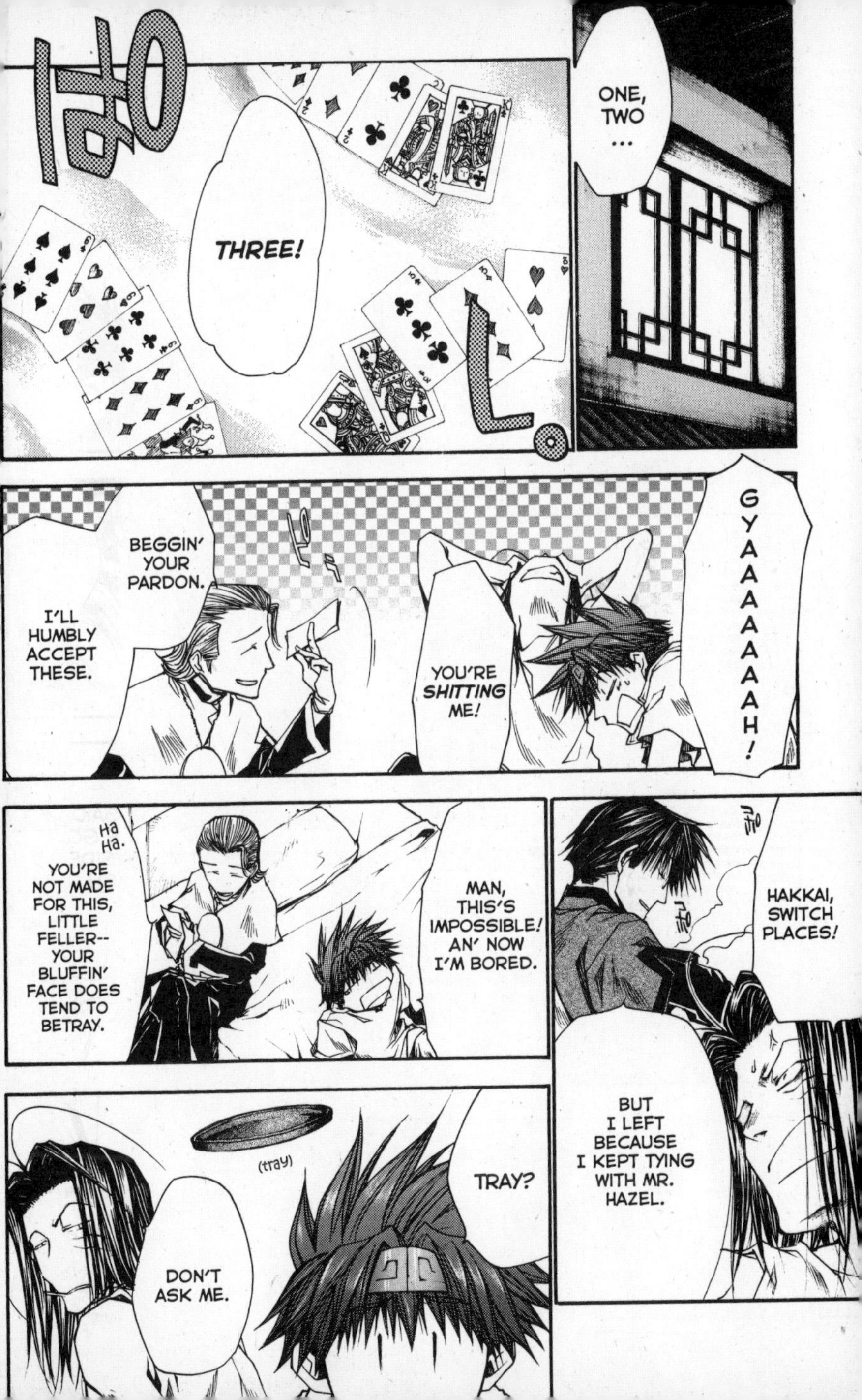
ONE, TWO ...
THREE!
GYAAAAAAAAH!
YOU'RE SHITTING ME!
BEGGIN' YOUR PARDON.
I'LL HUMBLY ACCEPT THESE.
HAKKAI, SWITCH PLACES!
BUT I LEFT BECAUSE I KEPT TYING WITH MR. HAZEL.
MAN, THIS'S IMPOSSIBLE! AN' NOW I'M BORED.
Ha Ha.
YOU'RE NOT MADE FOR THIS, LITTLE FELLER-- YOUR BLUFFIN' FACE DOES TEND TO BETRAY.
TRAY?
(tray)
DON'T ASK ME.

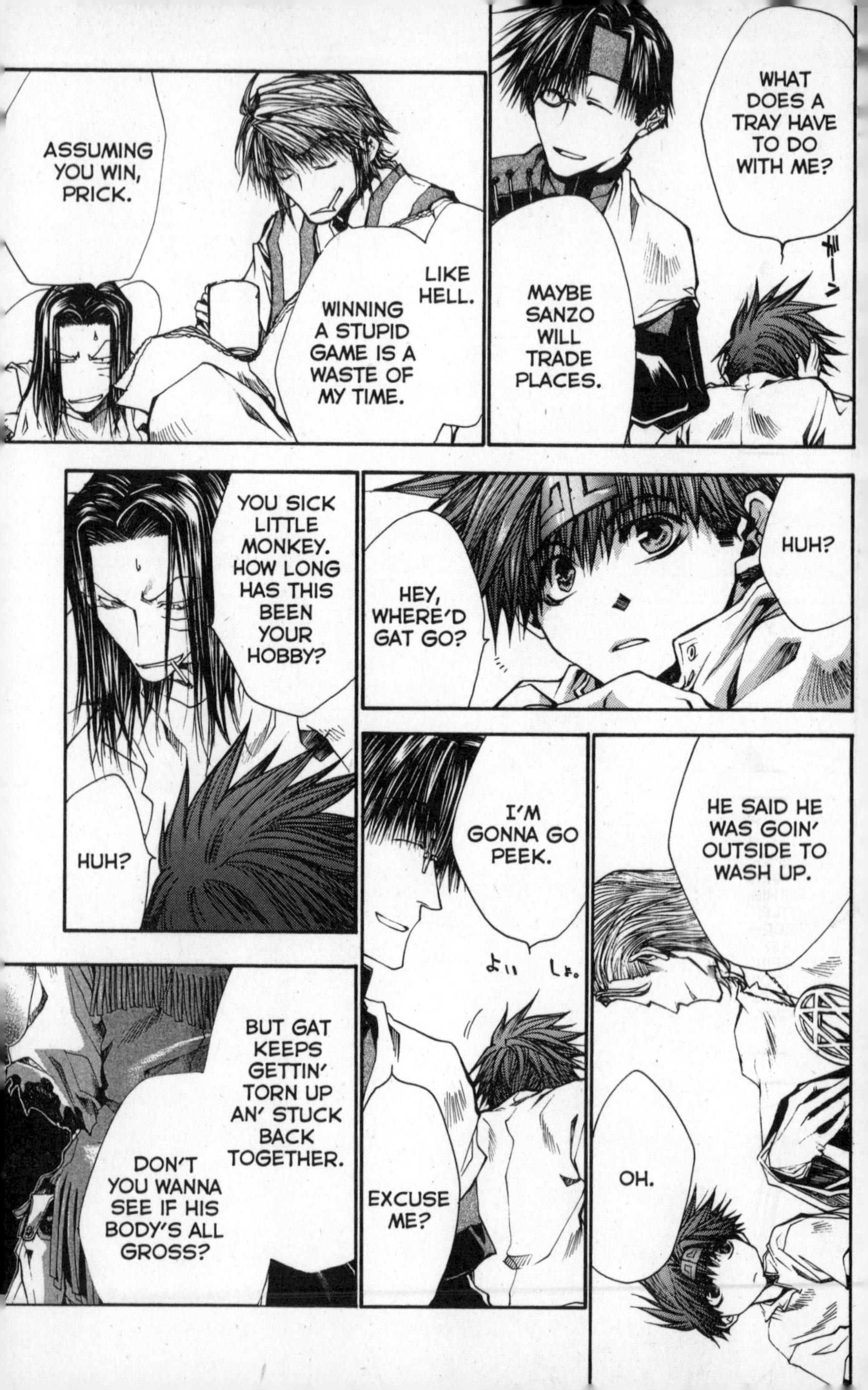
WHAT DOES A TRAY HAVE TO DO WITH ME?
MAYBE SANZO WILL TRADE PLACES.
LIKE HELL.
WINNING A STUPID GAME IS A WASTE OF MY TIME.
ASSUMING YOU WIN, PRICK.
HUH?
HEY, WHERE'D GAT GO?
HE SAID HE WAS GOIN' OUTSIDE TO WASH UP.
OH.
I'M GONNA GO PEEK.
よい しょ。
EXCUSE ME?
YOU SICK LITTLE MONKEY. HOW LONG HAS THIS BEEN YOUR HOBBY?
HUH?
BUT GAT KEEPS GETTIN' TORN UP AN' STUCK BACK TOGETHER.
DON'T YOU WANNA SEE IF HIS BODY'S ALL GROSS?

NOT THE TINIEST DAMN BIT.

'KAY!

TUP

LET HIM BE.

HM. CURIOSITY KILLED THE--

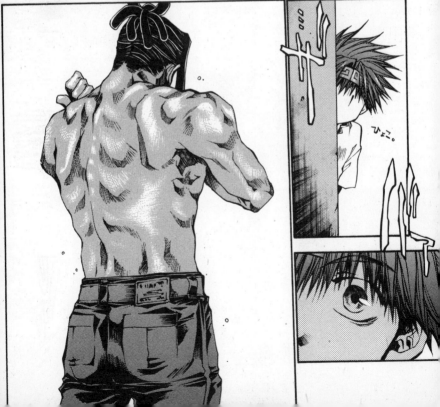

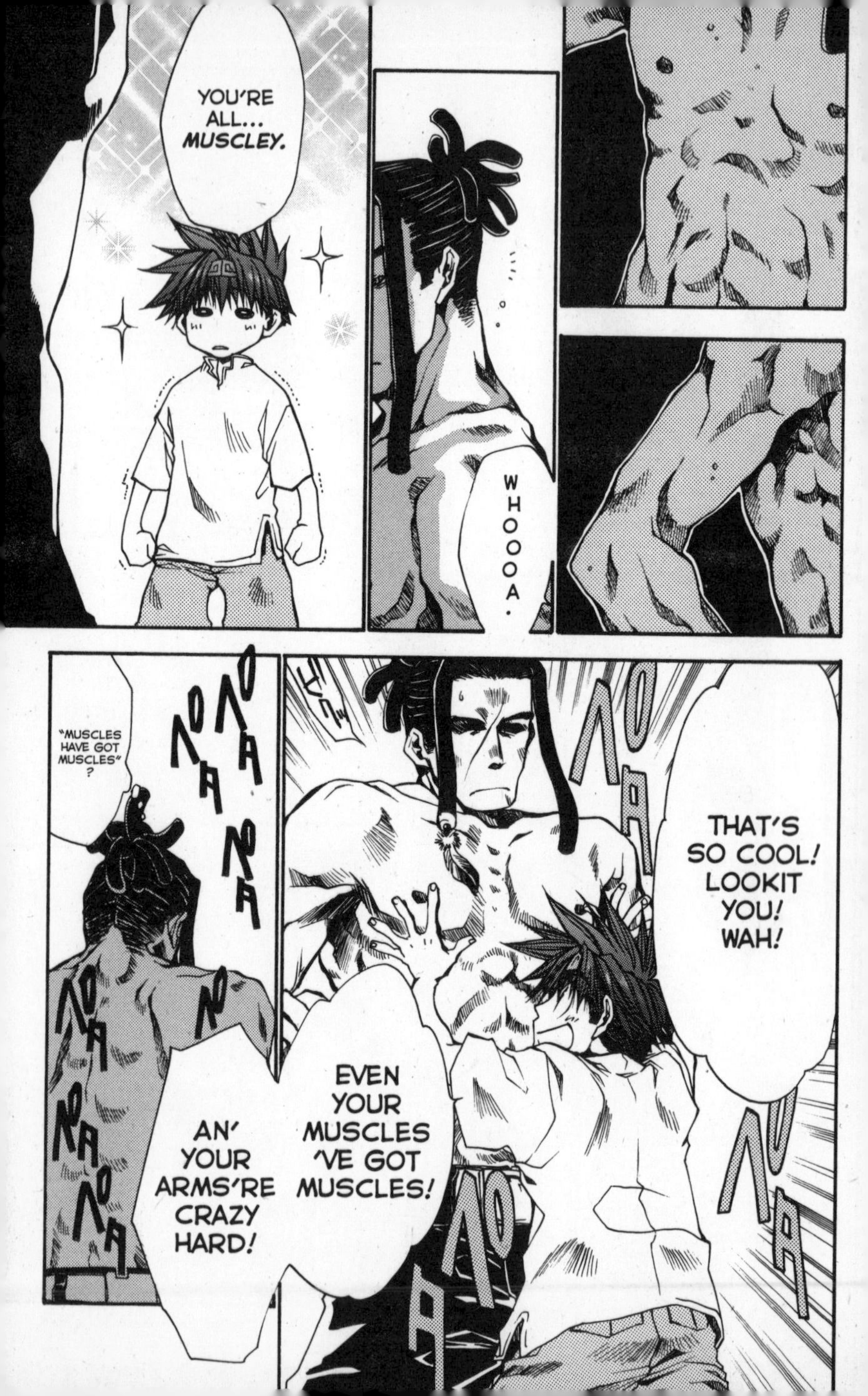
WHOOOA.
YOU'RE ALL... MUSCLEY.
THAT'S SO COOL! LOOKIT YOU! WAH!
EVEN YOUR MUSCLES 'VE GOT MUSCLES!
AN' YOUR ARMS'RE CRAZY HARD!
"MUSCLES HAVE GOT MUSCLES"?

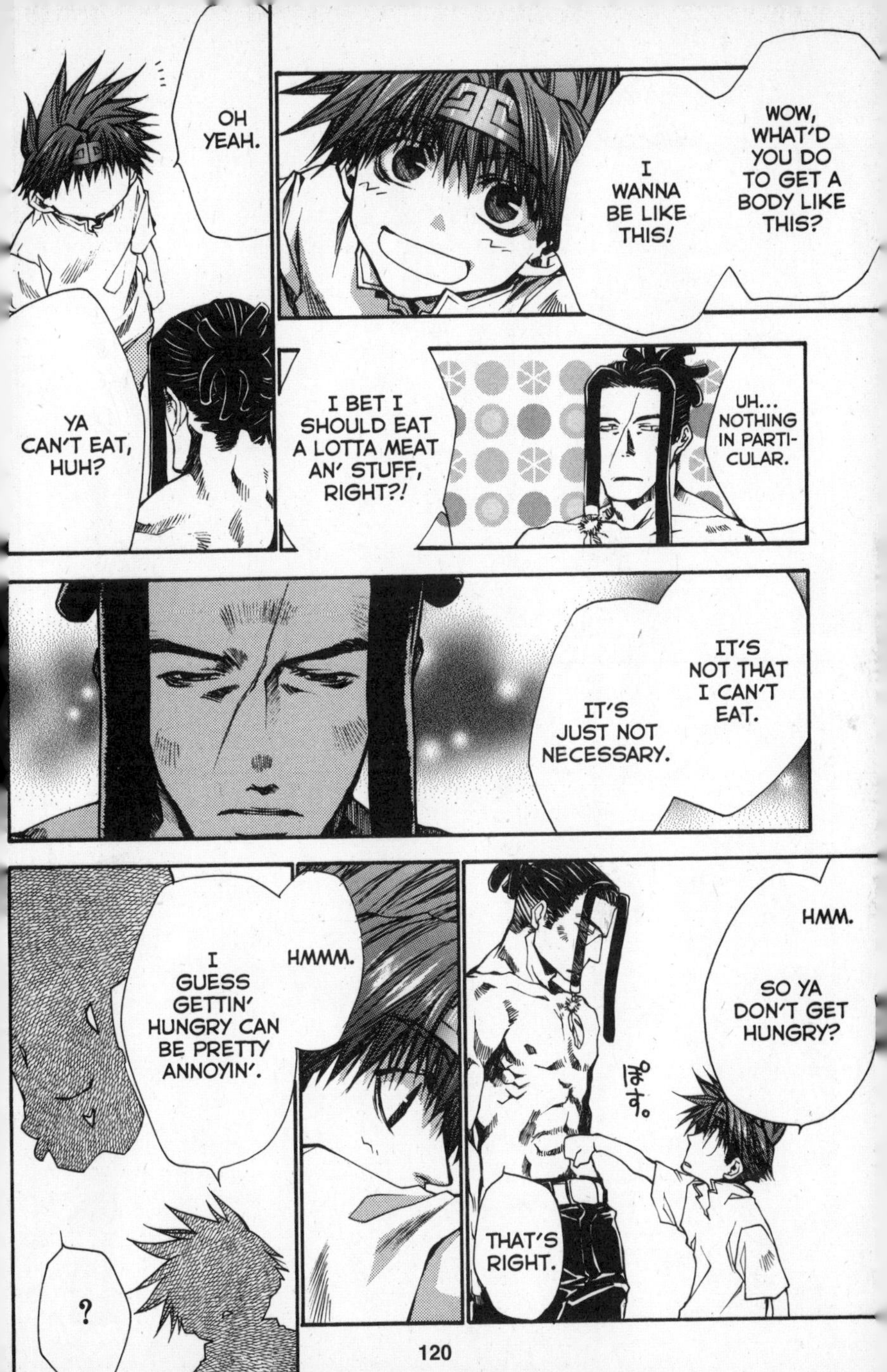
WOW, WHAT'D YOU DO TO GET A BODY LIKE THIS?
I WANNA BE LIKE THIS!
UH... NOTHING IN PARTI- CULAR.
I BET I SHOULD EAT A LOTTA MEAT AN' STUFF, RIGHT?!
OH YEAH.
YA CAN'T EAT, HUH?
IT'S NOT THAT I CAN'T EAT.
IT'S JUST NOT NECESSARY.
HMM.
SO YA DON'T GET HUNGRY?
ぽす。
THAT'S RIGHT.
HMMM.
I GUESS GETTIN' HUNGRY CAN BE PRETTY ANNOYIN'.
?

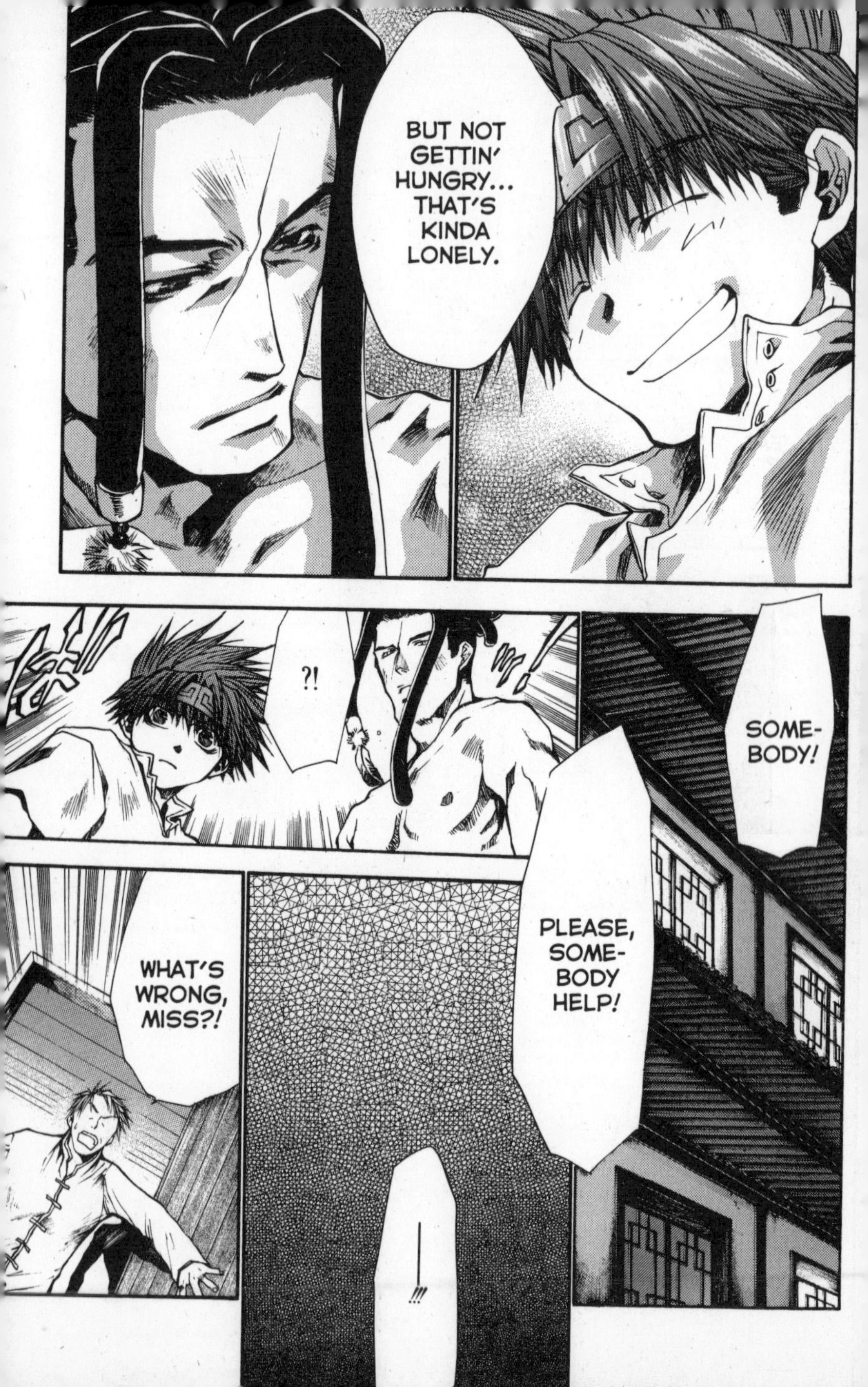
BUT NOT GETTIN' HUNGRY... THAT'S KINDA LONELY.
SOME-BODY!
PLEASE, SOME-BODY HELP!
?!
!!!
WHAT'S WRONG, MISS?!

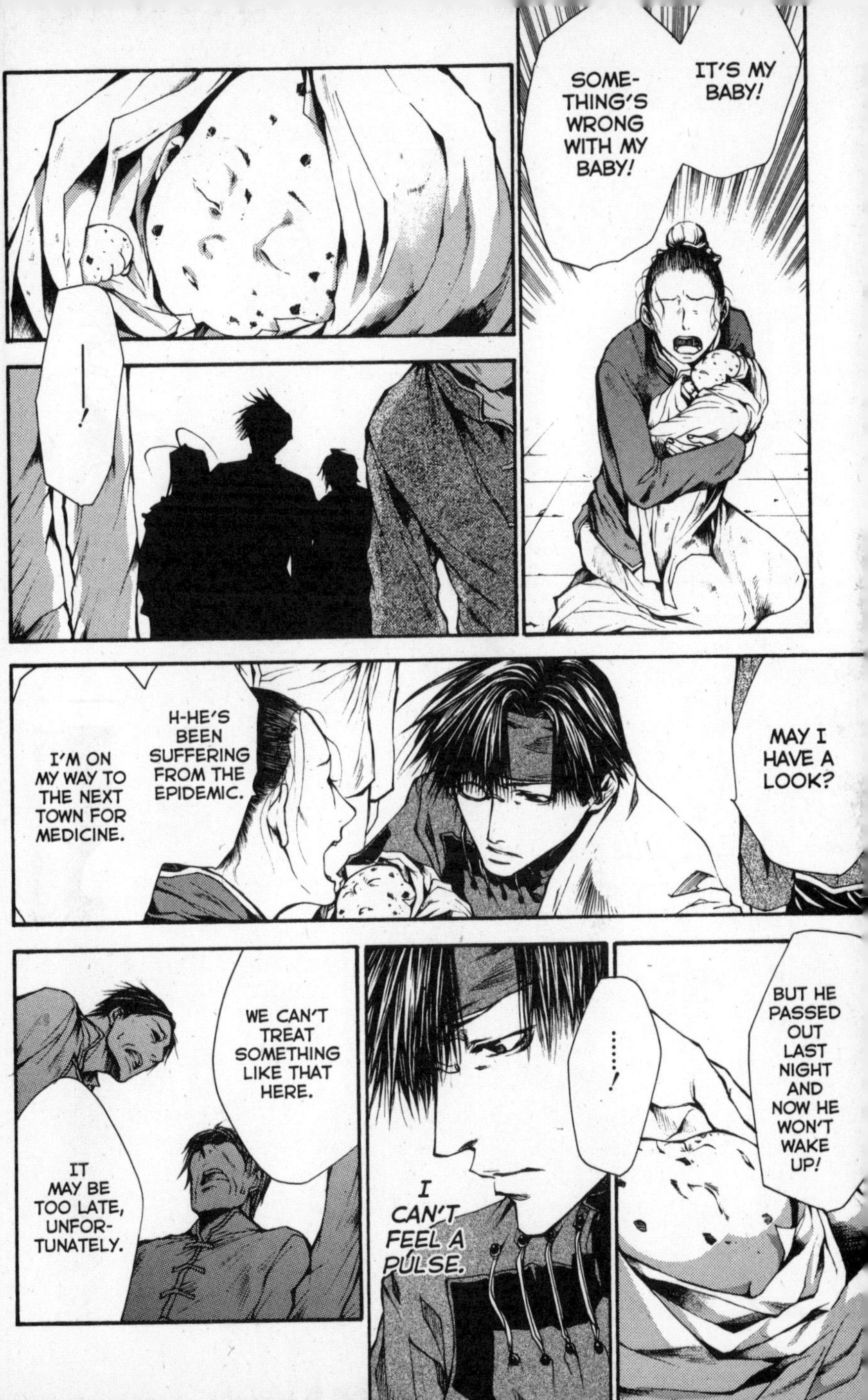
IT'S MY BABY!
SOME-THING'S WRONG WITH MY BABY!
!
MAY I HAVE A LOOK?
H-HE'S BEEN SUFFERING FROM THE EPIDEMIC.
I'M ON MY WAY TO THE NEXT TOWN FOR MEDICINE.
BUT HE PASSED OUT LAST NIGHT AND NOW HE WON'T WAKE UP!
......!
I CAN'T FEEL A PULSE.
WE CAN'T TREAT SOMETHING LIKE THAT HERE.
IT MAY BE TOO LATE, UNFOR-TUNATELY.

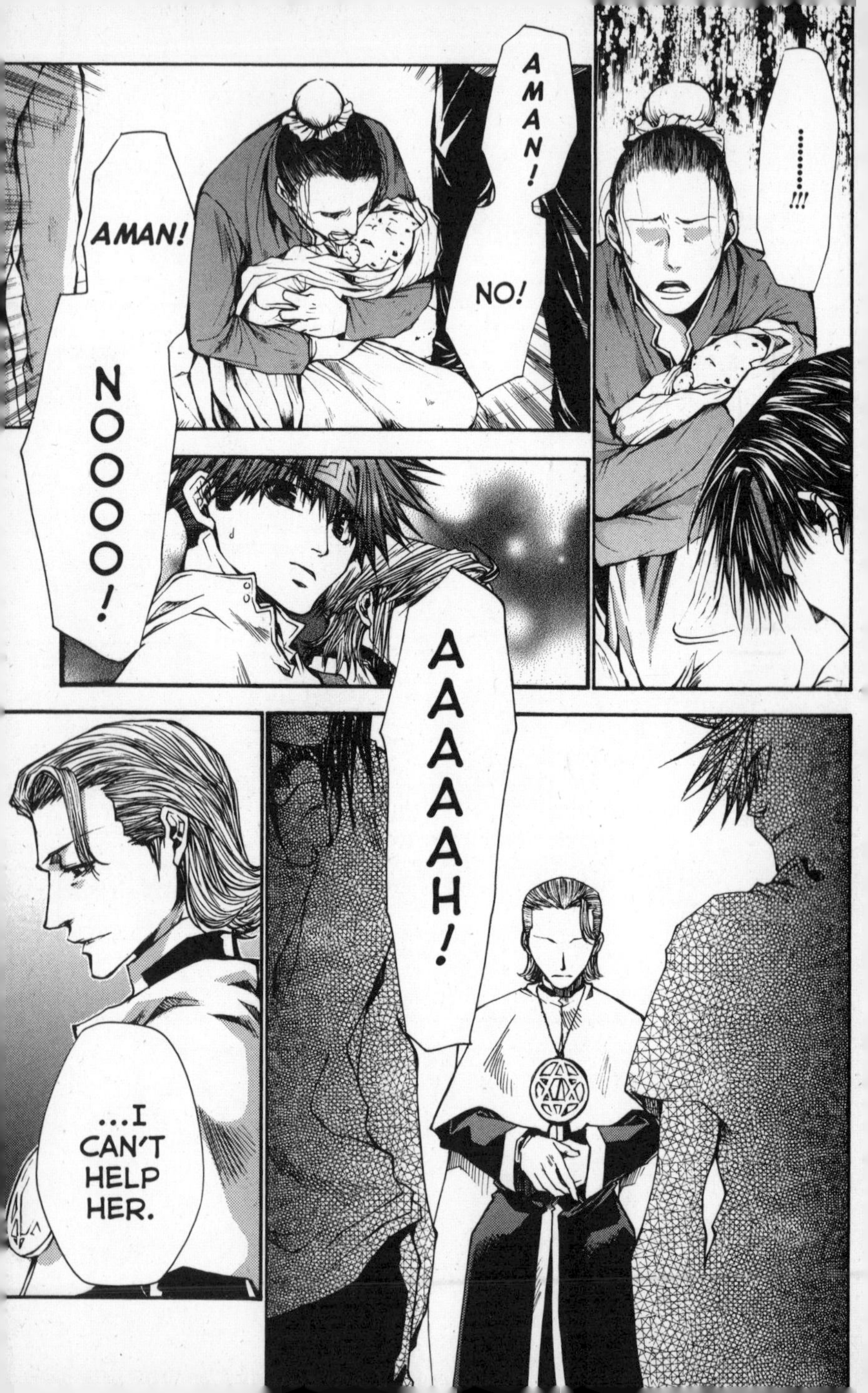
......!!!
AMAN!
NO!
AMAN!
NOOOOO!
AAAAAH!
...I CAN'T HELP HER.

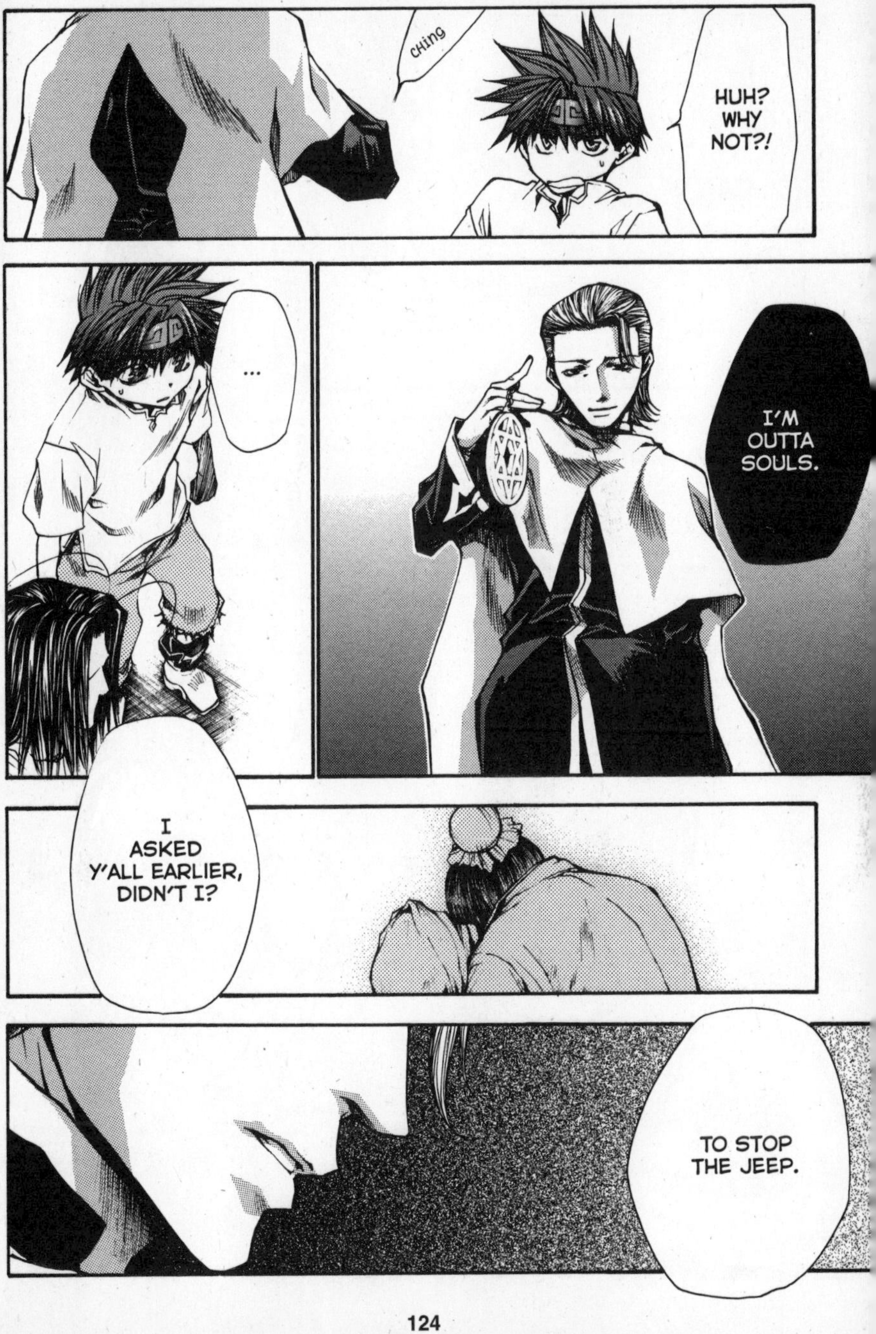
HUH? WHY NOT?!
CHING
I'M OUTTA SOULS.
...
I ASKED Y'ALL EARLIER, DIDN'T I?
TO STOP THE JEEP.

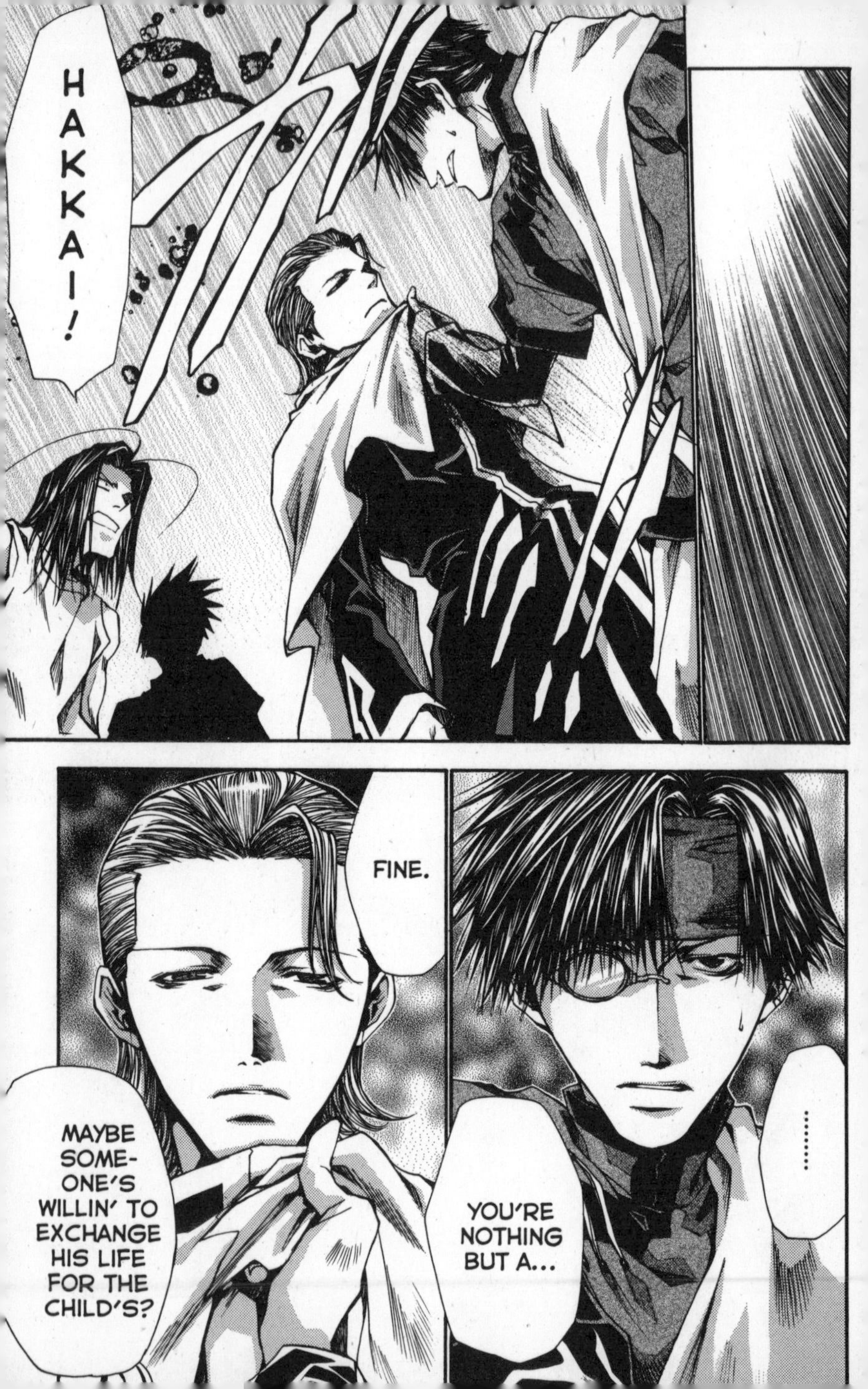
HAKKAI!
....
YOU'RE NOTHING BUT A...
FINE.
MAYBE SOMEONE'S WILLIN' TO EXCHANGE HIS LIFE FOR THE CHILD'S?

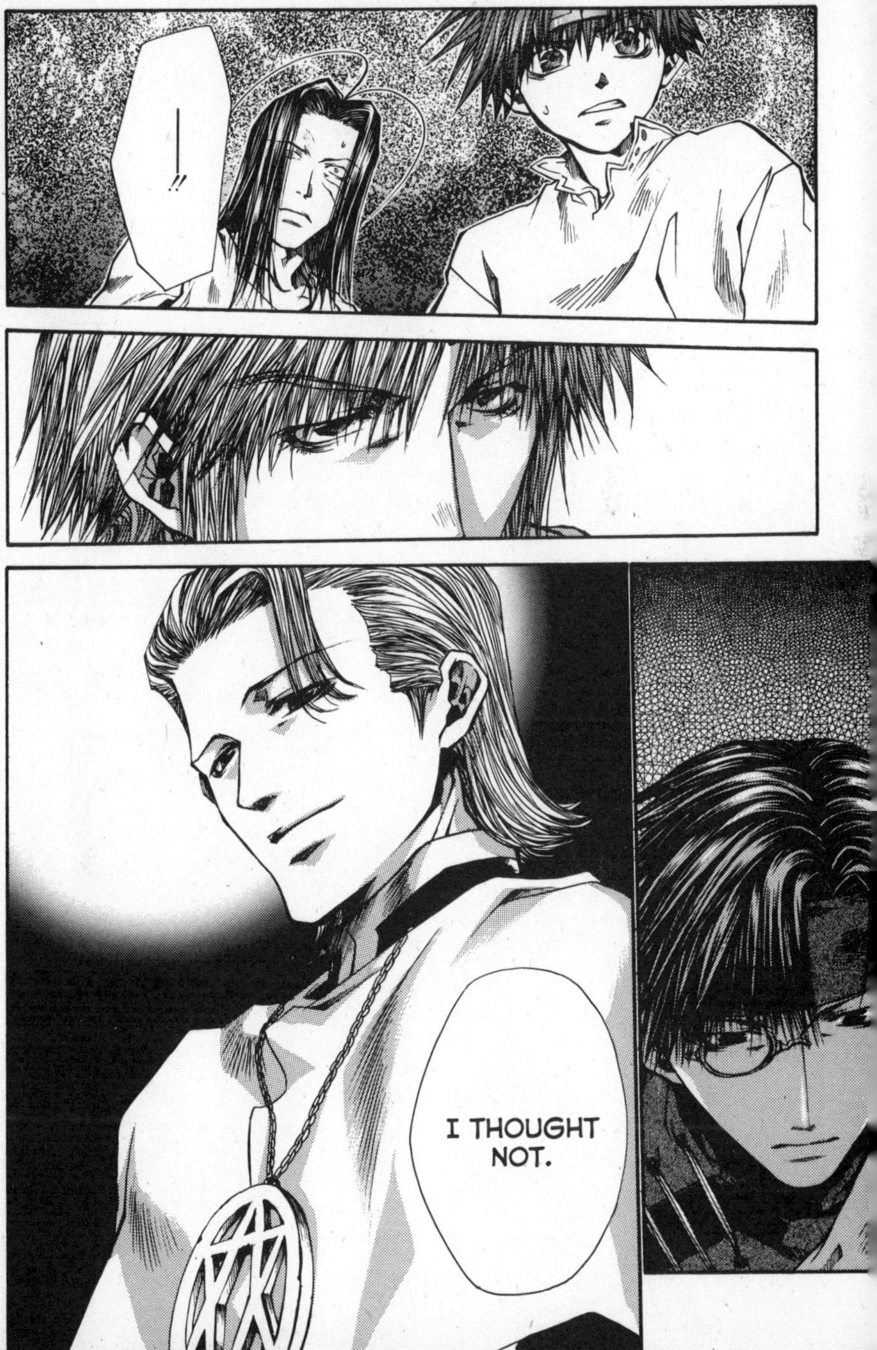
—!!
I THOUGHT NOT.

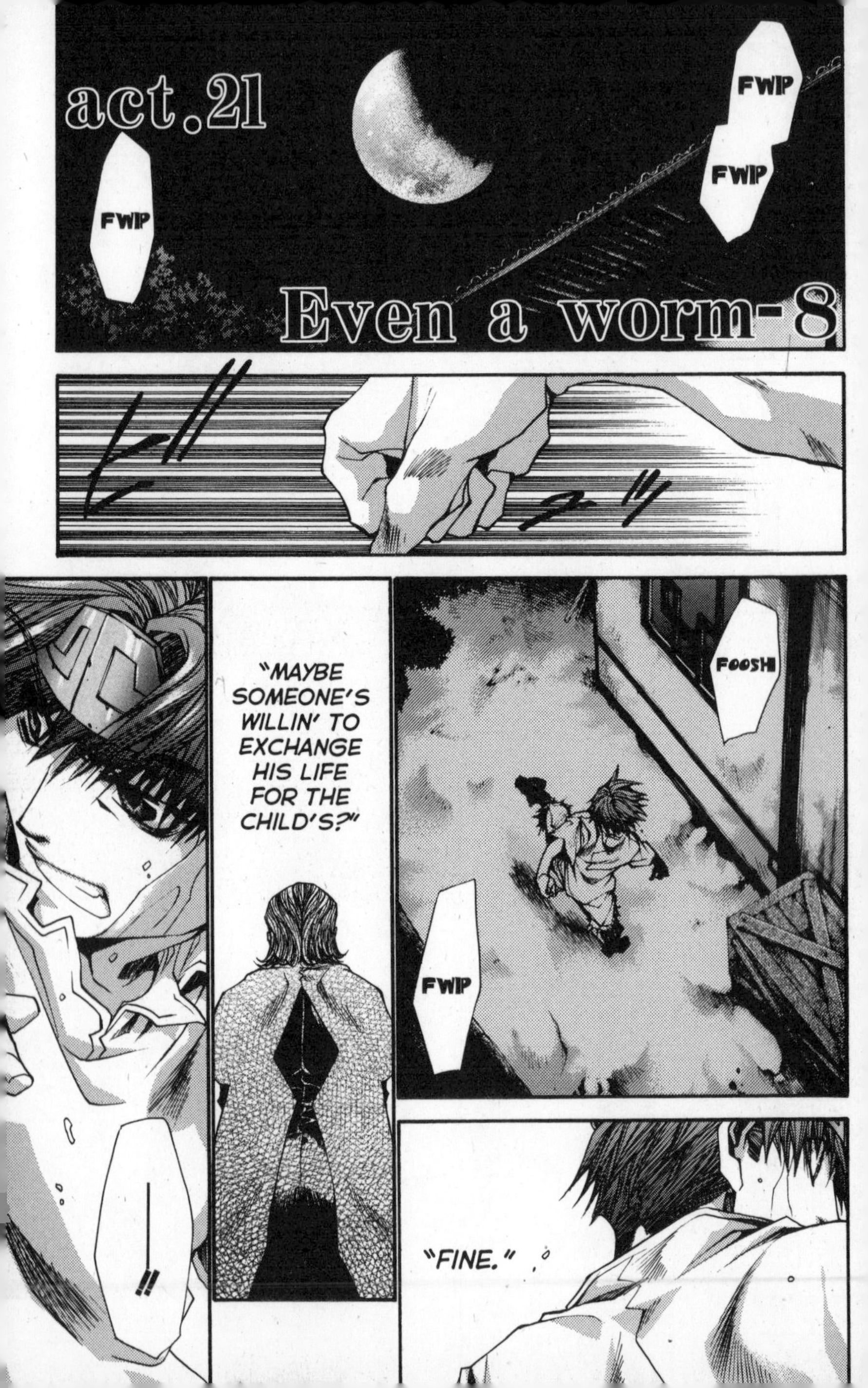
FWIP
FWIP
act.21
FWIP
Even a worm-8
FOOSH
FWIP
"FINE."
"MAYBE SOMEONE'S WILLIN' TO EXCHANGE HIS LIFE FOR THE CHILD'S?"
—!!

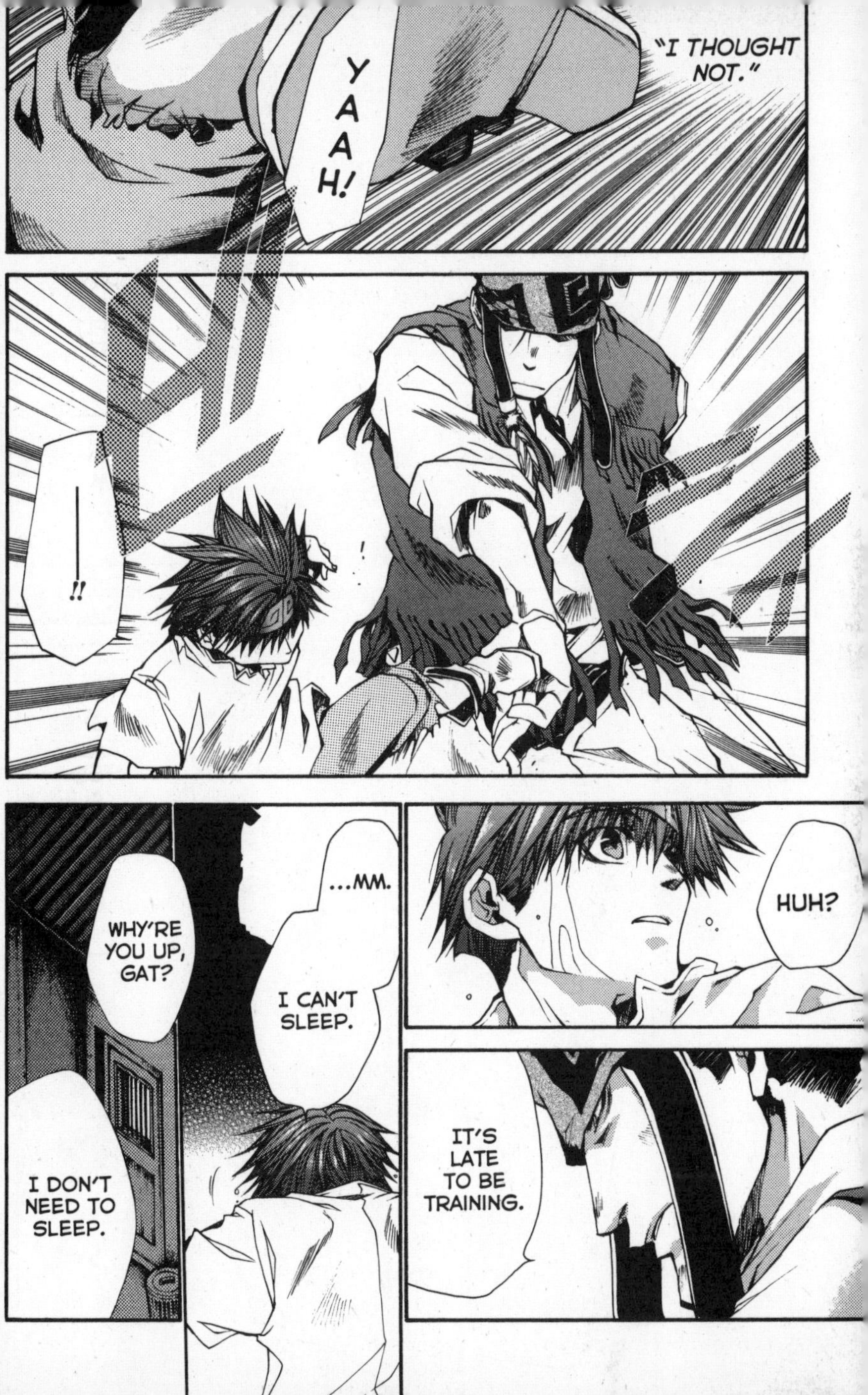
"I THOUGHT NOT."
YAAAH!
—!!
!
HUH?
IT'S LATE TO BE TRAINING.
...MM.
I CAN'T SLEEP.
WHY'RE YOU UP, GAT?
I DON'T NEED TO SLEEP.

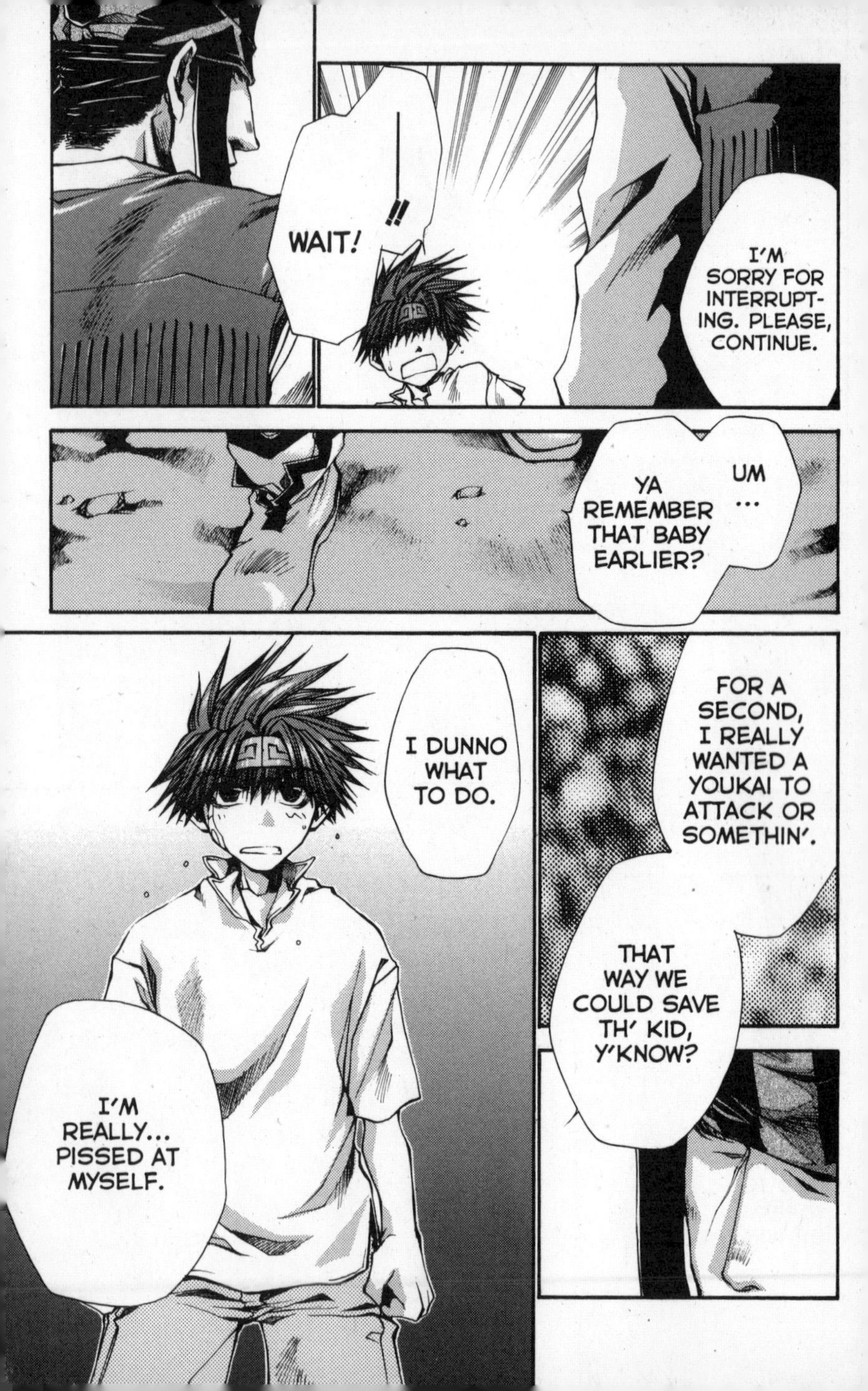
I'M SORRY FOR INTERRUPTING. PLEASE, CONTINUE.
WAIT!
!!
UM ...
YA REMEMBER THAT BABY EARLIER?
FOR A SECOND, I REALLY WANTED A YOUKAI TO ATTACK OR SOMETHIN'.
THAT WAY WE COULD SAVE TH' KID, Y'KNOW?
I DUNNO WHAT TO DO.
I'M REALLY... PISSED AT MYSELF.

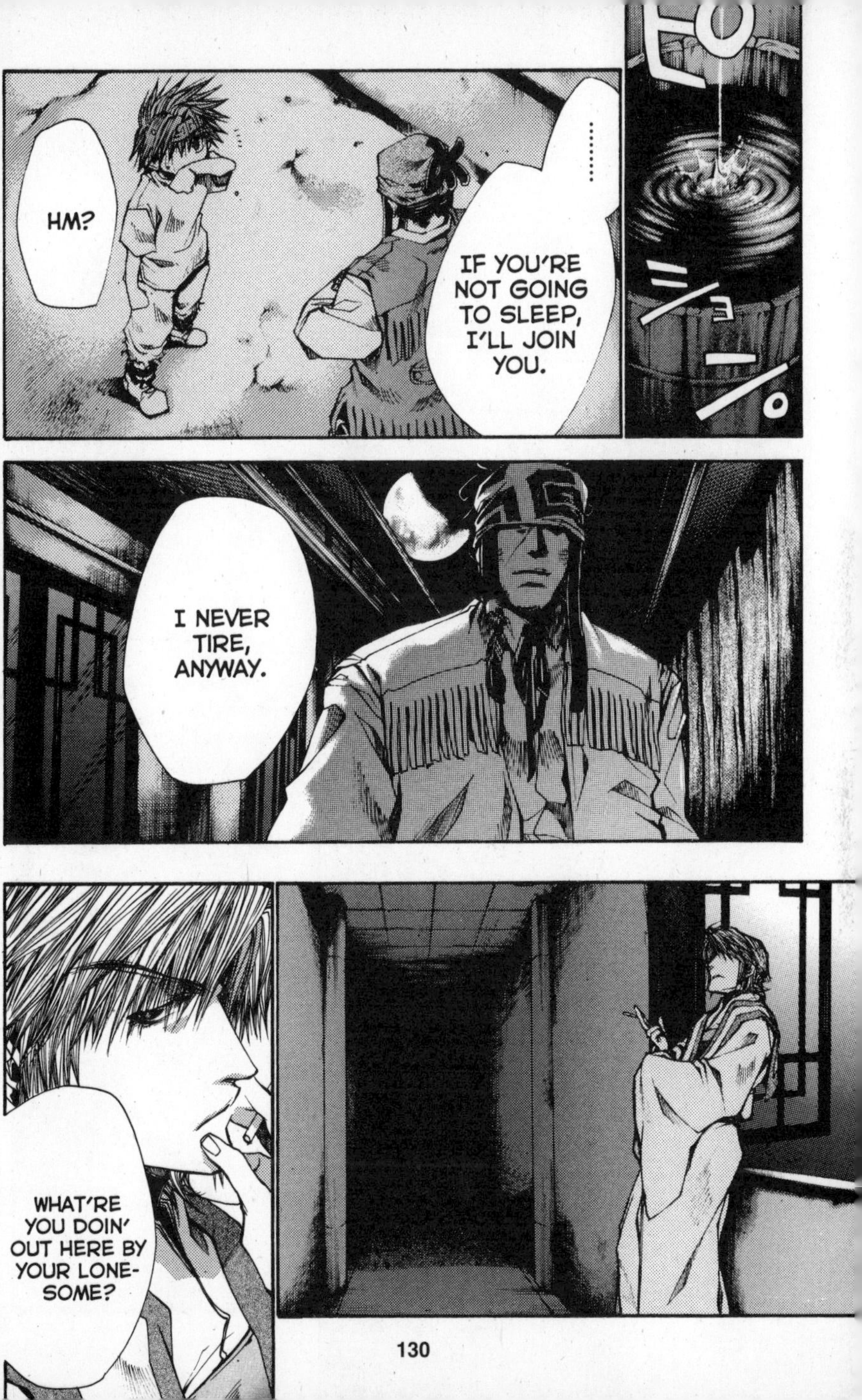
......
IF YOU'RE NOT GOING TO SLEEP, I'LL JOIN YOU.
HM?
I NEVER TIRE, ANYWAY.
WHAT'RE YOU DOIN' OUT HERE BY YOUR LONE-SOME?

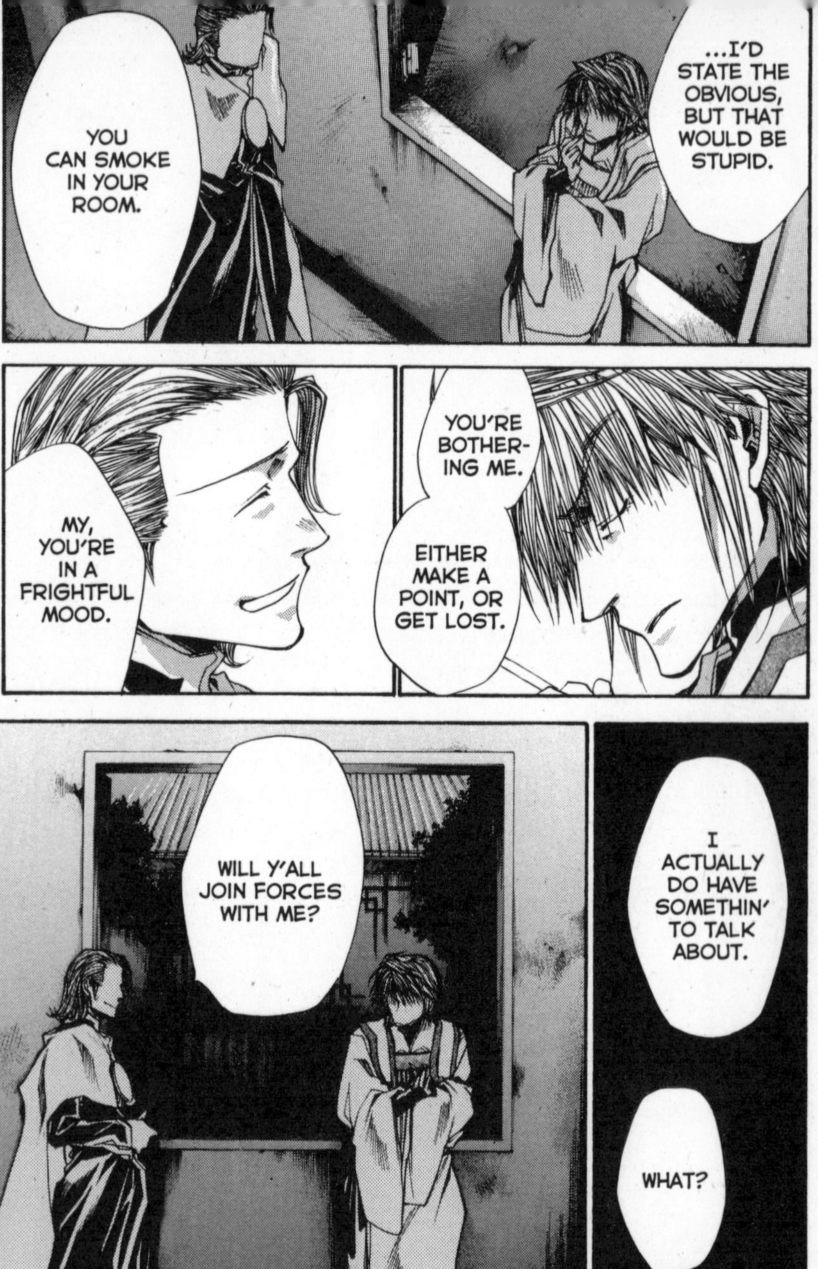
...I'D STATE THE OBVIOUS, BUT THAT WOULD BE STUPID.
YOU CAN SMOKE IN YOUR ROOM.
YOU'RE BOTHERING ME.
EITHER MAKE A POINT, OR GET LOST.
MY, YOU'RE IN A FRIGHTFUL MOOD.
I ACTUALLY DO HAVE SOMETHIN' TO TALK ABOUT.
WHAT?
WILL Y'ALL JOIN FORCES WITH ME?

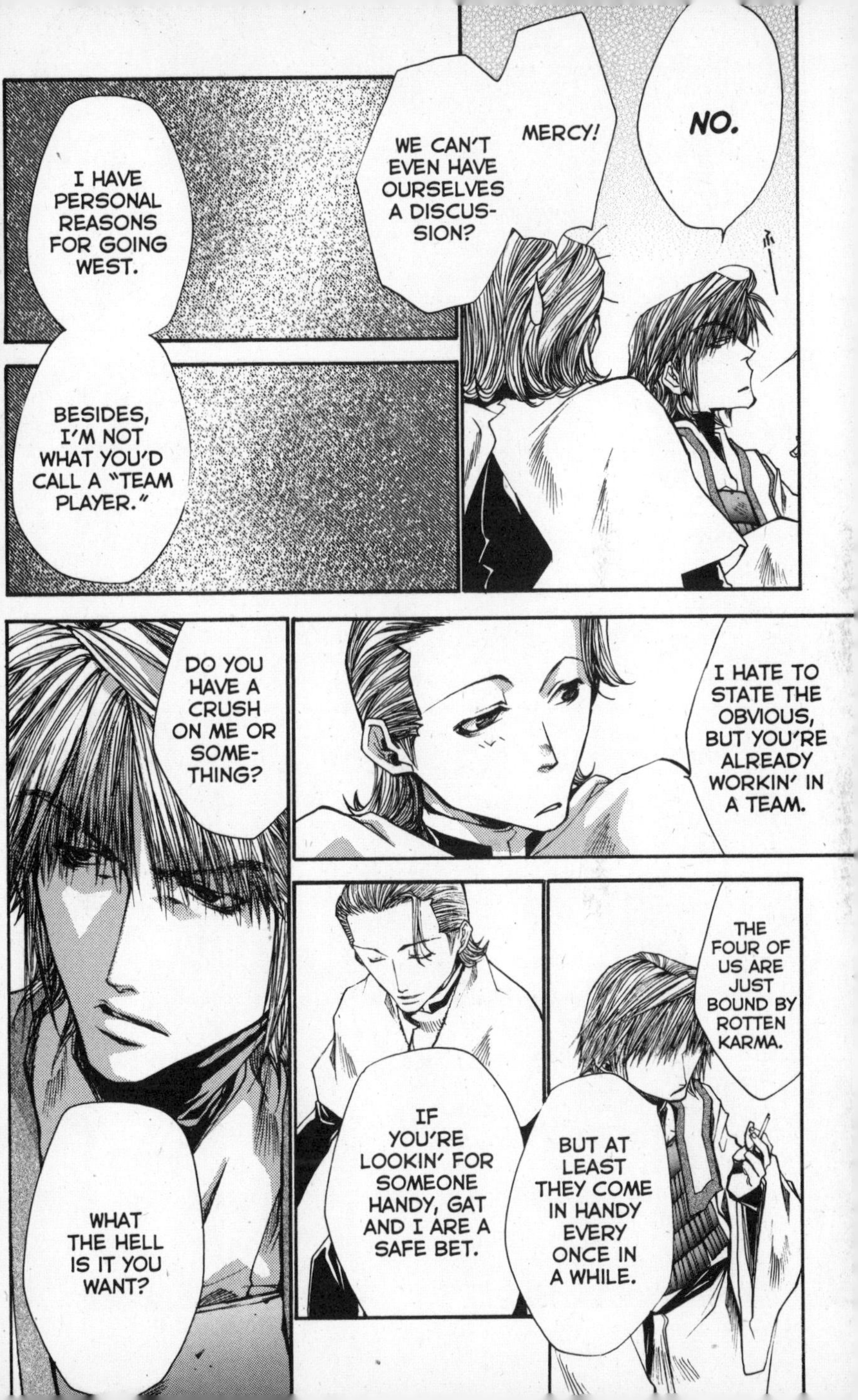
NO.
MERCY!
WE CAN'T EVEN HAVE OURSELVES A DISCUS-SION?
I HAVE PERSONAL REASONS FOR GOING WEST.
BESIDES, I'M NOT WHAT YOU'D CALL A "TEAM PLAYER."
I HATE TO STATE THE OBVIOUS, BUT YOU'RE ALREADY WORKIN' IN A TEAM.
THE FOUR OF US ARE JUST BOUND BY ROTTEN KARMA.
BUT AT LEAST THEY COME IN HANDY EVERY ONCE IN A WHILE.
IF YOU'RE LOOKIN' FOR SOMEONE HANDY, GAT AND I ARE A SAFE BET.
DO YOU HAVE A CRUSH ON ME OR SOME-THING?
WHAT THE HELL IS IT YOU WANT?

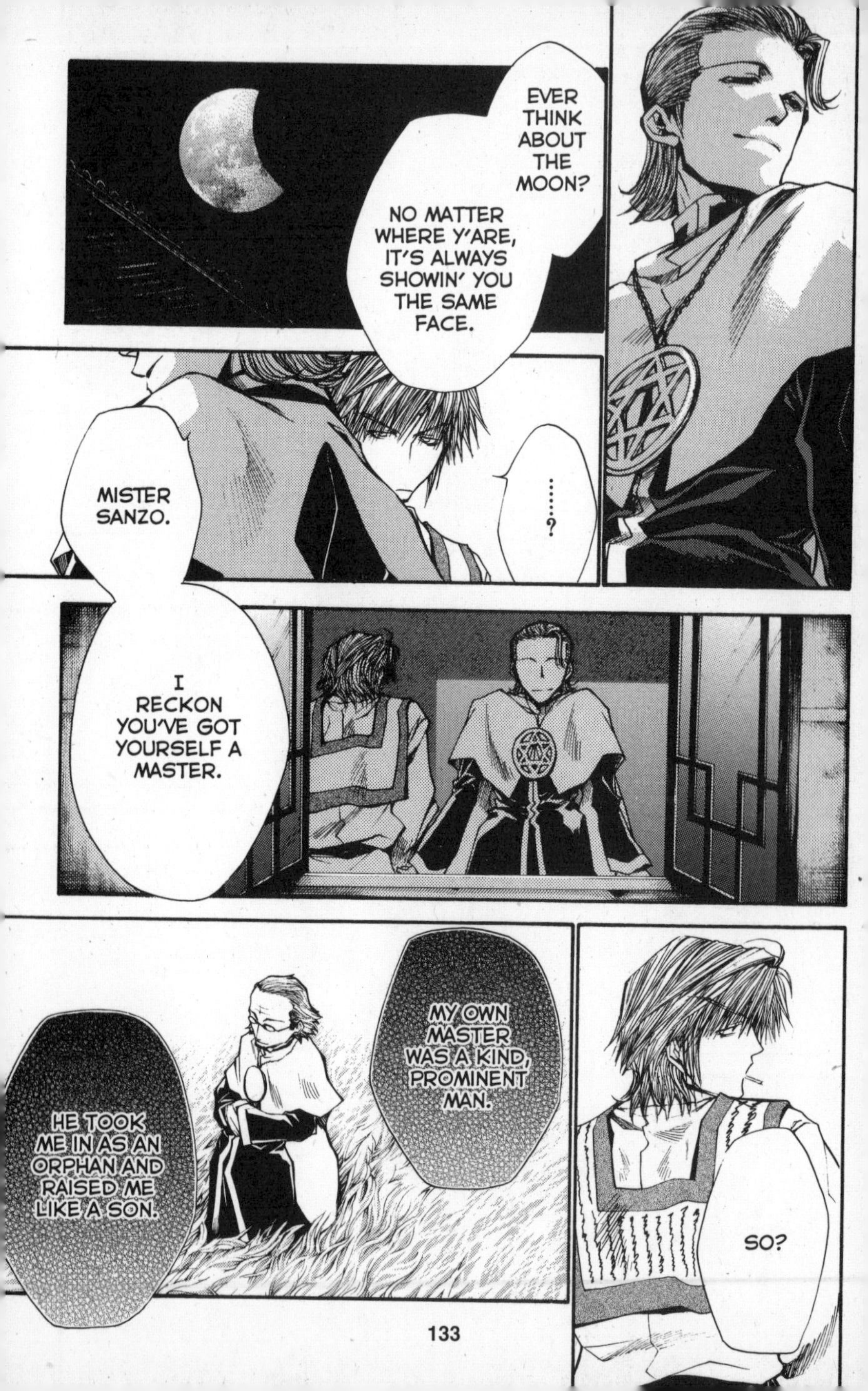
EVER THINK ABOUT THE MOON?
NO MATTER WHERE Y'ARE, IT'S ALWAYS SHOWIN' YOU THE SAME FACE.
......?
MISTER SANZO.
I RECKON YOU'VE GOT YOURSELF A MASTER.
SO?
MY OWN MASTER WAS A KIND, PROMINENT MAN.
HE TOOK ME IN AS AN ORPHAN AND RAISED ME LIKE A SON.

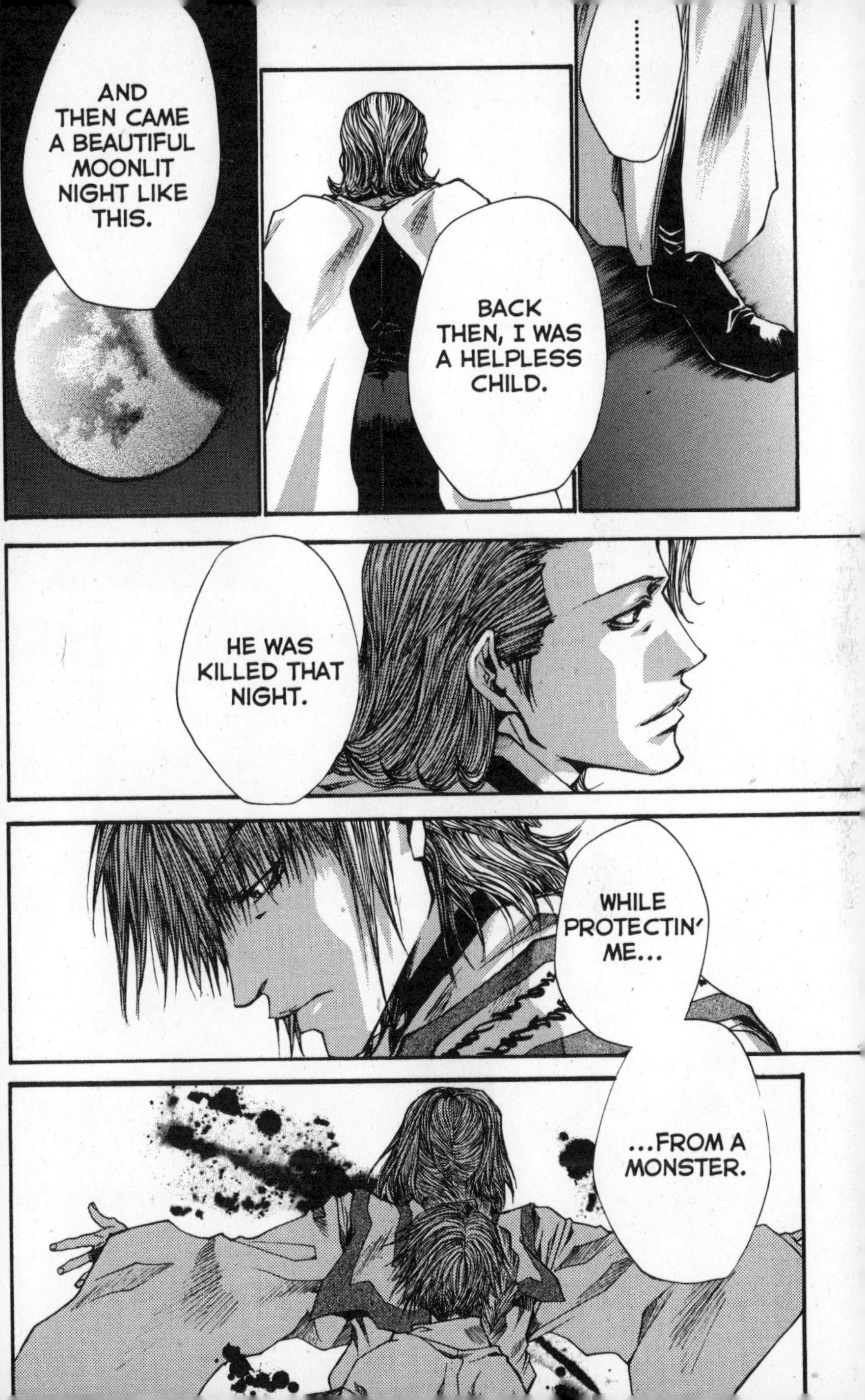

......
BACK THEN, I WAS A HELPLESS CHILD.
AND THEN CAME A BEAUTIFUL MOONLIT NIGHT LIKE THIS.
HE WAS KILLED THAT NIGHT.
WHILE PROTECTIN' ME...
...FROM A MONSTER.

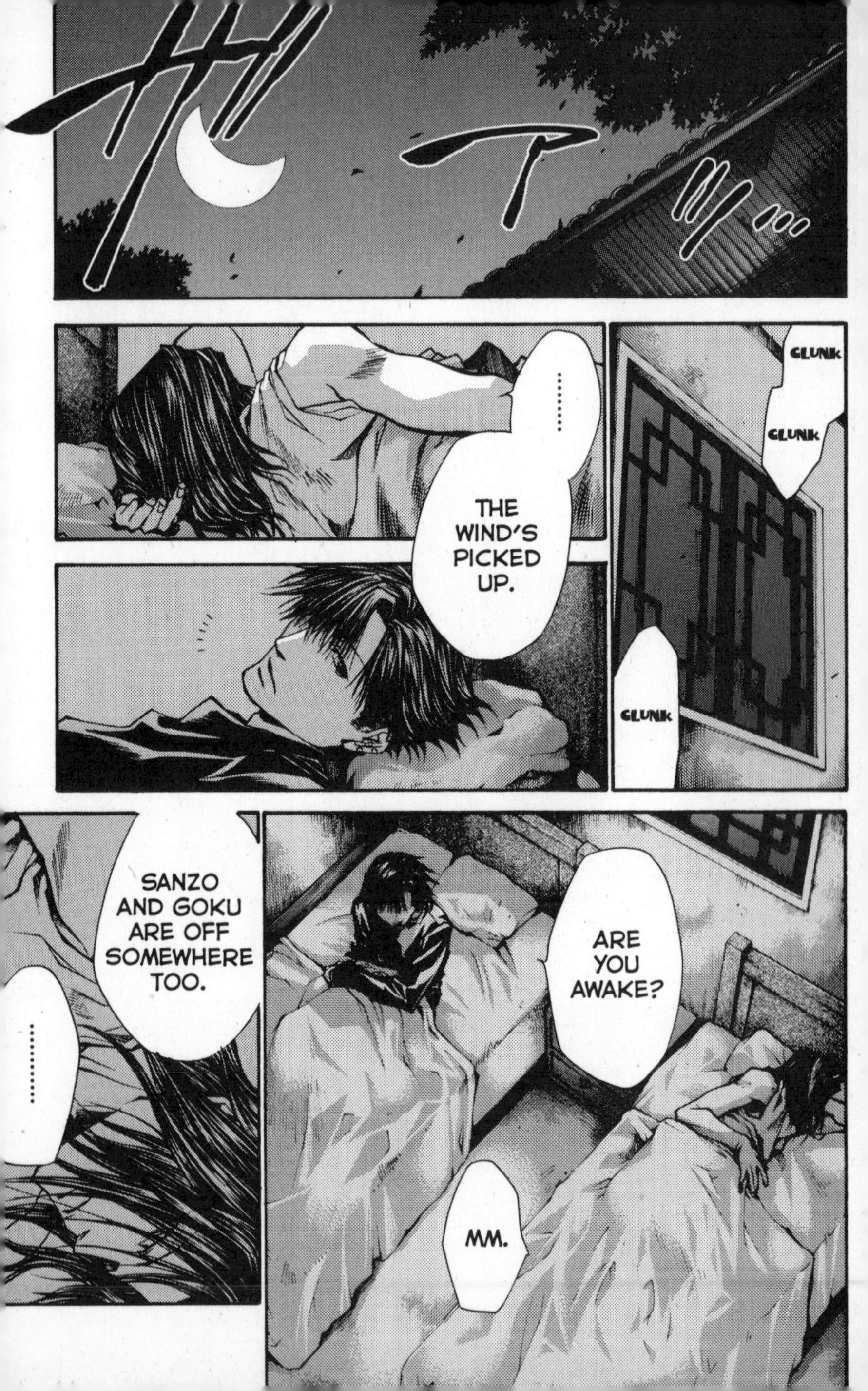

GLUNK
GLUNK
GLUNK
......
THE WIND'S PICKED UP.
ARE YOU AWAKE?
MM.
SANZO AND GOKU ARE OFF SOMEWHERE TOO.
......

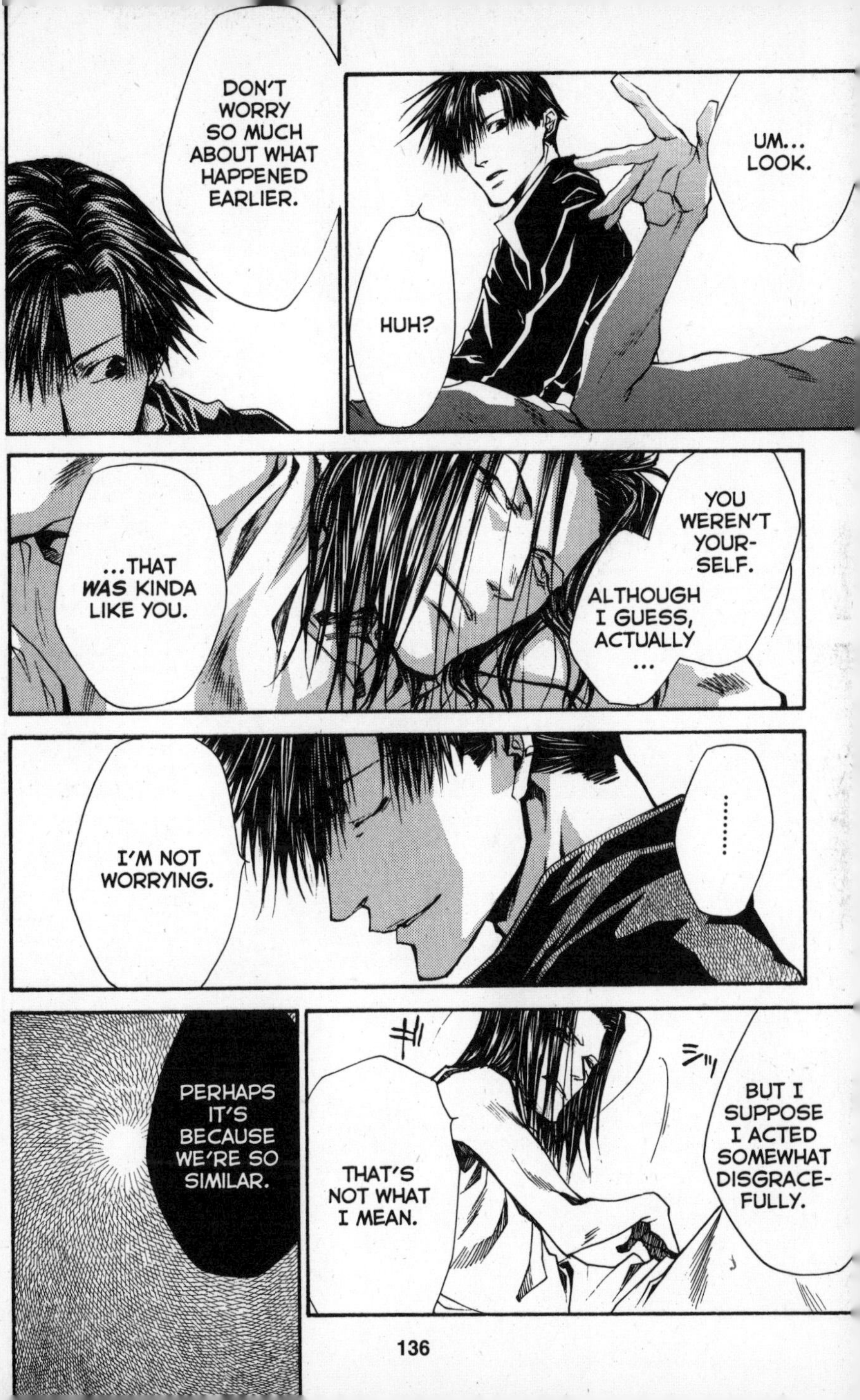
UM... LOOK.
HUH?
DON'T WORRY SO MUCH ABOUT WHAT HAPPENED EARLIER.
YOU WEREN'T YOUR-SELF.
ALTHOUGH I GUESS, ACTUALLY ...
...THAT *WAS* KINDA LIKE YOU.
......
I'M NOT WORRYING.
BUT I SUPPOSE I ACTED SOMEWHAT DISGRACE-FULLY.
THAT'S NOT WHAT I MEAN.
PERHAPS IT'S BECAUSE WE'RE SO SIMILAR.

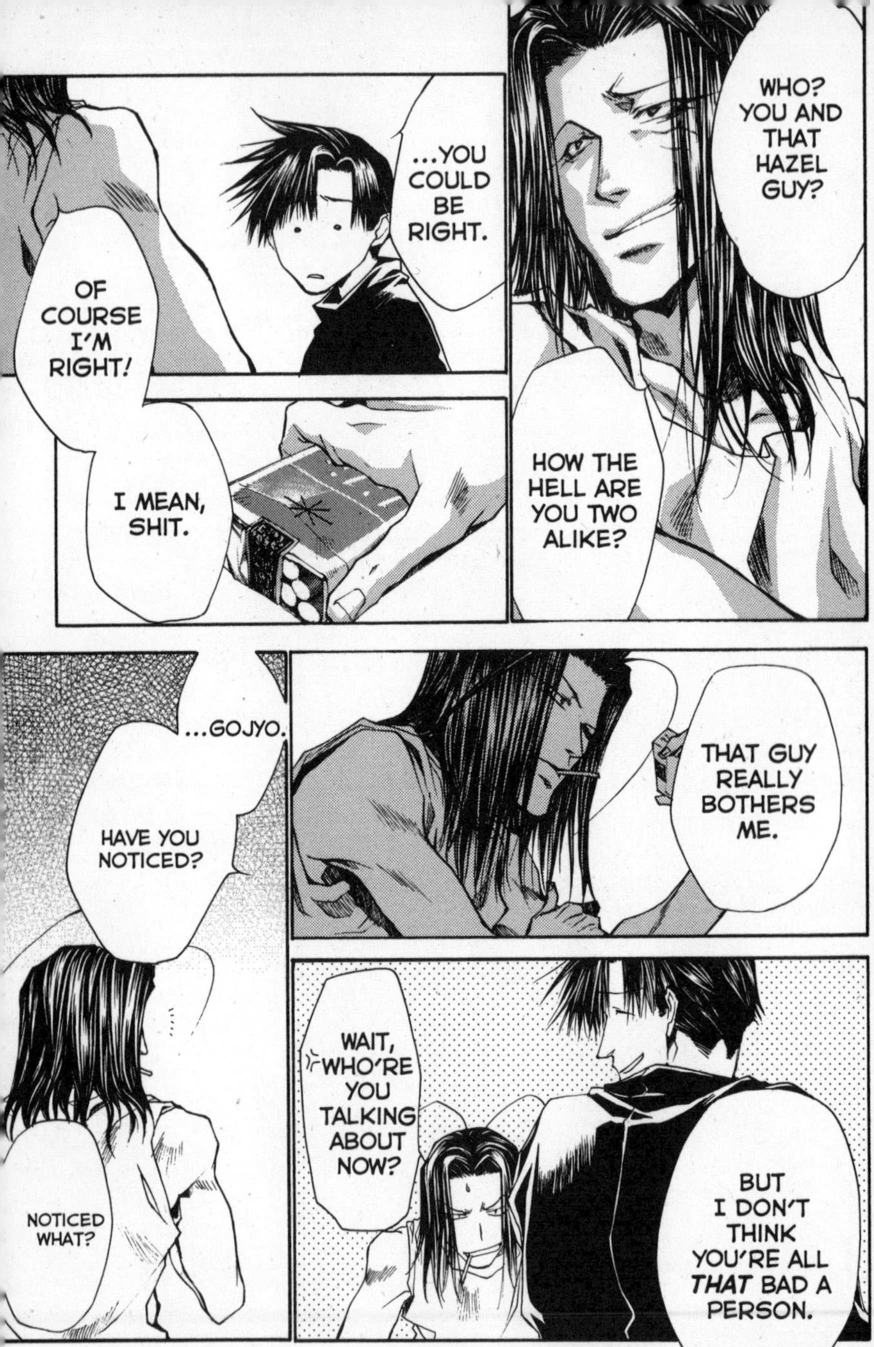
WHO? YOU AND THAT HAZEL GUY?
HOW THE HELL ARE YOU TWO ALIKE?
...YOU COULD BE RIGHT.
OF COURSE I'M RIGHT!
I MEAN, SHIT.
THAT GUY REALLY BOTHERS ME.
BUT I DON'T THINK YOU'RE ALL *THAT* BAD A PERSON.
WAIT, WHO'RE YOU TALKING ABOUT NOW?
...GOJYO.
HAVE YOU NOTICED?
NOTICED WHAT?

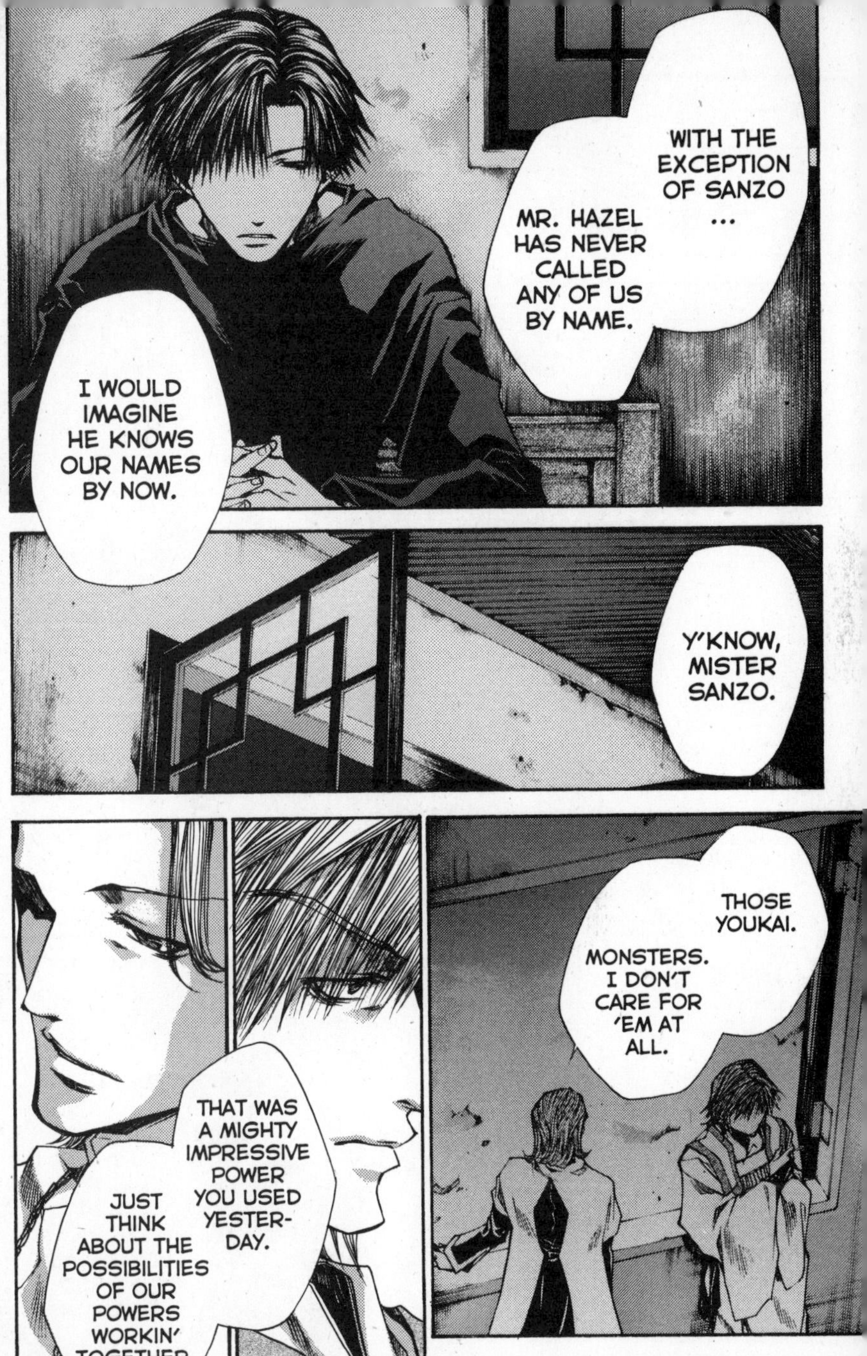
WITH THE EXCEPTION OF SANZO ...
MR. HAZEL HAS NEVER CALLED ANY OF US BY NAME.
I WOULD IMAGINE HE KNOWS OUR NAMES BY NOW.
Y'KNOW, MISTER SANZO.
THOSE YOUKAI.
MONSTERS. I DON'T CARE FOR 'EM AT ALL.
THAT WAS A MIGHTY IMPRESSIVE POWER YOU USED YESTER-DAY.
JUST THINK ABOUT THE POSSIBILITIES OF OUR POWERS WORKIN' TOGETHER.

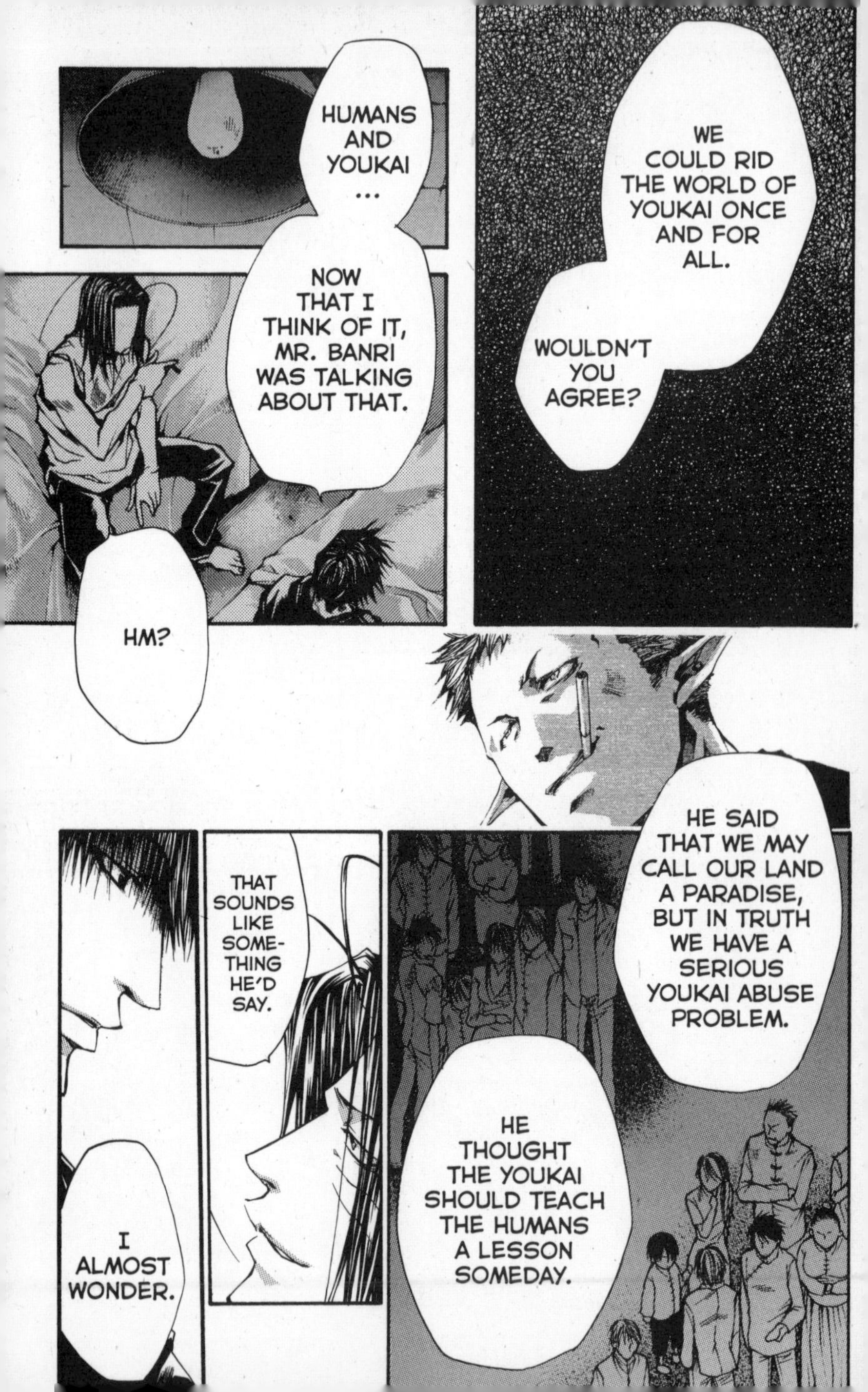
WE COULD RID THE WORLD OF YOUKAI ONCE AND FOR ALL.
WOULDN'T YOU AGREE?
HUMANS AND YOUKAI ...
NOW THAT I THINK OF IT, MR. BANRI WAS TALKING ABOUT THAT.
HM?
HE SAID THAT WE MAY CALL OUR LAND A PARADISE, BUT IN TRUTH WE HAVE A SERIOUS YOUKAI ABUSE PROBLEM.
HE THOUGHT THE YOUKAI SHOULD TEACH THE HUMANS A LESSON SOMEDAY.
THAT SOUNDS LIKE SOME-THING HE'D SAY.
I ALMOST WONDER.

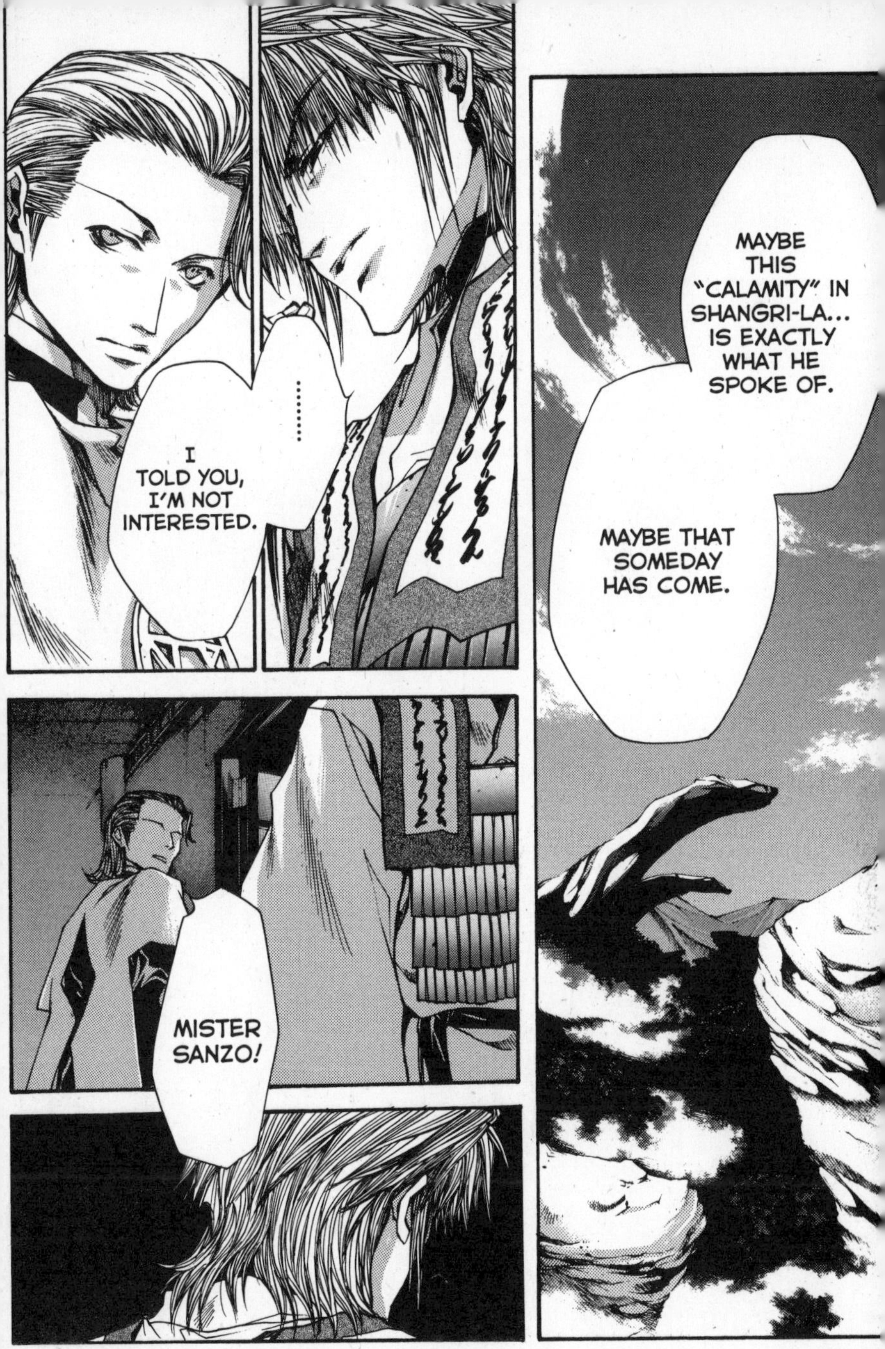
MAYBE THIS "CALAMITY" IN SHANGRI-LA... IS EXACTLY WHAT HE SPOKE OF.
MAYBE THAT SOMEDAY HAS COME.
......
I TOLD YOU, I'M NOT INTERESTED.
MISTER SANZO!

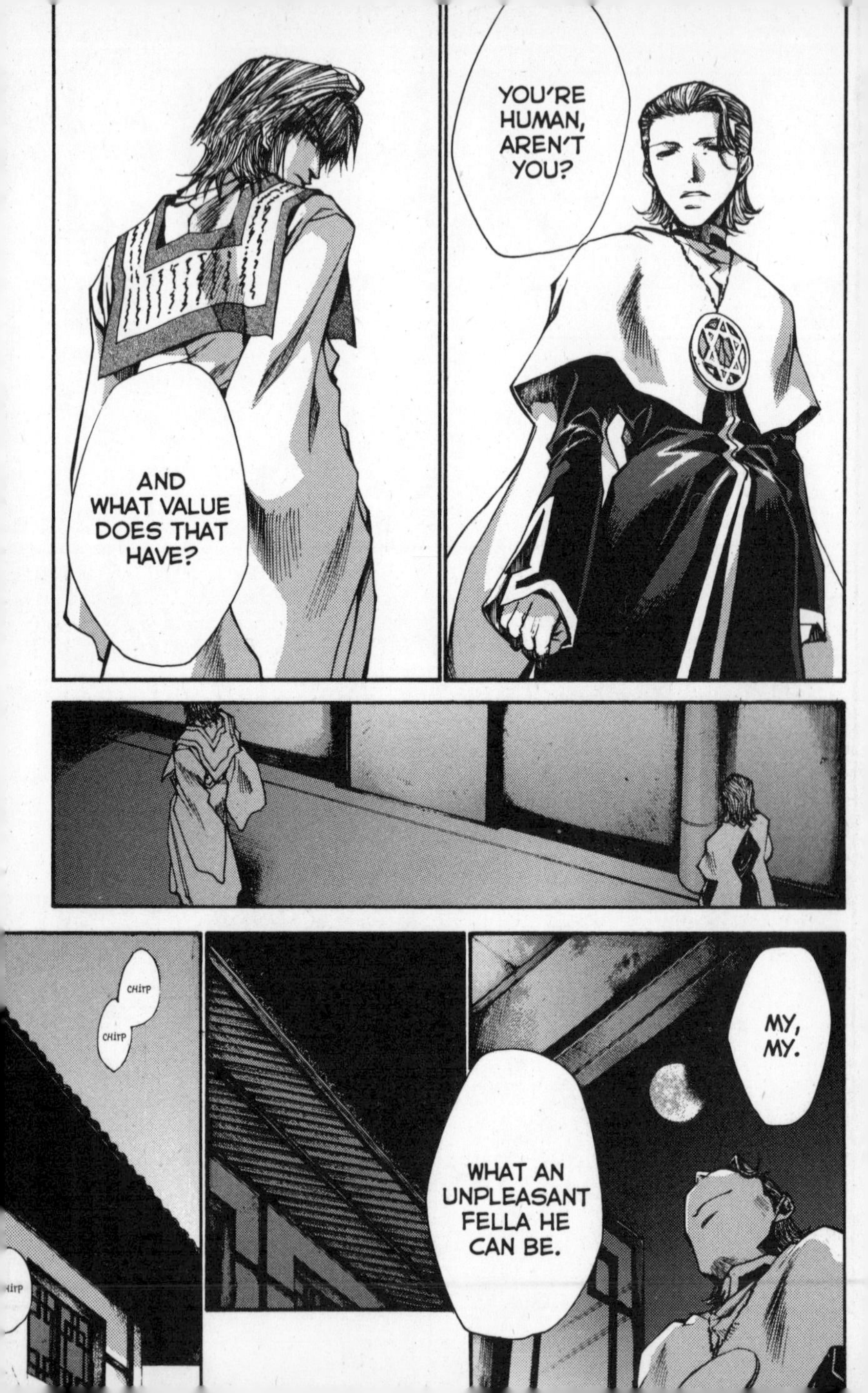
YOU'RE HUMAN, AREN'T YOU?
AND WHAT VALUE DOES THAT HAVE?
MY, MY.
WHAT AN UNPLEASANT FELLA HE CAN BE.
CHIRP
CHIRP

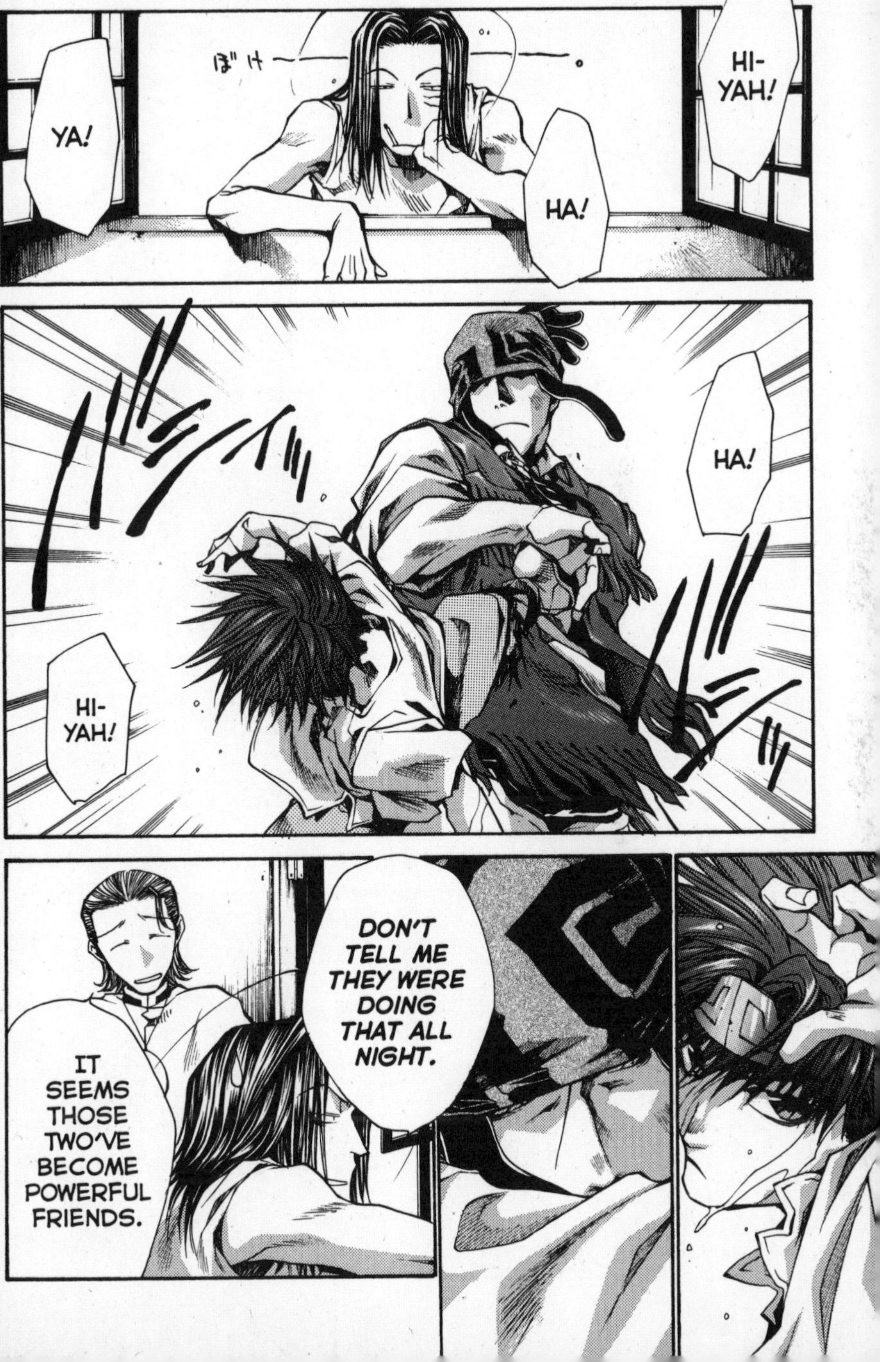
HI-YAH!
HA!
ぼけ〜
YA!
HA!
HI-YAH!
DON'T TELL ME THEY WERE DOING THAT ALL NIGHT.
IT SEEMS THOSE TWO'VE BECOME POWERFUL FRIENDS.

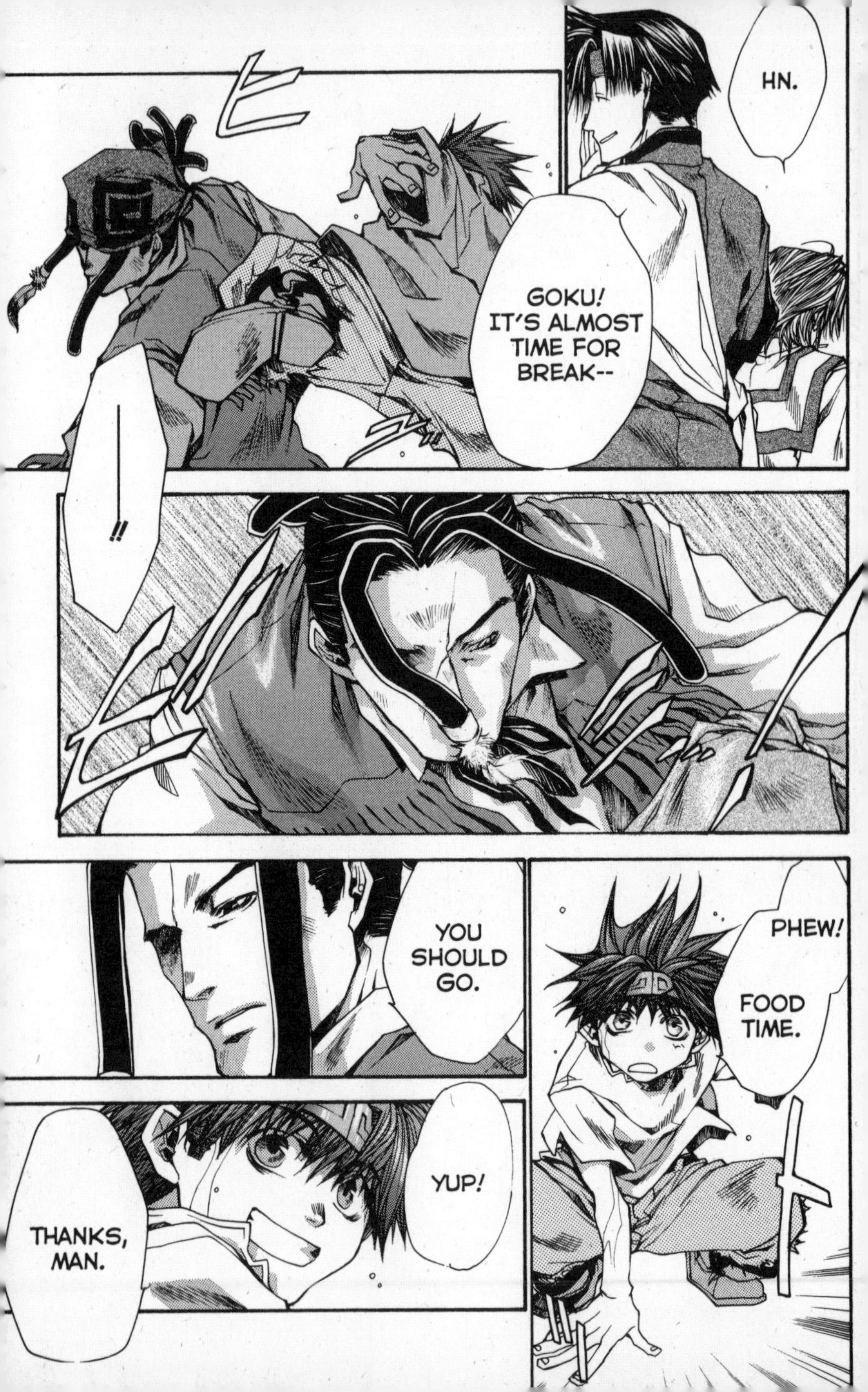
HN.
GOKU! IT'S ALMOST TIME FOR BREAK--
--!!
PHEW!
FOOD TIME.
YOU SHOULD GO.
YUP!
THANKS, MAN.

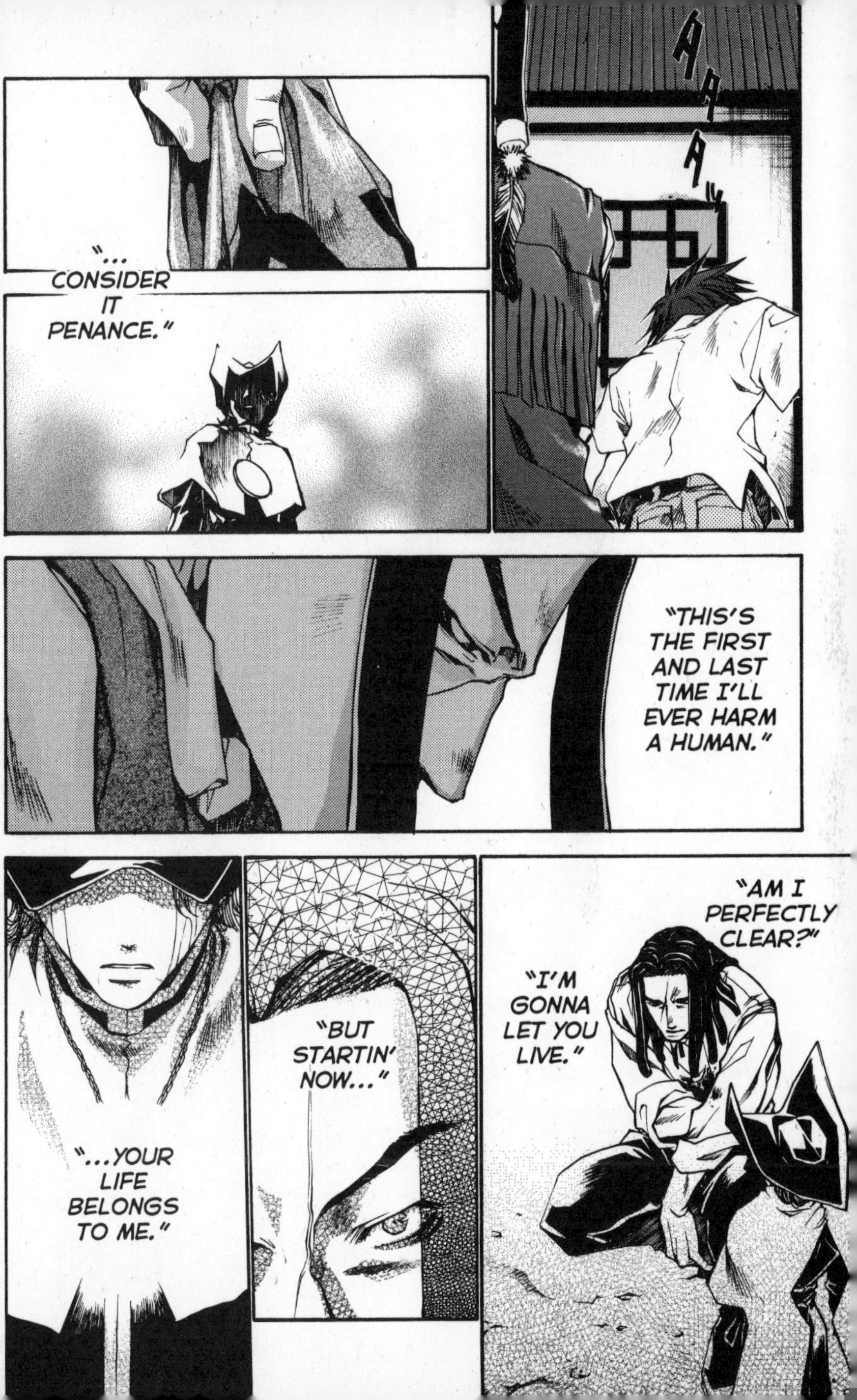

AAAA
"...CONSIDER IT PENANCE."
"THIS'S THE FIRST AND LAST TIME I'LL EVER HARM A HUMAN."
"AM I PERFECTLY CLEAR?"
"I'M GONNA LET YOU LIVE."
"BUT STARTIN' NOW..."
"...YOUR LIFE BELONGS TO ME."

HEADS UP!

IT'S NOT LIKE YA *CAN'T* EAT, RIGHT?

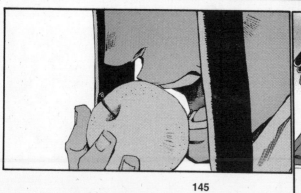

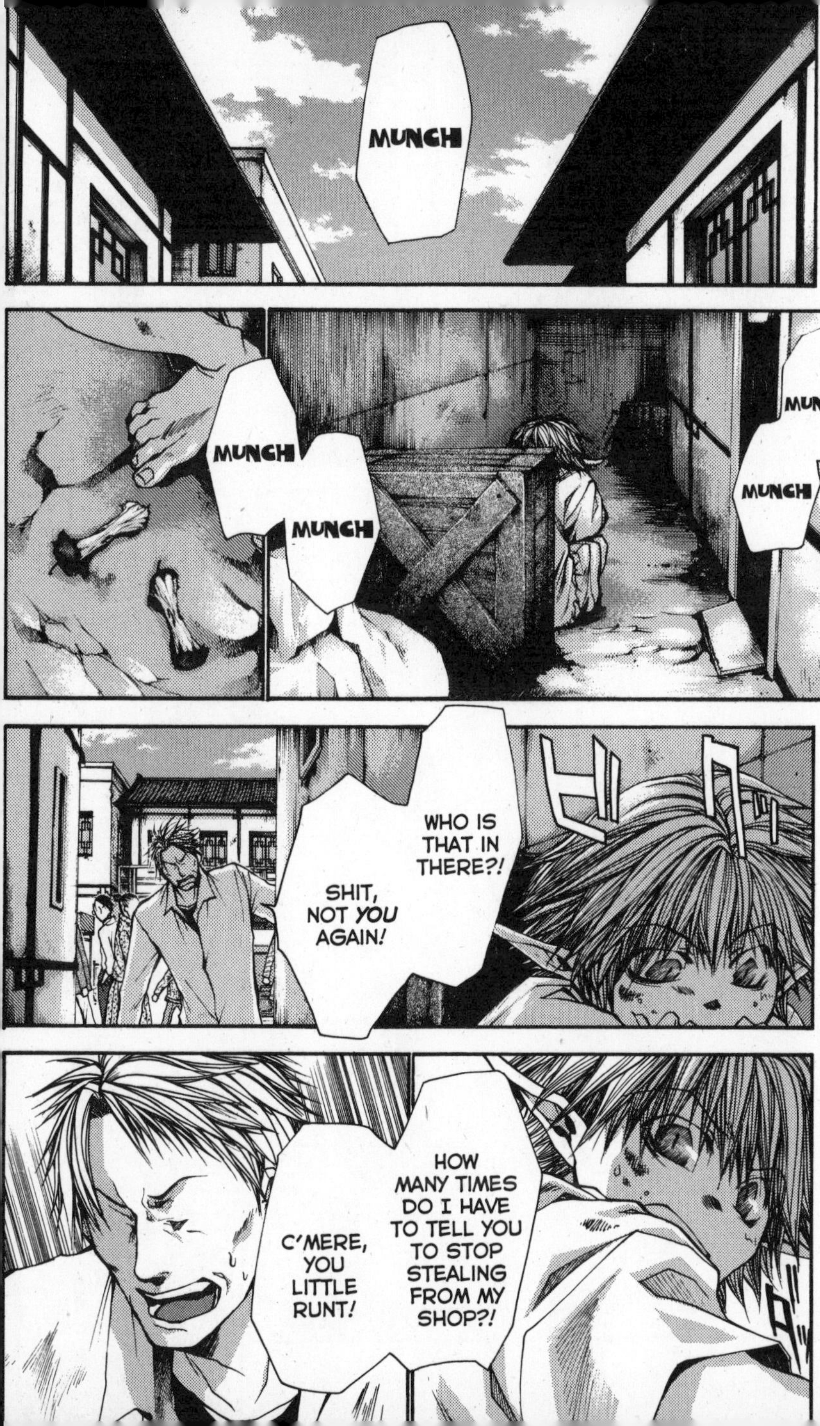
MUNCH
MUNCH
MUNCH
MUNCH
MUNCH
WHO IS THAT IN THERE?!
SHIT, NOT *YOU* AGAIN!
HOW MANY TIMES DO I HAVE TO TELL YOU TO STOP STEALING FROM MY SHOP?!
C'MERE, YOU LITTLE RUNT!

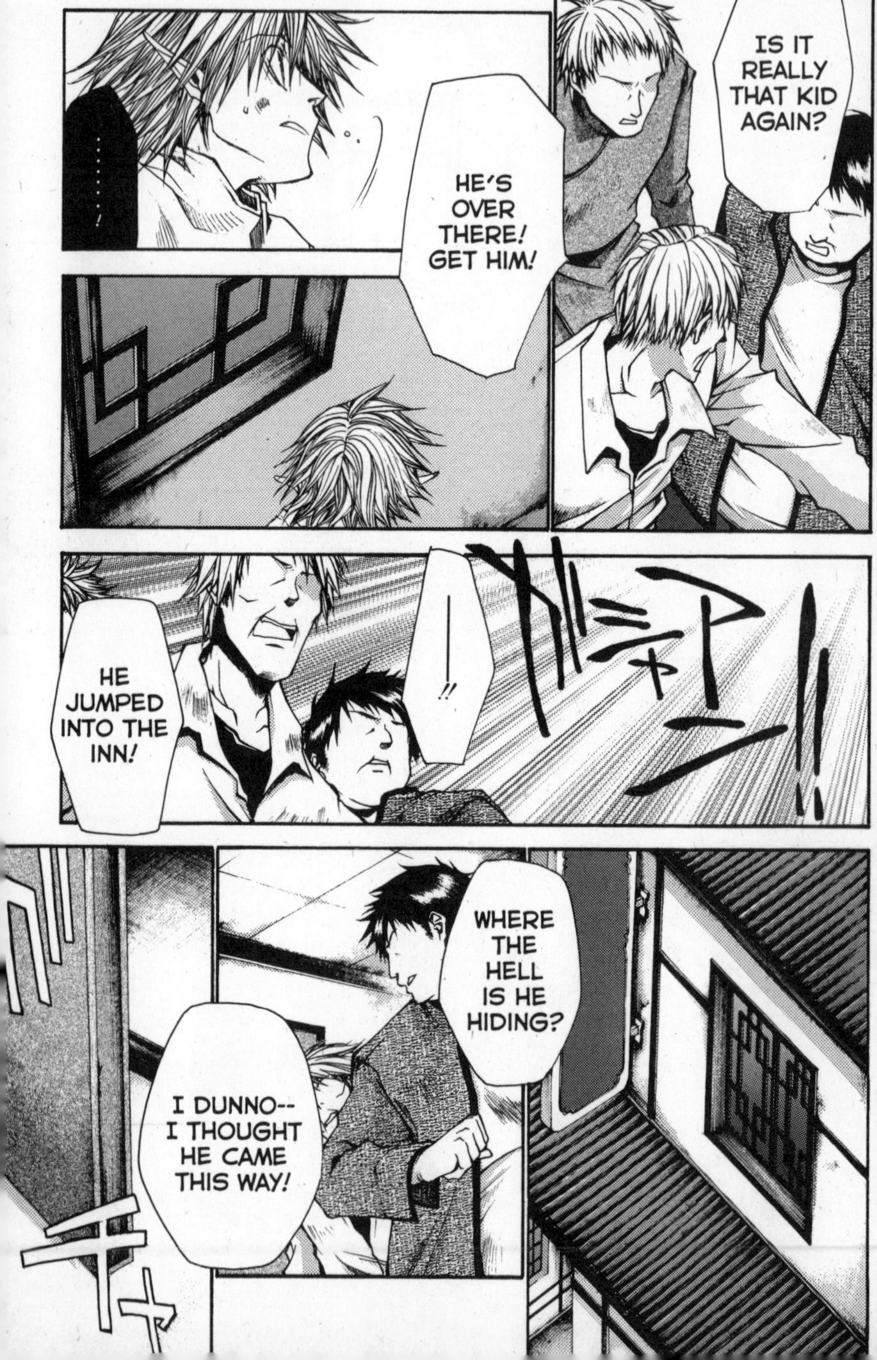

IS IT REALLY THAT KID AGAIN?
......!
HE'S OVER THERE! GET HIM!
ガシャーン!!
—!!
HE JUMPED INTO THE INN!
WHERE THE HELL IS HE HIDING?
I DUNNO-- I THOUGHT HE CAME THIS WAY!
ガチャ

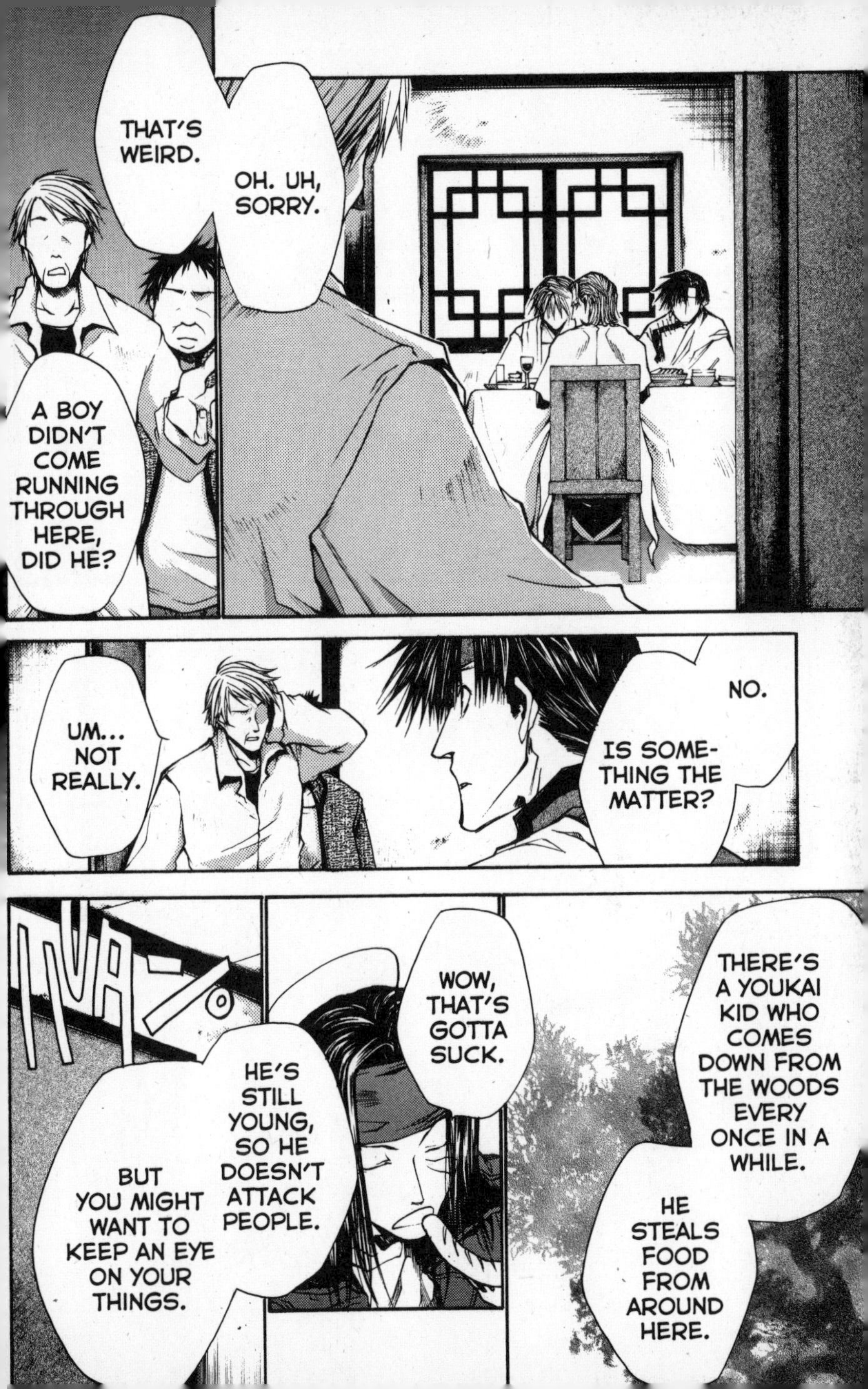
OH. UH, SORRY.
THAT'S WEIRD.
A BOY DIDN'T COME RUNNING THROUGH HERE, DID HE?
NO.
IS SOME-THING THE MATTER?
UM... NOT REALLY.
THERE'S A YOUKAI KID WHO COMES DOWN FROM THE WOODS EVERY ONCE IN A WHILE.
HE STEALS FOOD FROM AROUND HERE.
WOW, THAT'S GOTTA SUCK.
HE'S STILL YOUNG, SO HE DOESN'T ATTACK PEOPLE.
BUT YOU MIGHT WANT TO KEEP AN EYE ON YOUR THINGS.

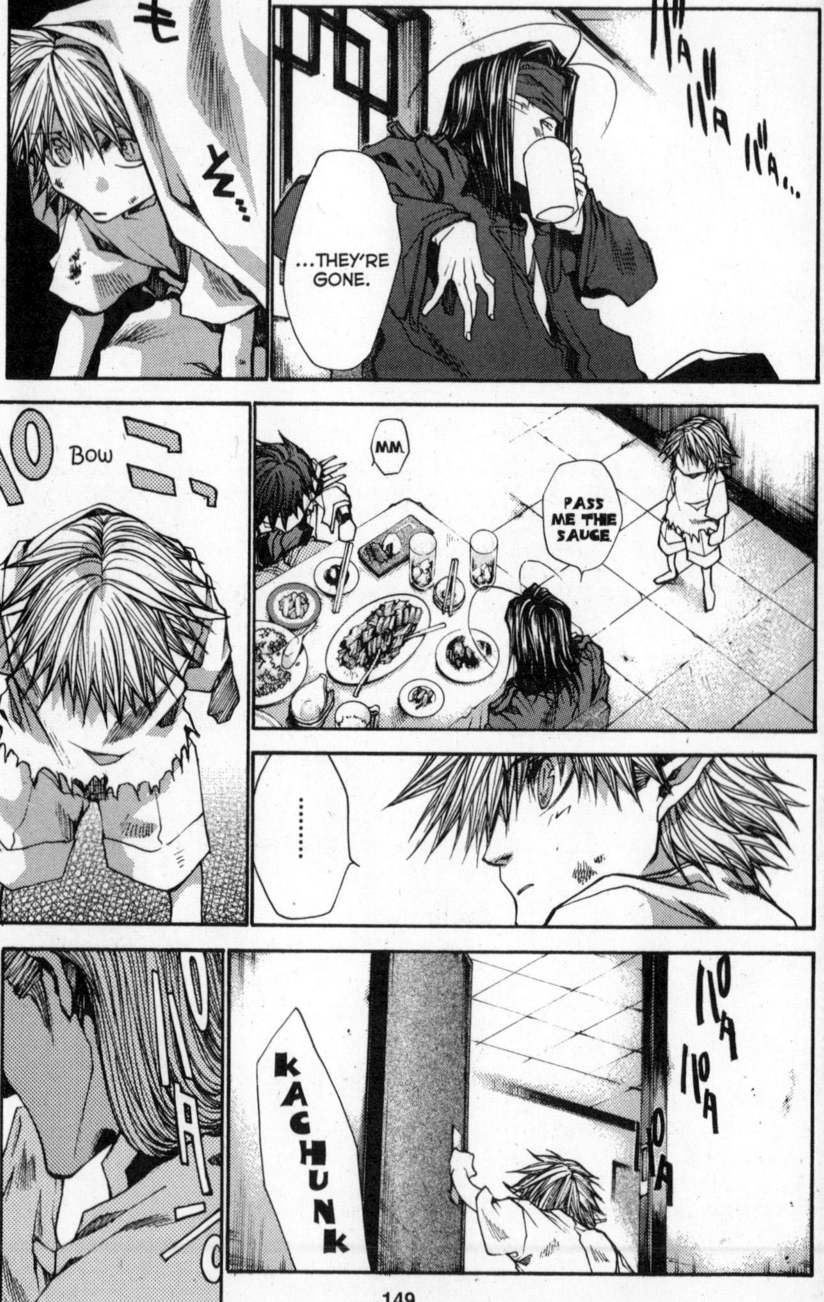
...THEY'RE GONE.
もぞ…
MM
PASS ME THE SAUCE
......
Bow
KACHUNK

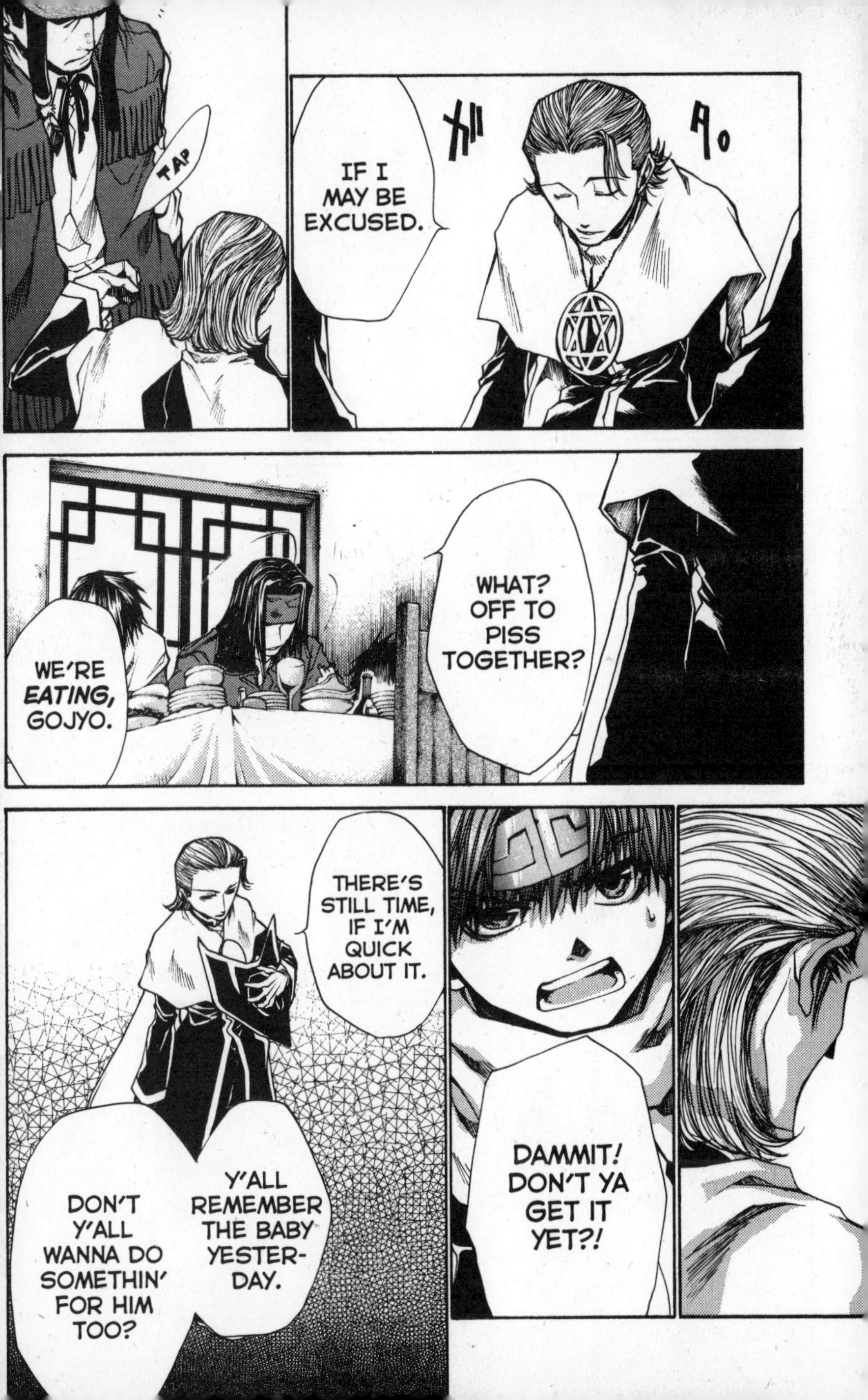
IF I MAY BE EXCUSED.
TAP
WHAT? OFF TO PISS TOGETHER?
WE'RE *EATING,* GOJYO.
DAMMIT! DON'T YA GET IT YET?!
THERE'S STILL TIME, IF I'M QUICK ABOUT IT.
Y'ALL REMEMBER THE BABY YESTER-DAY.
DON'T Y'ALL WANNA DO SOMETHIN' FOR HIM TOO?

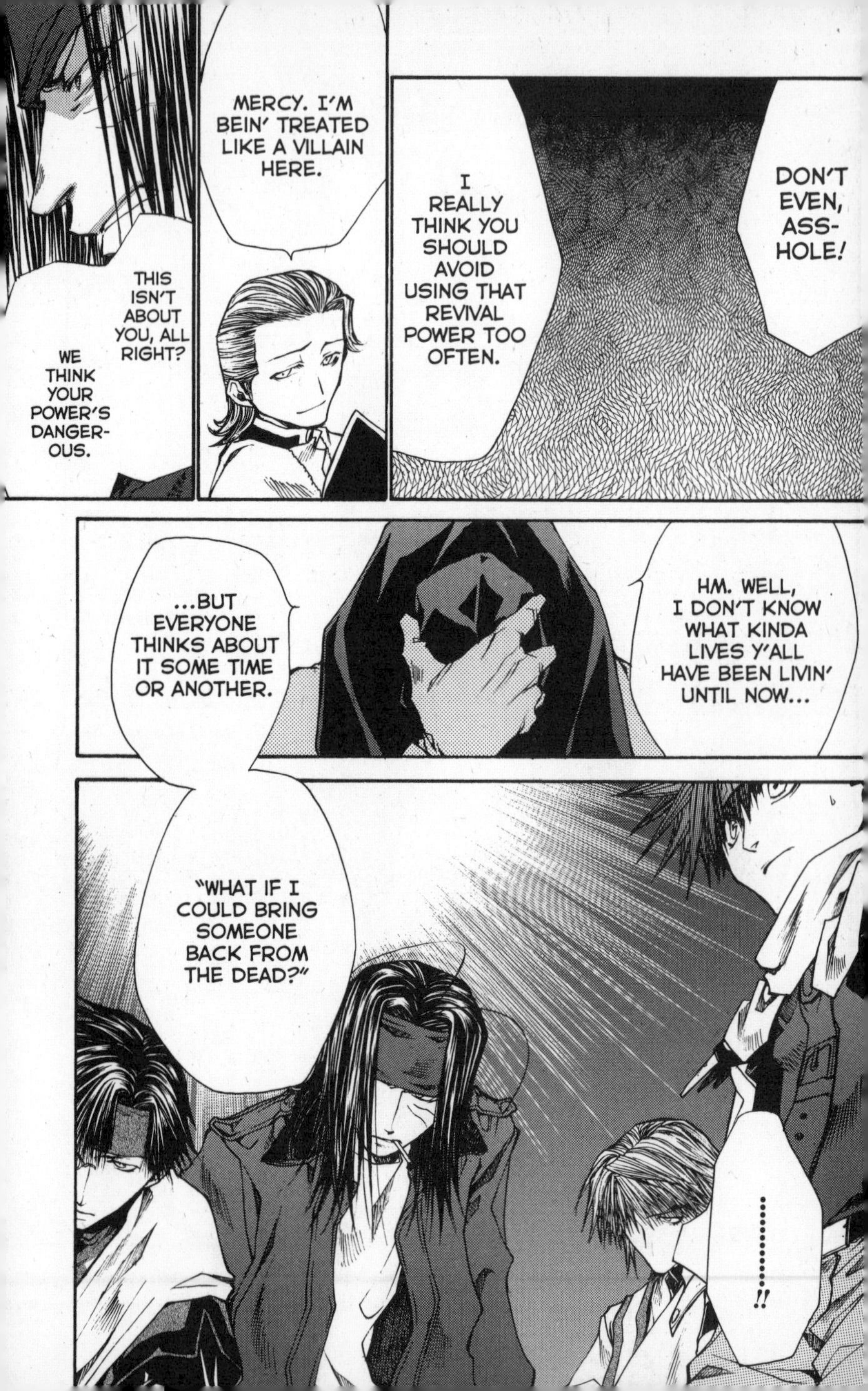
DON'T EVEN, ASS-HOLE!
I REALLY THINK YOU SHOULD AVOID USING THAT REVIVAL POWER TOO OFTEN.
MERCY. I'M BEIN' TREATED LIKE A VILLAIN HERE.
THIS ISN'T ABOUT YOU, ALL RIGHT?
WE THINK YOUR POWER'S DANGER-OUS.
HM. WELL, I DON'T KNOW WHAT KINDA LIVES Y'ALL HAVE BEEN LIVIN' UNTIL NOW...
...BUT EVERYONE THINKS ABOUT IT SOME TIME OR ANOTHER.
"WHAT IF I COULD BRING SOMEONE BACK FROM THE DEAD?"
.........!!

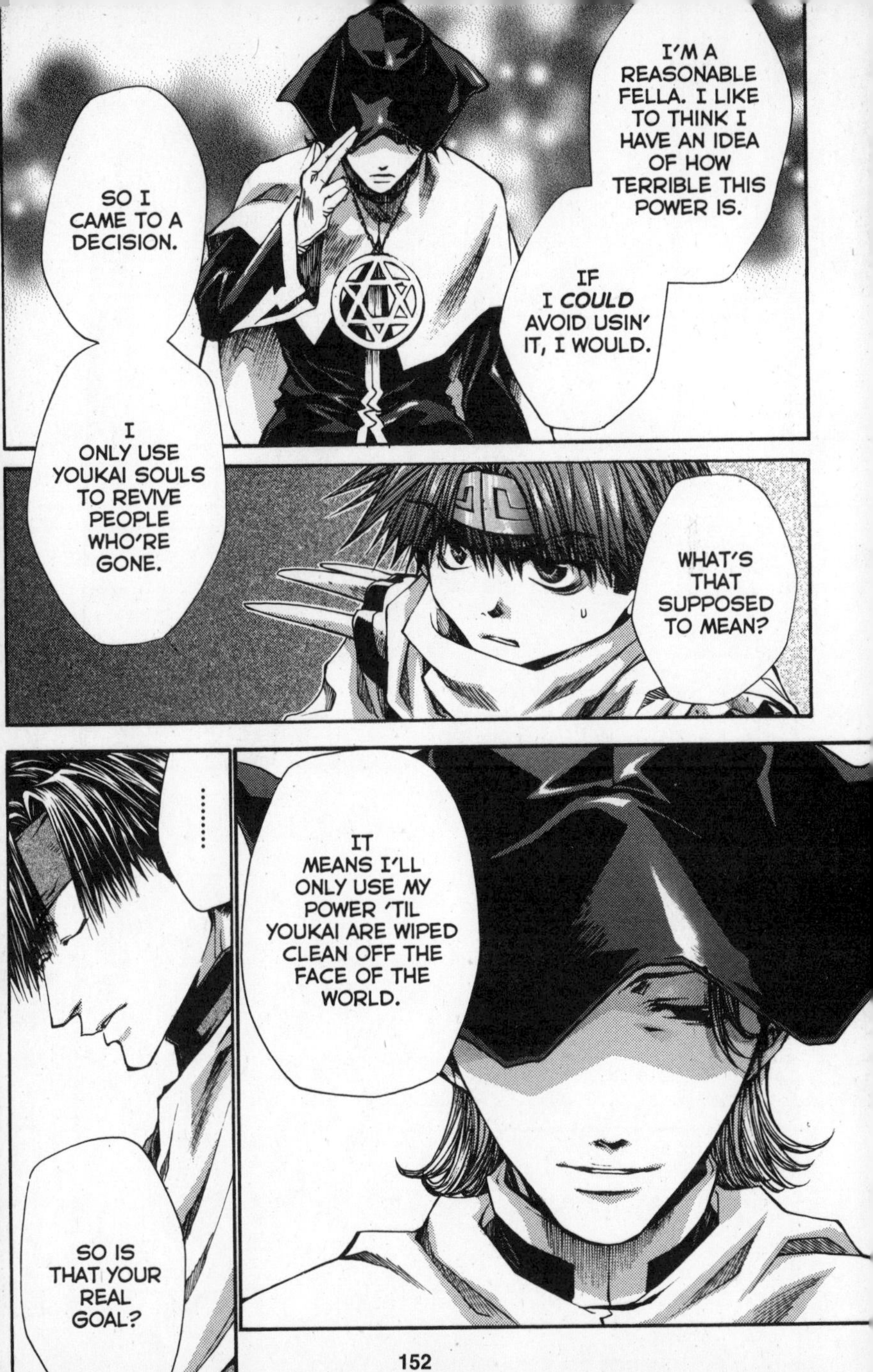
I'M A REASONABLE FELLA. I LIKE TO THINK I HAVE AN IDEA OF HOW TERRIBLE THIS POWER IS.
IF I *COULD* AVOID USIN' IT, I WOULD.
SO I CAME TO A DECISION.
I ONLY USE YOUKAI SOULS TO REVIVE PEOPLE WHO'RE GONE.
WHAT'S THAT SUPPOSED TO MEAN?
IT MEANS I'LL ONLY USE MY POWER 'TIL YOUKAI ARE WIPED CLEAN OFF THE FACE OF THE WORLD.
......
SO IS THAT YOUR REAL GOAL?

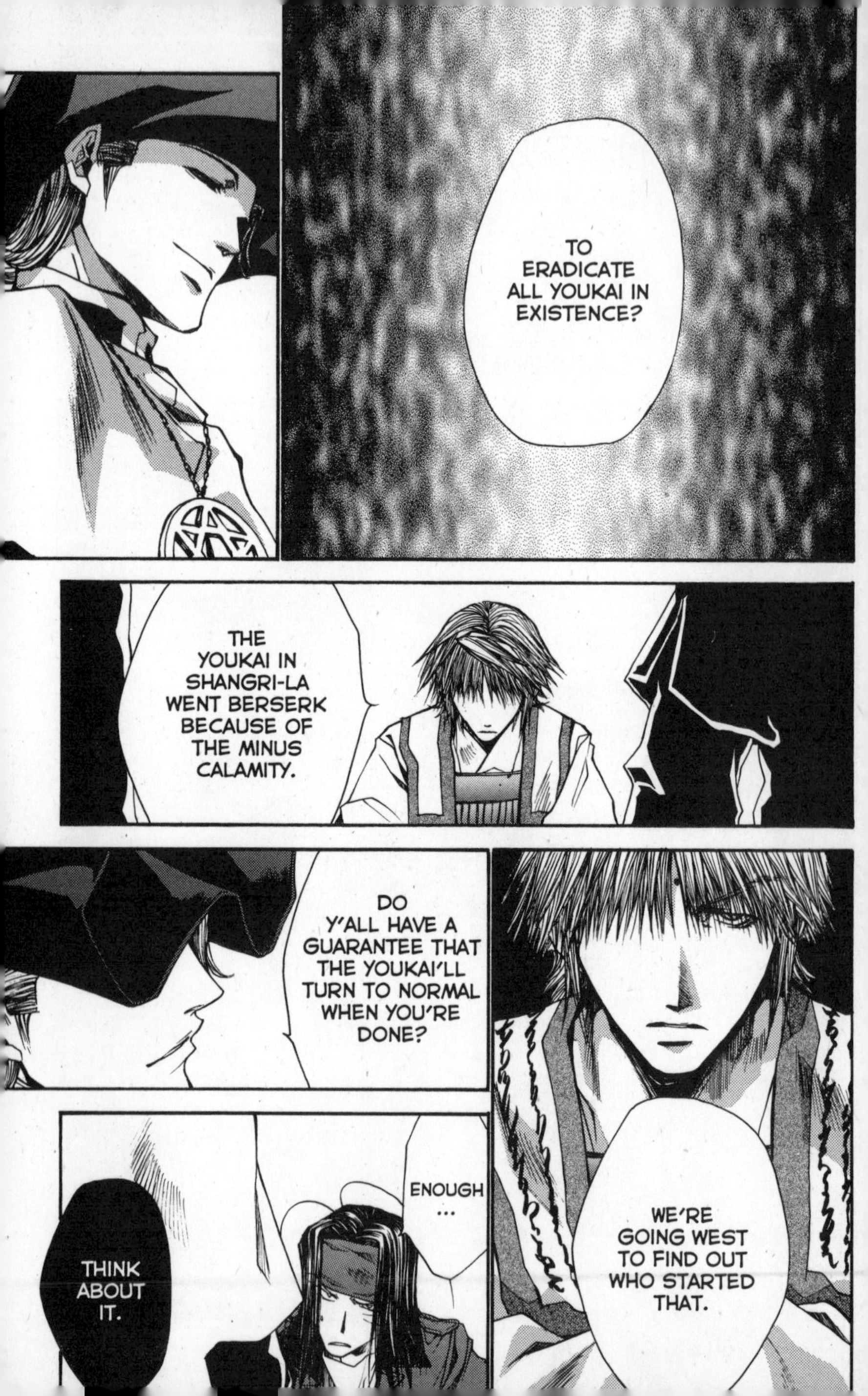
TO ERADICATE ALL YOUKAI IN EXISTENCE?
THE YOUKAI IN SHANGRI-LA WENT BERSERK BECAUSE OF THE MINUS CALAMITY.
WE'RE GOING WEST TO FIND OUT WHO STARTED THAT.
DO Y'ALL HAVE A GUARANTEE THAT THE YOUKAI'LL TURN TO NORMAL WHEN YOU'RE DONE?
ENOUGH...
THINK ABOUT IT.

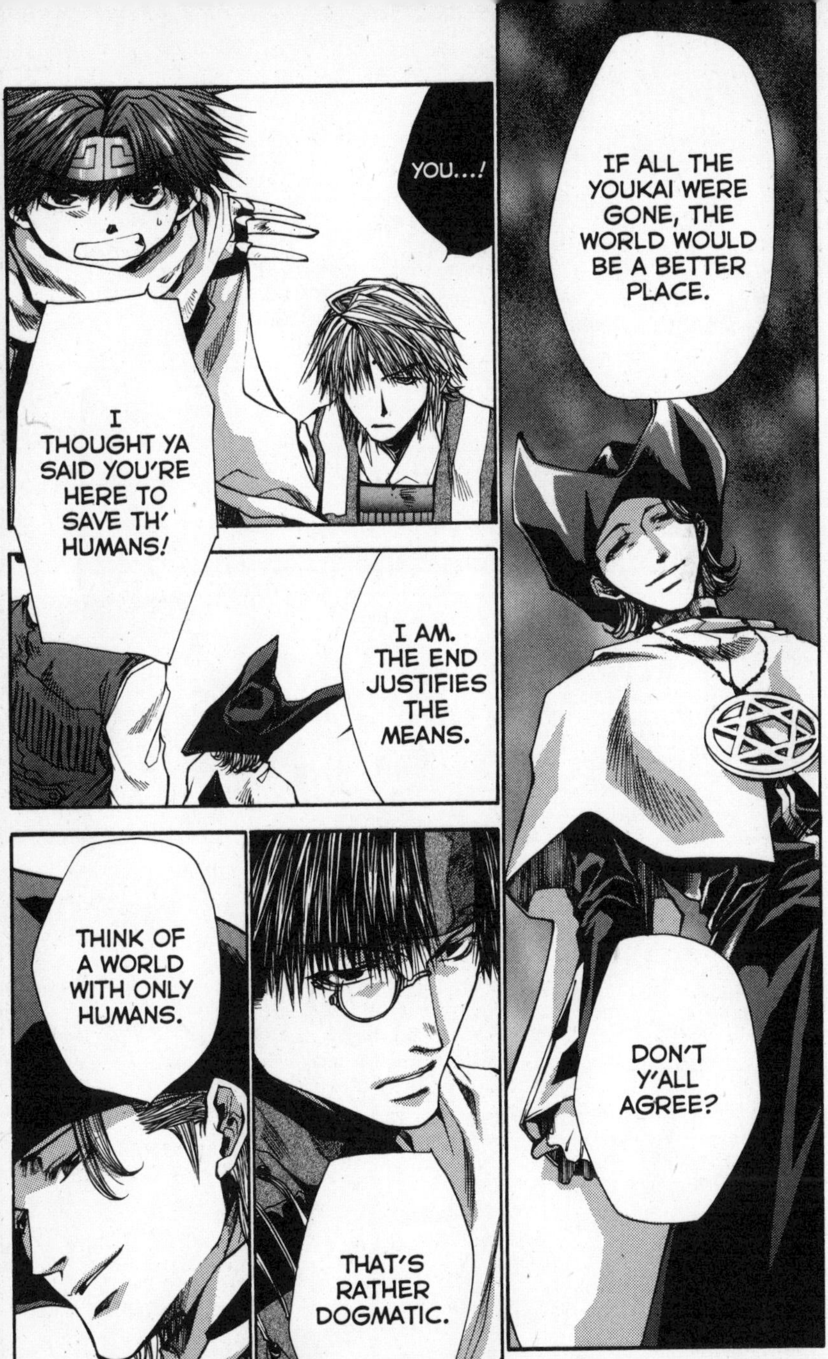
IF ALL THE YOUKAI WERE GONE, THE WORLD WOULD BE A BETTER PLACE.
DON'T Y'ALL AGREE?
YOU...!
I THOUGHT YA SAID YOU'RE HERE TO SAVE TH' HUMANS!
I AM. THE END JUSTIFIES THE MEANS.
THAT'S RATHER DOGMATIC.
THINK OF A WORLD WITH ONLY HUMANS.

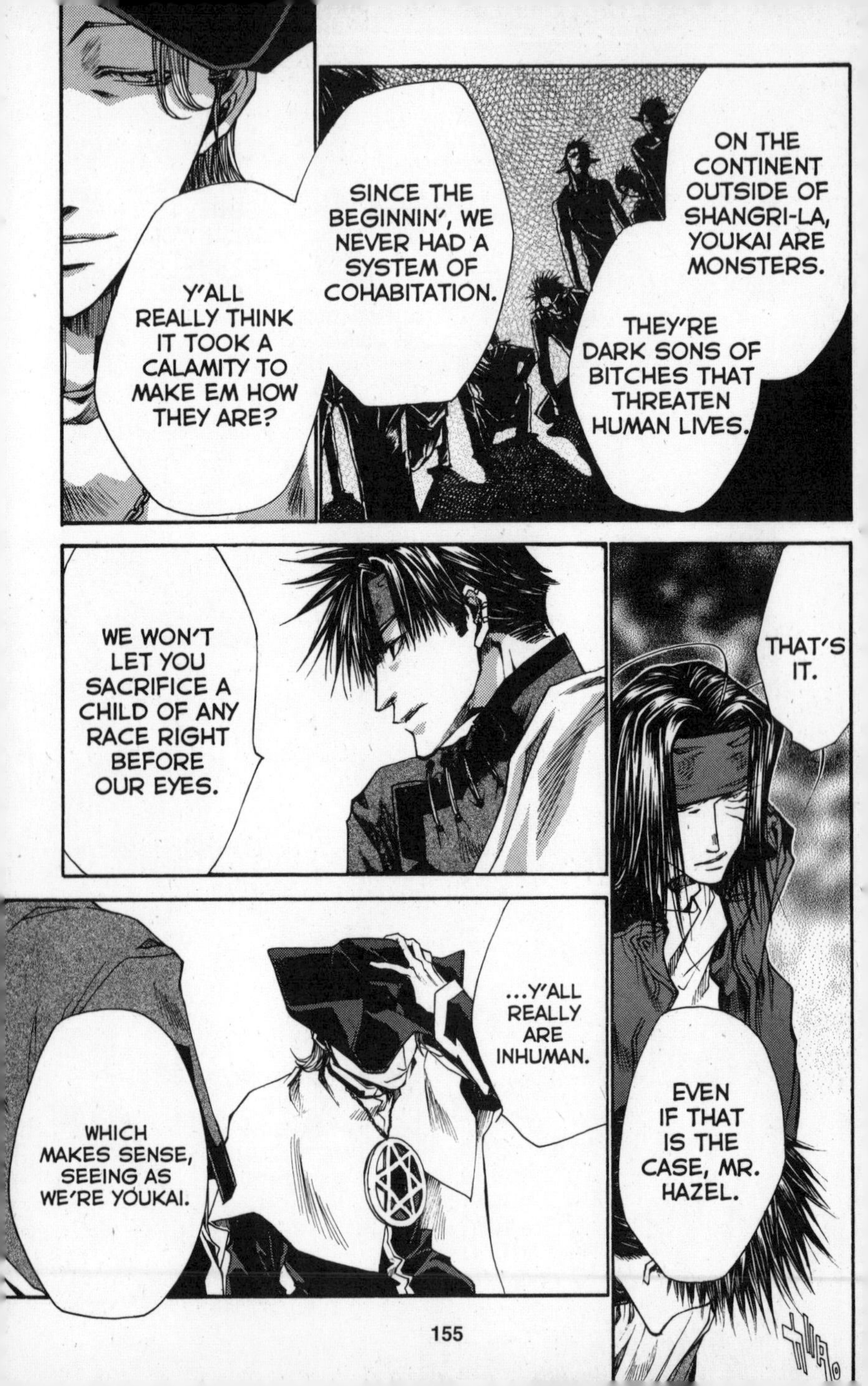
ON THE CONTINENT OUTSIDE OF SHANGRI-LA, YOUKAI ARE MONSTERS.
THEY'RE DARK SONS OF BITCHES THAT THREATEN HUMAN LIVES.
SINCE THE BEGINNIN', WE NEVER HAD A SYSTEM OF COHABITATION.
Y'ALL REALLY THINK IT TOOK A CALAMITY TO MAKE EM HOW THEY ARE?
THAT'S IT.
EVEN IF THAT IS THE CASE, MR. HAZEL.
WE WON'T LET YOU SACRIFICE A CHILD OF ANY RACE RIGHT BEFORE OUR EYES.
...Y'ALL REALLY ARE INHUMAN.
WHICH MAKES SENSE, SEEING AS WE'RE YOUKAI.

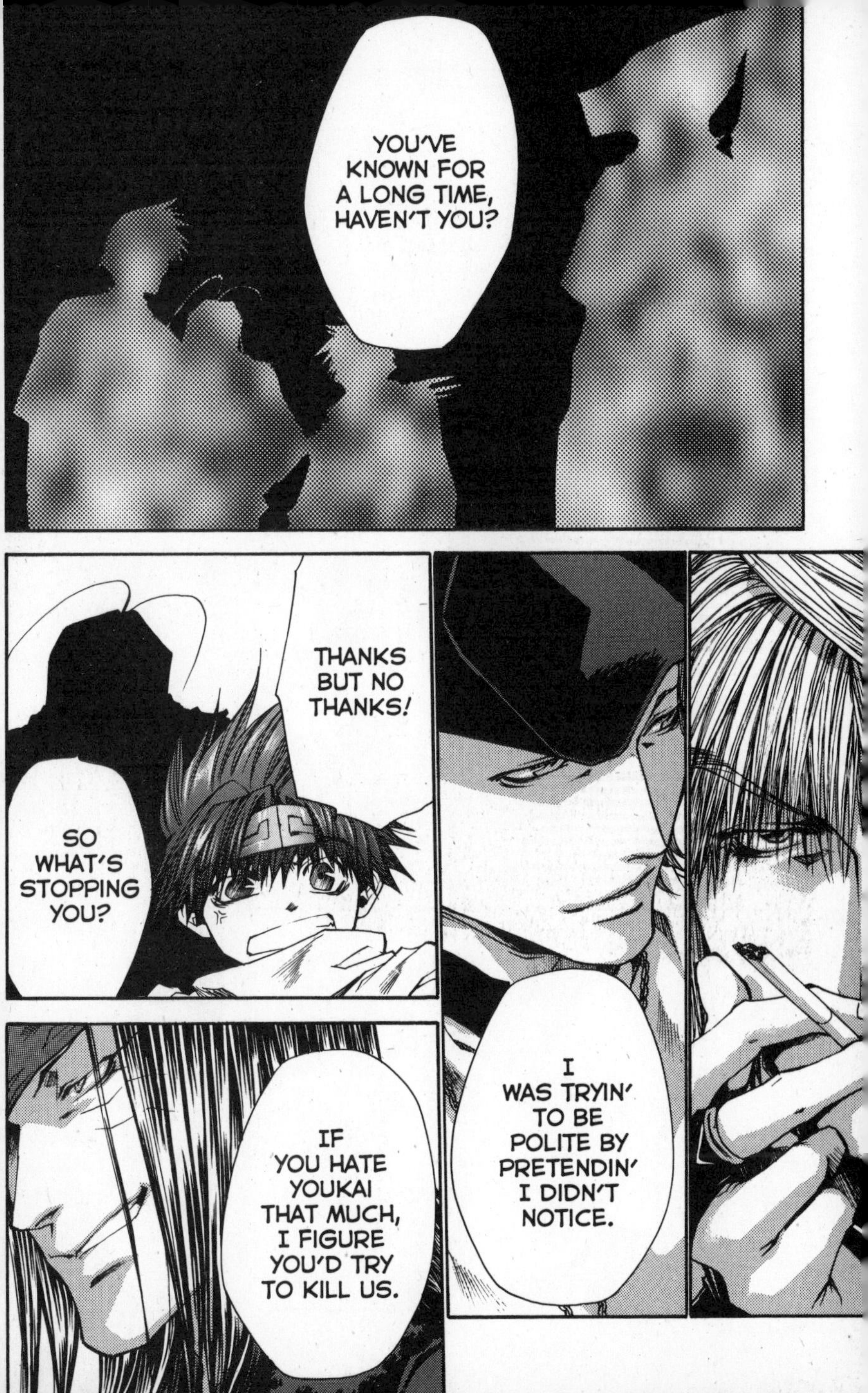
YOU'VE KNOWN FOR A LONG TIME, HAVEN'T YOU?
I WAS TRYIN' TO BE POLITE BY PRETENDIN' I DIDN'T NOTICE.
THANKS BUT NO THANKS!
SO WHAT'S STOPPING YOU?
IF YOU HATE YOUKAI THAT MUCH, I FIGURE YOU'D TRY TO KILL US.

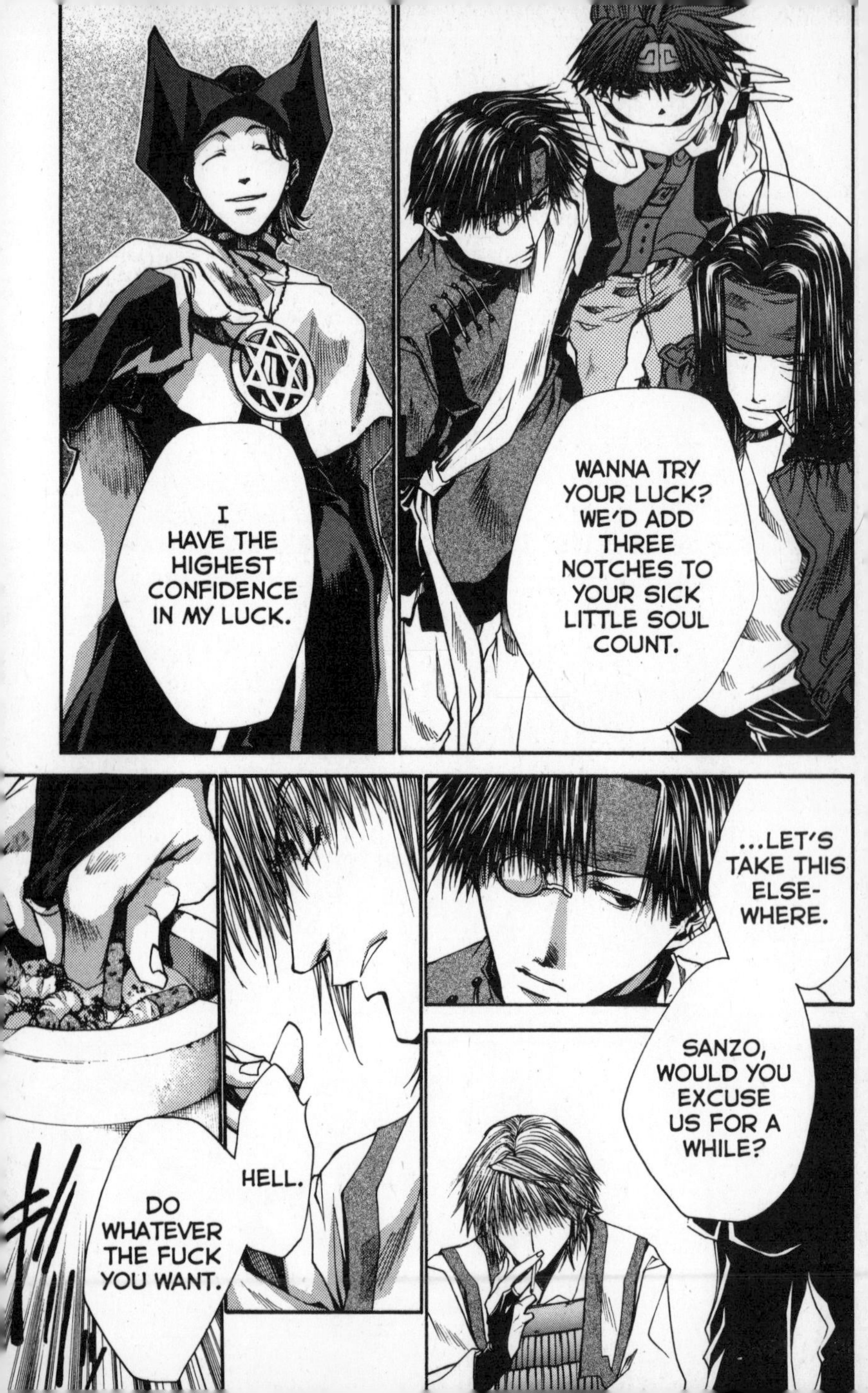
WANNA TRY YOUR LUCK? WE'D ADD THREE NOTCHES TO YOUR SICK LITTLE SOUL COUNT.
I HAVE THE HIGHEST CONFIDENCE IN MY LUCK.
...LET'S TAKE THIS ELSE-WHERE.
SANZO, WOULD YOU EXCUSE US FOR A WHILE?
HELL.
DO WHATEVER THE FUCK YOU WANT.

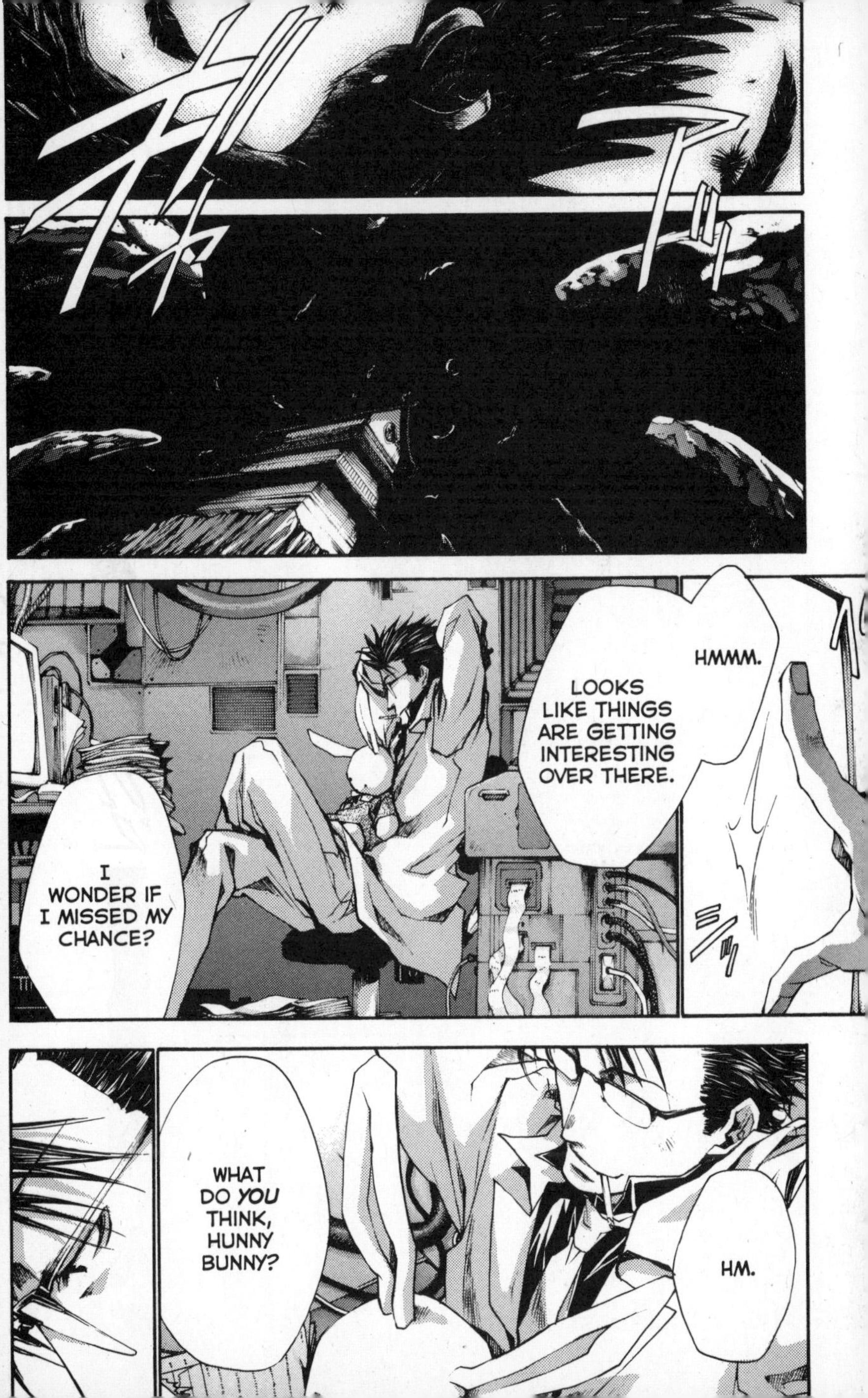
HMMM.
LOOKS LIKE THINGS ARE GETTING INTERESTING OVER THERE.
I WONDER IF I MISSED MY CHANCE?
WHAT DO *YOU* THINK, HUNNY BUNNY?
HM.

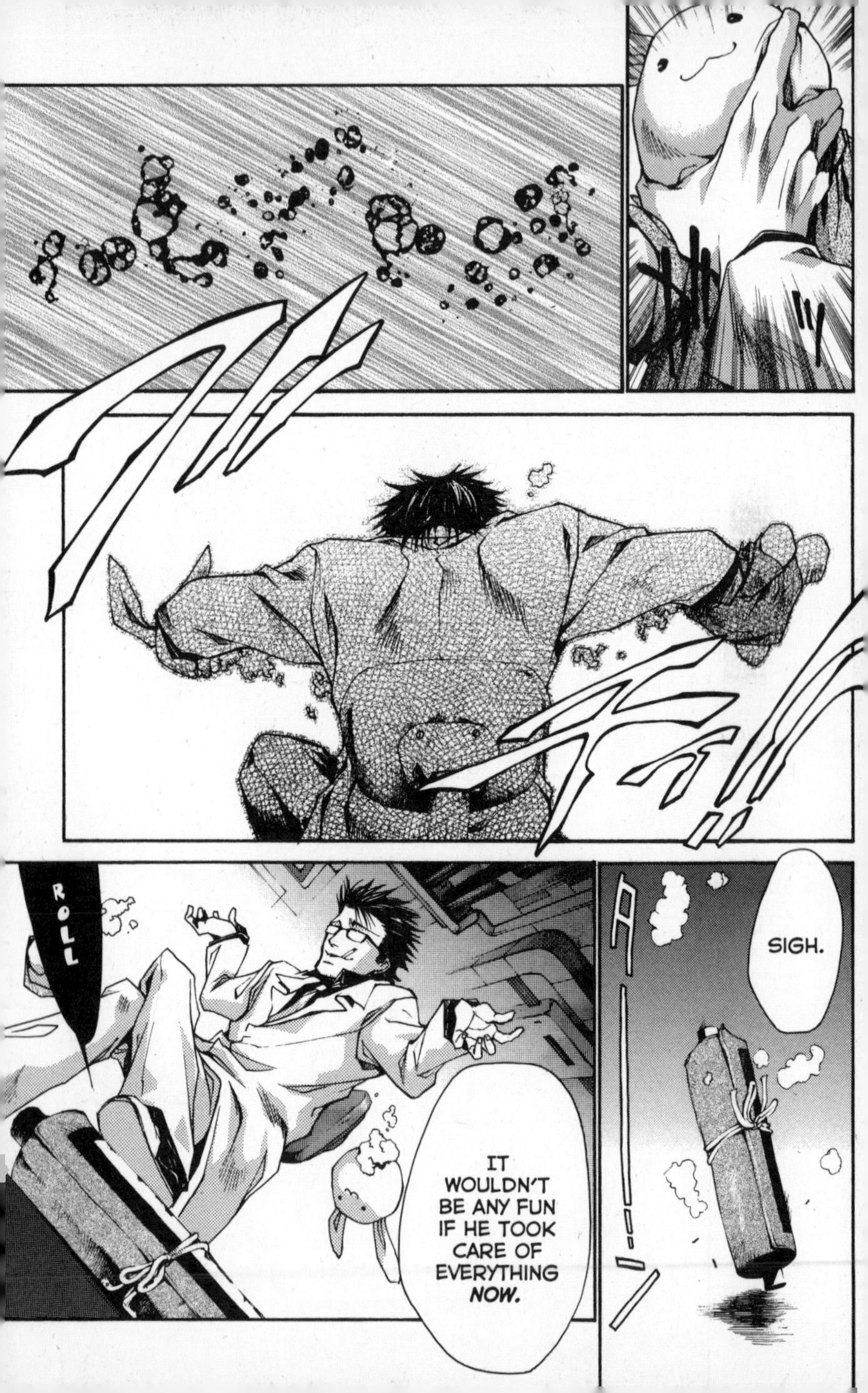
SIGH.
IT WOULDN'T BE ANY FUN IF HE TOOK CARE OF EVERYTHING *NOW.*
ROLL

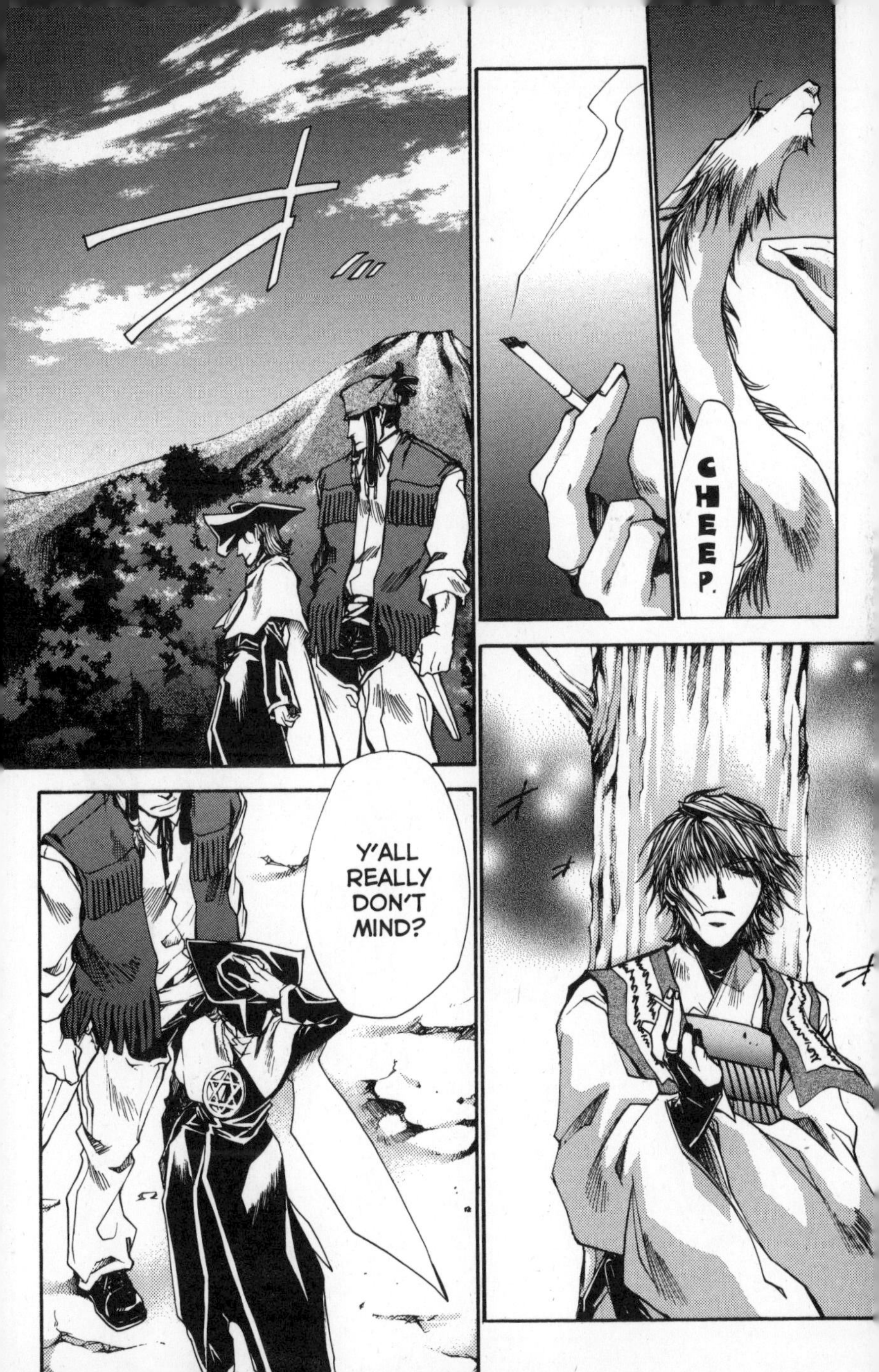
CHEEP.
Y'ALL REALLY DON'T MIND?

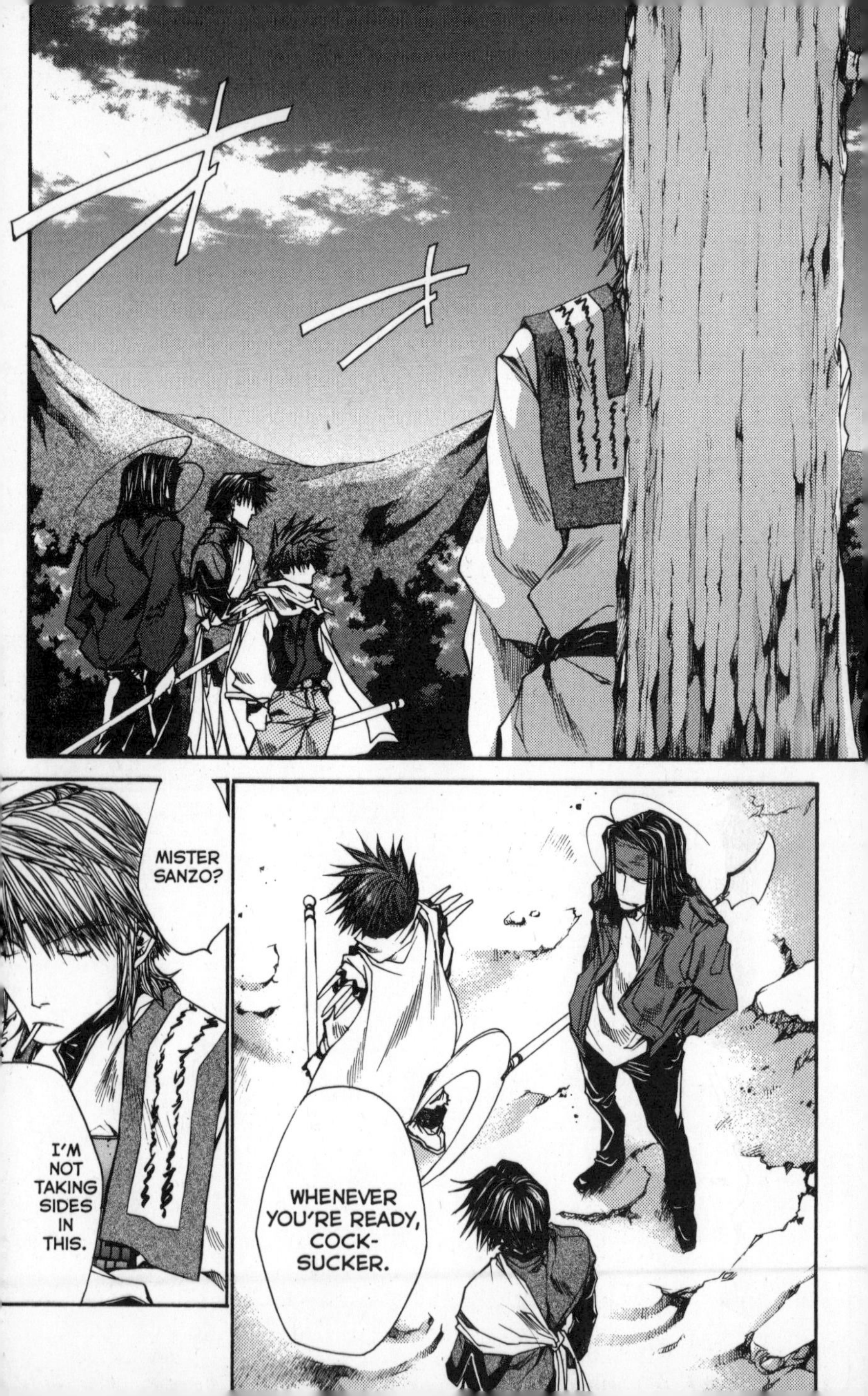
WHENEVER YOU'RE READY, COCK-SUCKER.
MISTER SANZO?
I'M NOT TAKING SIDES IN THIS.

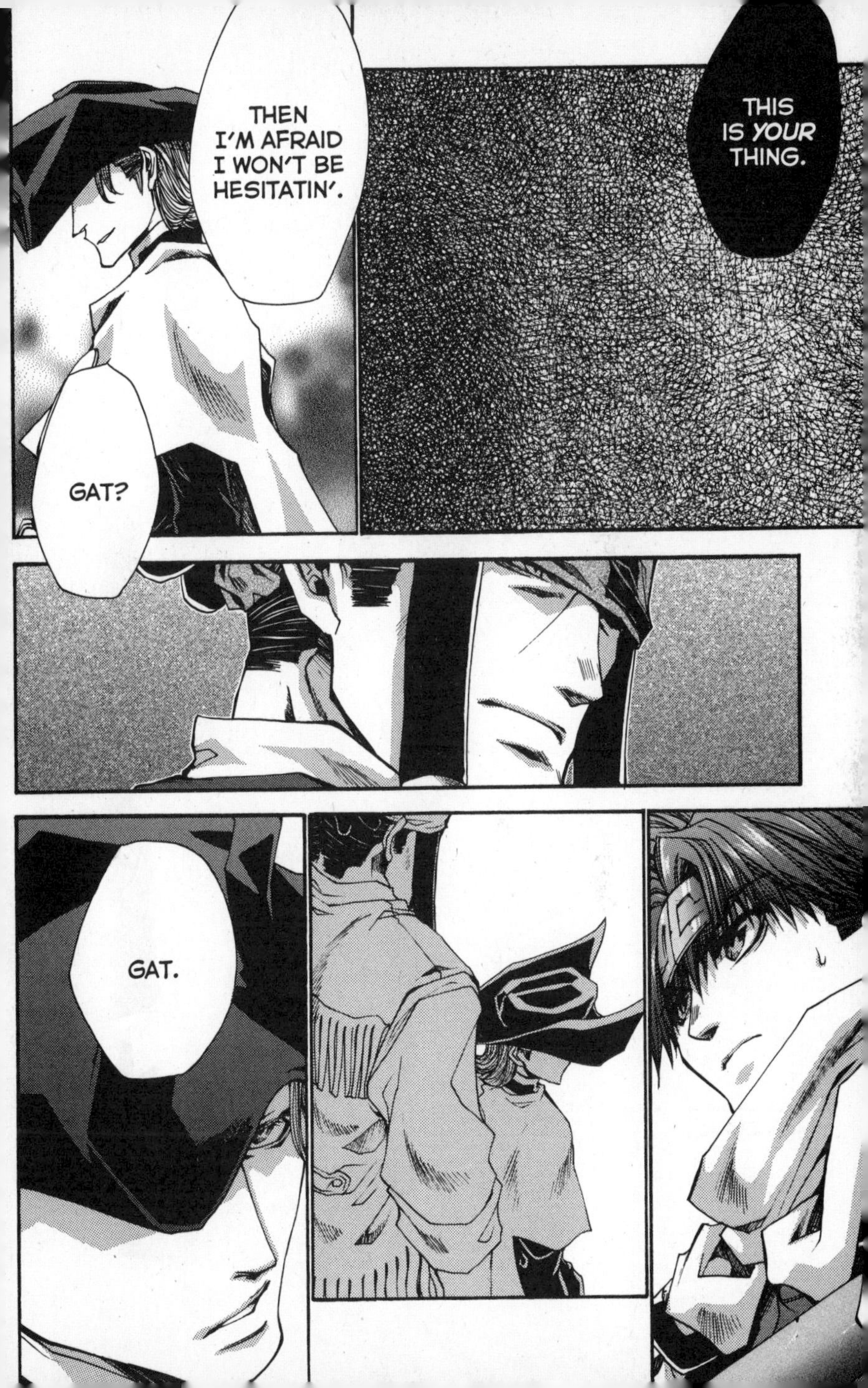
THIS IS *YOUR* THING.
THEN I'M AFRAID I WON'T BE HESITATIN'.
GAT?
GAT.

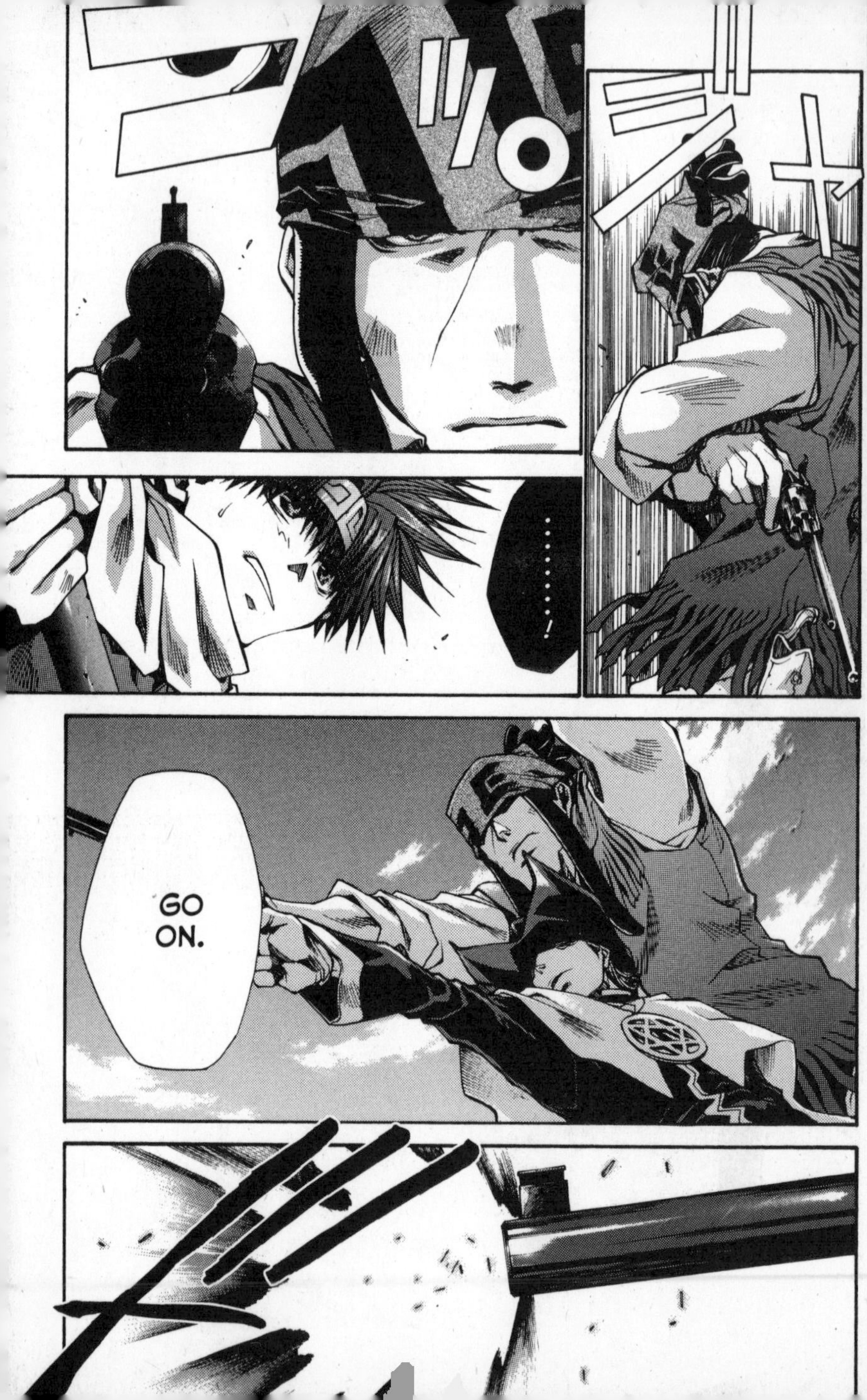
......!
GO ON.

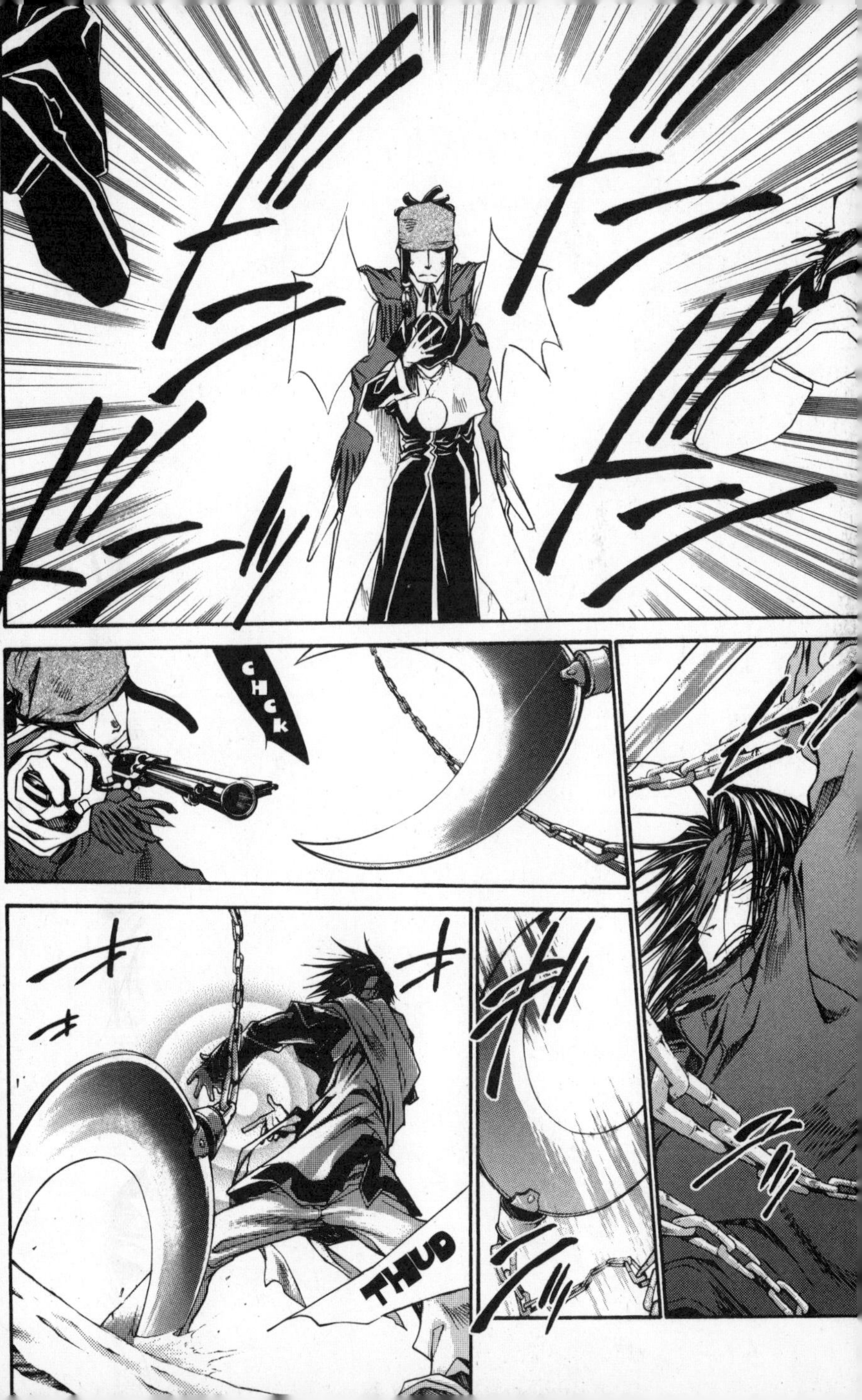
CHCK
THUD

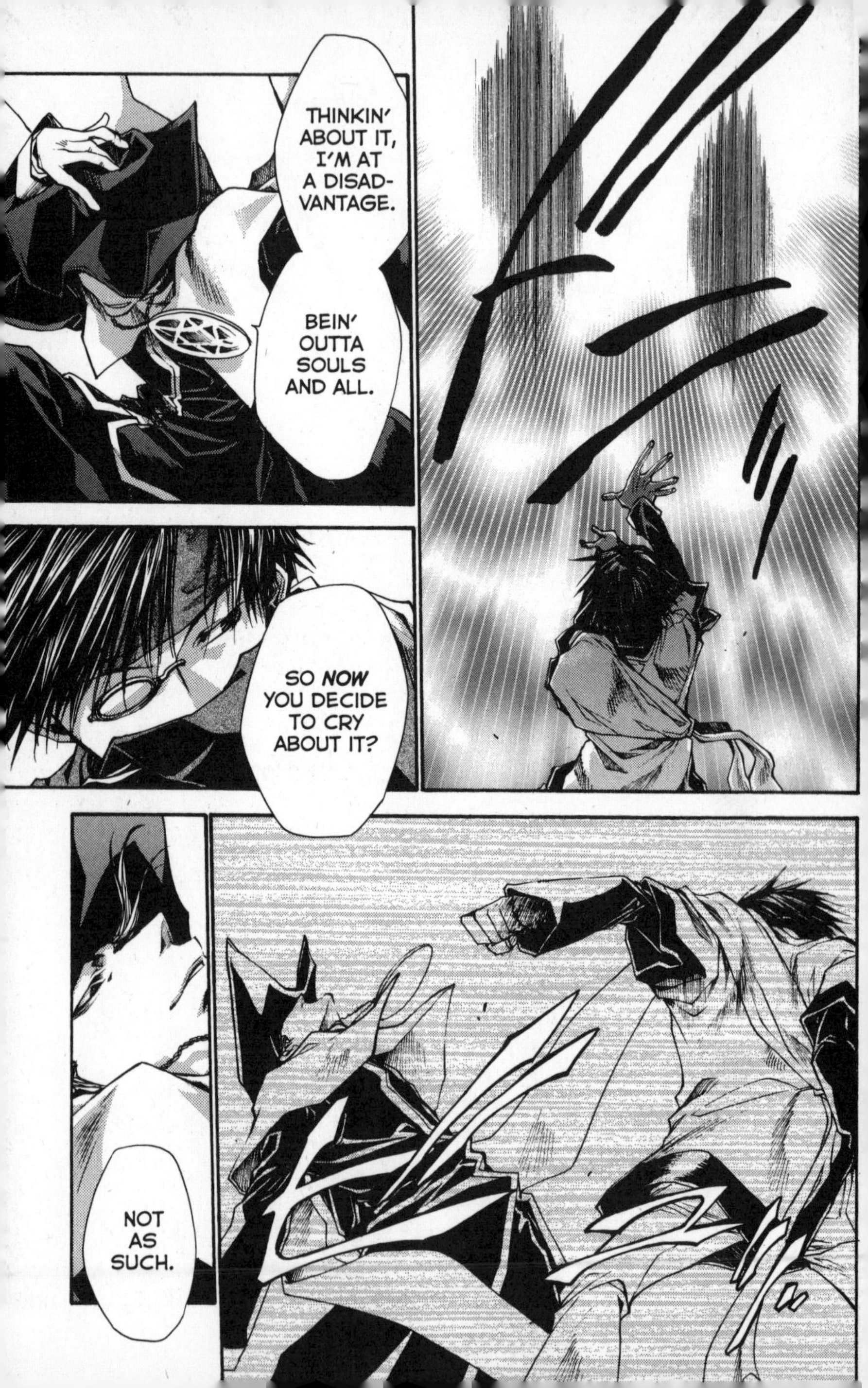
THINKIN' ABOUT IT, I'M AT A DISAD-VANTAGE.
BEIN' OUTTA SOULS AND ALL.
SO *NOW* YOU DECIDE TO CRY ABOUT IT?
NOT AS SUCH.

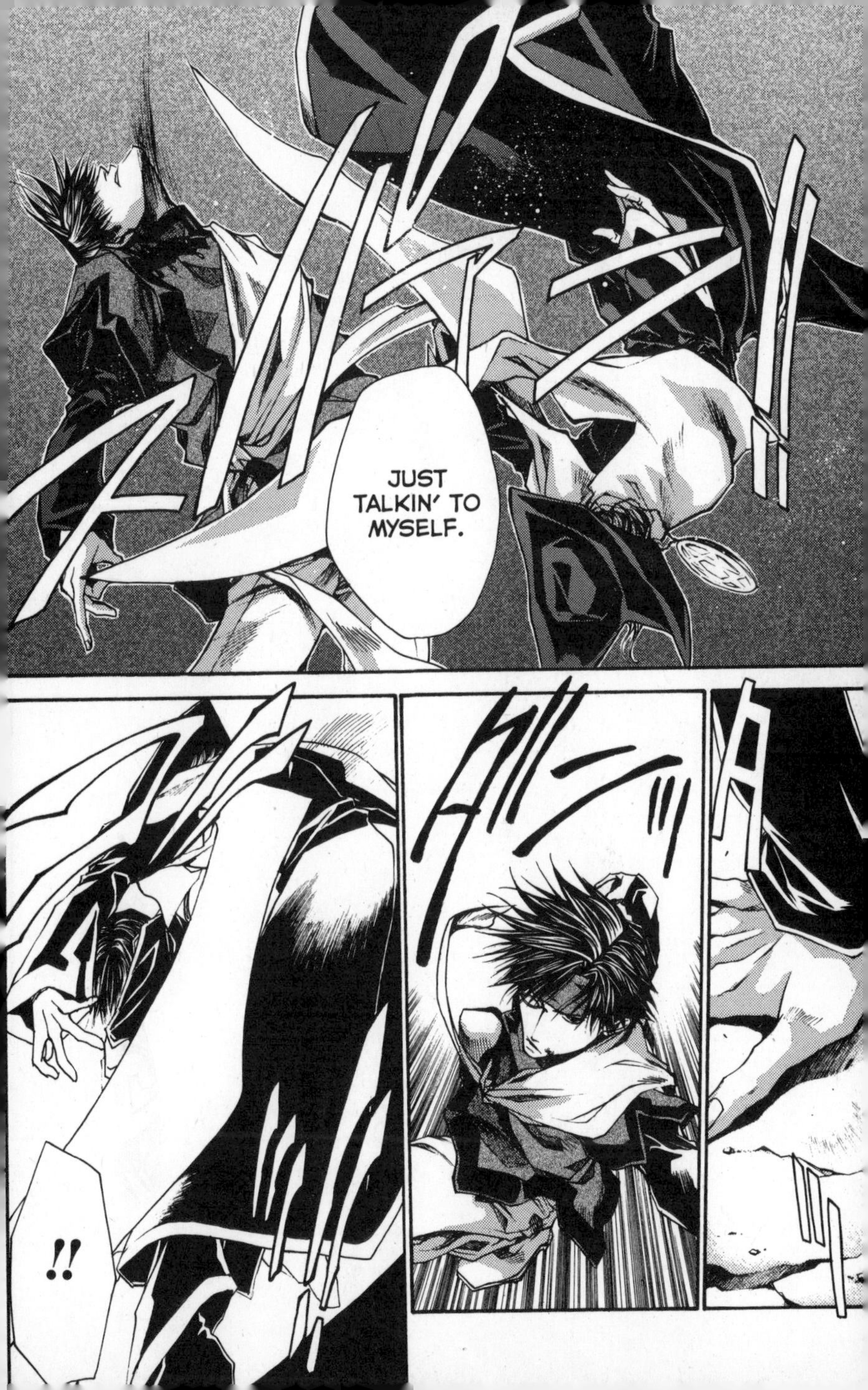
JUST TALKIN' TO MYSELF.
!!

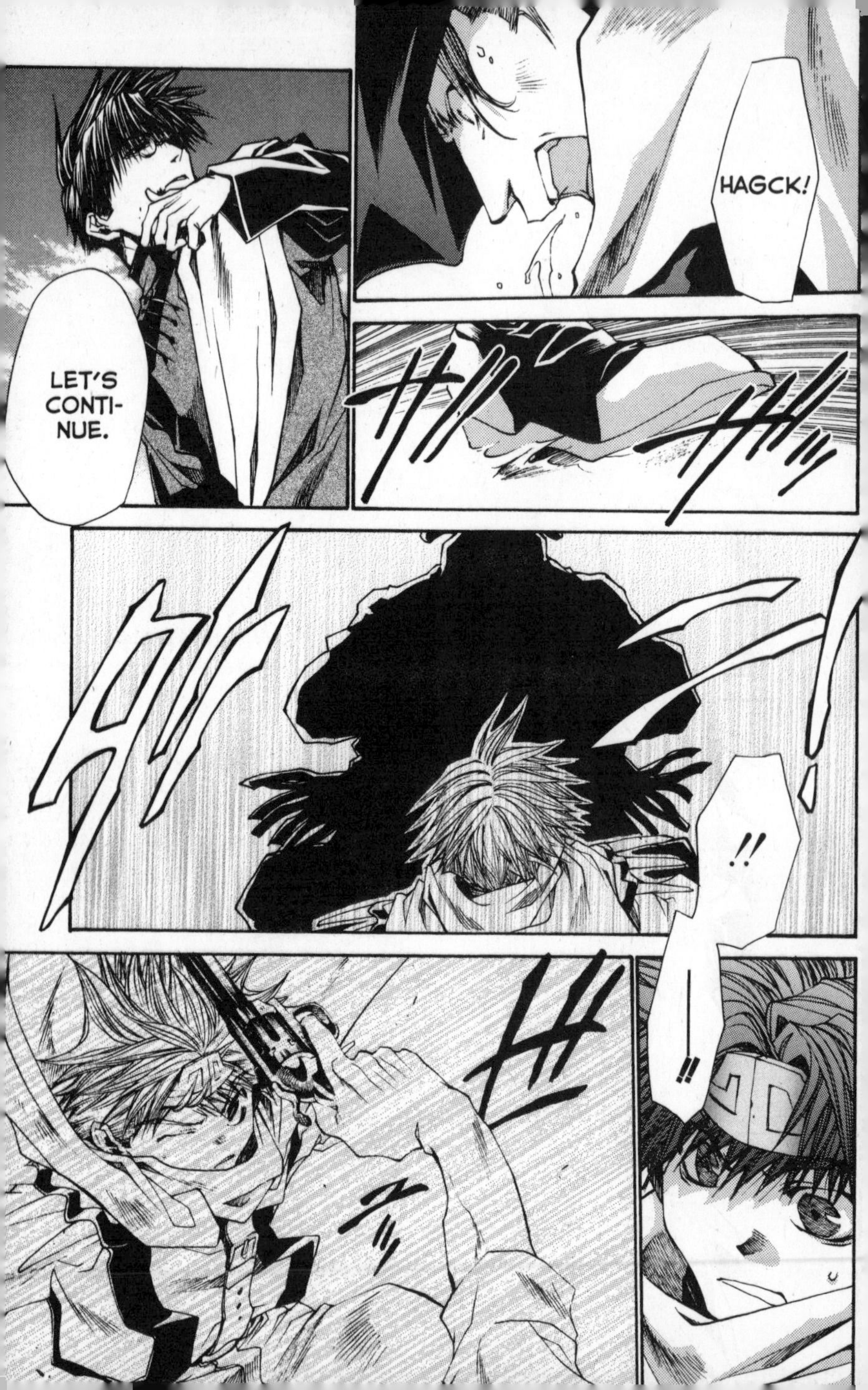
HAGCK!
LET'S CONTI- NUE.
!!
!!

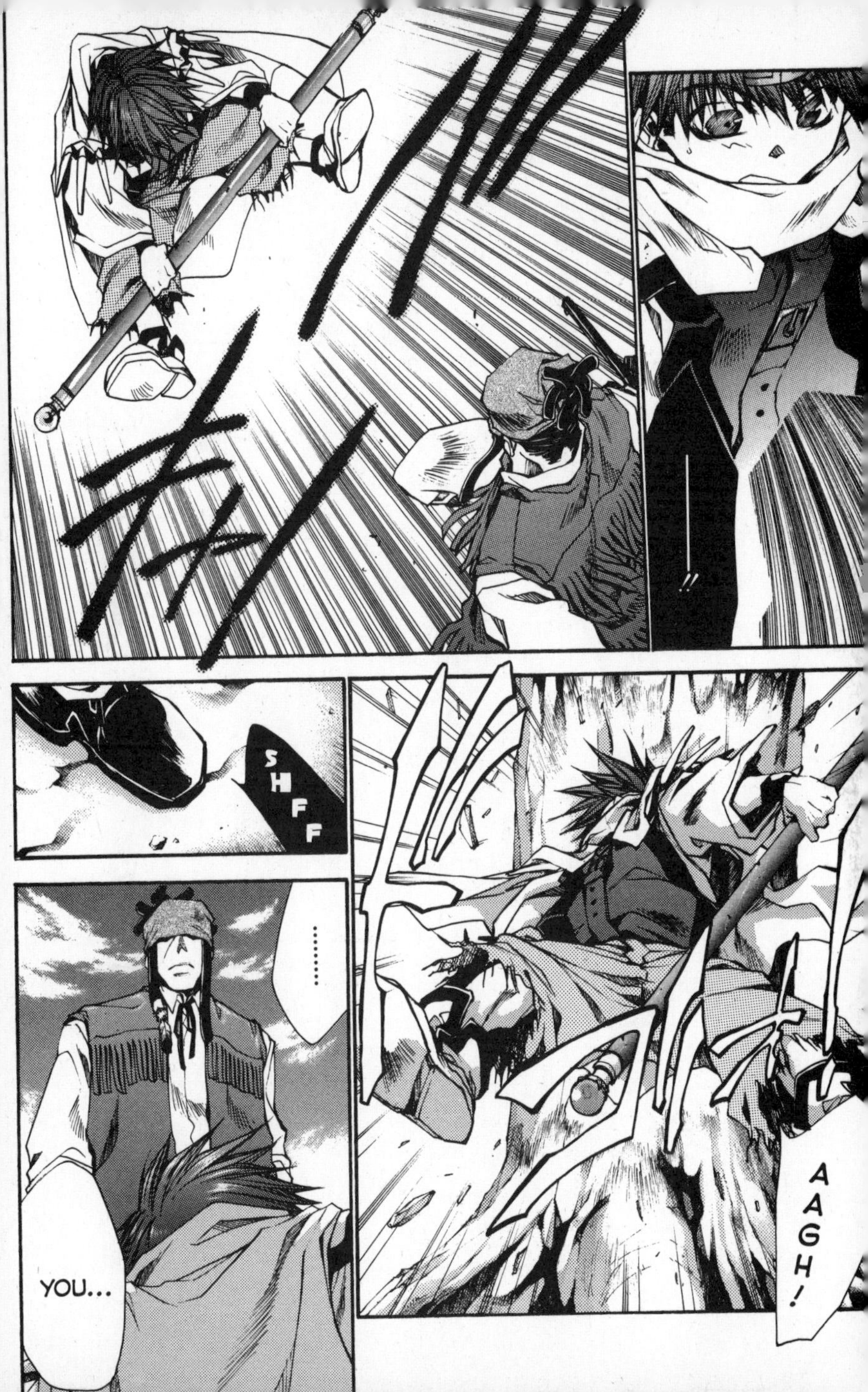
!!
AAGH!
SHFF
......
YOU...

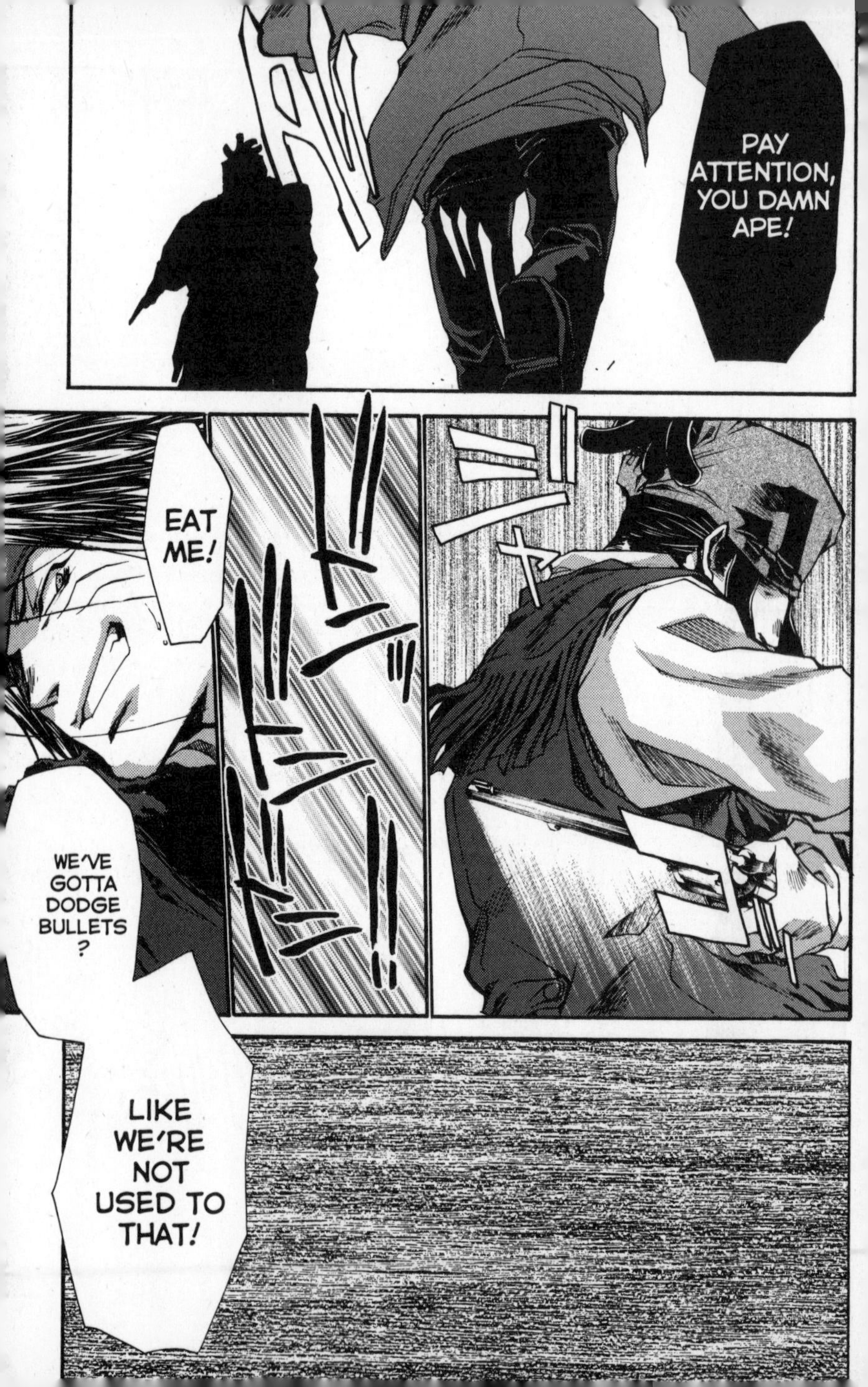
PAY ATTENTION, YOU DAMN APE!
EAT ME!
WE'VE GOTTA DODGE BULLETS?
LIKE WE'RE NOT USED TO THAT!

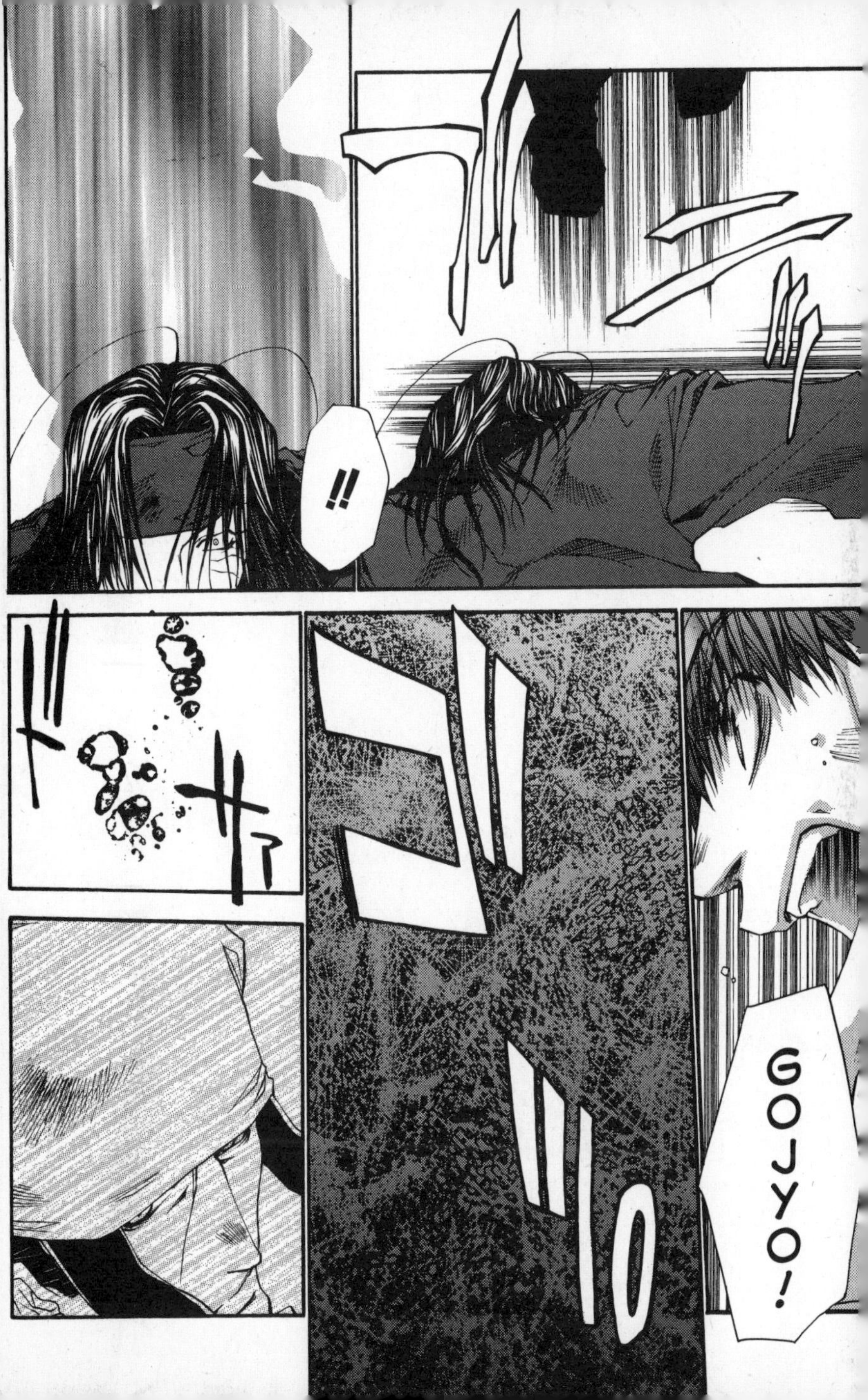
!!
GOJYO!

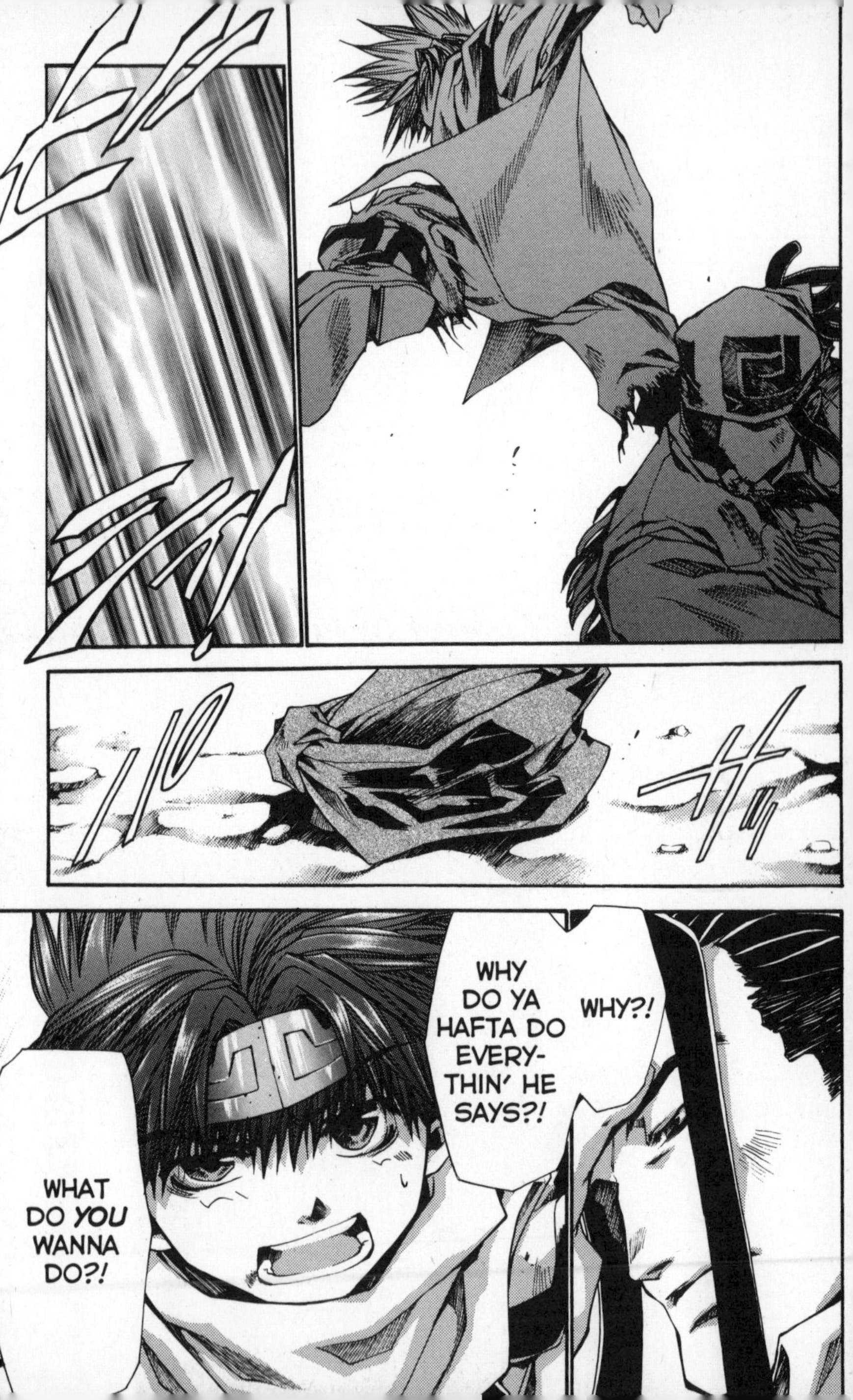
WHY?!
WHY DO YA HAFTA DO EVERY-THIN' HE SAYS?!
WHAT DO *YOU* WANNA DO?!

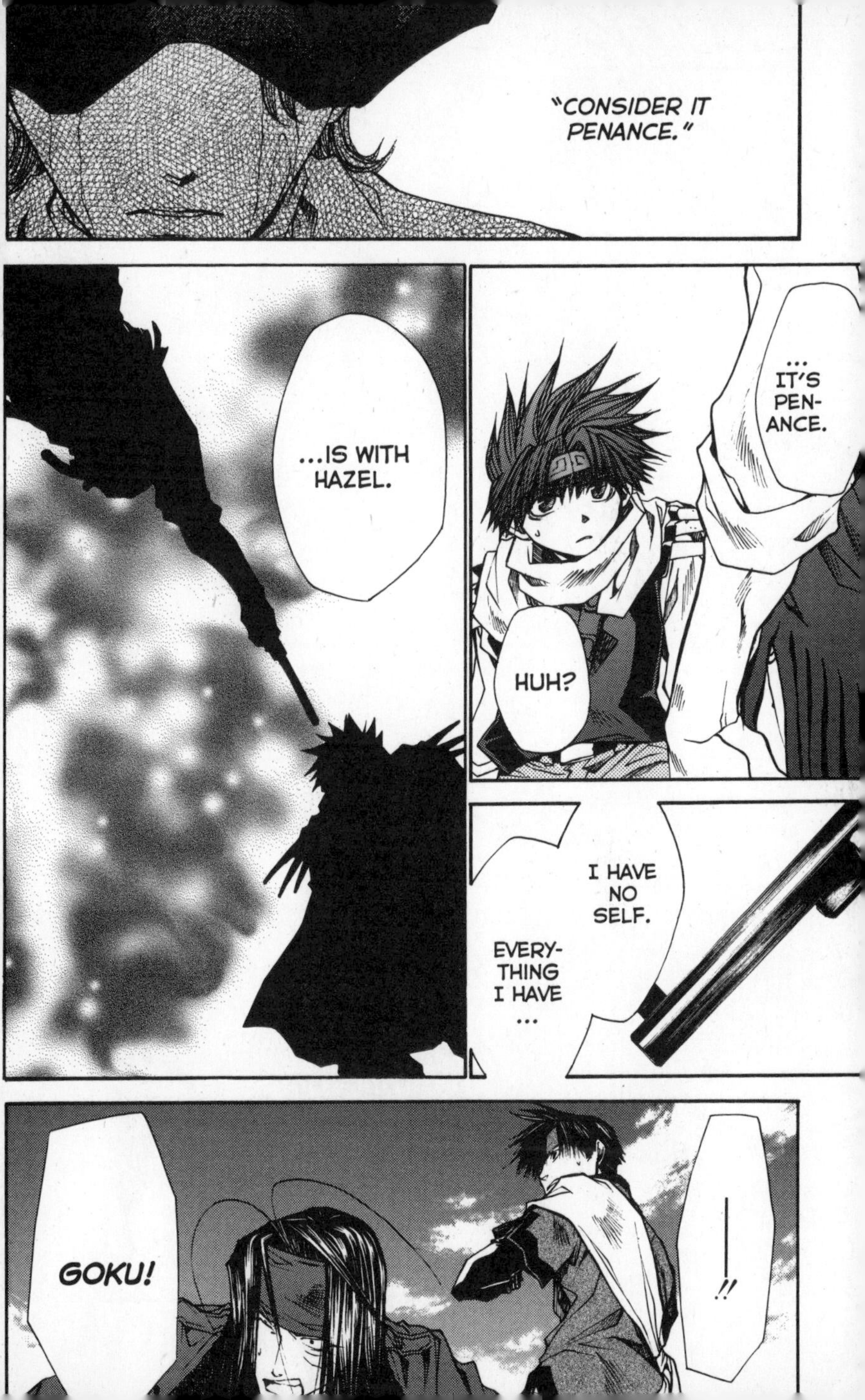
"CONSIDER IT PENANCE."
... IT'S PEN-ANCE.
HUH?
I HAVE NO SELF.
EVERY-THING I HAVE ...
...IS WITH HAZEL.
—!!
GOKU!

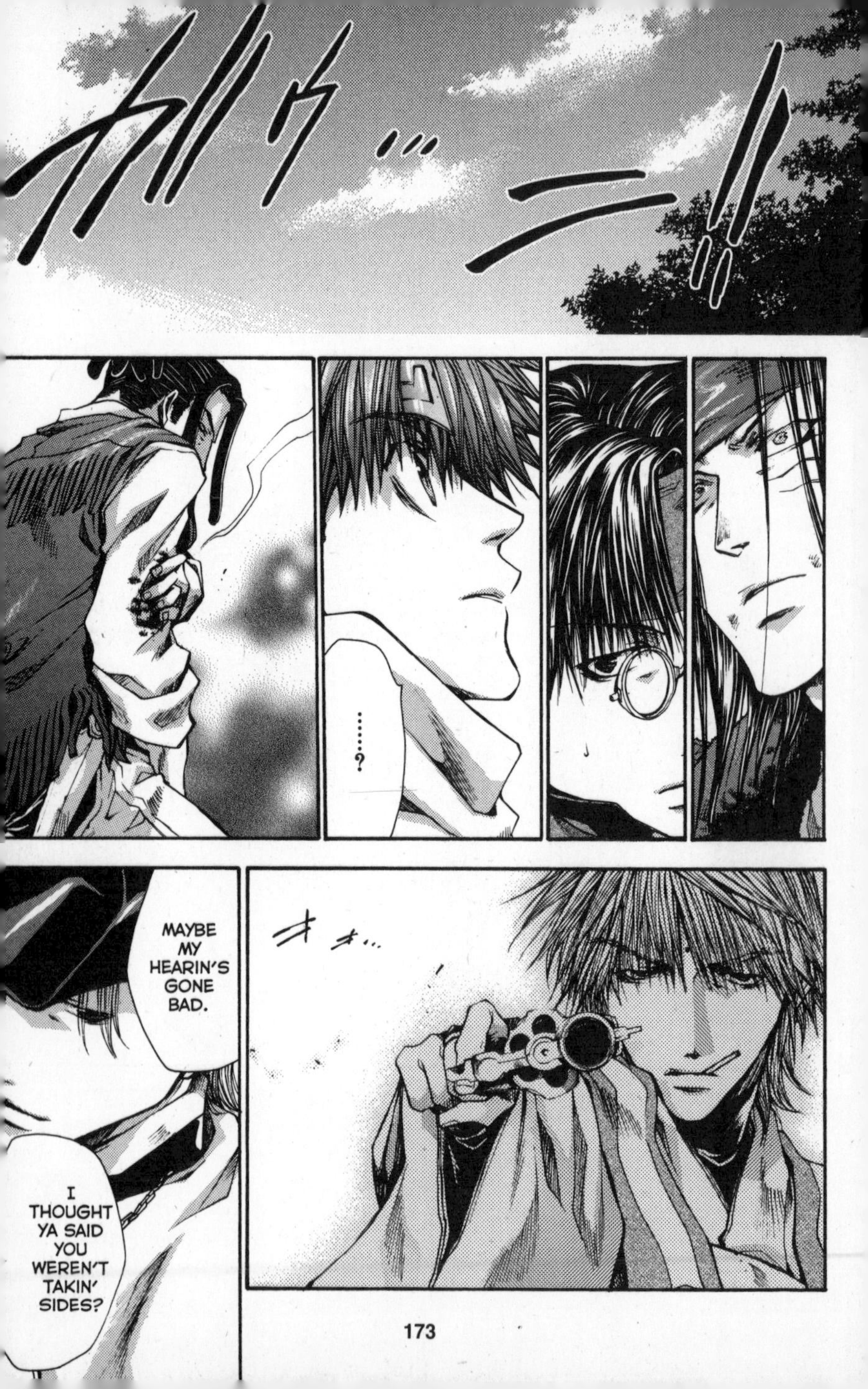
......?
MAYBE MY HEARIN'S GONE BAD.
I THOUGHT YA SAID YOU WEREN'T TAKIN' SIDES?

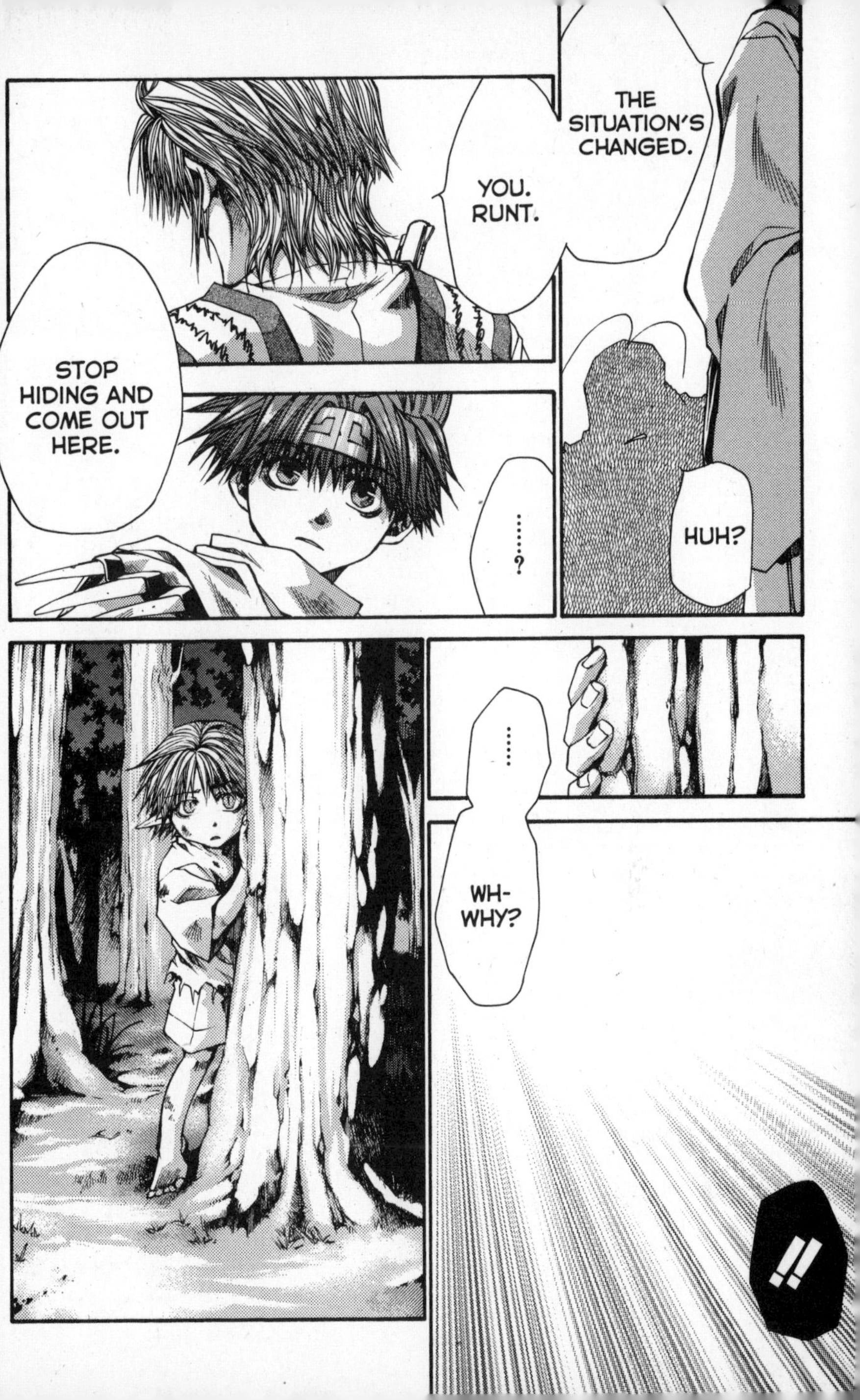
THE SITUATION'S CHANGED.
HUH?
YOU. RUNT.
STOP HIDING AND COME OUT HERE.
......?
......
WH- WHY?
!!

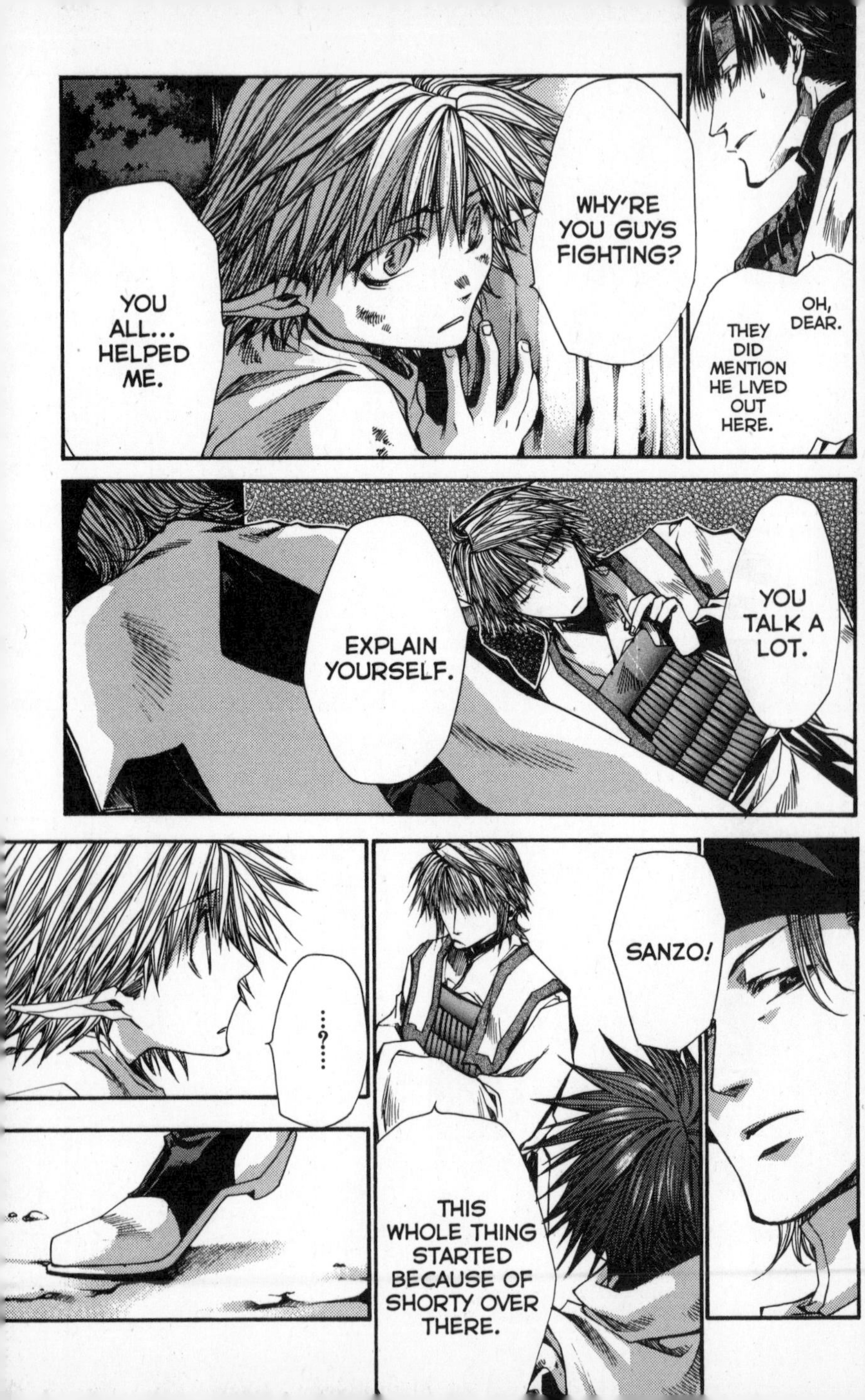
OH, DEAR.
THEY DID MENTION HE LIVED OUT HERE.
WHY'RE YOU GUYS FIGHTING?
YOU ALL... HELPED ME.
YOU TALK A LOT.
EXPLAIN YOURSELF.
SANZO!
THIS WHOLE THING STARTED BECAUSE OF SHORTY OVER THERE.
...?...

SHFF

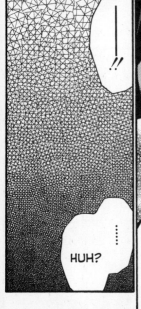

!!

......

HUH?

MR. BISHOP HERE...

...WANTS TO TAKE YOUR LIFE.

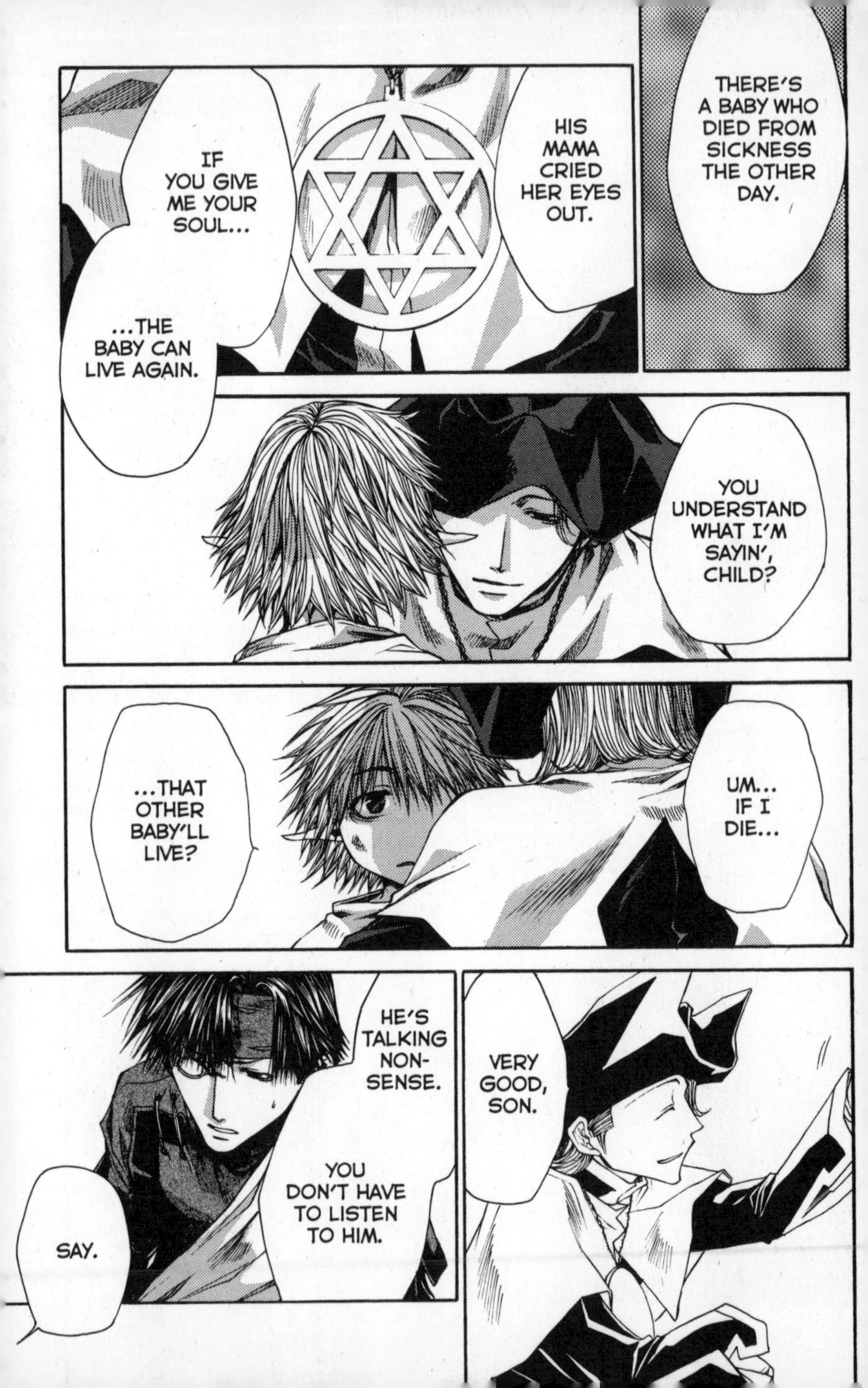
THERE'S A BABY WHO DIED FROM SICKNESS THE OTHER DAY.
HIS MAMA CRIED HER EYES OUT.
IF YOU GIVE ME YOUR SOUL...
...THE BABY CAN LIVE AGAIN.
YOU UNDERSTAND WHAT I'M SAYIN', CHILD?
UM... IF I DIE...
...THAT OTHER BABY'LL LIVE?
VERY GOOD, SON.
HE'S TALKING NON-SENSE.
YOU DON'T HAVE TO LISTEN TO HIM.
SAY.

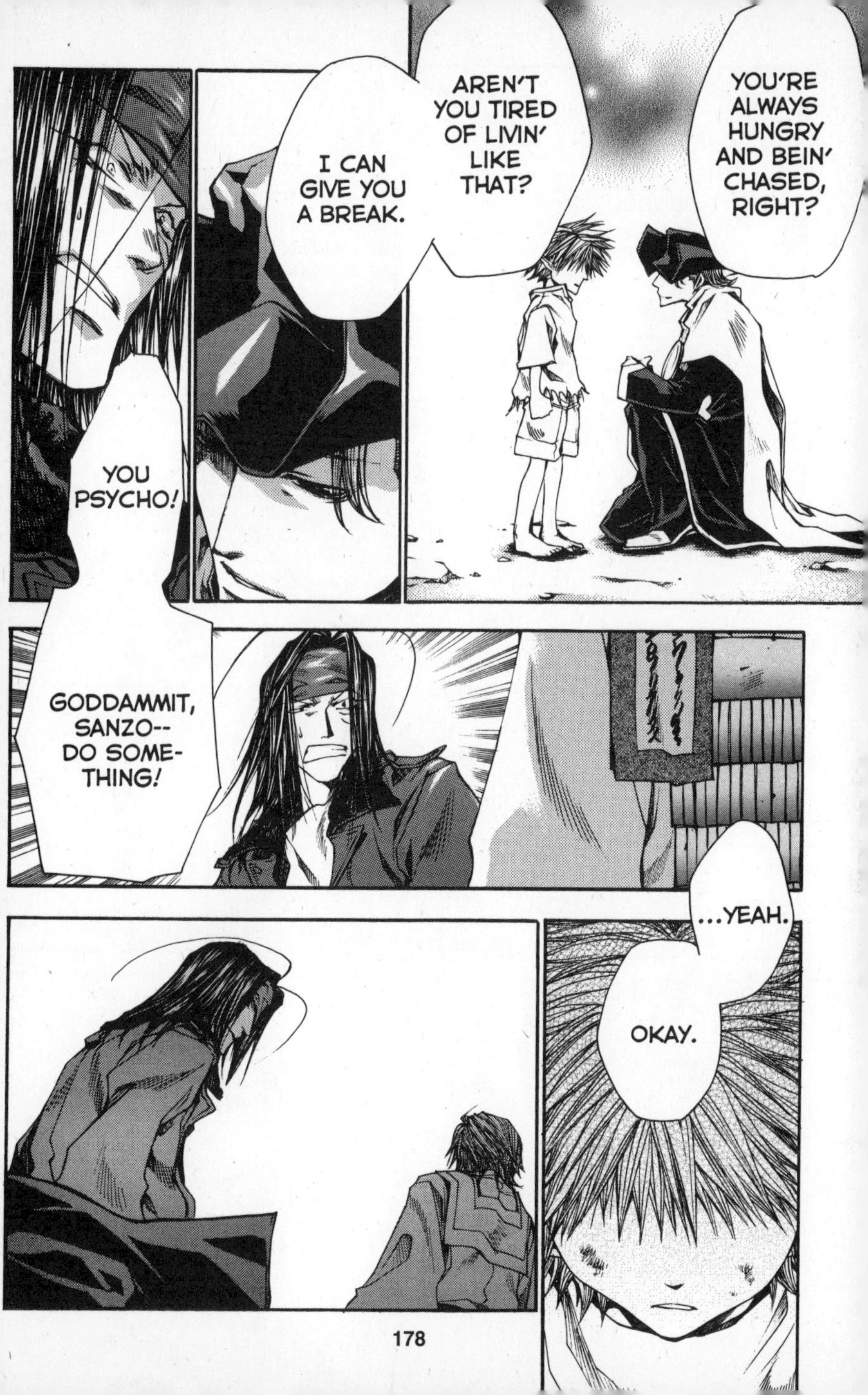
YOU'RE ALWAYS HUNGRY AND BEIN' CHASED, RIGHT?
AREN'T YOU TIRED OF LIVIN' LIKE THAT?
I CAN GIVE YOU A BREAK.
YOU PSYCHO!
GODDAMMIT, SANZO-- DO SOME-THING!
...YEAH.
OKAY.

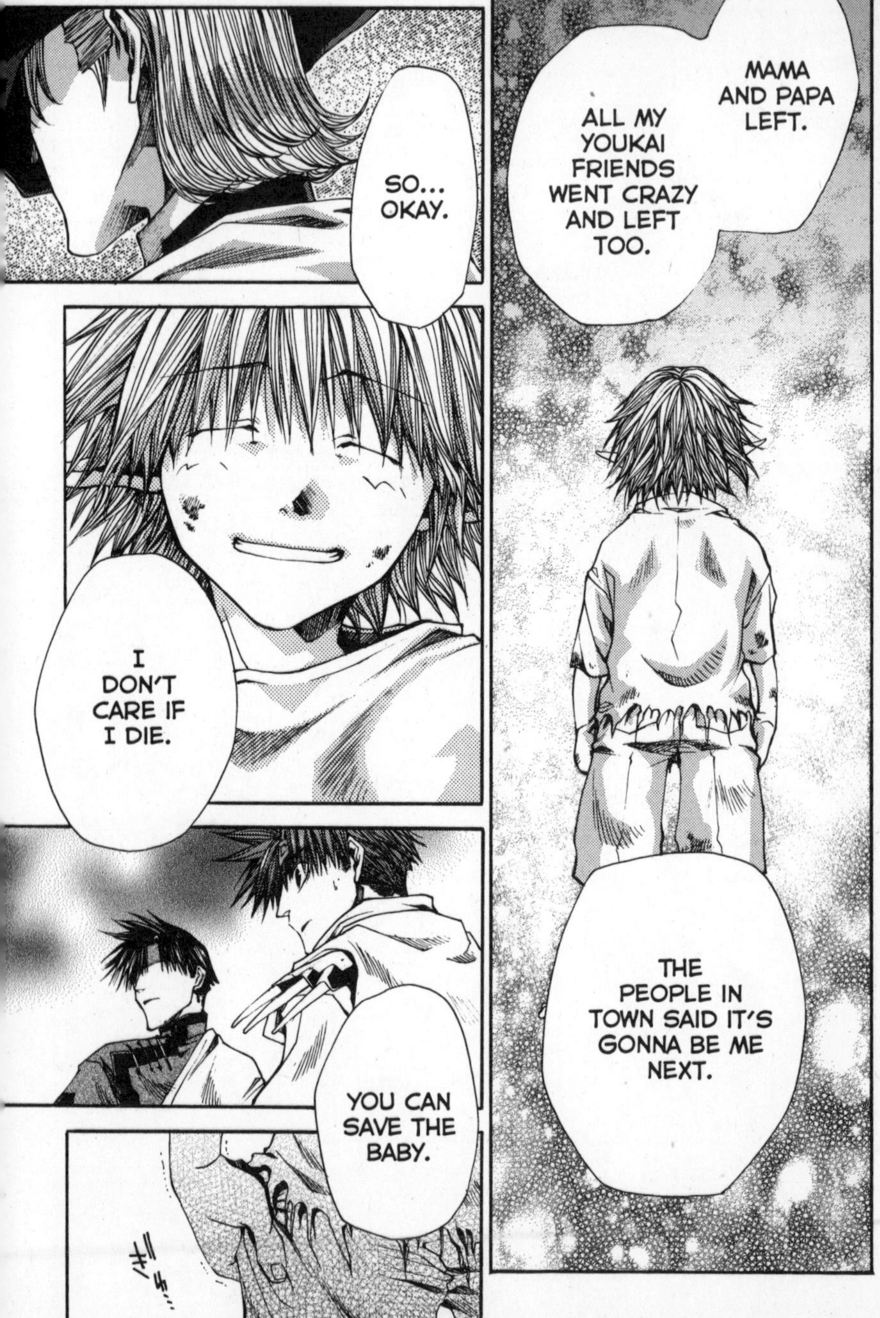
MAMA AND PAPA LEFT.
ALL MY YOUKAI FRIENDS WENT CRAZY AND LEFT TOO.
THE PEOPLE IN TOWN SAID IT'S GONNA BE ME NEXT.
SO... OKAY.
I DON'T CARE IF I DIE.
YOU CAN SAVE THE BABY.

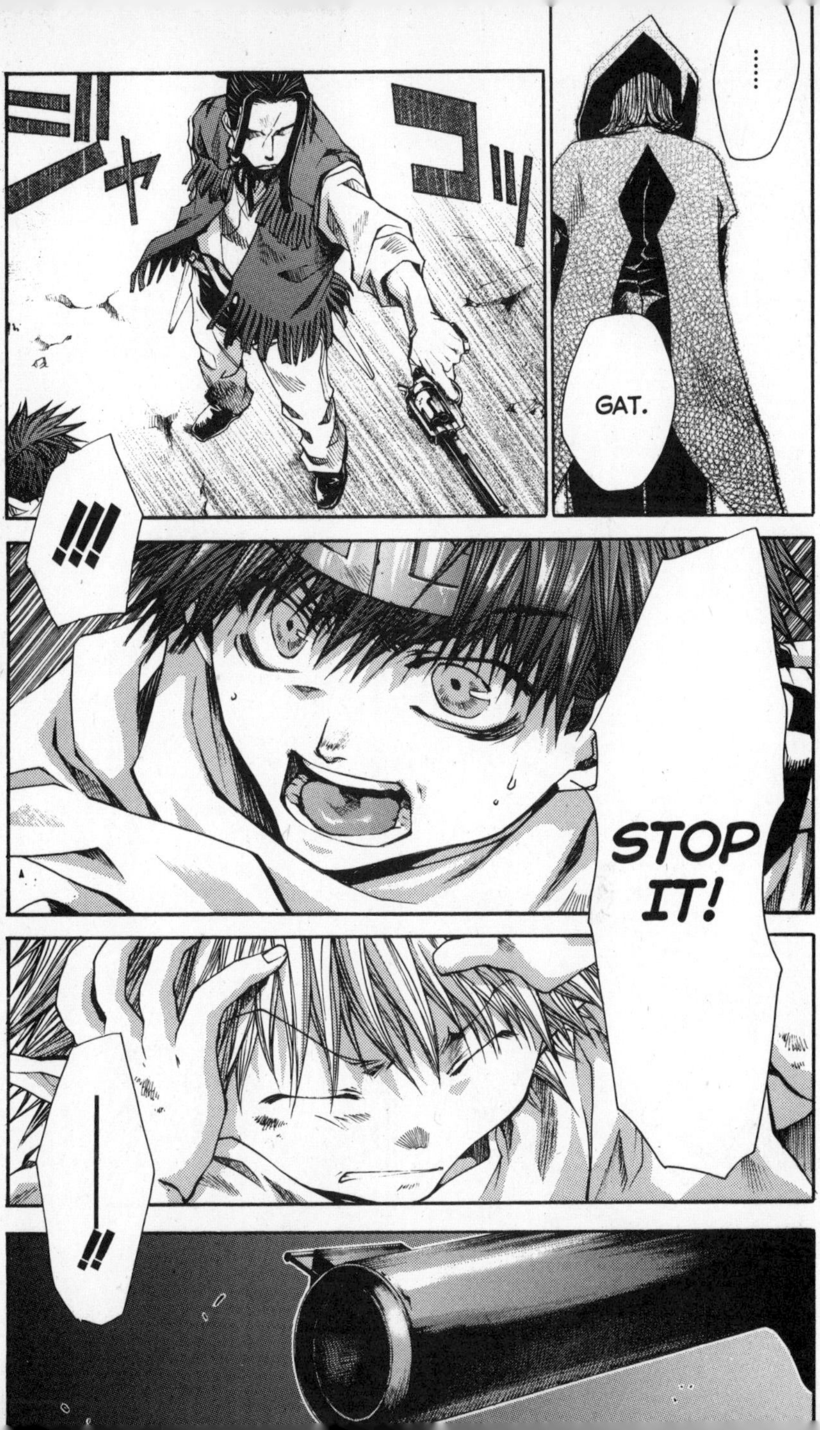
......
GAT.
ジャコッ
!!!
STOP IT!
——!!

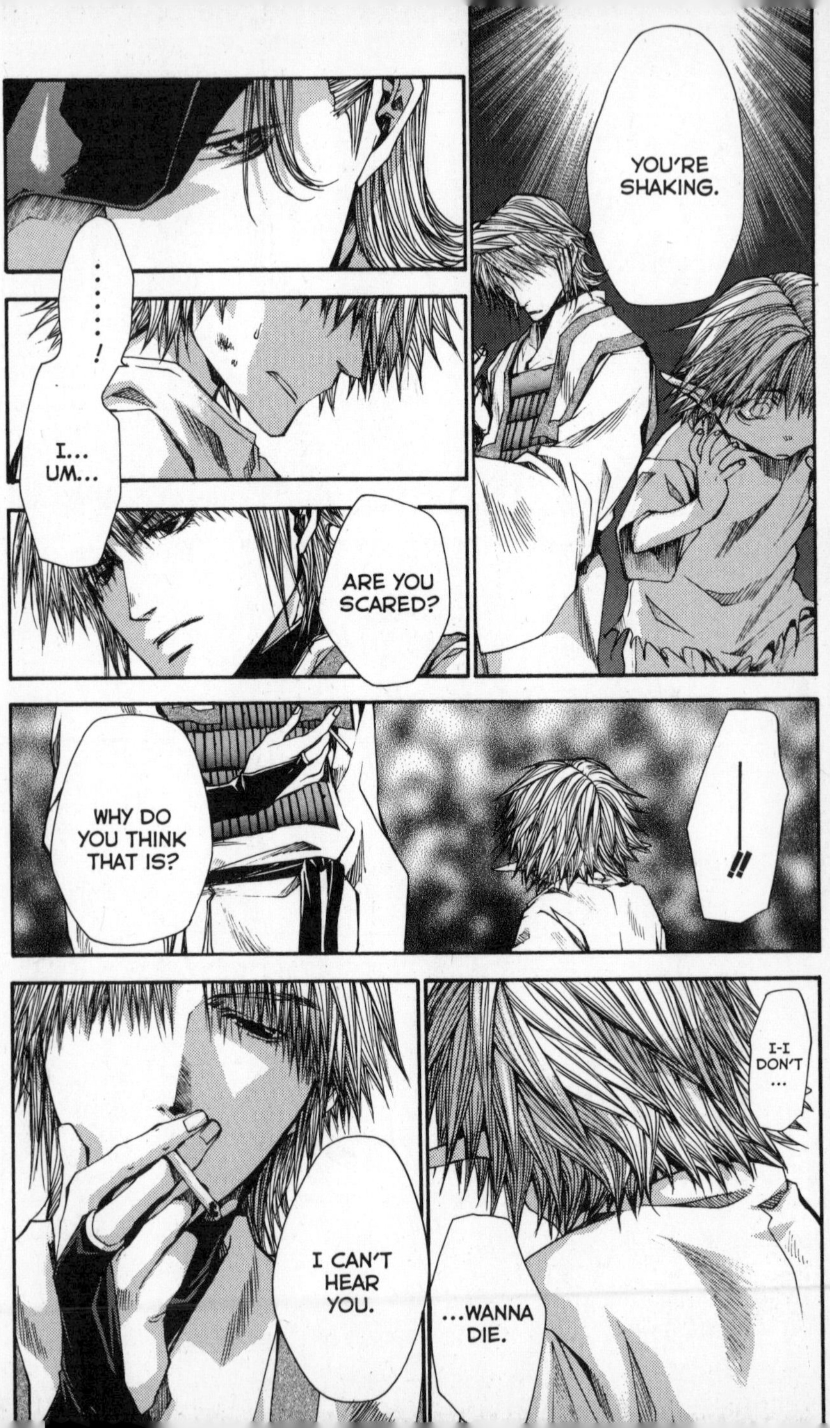
YOU'RE SHAKING.
......!
I... UM...
ARE YOU SCARED?
—!!
WHY DO YOU THINK THAT IS?
I-I DON'T ...
I CAN'T HEAR YOU.
...WANNA DIE.

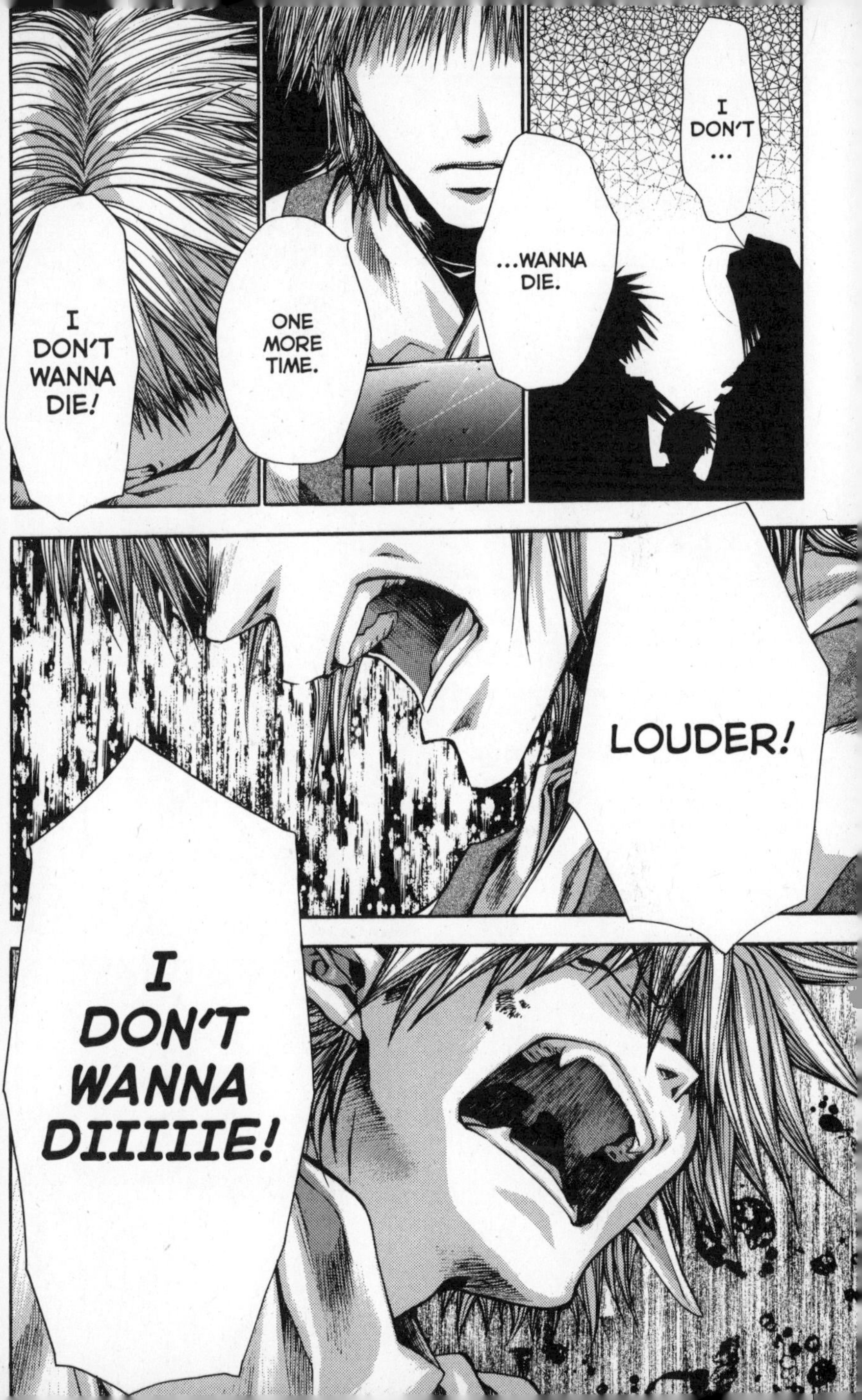
I DON'T ...
...WANNA DIE.
ONE MORE TIME.
I DON'T WANNA DIE!
LOUDER!
I DON'T WANNA DIIIIIE!

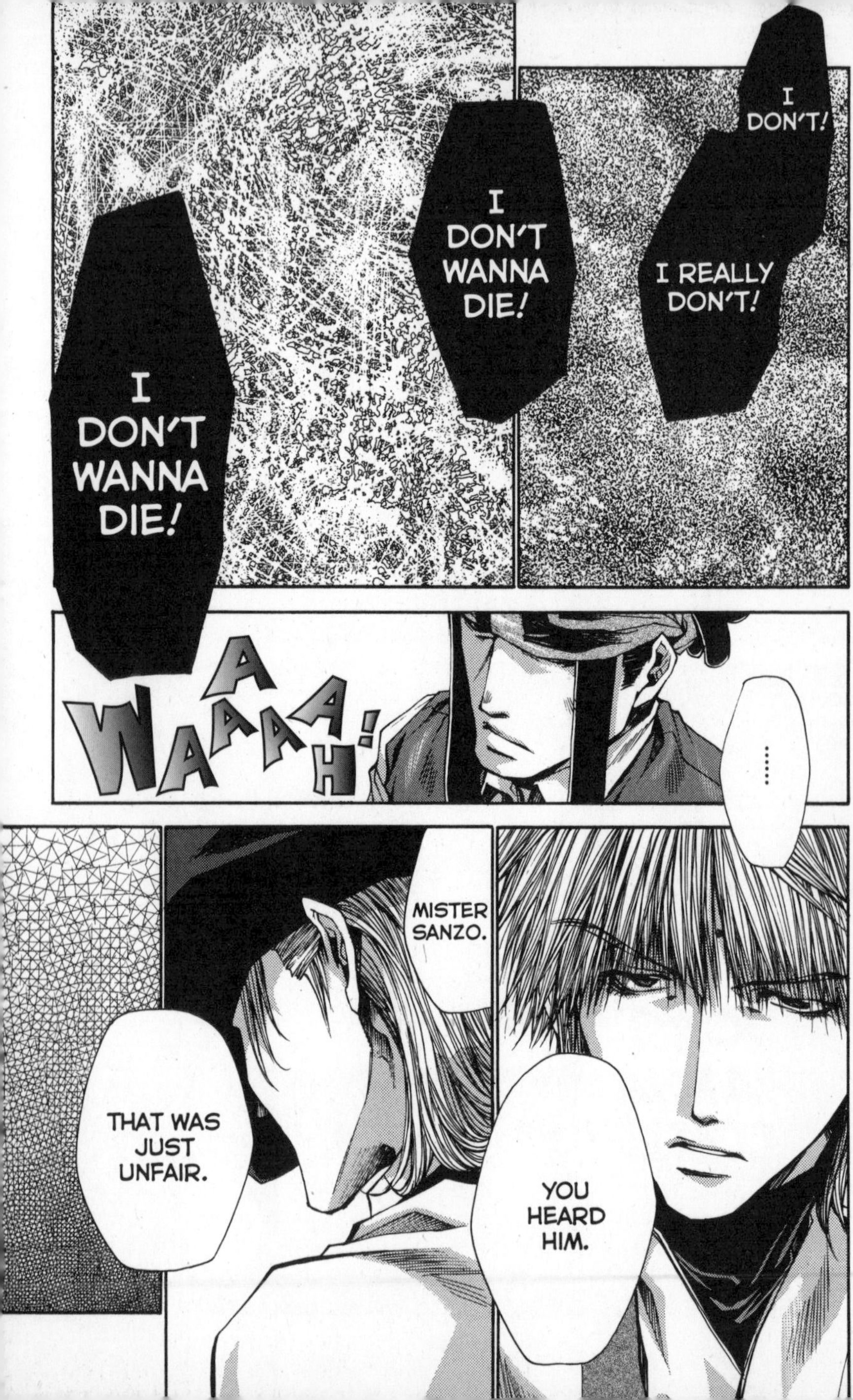
I DON'T!
I REALLY DON'T!
I DON'T WANNA DIE!
I DON'T WANNA DIE!
WAAAAAH!
......
MISTER SANZO.
THAT WAS JUST UNFAIR.
YOU HEARD HIM.

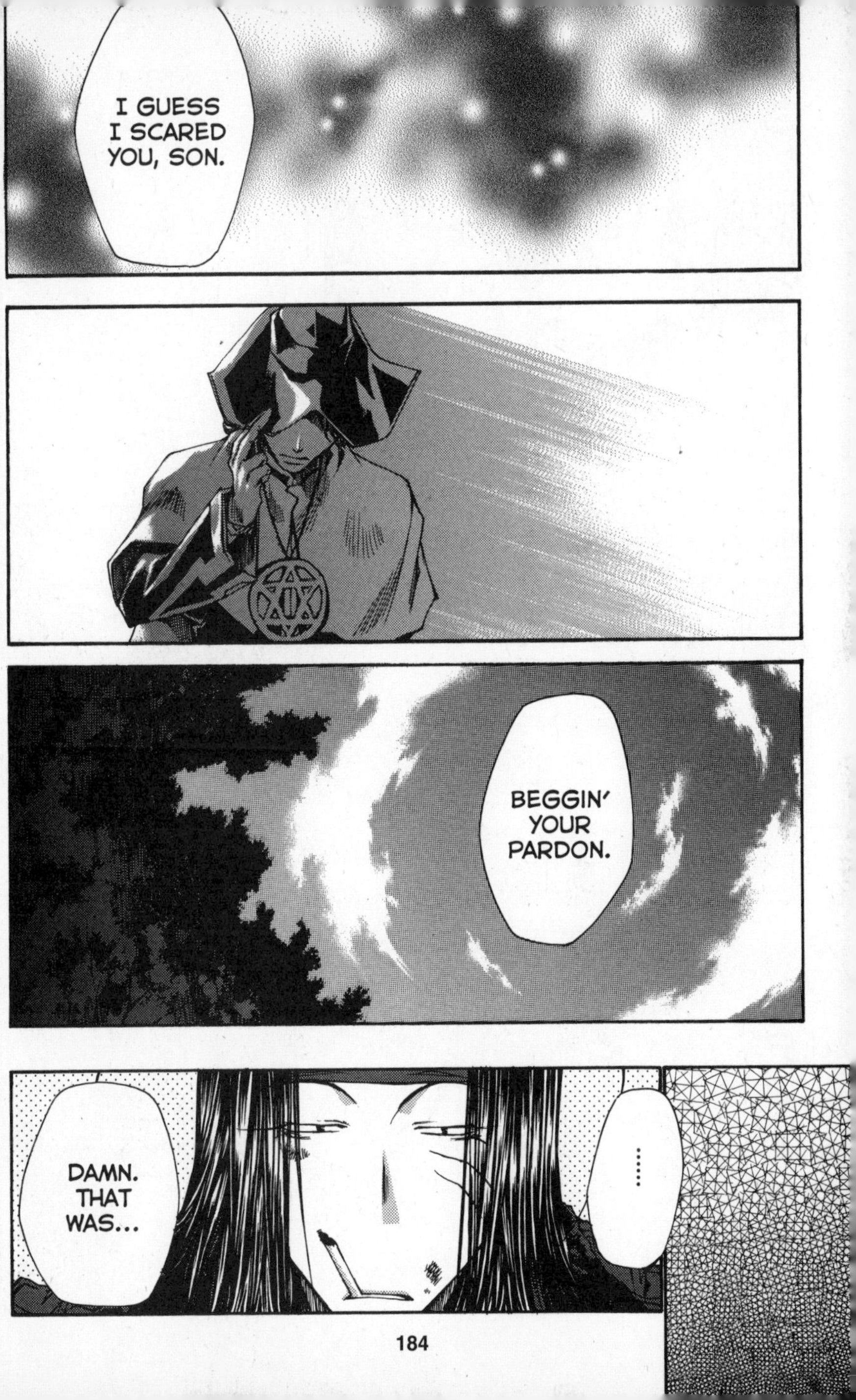
I GUESS I SCARED YOU, SON.
BEGGIN' YOUR PARDON.
......
DAMN. THAT WAS...

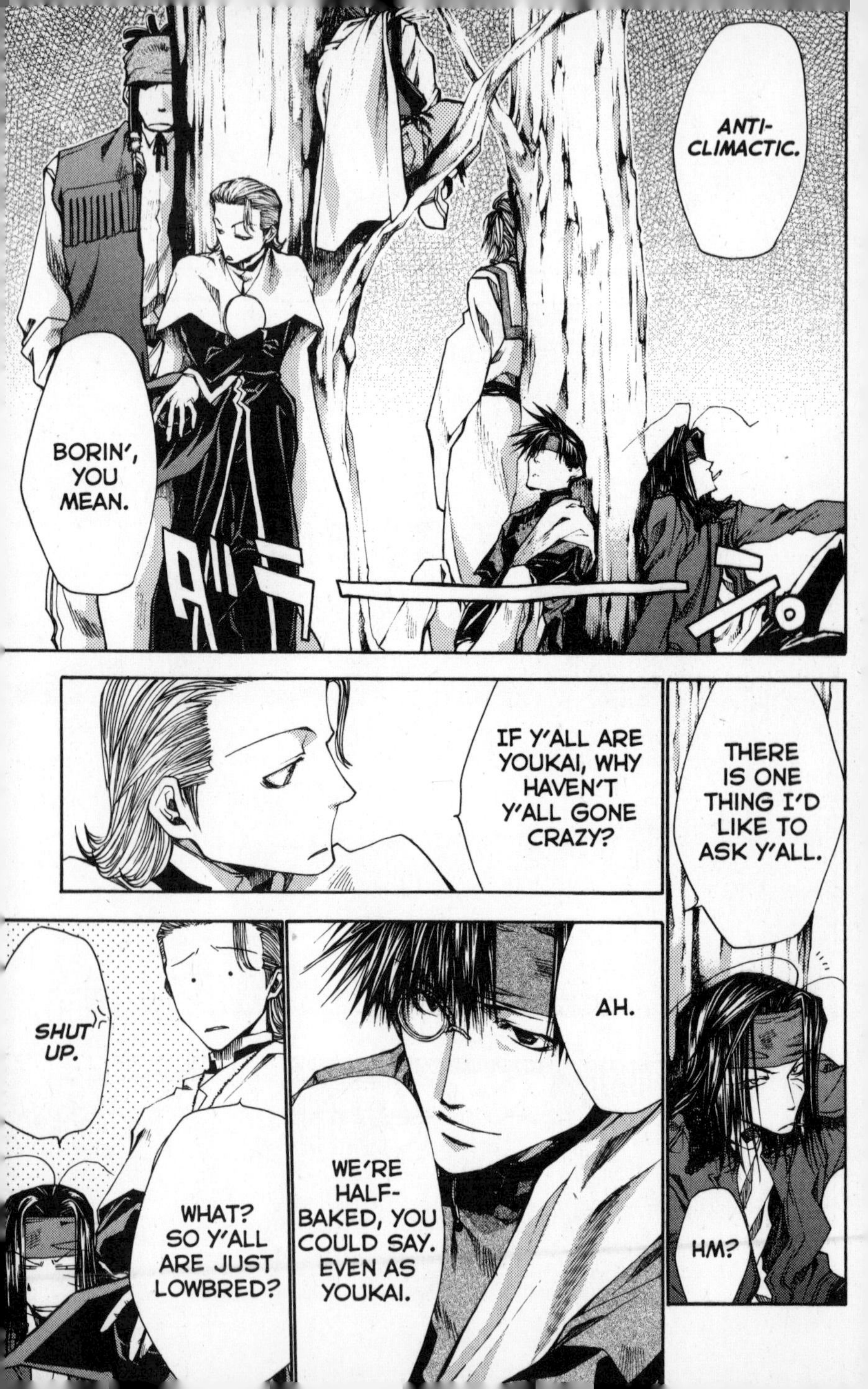
ANTI-CLIMACTIC.
BORIN', YOU MEAN.
THERE IS ONE THING I'D LIKE TO ASK Y'ALL.
HM?
IF Y'ALL ARE YOUKAI, WHY HAVEN'T Y'ALL GONE CRAZY?
AH.
WE'RE HALF-BAKED, YOU COULD SAY. EVEN AS YOUKAI.
WHAT? SO Y'ALL ARE JUST LOWBRED?
SHUT UP.

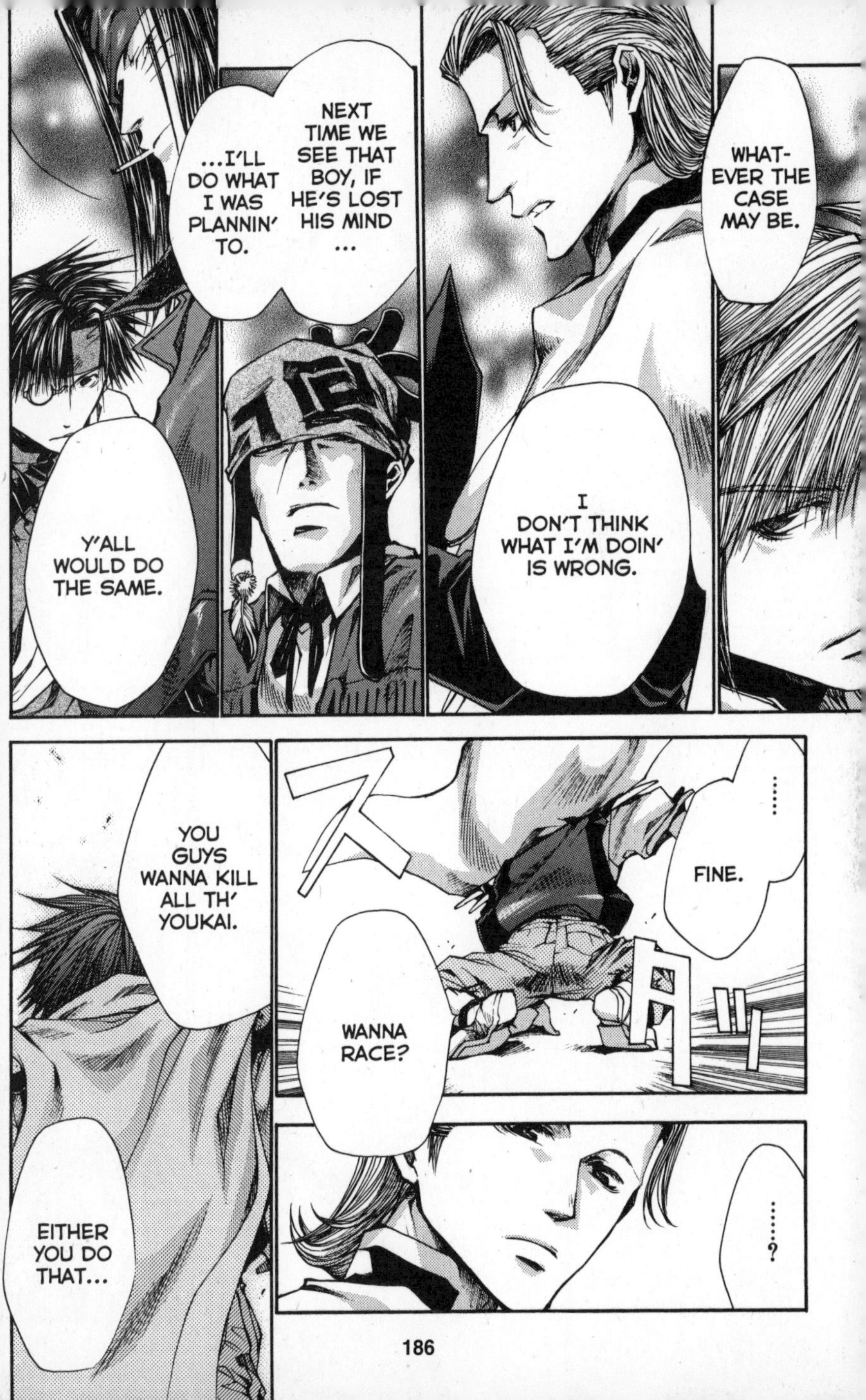
WHAT-EVER THE CASE MAY BE.
I DON'T THINK WHAT I'M DOIN' IS WRONG.
NEXT TIME WE SEE THAT BOY, IF HE'S LOST HIS MIND ...
...I'LL DO WHAT I WAS PLANNIN' TO.
Y'ALL WOULD DO THE SAME.
......
FINE.
ス
ダッ
WANNA RACE?
......?
YOU GUYS WANNA KILL ALL TH' YOUKAI.
EITHER YOU DO THAT...

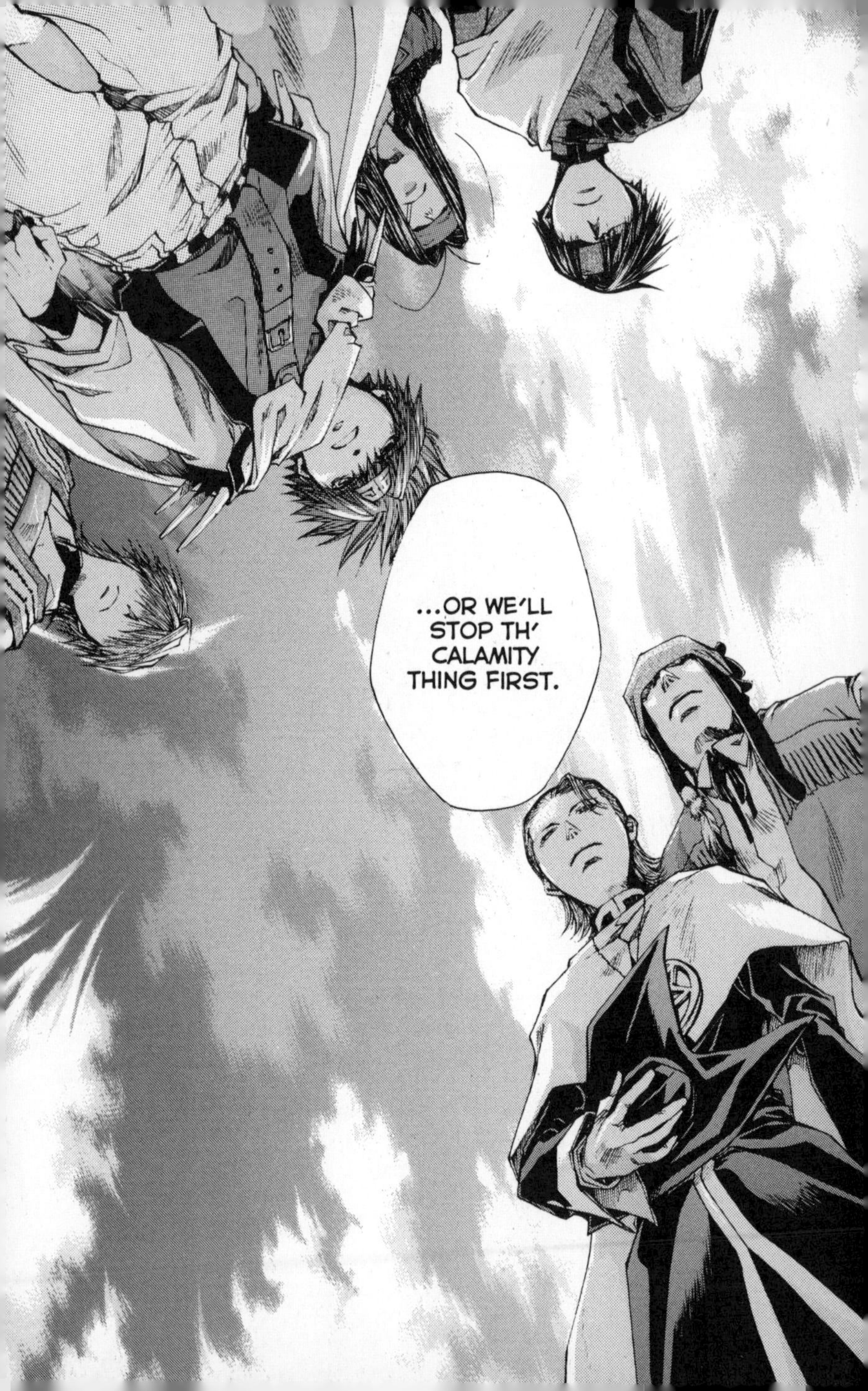
...OR WE'LL STOP TH' CALAMITY THING FIRST.

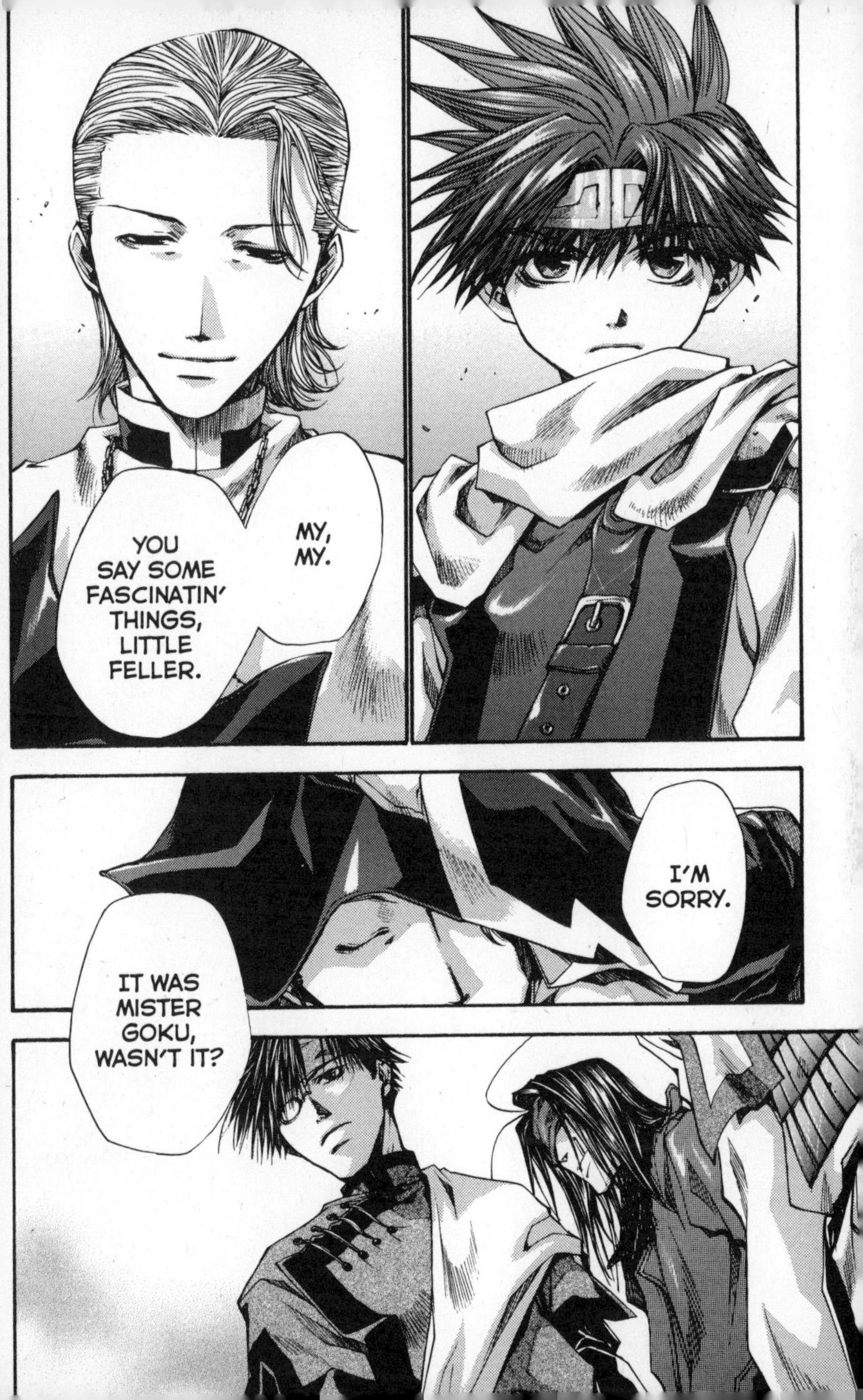
MY, MY.
YOU SAY SOME FASCINATIN' THINGS, LITTLE FELLER.
I'M SORRY.
IT WAS MISTER GOKU, WASN'T IT?

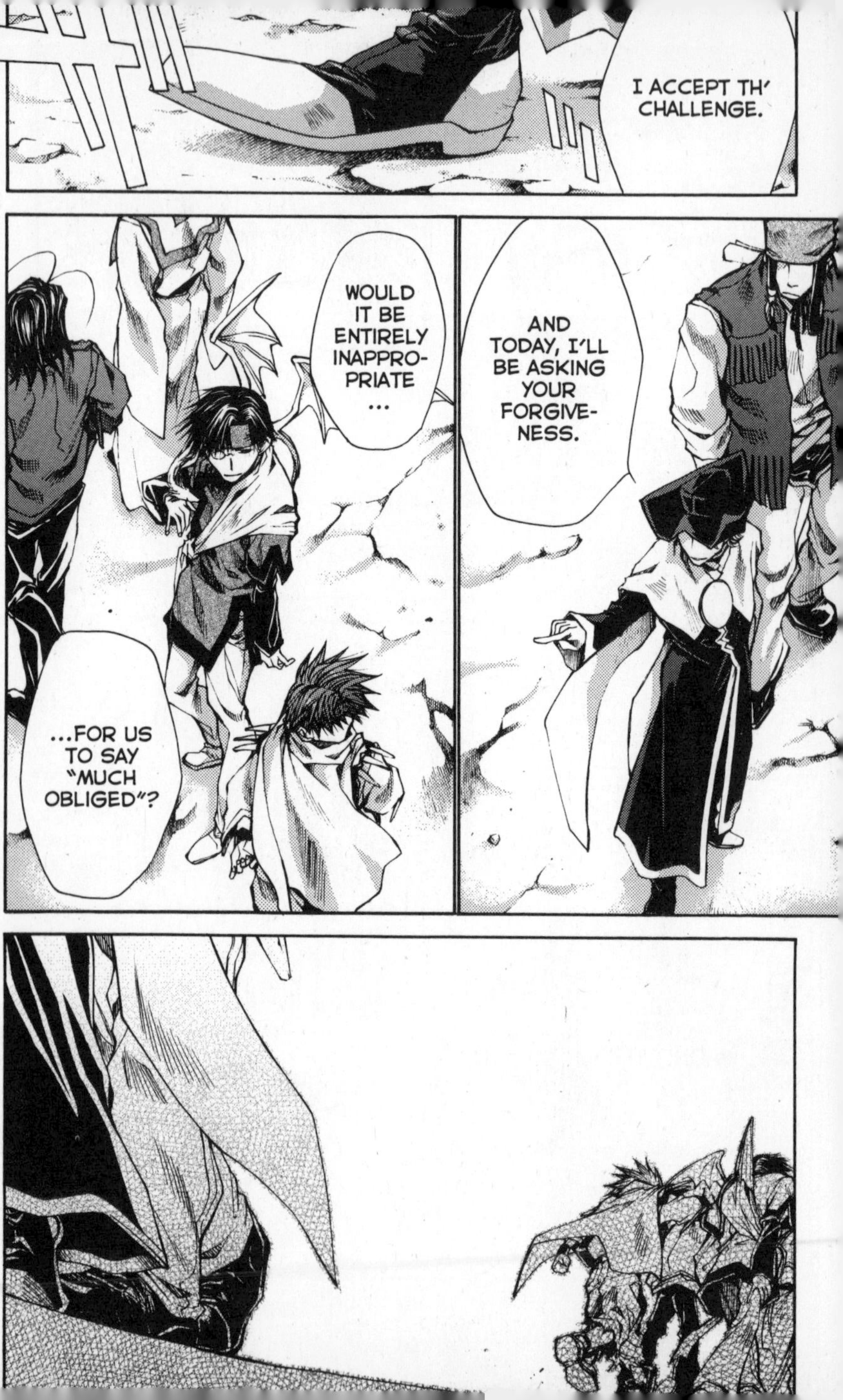
I ACCEPT TH' CHALLENGE.
AND TODAY, I'LL BE ASKING YOUR FORGIVE-NESS.
WOULD IT BE ENTIRELY INAPPRO-PRIATE ...
...FOR US TO SAY "MUCH OBLIGED"?

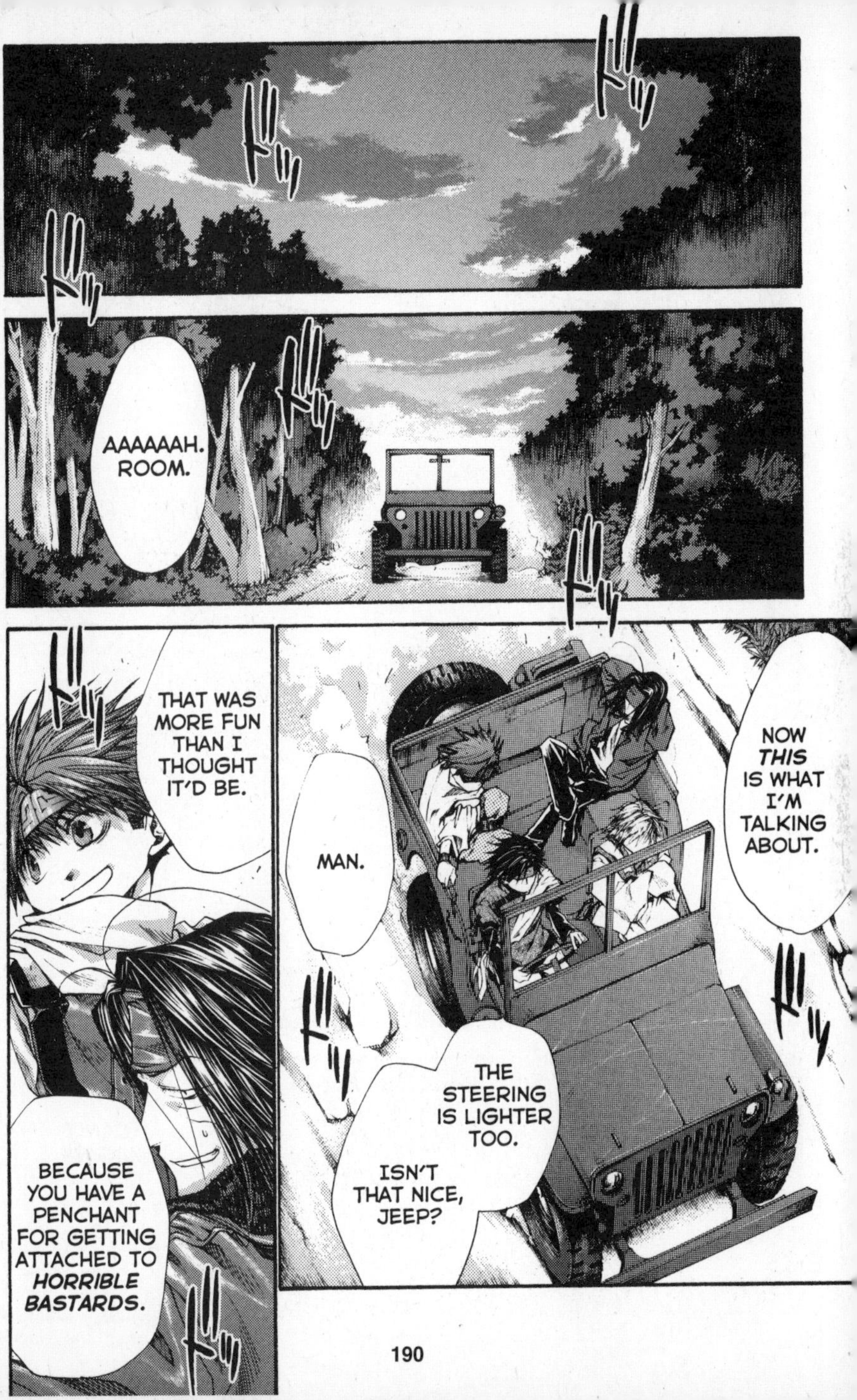
AAAAAAH. ROOM.
NOW *THIS* IS WHAT I'M TALKING ABOUT.
MAN.
THE STEERING IS LIGHTER TOO.
ISN'T THAT NICE, JEEP?
THAT WAS MORE FUN THAN I THOUGHT IT'D BE.
BECAUSE YOU HAVE A PENCHANT FOR GETTING ATTACHED TO *HORRIBLE BASTARDS*.

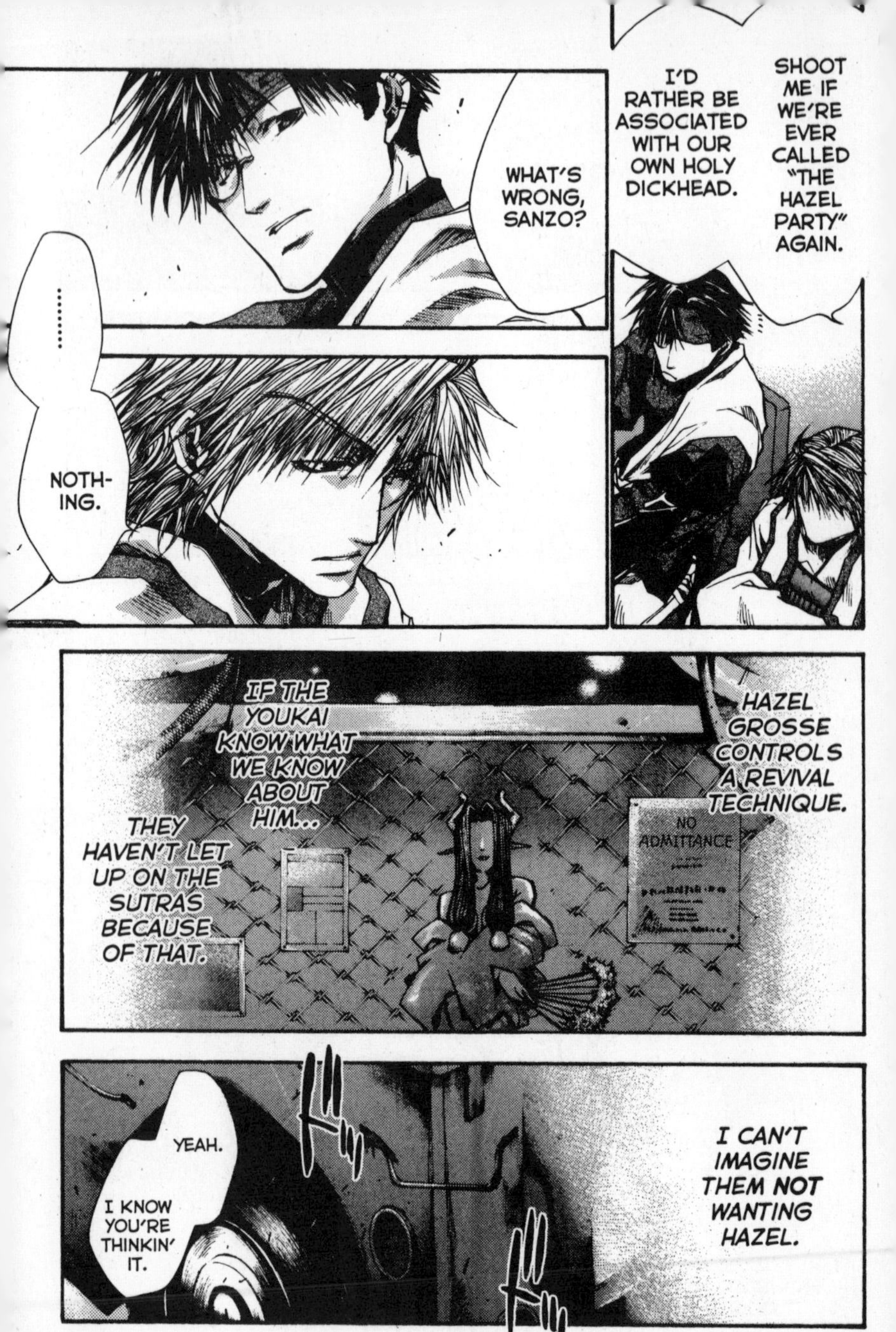
SHOOT ME IF WE'RE EVER CALLED "THE HAZEL PARTY" AGAIN.
I'D RATHER BE ASSOCIATED WITH OUR OWN HOLY DICKHEAD.
WHAT'S WRONG, SANZO?
......
NOTH-ING.
HAZEL GROSSE CONTROLS A REVIVAL TECHNIQUE.
IF THE YOUKAI KNOW WHAT WE KNOW ABOUT HIM...
THEY HAVEN'T LET UP ON THE SUTRAS BECAUSE OF THAT.
NO ADMITTANCE
I CAN'T IMAGINE THEM **NOT** WANTING HAZEL.
YEAH.
I KNOW YOU'RE THINKIN' IT.

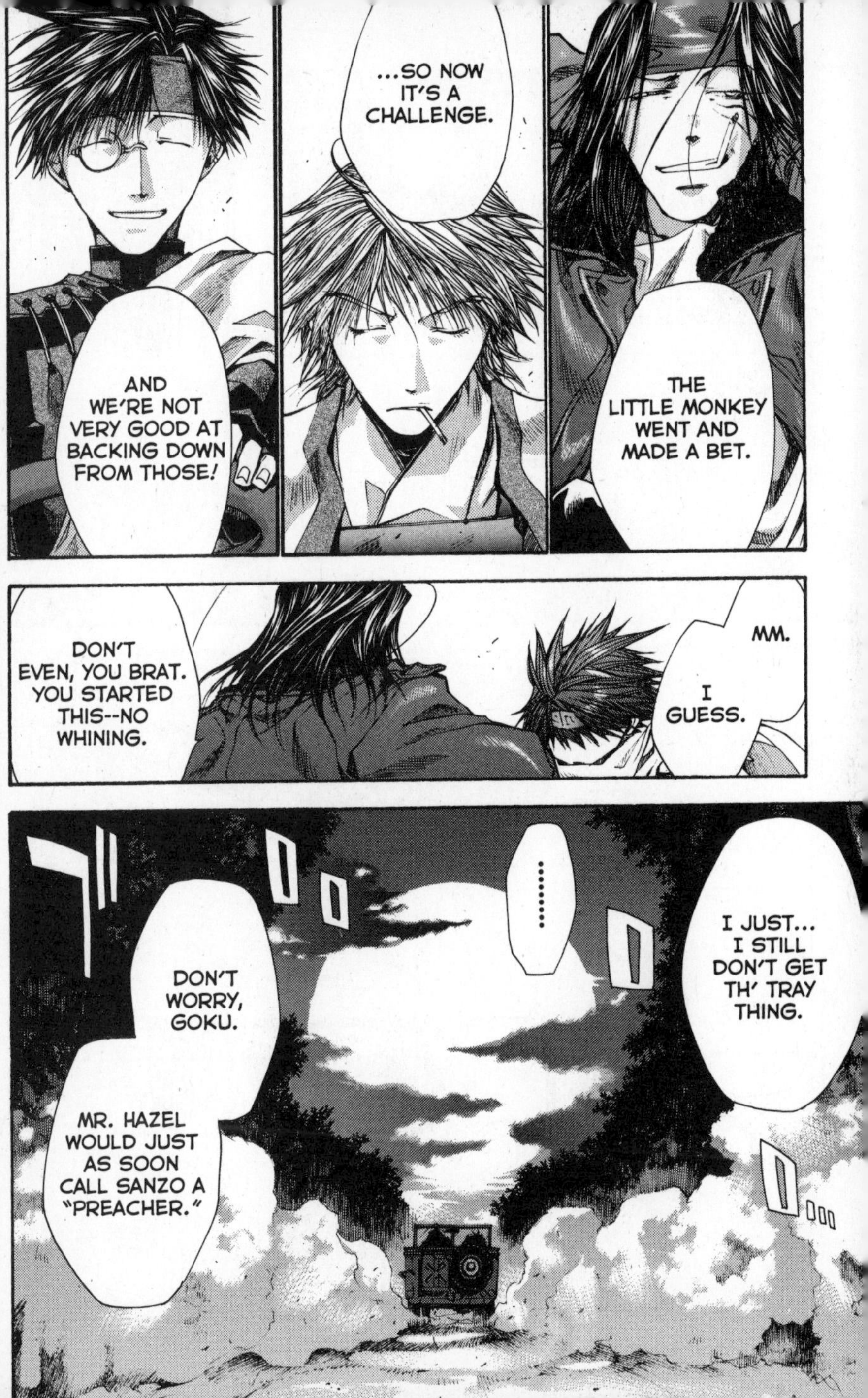
THE LITTLE MONKEY WENT AND MADE A BET.
...SO NOW IT'S A CHALLENGE.
AND WE'RE NOT VERY GOOD AT BACKING DOWN FROM THOSE!
MM.
I GUESS.
DON'T EVEN, YOU BRAT. YOU STARTED THIS--NO WHINING.
I JUST... I STILL DON'T GET TH' TRAY THING.
....
DON'T WORRY, GOKU.
MR. HAZEL WOULD JUST AS SOON CALL SANZO A "PREACHER."

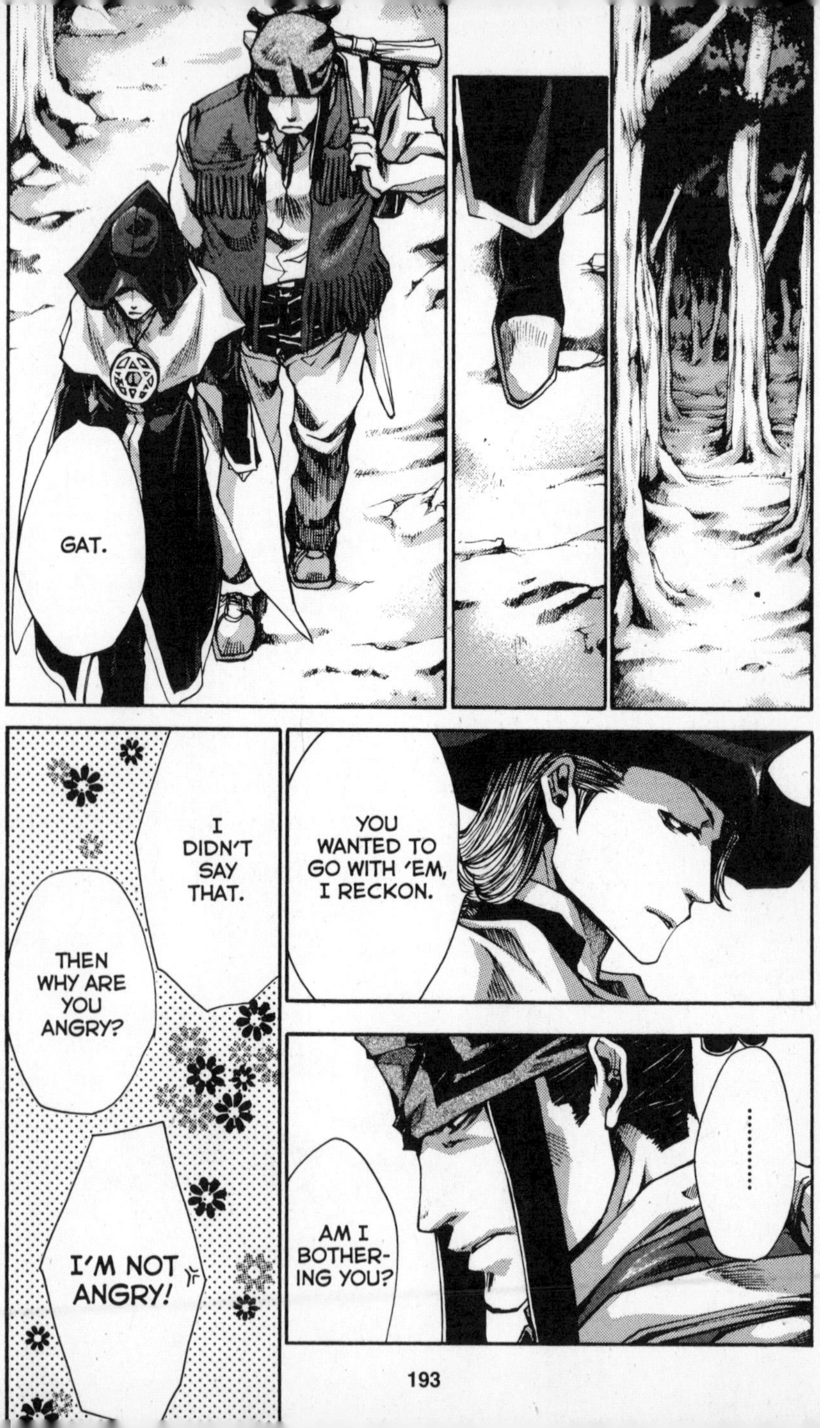
GAT.
YOU WANTED TO GO WITH 'EM, I RECKON.
......
AM I BOTHER-ING YOU?
I DIDN'T SAY THAT.
THEN WHY ARE YOU ANGRY?
I'M NOT ANGRY!

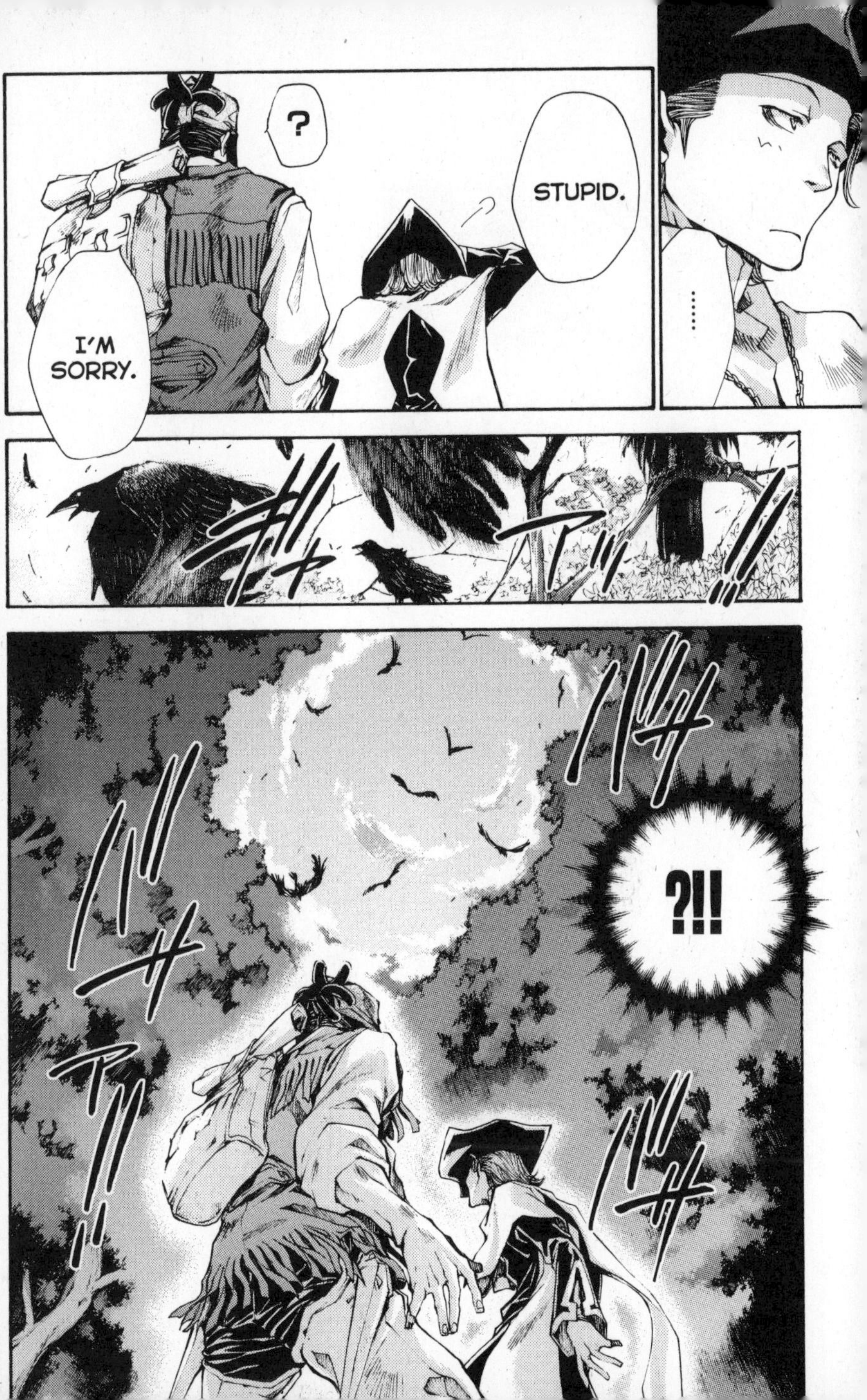

......
STUPID.
?
I'M SORRY.
ギャアッ!!
バサ
?!!
バサ
バサア!!

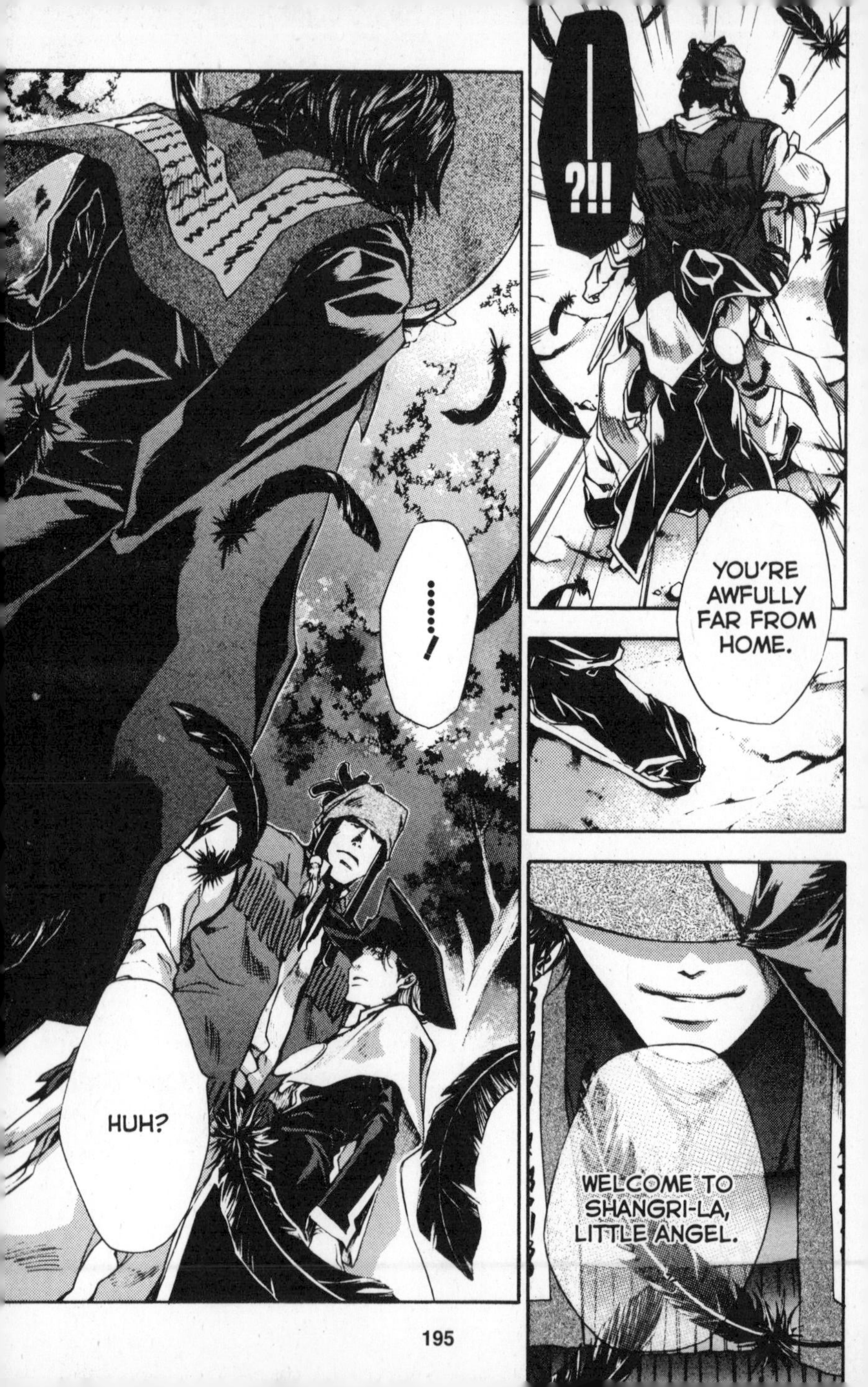

?!!
YOU'RE AWFULLY FAR FROM HOME.
WELCOME TO SHANGRI-LA, LITTLE ANGEL.
......!
HUH?

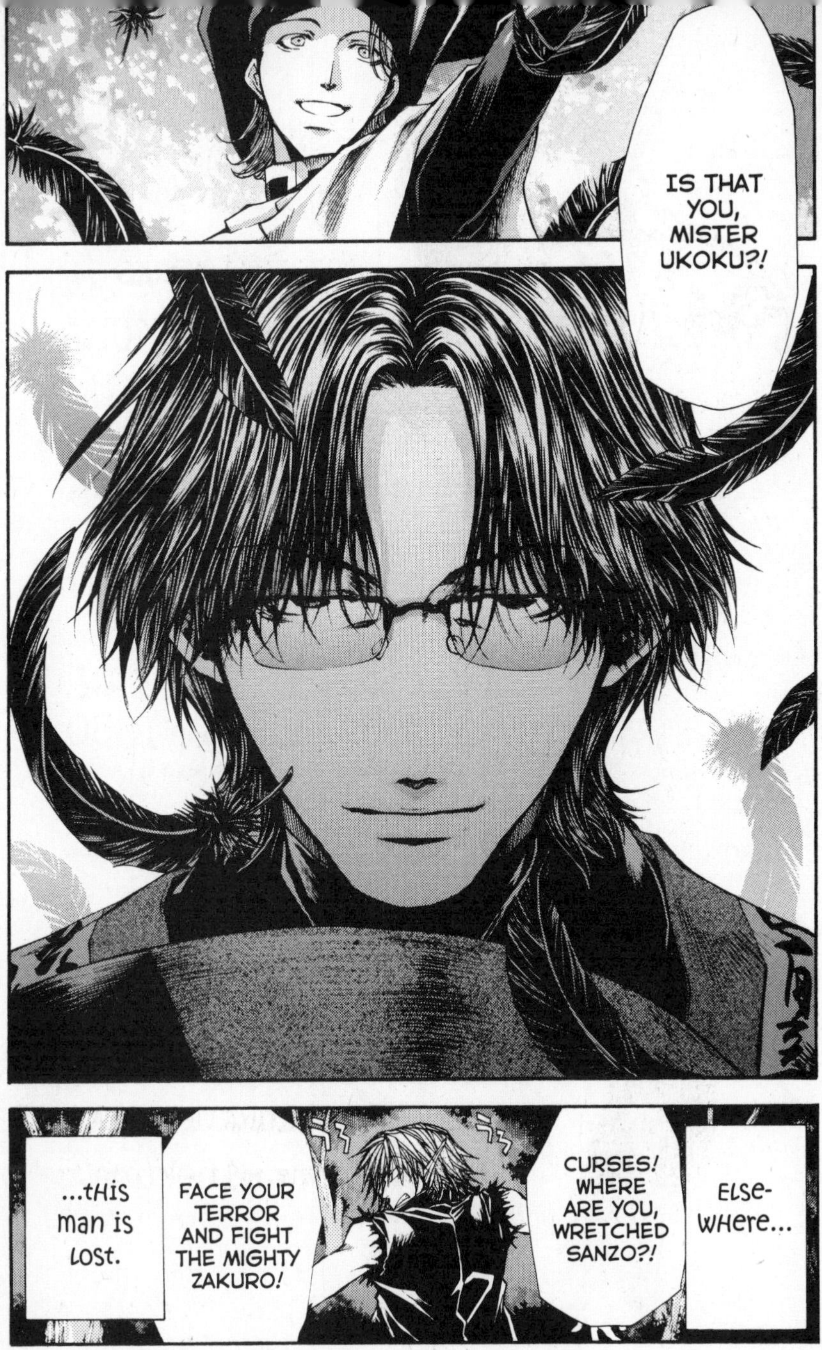
IS THAT YOU, MISTER UKOKU?!
Else-where...
CURSES! WHERE ARE YOU, WRETCHED SANZO?!
FACE YOUR TERROR AND FIGHT THE MIGHTY ZAKURO!
...this man is lost.

SAIYUKI RELOAD 5 THE END

STAFF

ORIGINAL WORKS
KAZUYA MINEKURA

ASSISTANT WORKS
KATSUYA SEINO
RIE TAHARA
TAKANO
TOMOMI NISHIYAMA
FUJIYOSHI KISHO
ASATO ASAHINA

EDITOR
YOUSUKE SUGINO

"KAZUYA MINEKURA OFFICIAL SITE"
http://www.minekura.com/

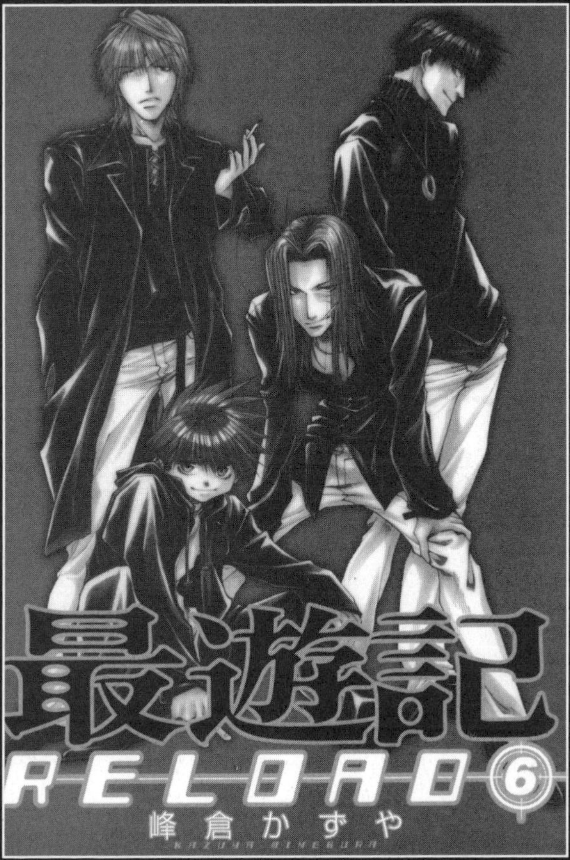
最遊記
RELOAD 6
峰倉かずや

Another volume, another town full of problems. Or is it? The latest stop on the Sanzo Party's trek west seems awfully peaceful and prosperous, considering the chaos going on throughout the land. What price will our heroes have to pay for their brief respite of quietude? Sanzo sat out the last round of battles, but how will he fare when he has to take on a horde of youkai all by his lonesome? And now Hazel suspects Goku of being the most dangerous youkai of them all...

SOUND EFFECT CHART

THE FOLLOWING IS A LIST OF THE SOUND EFFECTS USED IN *SAIYUKI*. EACH SOUND IS LABELED BY PAGE AND PANEL NUMBER, SEPARATED BY A PERIOD. THE FIRST DESCRIPTION (IN BOLD) IS THE PHONETIC READING OF THE JAPANESE, AND IS FOLLOWED BY THE EQUIVALENT ENGLISH SOUND OR A DESCRIPTION.

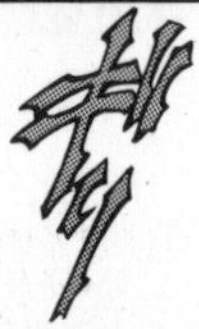

GIRI!

THIS USEFUL SOUND EFFECT HAS A COUPLE OF FUNCTIONS: IT CAN BE EITHER THE SOUND OF GRINDING TEETH OR TWO COMBATANTS STRUGGLING AGAINST EACH OTHER.

9.4	GYUN!: DIVE
10.1	GYUON!!: BWOOM
10.2	GYA!!!: CREE
11.3	GUI!: GRAB
11.4	BUN!: TOSS
12.2	DORUN!: VAULT
12.3	GO!: KICK
12.4	GAKA!: CRANK
12.5	GYUOO!!: SQUEAL
13.1	GYAGYA!: VROOM
13.2	GAGA!: KACHUNK
13.3	BURORORO: ENGINE RUMBLING
14.2	GARA!x3: CLATTER
14.3	BA!: BAM
14.4	GYAx3: CRASH
15.1	ZAZAA!: SKID
16.1	JIRI...: LOOM
16.2	DA!: DASH
16.3	BAKYA: CRONK
16.4	GO!: WHOCK
16.6	BUN!: WHAM
17.2	BASHII!!: BASH
18.1	BASHII: BASH
18.4	BUN!: WHAM
18.5	GAKI.: CLANG
18.6	DOSAA: THUD
20.1	PAN!: CRAK
21.2	BATAx3: SCRAMBLE
21.5	FURA: STAGGER
22.1	GU!: GRAB
22.4	DA!: DASH
22.5	GURA...: WOBBLE
23.2	ZA!: WHDD
25.1	GARANx4: DONG
26.3	GABAA!!: GRAB
27.4	TO!: STEP
27.6	ZAAA: RUSH
28.2	BASHAx2: SPLASH
28.3	GYU!.: SQUIRK
29.1	BASHA!: SPLASH
30.2	MUKYOU!: GRRR
30.3	SHAKOx2: BRUSH
30.4	SHAKO......: BRUSH
31.1	PE!: PTUI
32.1	KATSU!x2: SCARF
32.6	PAN!: CRAK
33.1	GO!.: KONK
33.5	GAPAA!!: SNARF

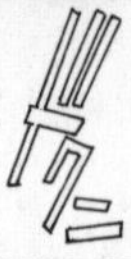

DOKUN!

IN MOST MANGA, A PLEASANT LITTLE "DOKI DOKI" IS THE PREFERRED SOUND FOR HEART-BEATS, BUT IN *SAIYUKI*, THEY NEEDED TO KICK IT UP A NOTCH. "DOKUN" IS THE SOUND OF A PARTICULARLY STRONG HEART-BEAT, USUALLY RESERVED FOR MOMENTS OF EXTREME SHOCK OR DEMONIC TRANSFORMATION.

67.2	BIKU!: TWITCH
70.5	PUHAA.: FSHOO
72.3	ZA!.: WHDD
73.2	ZA!: WHDD
73.3	DAAN!!: BAM
74.1	DON!x4: BOOM
75.3	PITA!.: HALT
77.2	ZAA!...: WHOOSH
78.4	BAAN!!: BAM
79.1	ZUZAA: SKID
79.2	ZOROx2: TRUDGE
79.4	GASHII!!: GRAB
79.5	BURAN: DANGLE
80.1	BUN!: SHOVE
80.2	DOKAA: CRASH
80.4	KII: ONNG
80.5	GOKYA!: KAWHACK
81.3	GUMI.: GRIND
81.6	HERA.: SMILE
82.1	DA!.: BAM
82.3	DOKAA!: CRASH
83.3	GIRI: TWIST
83.5	TA!: STEP
84.1	DAx4: DASH
84.2	GAAN: SHOCK
84.4	ZEEx2: WHEEZE
84.5	ZA!!: WHDD
85.1	ZAx2: WHDD
85.1	TO!: TAP
85.3	BAKYA.: KAWHAM
86.1	DAx5: DASH
87.1	DON!: WHAM
87.3	HYUNx2: FSSHHT
87.4	BA!: BAM
87.5	DO!x5: THOK
88.3	ZON!: SLICE
88.6	TSU: ZMM
89.1	FUO...: VMM
89.3	OOO..: WOOM
90.5	YORO..: STAGGER
90.6	ZURU...: SLUMP

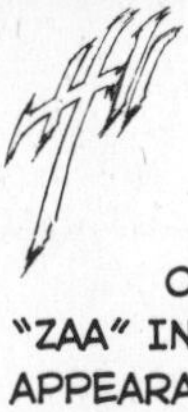

ZAA!

YOU'LL SEE THIS ONE A LOT IN *SAIYUKI*. "ZAA" INDICATES A DRAMATIC APPEARANCE. IF YOU WANT TO MAKE A LASTING IMPRESSION, ALWAYS COME IN WITH A COOL POSE AND A BIG "ZAA!"

33.6	ZUI!!: SHOVE
35.4	GAAN!!: CLANG
36.1	UOOOOO: ROOOAH
37.4	HYU...: WHOOSH
37.5	DON!x2: BOOM
38.1	DON!x3: BOOM
38.4	OOO...: HOWLING WIND
40.1	GOGAA!: KAPOW
40.3	JAKA!: KACHAK
40.5	DON!x3: BOOM
41.6	PISHI!.: SNAP
42.4	DON!x3: BOOM

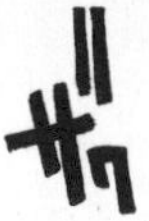

ZAWA!

NO ONE REALLY CARES WHAT ALL THOSE EXTRAS IN THE BACKGROUND ARE SAYING, RIGHT? THAT'S WHY MANGA-KA USE THIS HANDY SOUND EFFECT TO INDICATE BACKGROUND CHATTER. YOU'LL SEE IT HOVERING OVER CROWDED CITY STREETS OR CLASSROOMS THROUGHOUT MANGA. IT CAN ALSO BE USED TO INDICATE THE SOUND OF WIND BLOWING THROUGH THE LEAVES OF A TREE. AIN'T THAT SWEET?

43.1	DON!: BOOM
43.2	GESHII!!: WHAM
43.5	OOO: VOOM
44.1	DON!: BOOM
45.5	SHUOOO...: SHOOO
47.1	HA!: GASP
47.5	GAYAx2: MURMUR
53.3	CHARI.: CHING
54.1	SHIGEx2: STARE
55.4	HISOx3: WHISPER
59.1	BURORORORO: ENGINE RUMBLING
59.2	DO!x5: ENGINE RUMBLING
60.1	DO!x3: ENGINE RUMBLING
61.1	DO!x2: ENGINE RUMBLING
62.1	BURORO...: ENGINE RUMBLING
62.2	GAKO!: KAWHAM
66.1	OO..: OOH

91.1 DOSAA!: KATHUD
91.2 KA!: TAP
91.4 MICHI!.: SQUISH
93.1 GUI!!: GRAB
94.1 JAKO!: KACHAK
94.4 HERA.: SMILE
95.6 GUI!: GRAB
98.2 ZUSHA: SPLATTER
100.4 GAU...N: BANG
101.1 ZA!.: WHDD
101.4 CHUNx3: CHIRP
105.6 SHIN.: SILENCE

はっ

HAH!

THIS IS ONE OF THE MOST COMMON SOUNDS YOU'LL SEE IN MANGA. IT'S USED TO INDICATE SURPRISE AND IS USUALLY EQUIVALENT TO "GASP!" "H" ISN'T NECESSARILY VOCALIZED, THOUGH.

106.1 BURORORORO...: ENGINE RUMBLING
106.2 DO!x7: ENGINE RUMBLING
107.6 KA!: FLASH
108.1 GYAx3: SQUEAL
108.2 GYA!: SQUEAL
109.2 GA!: GRAB
109.3 TA!!: DASH
109.5 BURORORO: ENGINE RUMBLING
111.3 DO!x5: ENGINE RUMBLING
113.1 BURORORORO...: ENGINE RUMBLING
113.3 DOYAx2: KLOMP
113.4 GAKIN: YANK
114.4 SHURUx2: SLIP
114.6 GYAAx2: ARRGH
115.1 SUPAAN!: KASLAP
116.2 PASHI.: FLAP
116.3 PIRA: FLUTTER
116.4 KOPOx2: GLUG
117.1 GAAN: SHOCK
118.3 JAAAA: RUSSH
118.4 ...ZABAA: SPLASH
118.4 HYOKO.: PEEK
119.5 PETAx3: PAT
119.6 PETAx7: PAT
120.5 POSU.: POF
121.4 BA!!: BAM
125.2 GA!!!: GRAB
127.2 BYU!: WHOOSH
128.2 BISHI: BFF
130.1 PISHON.: PLIP
132.1 FUU: FSSHH
135.1 ZAA!...: WHOOSH
136.5 GISHI!: CREAK
142.1 BOKEE.: STARE
142.2 BASHI!x2: BASH
143.2 HYU..: WHOOSH
143.3 BI!...!: VWP
143.4 TO!: TAP
144.1 TAx3: DASH
145.2 HYU..: TOSS
145.3 PASHII!: CATCH
146.4 BIKU!: TWITCH
146.5 DA!: DASH
147.4 GASHAAN!!: CRASH
147.7 GACHA: CLATCH
148.6 PATAN.: SHUT
149.1 BATAx3: TROMP
149.2 MOSO...: CREEP
149.5 PEKO!: BOW
149.6 PATAx3: SCRAMBLE
149.7 PATAN.: SHUT
150.1 GATA.: SKOOT
157.6 GIRI!: GRIND
158.1 GYAA!: CAW
158.3 PESHI!: FLICK
159.1 GA!: GRAB
159.3 BUCHII!!: RRIP
159.4 TAA..N: DROP
160.3 OOO...: HOWLING WIND
161.1 OOO...: HOWLING WIND
163.1 JA: KA-
163.2 KO!.: CHAK
163.5 DO: BOOM
164.1 DONx4: BOOM
164.2 BYU!: WHOOSH
164.4 GIN!: CLANG
164.5 OOO: ONNG
165.1 DON!: BAM
165.4 BYU!..: WHOOSH
166.1 SUPAAN!!: KAWHACK
166.2 TA!: TAP
166.3 DAN!: BAM
166.4 GO!!!: WHAM
167.2 ZAZA!: SKID
167.4 DAN!: BAM
167.6 BYU!: WHOOSH
168.2 BAKYA!: KAWHAM
168.3 DOGOO!: KASLAM
169.1 DA!: DASH
169.2 JAKO!: KACHAK

169.3	DON*/*x3: BOOM
170.1	BUN*/*: BOING
170.4	GO*/*.: WHAM
170.5	DOSAA: KATHUD
171.2	BISHII*/*: KICK
171.3	PASA*/*: FLUTTER
173.1	GAU...N*//*: BANG
173.6	OO...: HOWLING WIND
176.2	FUWA: FLOAT
179.5	GYA...: GRIP
180.2	JAKO*/*: KACHAK
185.1	DARAAN.: BADABING
186.5	SUTA*/*: TMP
189.1	ZA*/*: WHDD
190.1	DO*/*x9: ENGINE RUMBLING
191.5	DO*/*x2: ENGINE RUMBLING
192.5	BURORORORO...: ENGINE RUMBLING
194.3	GYAA*///*: CAW
194.4	BASA*/*x3: FLAP
196.3	URUx2: TRUDGE
182.5	ZO..: SHIVER
182.6	GAN*/*: CHOP
182.6	BAKYA: WHACK
183.1	DA*//*: DASH
183.2	GASHAA*/*: CRASH

TOKYOPOP.com

STOP!

This is the back of the book.
You wouldn't want to spoil a great ending!

This book is printed "manga-style," in the authentic Japanese right-to-left format. Since none of the artwork has been flipped or altered, readers get to experience the story just as the creator intended. You've been asking for it, so TOKYOPOP® delivered: authentic, hot-off-the-press, and far more fun!

DIRECTIONS

If this is your first time reading manga-style, here's a quick guide to help you understand how it works.

It's easy… just start in the top right panel and follow the numbers. Have fun, and look for more 100% authentic manga from TOKYOPOP®!

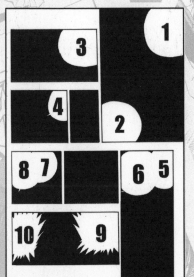

100% AUTHENTIC MANGA